CAUTION
GLASS
HANDLE WITH CARE
DO NOT PAINT

The Amazing Gooney Bird
The Saga of the Legendary DC-3/C-47

The Amazing Gooney Bird

The Saga of the Legendary DC-3/C-47

Carroll V. Glines

Schiffer Military/Aviation History
Atglen, PA

ACKNOWLEDGMENTS

In 1959, Lt. Col. Wendell F. Moseley and I co-authored *Grand Old Lady*, the first book ever published about the lovable old C-47 Gooney Bird that we both flew during our Air Force careers in World War II and afterward. It was followed by *The DC-3: The Story of a Fabulous Airplane* in 1965. Then, in 1979, we collaborated once more to produce *The Legendary DC-3*.

It is a publishing oddity that three different publishers decided to produce books on the same subject in a relatively short time span. But they did because they realized that the Gooney Bird was defying all odds about its survival as it passed its 30th, 40th, and 50th birthdays. Each successive book was updated and went through a normal course of hardcover sales and into paperback.

Now a fourth publisher, Peter Schiffer, recognizing that the lovable Gooney Bird has proven that it will outlive us all, asked me to prepare this saga of the DC-3/C-47 as it passed its 60th birthday milestone. This edition contains updated information and new photographs that have been obtained from a number of new sources.

During the research over the years, it was found that literally hundreds of people had stories to tell about the Grand Old Lady of the Skies. Sadly, only a few could be told here. But many of those who helped supply the stories, photos, and referrals to sources can be mentioned. They include the late Generals Maxwell D. Taylor and Anthony C. McAuliffe; Colonels Frank J. McNees and Troy Crawford; Lieutenant Colonels Charles A. Rawls, Perry C. Emmons, Donald A. Shaw, and Paul C. Fritz; Majors Annis G. Thompson, Archie G. Burdette, Harold T. Allen, Frank Sweeney, Donald V. Browne, and Francis L. Satterlee; and Master Sergeant Walter E. Jones.

Thanks are also reserved for Robert Kopitzke, retired curator for the History of Aviation Collection (HAC) at the University of Texas at Dallas (UTD) who provided archival materials from American Airlines, his former employer; William K. Jones, the HAC's aircraft maintenance expert; and George H. Williams, chairman of the HAC advisory board, author and World War I historian.

Donald W. Douglas, Sr. and Donald W. Douglas, Jr. cooperated graciously in the original version, plus a number of Douglas Aircraft Co. public relations specialists such as Joe B. Messick, Mrs. Ida Hershensohn, Harry Gann and Pat McGinnis.

Several historical studies by the Air Force and Navy were consulted in addition to materials furnished by various DC-3 operators. Those whose writings provided new insights into the fascinating history of the Gooney Bird include Jack S. Ballard, Office of Air Force History; Henry M. Holden, editor of the *DC-3/Dakota Journal* and author of *The DC-3 & C-47 Story*; Douglas J. Ingells, former Douglas employee and author of *The Plane That Changed the World*; Robert C. Mikesh, author of *Flying Dragons, a history of the South Vietnamese Air Force*, and Arthur Pearcy, British author and widely acknowledged DC-3 historian.

Carroll V. Glines
Dallas, Texas

To Mary Ellen, Karen, David, and Valerie who waited and watched for my Gooney Bird to come home.

Book Design by Ian Robertson.

Library of Congress Catalog Number: 96-67288

Printed in China.
ISBN: 0-7643-0064-4

We are interested in hearing from authors with book ideas on related topics.

Published by Schiffer Publishing Ltd.
77 Lower Valley Road
Atglen, PA 19310
Please write for a free catalog.
This book may be purchased from the publisher.
Please include $2.95 postage.
Try your bookstore first.

CONTENTS

Foreword

It affords me much pleasure and not a little prideful nostalgia to contemplate the DC-3's long and distinguished career. I do not believe that any of us who worked on the designs and nursed the development of the DC-1 and DC-2 quite realized at the time that we were really building the DC-3, an airplane that would outlast the working careers of us all—and indeed win for herself a fame worldwide and devotion unexcelled in the hearts of generations of those who flew her. But I think it is well to remember that it was the skill and talent, the courage and faith of the flyers themselves who made her great. Bold men and women in war and peace who loved aviation and found in the Grand Old Lady a response and faithfulness to reflect their own.

And so, in a parody of Ol' Man River, she flies on and on. And who knows? Perhaps she will fly on forever. I hope she does.

Donald W. Douglas, Sr.

Introduction

As the 20th century nears its end, the world has seen literally thousands of different models, shapes, and sizes of airplanes come and go. During this time four big wars and scores of small ones have proven the airplane to be a valuable weapon. Between wars, the airplane has been an instrument of peace and international commerce. It is now universally recognized that no more wars will be fought and no peace truly lasting without the airplane playing a dominant role as an instrument of power—either military or economic. In the span of this century, the airplane has changed from a mark of folly and daring to a symbol of national strength and vigor.

Of all the aircraft ever built that have contributed to aviation progress, the Douglas DC-3 is one which has surpassed all others in faithful service, dependability, and achievement. It has been parked on the ramps of the world's air terminals for over sixty years. It was the first airliner to offer predictable comfort and safety to a skeptical public and the first that could make money just by hauling passengers. During the years since its first flight, the DC-3 has also earned a reputation for longevity unequaled in aviation. Born during the days of wooden propellers, it is still flying as we engage in space exploration. From those who have flown it during the last six decades, whether in the cabin or the cockpit, the DC-3 has won more acclaim and affection than any other plane in the history of aviation.

This book is about that airplane: its birth, development, its adoption by the airlines and the military services, its uses during World War II, Korea, and Vietnam, its conversion to civilian use after the wars, its innumerable feats as an angel of mercy, its employment as a jack-of-all-trades, and finally its future.

This legendary airplane has earned many names, set many records and scored innumerable aviation "firsts." It has flown more miles, piled up more flying time, carried more cargo and passengers, and performed more "impossible" feats than any other winged craft in the world, even in this age of mammoth jet airliners.

The manufacturer called it the Skytrain and designated it the "DC-3." The airlines called it simply, "the Three." The U.S. Air Force dubbed it the "C-47" plus other designations, while the U.S. Navy labeled it the "R4D" with several suffixes. The British called it the Dakota. But these are official identifications. The men who flew and still fly this extraordinary flying machine have other names for it. Some airline pilots called it the "Dizzy Three." Civilian pilots and passengers have given it such names as "Old Methuselah," "Placid Plodder," "Dowager Duchess," and we named it "Grand Old Lady." Today, however, pilots everywhere refer to it with great affection as the "Gooney Bird" after the albatross, whose great powers of flight and ubiquity are legendary.

I first fell in love with the Gooney Bird as a teen-ager when I watched it come and go from the fence at the Philadelphia, Pennsylvania Municipal Airport. I dreamed of the day when I might be a pilot-in-command on one of these magnificent, stately birds. The great day came for me after I won my wings in January 1942 as a pilot in the U.S. Air Force.

This plane, of all the planes I have flown, doesn't seem inanimate, somehow. It has a distinct personality, a warmth, an identity, and a nobility that is unlike anything else man-made that I know of. It is dependable, forgiving, attentive, gracious and benevolent. I have flown it for hundreds of hours and, although I had a few moments of doubt, it always brought me home safely and full of gratitude for the qualities that were built into it by Douglas engineers and technicians, and for the care and maintenance by the Air Force ground personnel who serviced it.

I hope I can convey to the reader in the following pages what a remarkable flying machine Mr. Douglas built. If so, I will have partially repaid the kindly Gooney Bird for the years of progress it has brought to the flying art and the many hours of pleasure I had when it was in my hands. But let no one think that this book is a eulogy for the deceased. The Amazing Gooney Bird is still in the prime of life and will outlive all who read this work.

Carroll V. Glines
Dallas, Texas

1

"There Isn't a Plane in the World"

I came to admire this machine which would lift virtually any load strapped to its back and carry it anywhere in any weather, safely and dependably. The C-47 groaned, it protested, it rattled, it leaked oil, it ran hot, it ran cold, it ran rough, it staggered along on hot days and scared you half to death, its wings flexed and twisted in a horrifying manner, it sank back to earth with a great sigh of relief—but it flew and it flew and it flew.

Capt. Len Morgan
Braniff Airways

Captain Warren C. Tomsett, thirty-three-year-old pilot of the U.S. Air Force C-47 code-named Extol Pink stalked briskly out into the damp, pungent air of the Vietnamese night. Behind him followed his co-pilot, Captain John Ordemann, navigator Donald Mack, Technical Sergeant Edsol Inlow, and loadmasters Sergeants Jack Morgan and Frank Barrett. They had just been briefed to fly a flare drop mission in support of operations by South Vietnamese ground forces against the Viet Cong Communist guerrillas.

After three years of an undeclared war, the United States Air Force had perfected a system of coordination with the Vietnamese to counter the night terror raids on their fortified hamlets. It had been a truism among the villagers that they felt reasonably safe during the day but "the night belongs to the Viet Cong!"

Communist guerrilla strategy had been simple: Intimidate and terrorize the helpless South Vietnamese into submission and spread communist doctrine further into Southeast Asia. Surprise night attacks had been the most successful tactics used. The hard-pressed South Vietnamese government pleaded for some method of nullifying or preventing the nightly raids. The U.S. Air Force, committed to a national policy of advising the anti-Communist governments in air matters, came up with an answer to this vexing problem: USAF pilots could fly non-offensive reconnaissance missions but could not fire on the Viet Cong unless fired upon first. These missions were code-named "Night Angel" which proved to be the salvation for many outposts and strategic villages. Aircraft equipped with "paraflares" could maintain an all-night vigil in the skies overhead. When a call for help was received from a besieged outpost,

The DC-1, granddaddy of all Gooney Birds, poses with one of its engineers at Clover Field, Santa Monica, California, before its first flight in 1933. It bore the experimental Department of Commerce license number X-223Y and was TWA company plane number 300. In its first weeks of flight tests, it set numerous new national and international speed, distance and load records for transport aircraft. (Douglas Aircraft photo)

A model of the DC-1 undergoes wind tunnel tests at the National Advisory Committee for Aeronautics (NACA) facility. On April 30, 1935, the DC-1 was the first commercial transport to span the U.S. continent in less than half a day. (NACA photo)

The test program for the DC-1 was extensive. On one occasion, a mix-up of signals between the pilots in the cockpit caused an early retraction of the landing gear. The results are shown here. Fortunately, the only damage was two bent propellers. (Douglas Aircraft photo)

the planes would envelop the scene below in an umbrella of light. Often all that was needed to halt an attack was the brilliant illumination provided by the magnesium flares. If the ground attack continued, Vietnamese Air Force fighters from nearby bases were scrambled to make strafing and bombing attacks on the Viet Cong positions. From the time of the first flare drop mission, the night no longer belonged to the Viet Cong.

The aircraft chosen for the flare drop missions was not a new plane designed especially for this kind of operation. It was, by usual standards, an ancient aircraft, more than a hundred years old when reckoned by the expected life span of the average airplane. It was a 150-mile-an-hour transport plane with the military designation of "C-47" which had been designed in the mid-1930s and had already seen war service all over the world. It proved to be the only airplane for the job during the early years in war-torn Vietnam.

The C-47 assigned to Captain Tomsett that night of July 20, 1963, had over 10,000 hours on its airframe. It had been built in 1945 and earmarked for the scrap pile a decade later. It never got there because a newer type of aircraft to replace it had not been found. The C-47 had already been called "the airplane that won't wear out" and there had been over three decades, billions of passenger miles, and thousands of pilots who could vouch for that. Warren Tomsett didn't know it but he was on a mission that would win the Distinguished Flying Cross for himself and his co-pilot, and Air Medals for the rest of the crew. More than that, it would win for them the Mackay Trophy for "The Most Meritorious Flight of the Year."

Tomsett lifted his lumbering Gooney into the black sky above Bien Hoa a half hour before midnight and headed southwest over the lush delta area to his assigned patrol sector. He was in continual touch with the Air Operations Center at Bien Hoa as he cruised through the darkness guided only by the ground controller's instructions. The navigator sat at his table behind the pilots, keeping track of the plane's position, while the loadmasters in the rear listened on the interphone for orders to throw out the flares. It looked like the beginning of a long night.

"Extol Pink, this is Paris Control," a voice announced on the radio with a practiced calmness born of long experience. "Will you accept a rescue mission, repeat, rescue mission? Over."

Tomsett stiffened in his seat and reached for the mike. "Roger, Control. Understand you want me for a rescue mission. What's the urgency? Over."

"Six critically wounded personnel need immediate evacuation from Loc Ninh. Will you accept the mission? Over."

Tomsett knew nothing about the airstrip at Loc Ninh. He was told it was 3,600 feet long and sixty-five feet wide. Located seventy-five miles northwest of Saigon, it was only eight miles from the Cambodian border. It had been hacked out of the virgin jungle with trees 200 feet high forming an impenetrable wall at both ends of the runway. Daylight landings at Loc Ninh were tough enough, but night operations were deemed impossible because of the mountainous terrain and the lack of runway lights and navigational aids. Just to locate it in the pitch blackness would take extraordinary navigational skill. To make a landing and a takeoff would require all the skill—and guts—ever mustered by a pilot in wartime. Six Vietnamese soldiers lay dying near that strip. They would never see daylight if Tomsett refused to try a landing. But no one would blame him if he refused to risk his life and the lives of his five crewmen to save the lives of an equal number of men he didn't know and whose language he couldn't speak.

"We'll take it," Tomsett said firmly. "Are you sending up a flare ship to replace us? Over."

The Grand Central Air Terminal provided the backdrop for the DC-1 on a visit in 1933. Only one DC-1 was built but it was the forerunner of hundreds of DC-2s and DC-3s. Approximately 1,000 of the latter still ply the world's skies. (McDonnell Douglas photo)

The Douglas DC-1 carried twelve passengers and a crew of two. The man in uniform was the co-pilot who also acted as a steward and served beverages to the passengers. (McDonnell Douglas photo)

"Roger. Remain in your area until relieved in about an hour."

Tomsett turned the controls over to Ordemann and left his seat to talk to the navigator, Captain Don Mack. A former weatherman, the thirty-six-year-old Mack had completed navigation school in 1958 and had joined the Air Commando Wing in 1961. "Look up Loc Ninh and tell me everything you can about it," Tomsett said. "Then give me a course and an ETA (estimated time of arrival) over the strip when the relief flare ship gets here."

While Mack worked, Tomsett instructed Sergeant Inlow, the flight engineer, to verify the fuel consumption on both engines and discussed with Sergeants Morgan and Barrett, the load-masters, what they were to do to help load the wounded aboard.

By the time Tomsett had briefed Morgan and Barrett, Don Mack had finished his research. He gave both pilots a thorough briefing on headings, terrain features, locations of other airstrips and known Viet Cong concentrations, and the time to get to Loc Ninh after the substitute flare ship arrived.

At 2:30 a.m., Extol Pink was relieved by a Vietnamese flare ship and headed on the course Mack had plotted. When scattered clouds began to form at 500 feet above the ground, Tomsett knew he had to get below them. The visibility decreased as the clouds thickened. There were no lights or visible landmarks outside. Radar contact with the Operations Center was lost as the plane's low altitude took it off the radar scopes. Tomsett could only fly the course Mack had prescribed and wait until the ETA was reached.

"Two minutes to go for ETA," Mack suddenly announced.

The other five crew members stared through the blackness, looking for some sign of an airfield ahead.

"You should see it dead ahead...now!" Mack said as he watched the second hand on his watch creep around the dial.

Sergeant Inlow, standing between the pilots, was first to see several small fires outlining a runway directly under the nose of the aircraft. "There it is!" he shouted, pointing below.

TWA, the first operator of the DC-1, was proud that it had established a transcontinental record of 13 hours, 4 minutes from Los Angeles to New York on February 18-19, 1934. Licensed to carry passengers later, it was assigned Department of Commerce No. NC 223Y. (Photo by H. L. Kinsey, courtesy TWA).

The DC-1 ended its flying days at Malaga, Spain, in December 1940 when an engine failed on takeoff. Then operated by Sociedad Anomina de Transportes Aeros, later named Iberia, it had been used previously in the United States to test a Sperry automatic pilot linked to a radio compass and was later owned by Howard Hughes. (McDonnell Douglas photo)

Another view of the crashed DC-1, named Negron after a Spanish hero. Parts were salvaged and some of the aluminum stringers were used to construct platforms for religious festivals. (McDonnell Douglas photo)

Tomsett wheeled the C-47 into a left turn and studied the ill-defined runway he hoped to land on. The field was so small and poorly marked and the weather had deteriorated so much that had Mack's navigation been off even an eighth of a mile the crew would never have seen it. Its proximity to the Cambodian border had presented further demands on his skill since overflight would have caused an international incident.

Tomsett planned his approach carefully. He used full flaps and a steep, near-stall glide to insure missing the trees at the approach end and stopping before he reached the other end. On the approach he could see tiny flashes of light winking through the jungle foliage. The Viet Cong had completely surrounded the strip and were peppering away at the plane with small arms fire.

The official report of the mission states simply that the "landing was accomplished under blackout conditions," which meant that Tomsett's only reference to the ground was the light made by the tiny fires (actually two rolls of toilet paper jammed on sticks and soaked with gasoline) placed erratically on both sides of the strip. He taxied to the end of the strip and shut the engines off while the wounded were loaded aboard. An attempt was made to inspect the plane for battle damage, but since no lights could be used and another Viet Cong attack might come at any moment, Tomsett decided that as long as his controls and engines responded, he would try the takeoff.

Captain Don Mack and the three sergeants immediately improvised litters as there was only one aboard the aircraft. These were hastily made from parachutes and bamboo poles, and the six wounded Vietnamese were lifted aboard, all in critical condition.

The loading door was slammed shut as Tomsett started the engines and made a 180-degree turn on the runway. He decided to take off in the opposite direction to avoid staying too long on the ground. As he checked the engines, he discovered that the center instrument panel lights had failed and he couldn't see the instruments. Sergeant Inlow, an old hand at improvising, whipped out his flashlight and held its beam on the panel. "Let 'er go, Captain!" Inlow shouted.

Tomsett jammed both throttles forward to the stops, held the brakes momentarily and headed the lumbering transport down the narrow strip. Again, automatic weapons fire was seen winking out of the darkness, but the ghostlike plane was hard to see. Putting the creaking Gooney Bird into a maximum performance climb, the daring pilot escaped both the bullets and the murderous trees at the end of the runway.

En route to Saigon a U.S. Army medic, who had decided to go along at the last minute because of the reported serious condition of the Vietnamese, Captain Mack and the three sergeants cared for the wounded. By the time the plane arrived at Saigon, their uniforms were covered with blood. Colonel Gerald J. Dix, commander of the 1st Air Commando Wing, reported:

"After the wounded were delivered to the waiting ambulances the crew of Extol Pink returned to Bien Hoa at 0455, almost seven hours after their original scramble. Each member of the crew had contributed unselfishly to the success of both missions. Their professional performance, adaptability, and courage reflect great credit upon their country and the United States Air Force. Their efforts and gallantry helped to save the lives of comrades in arms in the fight against the common enemy and added immeasurably to the morale and effectiveness of the Army of South Vietnam.

"I consider this the most meritorious flight of the year. The entire flight crew exposed themselves to hostile action throughout the flight. The professional skill, daring and extraordinary heroism displayed by the entire crew was instrumental in the success of the mission."

The Douglas DC-2 evolved from the DC-1 and held fourteen passengers in stylish comfort. The first DC-2 was accepted by TWA on May 14, 1934, and made its inaugural run between Columbus, Ohio, and Newark, New Jersey. (McDonnell Douglas photo)

An American Airlines DC-2 is parked at Chicago Municipal Airport while an American Ford Trimotor takes on passengers at the gate. The arrival of the DC-2 signaled the end of the older, slower Ford, Stinson, Boeing and Curtiss transports. (Photo courtesy Robert Kopitzke)

General Curtis E. LeMay, Air Force Chief of Staff, agreed with Colonel Dix's observation and presented the modest sextet with the Mackay Trophy at a ceremony at the Air Commando base in Florida. But neither Warren Tomsett nor any of his crew members believe they should get all the credit for the success of their mission. "It's the airplane that earned the trophy," Tomsett told the author. "We just made it do what it has been capable of doing for many years. There isn't a plane in the world that could match it!"

The feat performed by the crew of Extol Pink in their C-47 was just one more in the unending saga of "impossible" accomplishments by an airplane that refuses to grow old. The C-47 that clawed its way into the safety of the skies that night in Vietnam was, according to the experts, long overdue for the scrap heap. It had been flying for twenty years (twice the lifetime of most military planes) for the Air Force; each year it and hundreds of sister ships were given a reprieve so that they could keep on doing their jobs which no other plane could do. Each year a replacement has been sought for the aging Methuselah of the Skies. Each year the world's plane manufacturers sheepishly admit that none can be found. The airplane—the magnificent DC-3 and its military versions—has become a legend in its own time and has proved its immortality many times over.

From whence did this legend spring? What is the origin of this airplane that refuses to die? What genius could design a plane that could haul more than 600 million passengers and millions of tons of cargo for ten billion miles and still show no signs of wearing out?

It all began with the DC-1.

The single most important date in the history of the Douglas Aircraft Co. (now McDonnell Douglas) is August 2, 1932. It was on that date that Jack Frye, vice president in charge of operations for Transcontinental & Western Air (TWA), a vigorous but desperate young airline, wrote letters to several aircraft manufacturers soliciting bids for "ten or more trimotor transport planes." TWA's specifications were clearly stated: An all-metal monoplane with a maximum gross weight of 14,200 pounds, a fuel capacity for a cruising range of 1,080 miles at 145 miles per hour, with a capacity for 12 passengers plus a crew of two. Frye's letter ended with a simple question: "Approximately how long would it take to turn out the first plane for service tests?"

Foreign airlines were quick to realize the potential of the DC-2. The aircraft pictured here was restored by the Dutch Dakota Association in 1987 and given the name "Uiver" (Stork) after the KLM DC-2 that placed second in the London-Melbourne Race in 1934. Only two DC-2s are believed still flying today. (Photo courtesy Dutch Dakota Association)

A Western Air Express DC-3 poses by its Douglas predecessor transport the Army Air Corps' first cargo plane designated the C-1. Two pilots sat in the open cockpit forward and above the passenger cabin. The commercial version was used by the airline on the route between Los Angeles and Salt Lake City. (Photo courtesy Western Airlines)

One of Frye's letters was addressed to Donald W. Douglas, thirty-eight-year-old president of the Douglas Aircraft Company, Santa Monica, California. Others were sent to Curtiss-Wright, Martin and Consolidated aircraft companies. The reason for Frye's invitation to the aircraft industry was obvious to all the recipients. The great Knute Rockne, famed Notre Dame football coach, had been killed on a TWA Fokker F.10 transport en route from Kansas City, Missouri, to Wichita, Kansas, on March 31, 1931.

Public condemnation of air travel was prompt and deserved, with the brunt of the criticism aimed at TWA and its ancient plywood- and fabric-covered Fokkers. TWA had turned to the all-metal Ford trimotors, but they offered little improvement and certainly were not more comfortable or economical to operate. To survive, TWA looked to the budding aircraft industry for help.

Donald Douglas has called the letter from Frye "the birth certificate of the DC ships" and deservedly so. As soon as he digested its contents he called in his staff of engineers and production men: J. H. "Dutch" Kindleberger, Arthur E. Raymond, Fred Herman, Lee Atwood, Ed Burton, Fred Stineman, and Harry E. Wetzel. Together they studied the specifications and came to some astounding conclusions. New, more powerful engines were under development, new techniques in metal construction were coming along, and the efficient variable pitch propellers might be combined to make an entirely new airplane with a slightly swept-back cantilever wing and efficient wing flaps.

In his memoirs, Arthur Raymond recalled: "The swept-back wing was not part of the original design, nor did it come out of the wind tunnel tests. The fact is that as the weight crew the balance moved aft and it was easier to sweep the outer wing panels than it was to move the entire wing."

In ten days of around-the-clock figuring, Douglas and his experts concluded that they could not only meet Frye's specifications but could exceed them. The plane they envisioned would be designed for passenger comfort as well as speed and safety. A retractable landing gear would be designed which could fold into the engine nacelles for better streamlining; they would use the NACA enclosed type engine cowl for radial engines. Unique among its innovations was that it would be a low-wing monoplane with the Northrop type of monococoque construction and would be powered by two engines instead of three. They also proposed going beyond the state of the plane manufacturing arts by proposing a "honeycomb" wing construction and the partial stressing of wings and fuselage with aluminum skin.

Designing planes that were different was not strange to this unusual collection of engineering talent. These same men had teamed up with Douglas in the early Twenties and had engineered and built a whole stable of Douglas planes. First was the Cloudster, designed, built and flown in 1920. Four years later came the World Cruisers in which U.S. Army Air Service flyers made the first aerial circumnavigation of the globe. Then followed the C-1, and then the M-1, -2, -3, and -4—the first planes designed specifically to carry mail.

It was decided that Harry Wetzel, general manager, and Arthur E. Raymond, then assistant chief engineer, would take the train to New York. Still with much work to do, they bundled their sketches and notebooks full of figures under their arms and Boarded the Pullman. As the countryside sped by, the two engineers kept working. Two weeks after Douglas had received Frye's letter, Wetzel and Raymond presented the Douglas design proposal to a TWA committee, which included Frye, Richard W. Robbins, TWA president, and its most famous stockholder and chief technical advisor, Colonel Charles A. Lindbergh.

The TWA executives were fascinated by the Douglas sketches. This was not only a new plane but embodied a new concept of

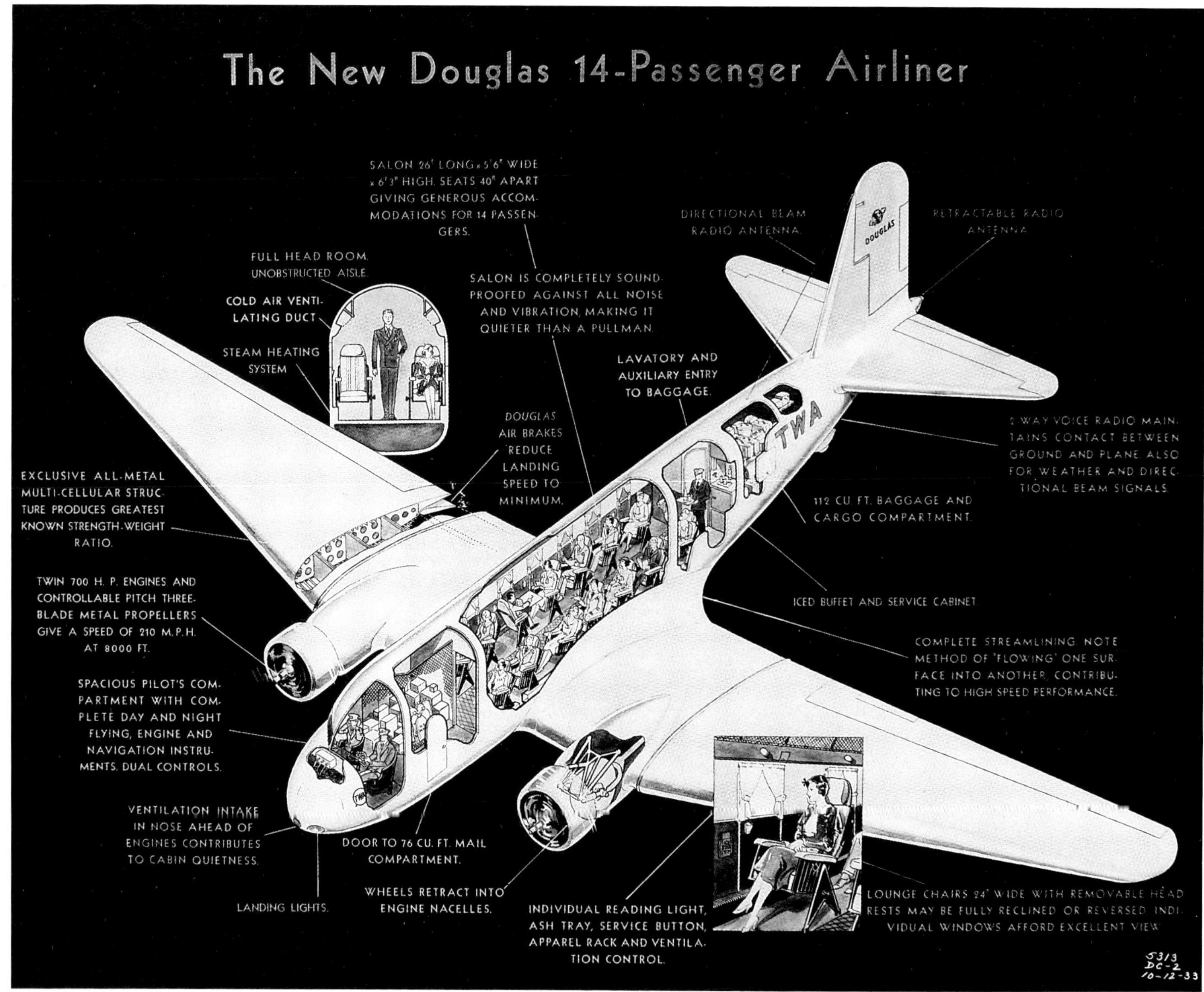

This 1933 drawing was used to persuade airlines to purchase the DC-2 and encourage passengers to fly in it. (Photo courtesy Robert Kopitzke)

aircraft design as well. "I like it," Frye said. "What do you think of it, Slim?"

Lindbergh was thoughtful for a moment. He remembered the tragedy of the Fokker that had killed Knute Rockne. "I recommend that we accept the concept, but I think Douglas must make one guarantee in addition to meeting all the points of their proposal. This ship should be able to take off with a full load from any point on the TWA route on one engine!"

Wetzel and Raymond looked at each other and took out their slide rules. The answer, as Raymond recalled later, was only about 90 percent Yes. The remaining ten percent could only be assured by actual test. "We'll try," was all Raymond could say.

The contract between Douglas and TWA was signed on September 20, 1932, and new life surged through the Douglas shops. The plant had been shut down, with only a skeleton force kept around to keep the rust off the machinery. The Great Depression had hit the budding aircraft industry hard. There was real cause for rejoicing when it was announced that Douglas was hiring its old hands back.

Weeks followed without any visible sign of an airplane being born. Then, slowly, the various shops began to get blueprints from which they were to make the thousands of parts that go to make up an airplane. Each print was marked mysteriously with the code "DC-1" which meant "Douglas Commercial—1st Model."

The fuselage, larger and longer than a Greyhound bus, slowly began to take shape on the assembly floor. As each skin panel was carefully fitted into place, the excitement among the employees rose. It was a graceful thing and it seemed so big. When the vertical stabilizer and wings were fitted on, it was a big airplane—the largest twin-engine landplane built in the United States up to that time.

The Los Angeles Terminal provided the backdrop for the DC-1 on a visit in 1933, the year of the first flight of the historic airliner. Although only one DC-1 was built, TWA and other airlines ordered more than 130 DC-2s, a slightly modified version of the DC-1. The world-famous DC-3, which flew for the first time in 1955, was simply the logical evolutionary development of the DC-1 and DC-2. Douglas Aircraft built more than 10,000 DC-3s, most of them as military tramsports designated the C-47.

Thirteen hundred miles to the north on February 8, 1933, the Boeing Airplane Co. in Seattle rolled out its answer to the growing demand for new transport planes; The Model 247.

The shiny aluminum of the DC-1 sparkled in the sunlight when it was pushed out of the Douglas hangar on June 22, 1933. Sleek and smooth in shape, it looked like a giant eagle as it was guided to the center of the parking ramp. The fuselage measured sixty feet from nose to tail and the wings stretched eighty-five feet from tip to tip. The nose tilted toward the sky majestically as the plane rolled on its two main wheels and smaller tail wheel. Two Wright Cyclone 710-horsepower, nine-cylinder, air-cooled engines were fitted to the forward edges of the wings. Three-bladed Hamilton Standard propellers, whose pitch could be controlled in the cabin by the pilots for most efficient takeoff and cruise power, were attached.

Inside the cabin were two rows of six seats in tandem with a broad aisle between. A small galley was located near the door at the rear of the fuselage for preparing meals in flight. There was also a lavatory and a toilet in a small rear compartment—more "firsts" for passenger comfort. Passengers could stand up and walk around in the cabin. Soundproofing insulation had been installed and cabin heaters to overcome the well-justified complaints of passengers who had huddled under blankets in the Fords, Fokkers and Boeings.

In the cockpit were more innovations. Dual controls and side-by-side seating for the pilots had been provided. New gyroscopic instruments were installed that would make blind flying easier and safer. Included was the new Sperry automatic pilot which could enable the pilot to fly "hands off"—the first commercial transport plane to be so equipped. To test the strength of the multi-cellular wings, a steamroller was driven over them and hundreds of pounds of shot bags were placed on the ailerons.

But beautiful, big and strong as it appeared to be, one question remained uppermost in everyone's mind: Would it fly?

Saturday, July 1, 1933 was bright and clear. On that day, the National Air Races were beginning in Los Angeles but few at the Douglas plant at nearby Santa Monica cared. A group of mechanics busied themselves around the maintenance shed. To them the first flight of a new airplane meant hours and sometimes days of tinkering with engines, fuel lines, pumps, and the hundreds of little things that, if neglected, could mean the difference between life and death for the test pilots.

It had been announced that the first flight of the DC-1 would be made by Carl A. Cover, test pilot and vice president in charge of sales. Attired tastefully in a tweed suit and a bright green hat, he climbed aboard with Fred Herman, a project engineer who would be the copilot. Crowds of onlookers were lined up on both sides of Santa Monica's Clover Field runway. Santa Monica residents had gotten used to Douglas "first flights" but there was always the same

The instrument panel of the first American Airlines' DSTs reflects the early flight and engine instruments being used in 1936. Later panels in the military versions reflected the increase in complexity required for military operations. (Douglas Aircraft Co. photos)

fascination. Everyone wanted to see if this new Douglas giant would fly—and if so, how well.

Cover busied himself in the cockpit, checking switches, hydraulic pressure and instrument readings. When both men were satisfied, Cover leaned out the left cockpit window and shouted "Clear!"

A mechanic standing nearby, hand on a fire extinguisher, gave the all clear signal. Cover touched the starter switch on the port engine. The starter growled and the propeller turned a few revolutions. Then the engine fired and broke into a roar. The other engine was started and Cover taxied into take-off position. After running the engines up and checking the magnetos and controls, Cover pulled out onto the runway. Instead of taking off, however, he taxied up and down the runway, testing brakes and, again, controls and engines. Finally, he nosed the plane into the wind, pushed the throttles forward and headed down the field.

Full of life, the gleaming craft sped straight ahead, a beautiful sight in the bright California noonday sun. The tail came up slowly, then the main wheels were off the ground at exactly 12:36 P.M. The engines purred as smoothly as a new watch.

Suddenly, without warning, just as Cover pulled the nose up into a gentle climb, the left engine sputtered and quit. The crowd gasped. A woman screamed. The craft nosed down momentarily and, as it did, the engine caught again. The crowd sighed. Cover cautiously lifted the nose and, as it did, both engines quit with that awful silence, the full meaning of which all pilots can appreciate. Again Cover jammed the nose forward, and again the twin engines roared back to life.

Cover, his hands busy in the cockpit, had no time to think. He was an old hand at the flying game and his old reflexes to maintain flying speed had saved his and Herman's lives and the airplane. The reflex that told him to get the nose down when he lost engine power was the very reflex that made the engine cut back in again. The second time it happened he reasoned that he would have to climb very carefully. He nursed the plane carefully up to about 1,000 feet, turned slowly, flew a wide traffic pattern and bounced to a safe, controlled landing.

As Cover taxied to a stop before a crowd of anxious spectators, Donald Douglas, maintenance men and engineers rushed up. "What happened, Carl?" they asked in unison.

"The damned engines cut out. That's all I know. Every time I tried to get the nose up, they cut out. I think you'd better check those carburetors. There's something screwy about them."

After the plane was towed back to Clover Field, engine mechanics and representatives from the Wright company took off the engine cowlings and dismantled the engines. Ivar Shogran, the engine specialist, and his men took the engines apart and put them back together several times. They put the engines on test stands and ran them for hours without a single sputter. It was some time before they concluded that the carburetors were indeed the problem. The floats had been designed with the floats hinged in the rear with the fuel lines feeding gas from the same direction. When the plane was put into a climbing attitude, the gasoline would not flow upward into the engines and the fuel would shut off. The floats were merely turned around 180 degrees, and the trouble was permanently corrected.

For the next six weeks, the DC-1 was subjected to the most intensive series of tests any Douglas plane had ever had to endure. Edmund T. Allen, a freelance test pilot hired by Douglas, Frank Collbohm as copilot, TWA pilots, and Jack Frye himself, a qualified airline pilot, wrung it out so much everyone was amazed that no structural failures resulted. There was concern that the wing structures would not withstand the strain. After all, butting the wings into the outer wing panels was a new engineering concept for a plane so large.

To test the DC-1's load-bearing capability, 18,000 pounds of sand bags and lead ingots was stowed aboard and the plane was lofted to 22,000 feet. Landing and takeoff trials were conducted and it was found that with a simulated load of passengers and baggage, it could get off in less than 1,000 feet, helped with the aid of new wing flaps that also allowed for a landing speed of about sixty-five miles per hour. Speed tests were flown over a measured course at various altitudes; on one of them, the DC-1 showed a speed of 227 miles per hour, better than most racing planes of that era.

But the test program for X223Y, the number assigned to the plane by the U.S. Department of Commerce, was not without incident. On one occasion a mechanic put heavy engine oil in the automatic pilot instead of hydraulic fluid and the controls became so stiff that it took the full strength of both pilots to get the plane back on the ground. On another occasion, with test pilot Eddie Allen at the controls, the landing gear was forgotten in a mix-up of cockpit signals and a belly landing was made. The only damage, however, was a pair of bent propellers and the egos of two red-faced pilots. As a result, the gear warning system was improved. Originally pumped down by hand, a motor drive was put in. The flaps were also manually operated at first, with a long lead screw that took many turns and a long time to lower them so it was also motorized.

Art Raymond adds: "As was usual in those days, some modifications in the tail surfaces were necessary to improve stability and control and to achieve the proper stick forces, but these were minor. The stalling speed came out a little high and we tried an auxiliary wing between the nacelles and the fuselage to see if this would help. It did lower the stalling speed but it made the stall so abrupt that we decided against it."

The DC-1 was put through test after test and it passed them all, surprising even the most skeptical engineers. During the trials, W. B. Oswald and Franklin R. Collbohm devised engine power tables to arrive at the best engine cruise power settings for different altitudes and discovered that the DC-1 was twenty percent more economical and faster than any other transport in the skies. Then came the day when it had to pass the test Lindbergh had added to the specifications—the single-engine takeoff from TWA's highest airport with a load simulating twelve passengers and their baggage. It was September 4, 1933. Eddie Allen was the pilot, and D. W. Tomlinson was copilot. The test was to be conducted at Winslow, Arizona, 4,500 feet above sea level where the thinner air meant the engines would be less efficient.

Allen gave full throttle to both engines and the fully loaded plane, slowly gathered speed. Just as the wheels left the ground, Tomlinson suddenly reached up and cut the ignition switch on the right engine. The plane lurched to the right, but a surprised Allen caught it in time, feathered the dead engine and held the ship straight ahead. Slowly but surely, the half-powered plane climbed to 8,000 feet and leveled off. Still flying on one engine, Allen flew to the next stop on the TWA route—Albuquerque, New Mexico, 280 miles away. Not only did the One make it in good time but it arrived 15 minutes ahead of one of TWA's Ford trimotors which had departed Winslow before the DC-1. If there were any doubts before this test, they were now completely swept away. TWA accepted the DC-1, the only one ever built, and immediately placed orders for twenty-five more but with a few modest structural changes.

The DC-1 contract price was $125,000, but it had cost Douglas $307,000 to build it. The original agreement was that TWA would have an option to buy up to a total of sixty planes at $58,000 each, later increased to $65,000 per plane. The net result was that Douglas lost over a quarter of a million dollars on the first order of twenty planes. Willing to take the gamble because he saw that his planes already outperformed the only real competitor, Boeing's 247 transport, he felt sure he would recoup his loss with sales to other airlines. Actually, his engineers had already come up with new sketches and blueprints based on a hint that Frye himself had dropped before the DC-1's first flight. He said he would be interested in placing a larger order if improvements could be made. The Douglas engineers went to work to see what they could do.

Meanwhile, TWA officially took delivery on the DC-1 in December 1933 in a ceremony at Los Angeles Municipal Airport. Although the company started taking delivery of the initial twenty-five DC-2s a few months later at a total cost of $1,625,000, it continued to use the DC-1 for experimental purposes. It was "plushed up" with carpeting on the floor, insulation to deaden engine noise, a cream-and-blue decor and comfortable, reclining leather seats. It became known to the press as the "laboratory plane" and became the model for the interiors of the DC-2s to follow. For the first time, passengers had individual reading lights, seats that would face forward or rearward, foot rests, safety belts and cabin heating. A small galley was provided in the rear with space for thermos jugs, a hotplate and space for box lunches.

A test that would prove its capability and garner much public interest in the plane occurred on February 9, 1934, when President Roosevelt signed an Executive Order canceling all air mail contracts with civilian companies. He directed that the Army Air Corps take over the job of flying the mail over the airline routes. There had been allegations of fraud and favoritism in the award of air

All inaugural flights by the airlines were preceded with much fanfare. This was the christening scene at Chicago when American Airlines began service with DC-3s between Chicago and New York. (Photo courtesy Robert Kopitzke)

mail contracts by the Post Office Department which threatened to malign his New Deal programs.

When Jack Frye heard about the order, he called Capt. E. V. "Eddie" Rickenbacker, America's top World War I ace and vice president of Eastern Air Lines. They agreed that to make a strong point with the public about the unfairness of the cancellation, they would team up to set a cross-country speed record in the DC-1 from Burbank, California, to Newark, New Jersey, taking the last load of eastbound mail before the president's order went into effect. When they landed on February 19th, they had set a new transcontinental record of 13 hours, 4 minutes, including stops at Kansas City, Missouri, and Columbus, Ohio.

Later in 1934 the Department of Commerce and the Army Air Corps used the DC-1 to test a Sperry automatic pilot which was linked to a Kreusi radio compass and used for navigation experiments; night flying equipment was installed and tests were made to increase engine power at high altitudes. Tests were made with deicing boots on the wings and anti-icing systems for the propellers. Additional gasoline tanks were installed and the fuel capacity was boosted from 500 to 1,600 gallons. Pratt & Whitney Hornet engines were installed briefly, then replaced by more powerful Wright engines.

In 1935, two years after its maiden flight, the DC-1 was authorized by TWA to be made available to the National Aeronautic Association to attempt to set new national and international records for load, speed and distance. Within a three-day period, it smashed nineteen speed records, including a new west-east transcontinental mark of 11 hours, 5 minutes, thus eclipsing a record set by Roscoe Turner in his own racing plane on July 1, 1933, the day the DC-1 had flown for the first time.

In 1936, Howard Hughes, millionaire sportsman and largest holder of TWA stock, planned a record-breaking round-the-world flight. He decided that the DC-1 was the best plane for the job and bought it from TWA in the summer of 1936. He modified it by increasing the fuel capacity to give it an unprecedented range of more than 6,000 miles and changed engines to more powerful Wright models. After exhaustive tests, however, Hughes chose the faster Lockheed 14 in which he later circled the globe in 1939 in a record-setting time of 72 hours, 8 minutes.

Having bypassed the DC-1 for the world flight, Hughes sold it eventually to an Englishman, Viscount Forbes, the Earl of Granard, in May 1937. By that time, the DC-1 had accumulated 1,370 flying hours. The DC-1's new owner wanted to fly the Atlantic in it but Hughes talked him out of it. Taking the advice, the viscount shipped it to England on a freighter in June 1938. He flew it for several months and then sold it to a French company. Its whereabouts were not known for a while but it surfaced in Spain where it had been purchased by the Republican government for Lineas Aeros Postales Espanoles (L.A.P.E.) as a mail, cargo and personnel carrier and, painted in camouflage colors, was later used during the Spanish Civil War for reconnaissance. In 1939, just as the Spanish Civil War was drawing to a close and the Republican government was collapsing, it was used to evacuate officials from Spain to exile in France. When the war ended, it was seized by the Nationalists, stripped of its war paint and named "Negron" after a heroic Nationalist pilot. It was used by Sociedad Anonima de Transportes, which later became Iberia Air Lines, to link the major cities of Spain.

The end of the DC-1 as a flying machine came about in December 1940 during a landing at Malaga in southern Spain. After arriving from Tetuan, several passengers were loaded aboard and the wheel chocks were removed (the DC-1 had no parking brakes). The pilot taxied to the end of the runway, lined up for takeoff and started down the runway. An Iberia Air Lines pilot who was there tells what happened:

"The plane came roaring toward us. Then, suddenly, when her wheels were only inches from the ground, one engine sputtered and quit. The next instant, she was mushing down on her belly in a cloud of dust. When the dust cleared away, the plane was a pile of junk at the end of the runway."[1]

Fortunately, no one was injured but the DC-1 was never to fly again. Since World War I had begun and few aircraft spare parts were available, the airline decided to write it off the books. Mechanics towed the wreckage to a corner of the field and salvaged what spare parts might be useful on other types of planes.

As an airplane, the DC-1 was history but it had made an indelible mark in aviation history with an unmatched series of records. But, remarkably, this forefather of a long line of offspring, is still alive—in a way. Monks from the nearby Catedral de Malaga needed a light but strong andas, or portable platform, which could be used

[1]*As quoted in The Plane That Changed the World by Douglas J. Ingells. Fallbrook, Calif. Aero Publishers, 1966. P. 65.*

to carry the image of the Blessed Virgin through the streets on religious holidays. Metal spars and skin from the skeleton of the DC-1 were the answer. Thus, the grandfather of all Gooney Birds is still doing a job that requires strength and dependability.

While the DC-1 had been setting records, the Douglas factory at Santa Monica had tooled up for production of the updated, stretched version. Douglas engineers, pleased with the DC-1's performance, had come up with a new thought. With the extra margin of performance that had been engineered into the DC-1, why not try to stretch it about 30 inches and give it space for 14 seats instead of 12 and thus add a bonus of a little more productivity for the airlines. The engineers added two more feet in length and two more windows on each side and gave it a new company designation: DC-2. TWA promptly ordered twenty-five. A TWA press release glowingly described the airline's new "queen of the skies":

"The silver ship is a low-wing cantilever monoplane. The entire external appearance of the transport is remarkable for its complete freedom from struts and control system parts. In harmony with clean design, the wheels retract into the engine nacelles but are so arranged that emergency landings are possible while the gear is in the retracted position.

"The passenger salon is twenty-six feet, four inches long, five feet six inches wide, and six feet three inches high. The great height of the passenger salon permits even the tallest person to walk fully erect in the cabin for its entire length. The compartment is fitted to accommodate fourteen passengers in two rows of specially-designed lounge chairs 40 inches wide and separated by a central aisle 16 inches wide. Chairs are deeply upholstered and fully adjustable for reclining or reversing to face the passenger behind. Each seat has a private window and because of the height of the seat above the wing, there is excellent vision from all chairs.

Six Braniff Airways DC-2s fly in loose formation for the camera. Braniff's first DC-2 was purchased from TWA. Organized originally in 1930, Braniff eventually stretched its network to Buenos Aires, Argentina. (Photo courtesy of History of Aviation Collection, Univ. of Texas, Dallas)

"The transport is equipped with two 710-horsepower Wright Cyclone motors, which are supercharged to insure a fast cruising speed at high altitudes. Two controllable-pitch, three-bladed, two position, hydro-controllable Hamilton Standard propellers pull the 12,000-pound plane through the air. The propeller pitch is controlled by the pilot and is changed by oil pressure for climb and cruising speed.

"There are two main fuel tanks of 180 gallons capacity each and two auxiliary tanks of 75 gallons each, making a total of 510 gallons maximum fuel supply, enough to fly non-stop 1200 miles.

"The fuselage is of semi-monocoque construction with smooth riveted skin. The material used is a new extra light aluminum alloy having a thin coating of pure aluminum to give it high resistance to corrosion. The entire interior is accessible from nose to tail. The empennage is built integral with the fuselage to insure absolute rigidity.

"The Douglas air brakes—split trailing edge flaps—are built into the lower side of the wing to increase the lift and drag for slow, restricted landings. The flaps when hinged full-down cause a gain in lift of 35 per cent and a slow-down increase of 300 percent. They are operated by a hydraulic system controlled from the cockpit."

TWA also claimed optimistically that the DC-2 would reach a maximum speed of 212 miles per hour at 14,000 feet and 225 miles per hour at 18,000 feet. The service ceiling was projected to be 23,600 feet and its "absolute" ceiling was said to be 25,400 feet. Through the use of the flaps, landing speed was reduced to only 58 miles per hour. Its single-engine ceiling was 9,000 feet.

Although the general shape of the Two was similar to the DC-1, it required new blueprints, new tooling, and more structural analysis, including extensive wind tunnel tests. Despite the work required, the first of the new models rolled off the line and was accepted by TWA on May 14, 1934. Four days later its first scheduled run was made between Columbus, Ohio, and Newark, New Jersey, via Pittsburgh, Pennsylvania. When it began service between New York and Chicago, it broke the speed record between the two cities four times in as many days.

In addition to the new comfort that passengers could enjoy in the DC-2s, TWA and Eastern Air Lines showed the first inflight motion pictures to passengers. The first was shown on January 3, 1935 in an Eastern Air Lines plane that departed Newark and also flew over New York City. The copilot was Capt. Eddie Rickenbacker. The film was the premier showing of the film "Baboons." TWA added its "first" the following year. A motion picture entitled "Flying Hostess," produced by Universal Pictures, was previewed by critics in a TWA DC-2 in the air over New York City. It was the first film to portray the training of airline flight attendants. One writer described the functions of the then-called airline hostesses this way:

"Their duties were to bolt the seats to the floor before each flight, offer cotton for passengers' ears to muffle noise, make sure the passengers chose the door to the toilet instead of the nearby emergency exit, warn against throwing lighted cigar butts out the window and 'carry a railroad timetable in case the plane is grounded somewhere.'"[2]

As the Two was proving itself daily, more orders were placed by eager airline buyers who realized that this was the plane that could sell air travel to the public. One of them was sold to KLM Royal Dutch Airlines, one of the world's oldest carriers that had begun operations in 1919. It was christened "Uiver" (Stork) and was earmarked to participate in the Melbourne Centenary Air Race, better known as the London-to-Melbourne Race. It was to be a grueling 11,000-mile race sponsored by Sir Macpherson Robertson, a wealthy Scotsman and head of the MacRobertson Chocolate Company. Touted by the press as "the race of the century," a first prize of $15,000 was offered for the first crew entering the speed category to span the distance from Mildenhall near London to Melbourne, and $10,000 to the winner in a handicap category. The Royal Aero Club of England agreed to organize the race and enforce the rules. Robertson insisted on two main rules: the race must be international in character, and everything reasonable must be done to reduce the risk of accidents. He also stipulated that the race had to be completed within sixteen days. The Royal Aero Club made additional rules which included five control points for landings: Bagdadh, Iraq; Allahabad, India; Singapore, Malay Straits; Darwin and Charleville, Australia. The race was scheduled to begin on October 20, 1934.

Sixty-five entries were received from the pilots of fifteen nations; seventeen pilots from the United States had sent in their entry fees. However, by starting day there were only twenty planes representing seven countries ready for the race. The only American pilots left on takeoff day were Roscoe Turner, Clyde Pangborn, and Reeder Nichols, radio operator, in a Boeing 247; Jacqueline Cochran and Wesley Smith flying a Granville Supersportster; and Jack Wright and John Polando in a Lambert Monocoupe. An American-built Lockheed Vega was also entered which was flown by two Australians, John Woods and D. Bennett. KLM's DC-2 was piloted by Captains Koene D. Parmentier and Jan Moll. The pair favored to win were Britons C.W.A. Scott and Thomas Campbell-Black flying a de Havilland Comet, one of three designed especially for the race. Both pilots had flown the course in other types of aircraft several times before.

The starting positions were decided by a drawing. Captain James Mollison and his wife Amy Johnson Mollison, flying one of the Comets, drew first place. Roscoe Turner drew the second takeoff position. The KLM DC-2 took off fifth with about 30,000 letters and three adventurous passengers who had bought tickets to destinations along the regular KLM route.

Plane after plane became airborne at 45-second intervals, and as the last one disappeared, so did the crowd. They went home to tune in their wireless sets to follow the race to completion. The

[2]*Airline Builders by Oliver E. Allen. Alexandria, Va. Time-Life Books, 1981. P. 136.*

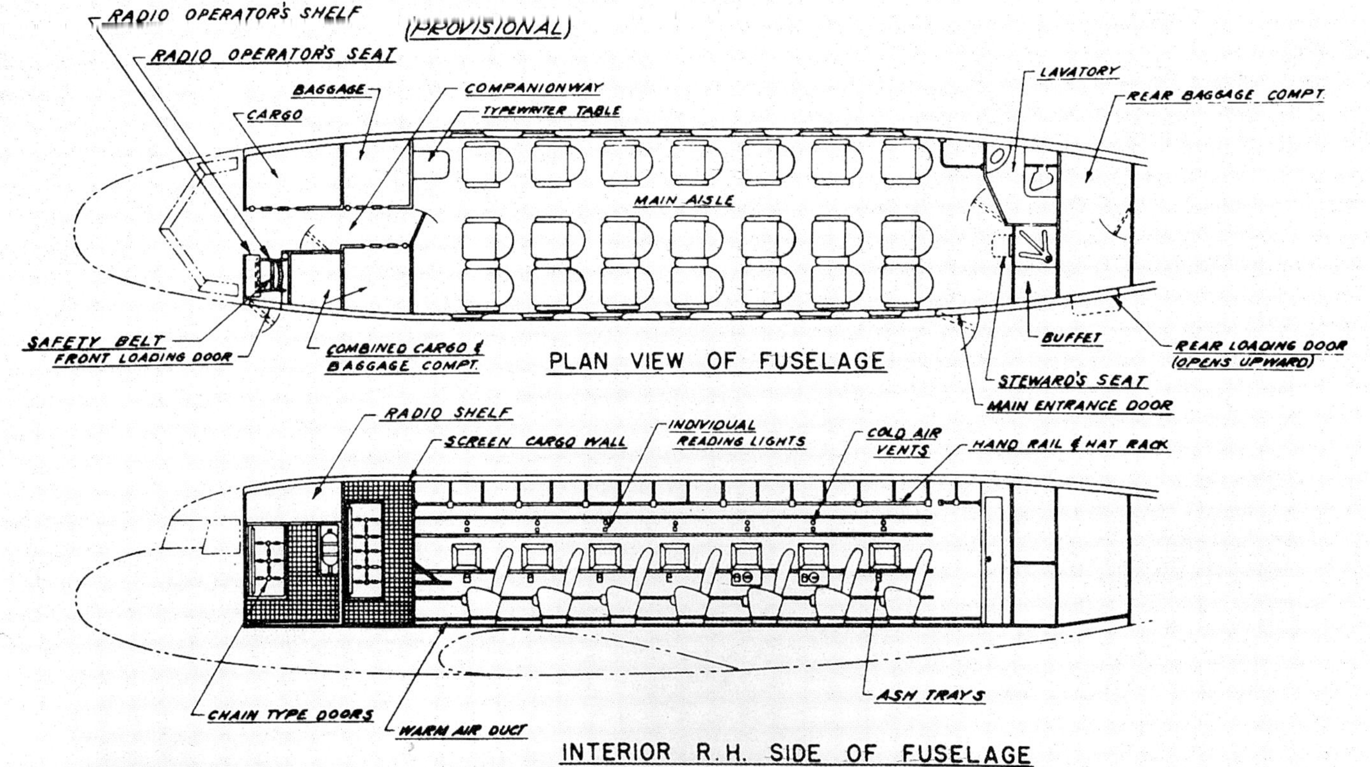

The interior of the Douglas DC-3 typically accomodates 21 passengers in three-abreast seating, although the Douglas Sleeper transport (DST) version carried only 14, and other arrangements provided for 28 passengers, or as many as 32 in maximum density seating. (Douglas Aircraft Co. Photo)

lower fares. In 1927, it cost $400 to fly from San Francisco to New York and it took 33 hours. By 1937 it was a 15-hour flight and cost only $149.50.

The luxury of the Skylounge with its swiveling chairs, fine chinaware and hot meal service cost only about $5 more for the coast-to-coast run and was immediately popular. Later, a "Half-Sleeper" was ordered by United Airlines, with sleeping berths for eight and reclining chairs for seven. Conversions to carry 23 passengers for daylight flights were also available.

In the short span of five years after its initial flight, the DC-3 was fast becoming the standard equipment for every major airline in the world. Orders were filling the mailboxes daily at the Douglas factory in Santa Monica. The Lockheed Electras, the flying boats and all of the trimotors were now obsolete. The number of the DC-3s that could be produced was limited only by the facilities at the factory. By 1938 the DC-3 was carrying nearly 95 percent of the nation's air traffic. By the next year, 90 percent of the world's airline passengers were being flown in DC-3s. Licenses to manufacture them were granted to the Fokker Co. in the Netherlands, although none were produced there. The Nakajima Co. in Japan was granted a license and the first DC-3 was produced there in September 1938 at Tokyo's Haneda Airport. The USSR bought many tools and jigs, plus eighteen DC-3s between November 1936 and March 1939. By the middle of 1940, about 40 were being produced monthly. Designated the PS-84 at first and later the Lisunov Li-2, they were flown by Aeroflot, Russia's state-owned airline. When the Germans overwhelmed Czechoslovakia in 1938, a number of DC-3s were captured and used by the Nazis during the invasion of the Netherlands. At least one DC-2 which had been obtained from the Fokker company had already been tested by the Luftwaffe.

By 1939 when it appeared that there would be an international air transportation system developing, the major nations of the world were being aligned politically or were at war with either the Allied forces led mostly by the United States, Great Britain, and France, or the Axis powers of Germany, Italy and Japan. Strangely, the DC-3, a people transport built for peace, was to play an unusually vital role in the outcome of the great world war that was to come.

2

The DC-3 Saves the Airlines

The DC-3 freed the airlines from complete dependence upon government mail pay. It was the first airplane that could make money just by hauling passengers.

C. R. Smith
President, American Airlines

While Douglas employees were putting the finishing touches on DC-2 Number 185, the first DC-3 was rolled out on the ramp beside it. Others followed quickly and the new version created much attention from the nation's top airline executives. They were invited to Santa Monica to witness its inaugural flight on December 17, 1935, the thirty-second anniversary of the Wright brothers' epic flight. They learned that Douglas would produce the DC-3 in several models and soon found that the new Three flew higher, faster and had more innovations for passenger safety and comfort than the DC-2.

There was a rush to place orders with Douglas and it was soon clear that the DC-3 had ushered in a new era for the air traveler. When American Airlines became the first airline in the world to put the new airliner into service, it was a day that marked the end of profitless flying.

A week later, on July 1, 1936—exactly three years since the day when the DC-1 made its first flight—Donald W. Douglas stood in President Roosevelt's Oval Office at the White House and was presented with the coveted Collier Trophy for having developed "the most outstanding twin-engined transport plane."

"The airplane," President Roosevelt said, "by reason of its high speed, economy, and quiet passenger comfort has been generally adopted by transport lines throughout the United States. Its merit has been further recognized by its adoption abroad and its influence on foreign design is already apparent."

No longer was the hapless passenger forced to balance his box lunch on his knees while munching a cold sandwich or an apple. No longer would he suffer from deafness, gastric disturbances, cold feet, and lack of sleep. Now chic stewardesses wearing white gloves brought handy trays containing full course meals from soup to nuts. And the meals were free. Between meals the stewardesses, all reg-

American Airlines ordered its early DSTs and DC-3s with passenger access doors on the right side of the fuselage. Later DC-3s and all military versions were standardized with doors on the left side. The DST is distinguishable by the small slit windows above the main passenger windows for the benefit of upper bunk passengers. (Photo courtesy Robert Kopitzke)

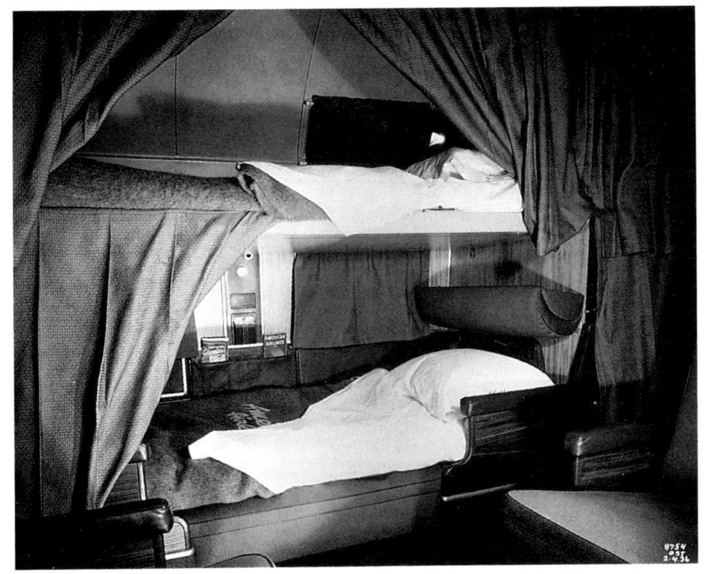

The Douglas Sleeper Transport (DST) was the first airliner designed and built initially as a sleeper. Arrangement of the passenger salon provided sleeping accommodations for sixteen. At the rear of the salon were two dressing rooms with adjoining lavatories and a baggage compartment that was accessible in flight. (McDonnell Douglas photo)

istered nurses, served chewing gum, hot bouillon or coffee and cookies. They chatted with the passengers, pointed out interesting places along the route and answered questions about the plane.

By the end of 1936, most of the nation's airlines had formed their fleets with the DC-3 as the main aircraft or were planning to convert to it. A new record was set that year, despite the Depression: one million passengers had boarded the scheduled airlines for the first time. The American public, because of the profound influence of this new airplane, was slowly becoming airminded. In the next three years the two million passenger mark would be passed.

Slowly, as the accountants totaled their profit-and-loss statements, the airlines found that the stretched version of the DC-2 spelled the difference between profit and loss and removed what was the greatest danger in commercial flying at that time—the near certainty of going broke.

The airlines then took on a new source of profit-making never before possible to any great extent: air freight. Maine lobsters, which previously had been placed in bulky containers and packed in several layers of ice to prevent spoilage on long rail journeys, were now shipped fast in lightweight containers across the country in less than a day. People on the West Coast and in the South who had never tasted Maine lobsters found they could enjoy them often. Orchid growers were able to ship fresh flowers to any part of the United States by air. Fresh fruits and vegetables, and even live animals, were flown in DC-3s. It was then that the railroads began to take notice. Their business was beginning to decline because airplanes could haul freight over long distances at faster speeds on regular schedules and do it safely. A whole new industry had been born!

With each hour in the air, DC-3 pilots grew more experienced at flying the new all-metal planes. They were easier to fly than the old Fords, Stinsons and Fokkers. Before too many years passed, there were pilots who had accumulated a great number of hours. When a pilot reached a certain point in his flying career he became a "Million Miler."

Captain Charles W. Myers, a retired Eastern Airlines pilot, was one of those Million Milers. He, like others, had many stories to tell about the DC-3:

"During my years with Eastern I put in about 9,000 hours in DC airplanes," he told the author. "Other than occasional minor difficulties, I had no serious mechanical failures. This, to me, points out the fine engineering that went into Douglas airplanes. We on the airlines should know. We flew them through thunderstorms, ice, sleet, hail, and hurricanes. As far as I know, none were lost because of mechanical or structural failure. At times we thought the big wings might buckle in a storm because we could actually see them wiggle. But this, as far as I know, never happened. They were sturdy, to say the least.

"The DC-3 was, in my opinion, the steppingstone for pilots from the Ford and Stinson trimotors, the Condors and Boeings to the modern airliner. It was just the schooling and transition airplane we needed for the complicated jet airplanes of today.

"We who flew the DC-3 had complete confidence in it. I might relate one incident that will serve to show how we got that confidence.

"I had left Atlanta one night headed for Chicago, with scheduled stops at Chattanooga, Nashville, and Louisville. Out of Atlanta the weather in front of us was anything but the best. Chattanooga, Nashville, and Louisville were socked in, and Atlanta went down to zero right after take-off. Over Chattanooga we rammed into a cold front full of wet snow and ice. We were at 5,000 feet

This is the most famous cockpit in the world. It has been estimated that DC-3/C-47 aircraft flew more than 100 million miles during World War II in airline and military service. No one has dared to estimate the miles it has flown since in military and commercial operations or by private owners. (Douglas Aircraft Co. photo)

when one engine began to pose power because of an iced-up carburetor. I turned on the carburetor heat control but it simply wouldn't melt the ice. The power dropped off so rapidly that I knew I had to do something fast.

"My copilot, Hank Freese, had been a barnstormer back in the early days as I had been. I reminded him of the days when we were often bothered with ice and said, 'Hank, lean it out until it backfires, like we used to do.' Hank pulled back the mixture control until the engine backfired several times and blew the slushy ice out of the carburetor.

"About this time, we hit the front that was causing all the foul weather. We were kicked upstairs, at higher altitude. What I mean is this: We hit a bad updraft that threw us from 5,000 feet up to 13,000 in nothing flat. Then we shot back down, fast, then on up to 10,000 and finally back down to 5,000 feet again. Talk about being busy! All that concerned me was keeping my air speed within the safety limits and keeping the bird straight and level. I wasn't particularly concerned how high the updrafts took us, but I would have worried some if it had started tossing us down below the 5,000-foot mark.

"While we were jockeying up and down in the dark sky, the second engine carburetor froze up and we had to blow out the ice like we had on the other one. There is always a danger of catching fire when you resort to this method but when the ice is too heavy for the heat control to melt it you don't have much choice. Besides, we had engine fire extinguishers that could be released if an engine caught fire.

"Chattanooga, Nashville and Louisville continued to be all socked in. The weather was so bad in places we couldn't even think about landing. By this time the wings, propellers, and tail surfaces were loaded with ice and we were carrying about all the power the

The Douglas Aircraft Co. offered a number of seating configurations for the DC-3s. C. R. Smith, president of American Airlines, was first to order the Douglas Sleeper Transport (DST), forerunner of the DC-3 and started the famous "Flagship Fleet." W. A. "Pat" Patterson, head of United Airlines, asked for a 14-passenger "Sky Club" arrangement similar to railroad club cars. (Douglas Aircraft Co. photo)

Clothing and baggage manufacturers adopted the Skysleeper concept and advertised their wares, along with models of the DC-3, in their show windows. (Photo courtesy Robert Kopitzke)

engines would stand to keep the bird in the air. Every once in a while the ice would break loose from the propellers and crash against the side of the airplane. I know the passengers were wondering what was going on outside, and I am sure they were a bit concerned. For certain, I was!

"The nearest place I figured we could set the big plane down was Indianapolis. I checked the weather there and it was bad. When you're flying a route like this you have to figure the odds in every case. I had already passed over three landing places and wasn't overloaded with fuel, by any means. Sooner or later I had to set down somewhere and not endanger the lives of the people for whom I was responsible. Besides, I cared a little for my own neck, too.

"Stumbling around in the darkness with poor radio reception, we finally found Indianapolis radio range station and circled for a clearance. I tried a landing but found that my windshield was so covered with ice that I couldn't see ahead. I pulled back up, took the hand fire extinguisher and slammed it against the left corner windshield and broke it. The cold air rushed in and chilled my face, momentarily blinding me, but at least I could see the runway to make my next approach. Looking cockeyed out of the corner glass, I finally got the bird on the ground.

"On the ramp my copilot and I looked the bird over. There were about two inches of ice on the wings, tail and nose, and it was solid. From that moment on, Hank Freese and I were convinced that we were flying the only airplane in that world that could do what that airplane did for us that night. Believe me, any time you can take an airplane, load it with a ton or more of ice, plus a load of passengers, baggage and mail, fly solid instruments from Atlanta to Indianapolis and do it all with partial or intermittent power, that's the airplane for me. I think I can speak for all the old DC-3 pilots—and there are lots of them around, probably still flying—when I say that all of us have deep respect for the old girl. It does my heart good to see them still flying. I'm sure they will never wear out."

A lineup of American Airlines DC-3 flagships awaits passengers at LaGuardia Field, New York, in 1941. The number of spectators to view ground operations closely was typical of the pre-war era before most Americans had flown. (Photo courtesy Robert Kopitzke)

While the airlines were having a heyday with their new airplane and bursting with happiness that the Three was bringing them out of the red into the black, war clouds loomed ahead for the nation. A mustached, former paperhanger named Adolf Hitler was screaming his defiance to the world.

Germany had been shorn of its military aircraft after World War I and was supposedly at the bottom of the list in numbers of trained pilots and airplane mechanics. But under Hitler's leadership, the Third Reich had secretly grown in military air strength. Hundreds of pilots and aircrewmen had been trained in gliders and commercial aircraft. As a result, Germany's airlines grew, and by 1939 Germany had a network of airlines linking the Fatherland with Africa and the Middle East. German-run airlines also stretched the length and breadth of South America. A vital air lifeline—the 2,600-mile stretch running from Lima, Peru, to Rio de Janeiro—was being spanned daily by a German company. This route was slowly expanded north through Ecuador to Colombia and south to Uruguay, Paraguay, and Argentina. By 1939 the transcontinental thread had become an economic chain.

In Brazil a Nazi syndicate had built landing fields on the strategic shoulder of land jutting out into the Atlantic where bombers and troops could be landed from Africa. Innocent-appearing merchant vessels could, and did, reconnoiter the ocean and guide German U-boats to their unsuspecting prey. In addition, these same ships warned blockade-running Axis vessels of the presence of Allied warships. The extensive planning for war placed the Germans in an excellent position to rush in planes and troops to take advantage of the political vacuum that might be caused by a revolution in any South American country.

The best part of the plan, from Hitler's viewpoint, was that it threw a monkey wrench into the war plans of the United States. America couldn't make a decision to strike east or west as long as there was the danger of enemy bombers coming from the south to blast the locks of the Panama Canal, attack Caribbean bases, or bomb American cities.

The United States did have a sword, however, with which to lop off Hitler's hold on South America. If the sale of gasoline from the refineries of the United States were cut off, Axis planes would not fly. But the sword was double-edged. If it were used without a declaration of war, there was the danger of cutting the bond of friendship with the countries of South America which was a vital part of the U.S. anti-Nazi strategy.

The Germans had no doubt thought of this possibility. While the U.S. had kept its activities strictly on a commercial basis in South America, Germany had been overly generous to the small struggling nations. The airlines had been established there by the Germans without regard to cost or profit; passengers and freight were benevolently flown over the entire continent at a continual

American Airlines inaugurated its Flagship Airfreighter service during World War II with older DC-3s. In some planes, the windows were covered over to protect them from damage by shifting cargo. (American Airlines photo)

loss. As a result, the countries became dependent upon the German airlines and took ever-increasing advantage of the low fares and dependable service.

The menace grew daily. As Hitler made his moves to dominate and occupy all of Europe, tons of airplane spare parts began to flow into the strategic shoulder of Brazil. The German-owned Condor Airlines had established some 3,000 miles of air routes where traffic possibilities were practically nonexistent. But the strategic impact was obvious to trained American observers. At the same time, Lufthansa-Peru and Sedta Airlines increased their networks, and Lati, an Italian transoceanic airline, doubled its schedule, thus providing an invaluable channel for inter-Axis diplomatic mail, wireless transmitting sets, and Axis agents.

The German menace, which comprised over 30,000 miles of air routes by the time war was declared against Great Britain in September 1939, had to be stopped quickly. Washington strategists decided to duplicate all the German air routes and have them flown by American crews and aircraft. Since the German airlines were popular, as well as cheap, it meant that superior service would have to be provided by U.S. airlines in order to make the plan feasible.

Pan-American Airways was the obvious organization to tackle the enormous task. Having started operations in Latin America in 1927, it had formed a system of trunk airlines linking all the capitals of South America with the United States and, in so doing, had won the confidence of all the Latin-American governments. Pan-American chose the DC-2s and -3s as its major aircraft for the task. Nineteen planes were assigned to the Eastern Division, while Panagra, the name of the South American West Coast system, was boosted to fourteen aircraft. The strategy was to cut flying time, stress safety, and operate on-the-minute schedules and thus attempt to drive the Axis operations out of business by sheer efficiency of service.

Panagra duplicated Sedta's routes early in 1941, and was shortly carrying three times the German company's volume of freight and passengers. Pan-American increased its schedules between Buenos Aires, Argentina, and Santiago, Chile, and paralleled Condor's operations over the Andes. At the same time, in the vital Colombian area, Panagra, which owned 80 percent of the stock, bought up the contracts of all the German employees of Scadta and reorganized it into a strong national company called Avianca. Then Panagra purchased a new airline which discharged German employees had or-

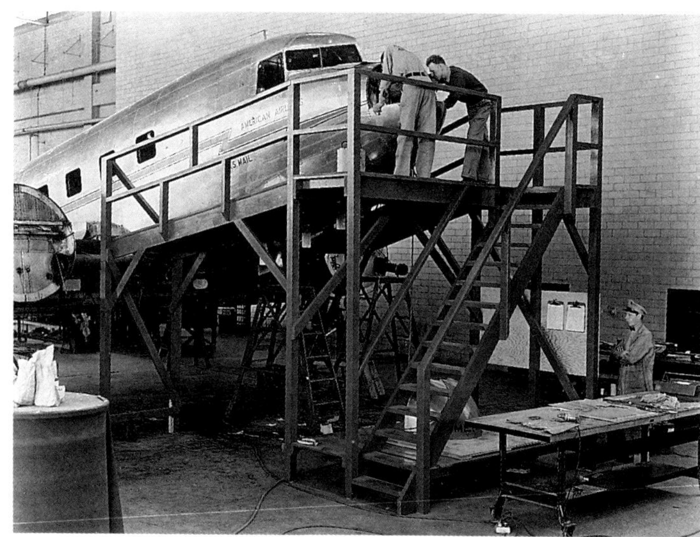

Wood trestles were constructed for easier access by American Airlines DC-2 and DC-3 mechanics. Engine and flight instruments were sometimes repaired and replaced through the nose cone as shown. (American Airlines photo)

The American Airlines DST Flagship Texas makes a stop at a desert airport to await passengers. It was the co-pilot's job to place the airline's trademark flag in a holder outside his window after landing and retrieve it before takeoff. (Photo courtesy Robert Kopitzke)

ganized, and thus completely terminated all Axis influence in the proximity of the vital inter-ocean link, the Panama Canal.

Panagra increased the DC-3 service on the trunk lines running north and south, making it possible for Peru to cancel Lufthansa's permits and expropriate its equipment when the Germans sabotaged interned ships in the harbor at Callao. One after another the Latin countries were able to cancel or take over the German airlines for cause. When the United States, in agreement with the Brazilian government, shut off Condor's gasoline supplies, that most important of the German airlines ceased to exist without any inconvenience to the Brazilian public. When the Japanese bombed Pearl Harbor on December 7, 1941, all that remained of Lufthansa's South American empire was a short 70-mile stretch over the Andes. It ceased operation within a week.

After World War II, the airlines bought surplus C-47s and had them modified to conform to federal regulations for passenger-carrying. Here TWA mechanics disassemble and rebuild them into DC-3s. (Douglas Aircraft Co. photo)

When this undeclared airline war had started, the Axis-owned or controlled airlines in South America were operating over some 33,000 air-route miles, whereas Pan-American, with its affiliated companies, had only 18,460 route miles. A week after Pearl Harbor the Pan-American system expanded to some 59,000 miles.

What makes this story relevant to the saga of the DC-3 is that the Axis could not have been squeezed out of South America if American-built planes had not been available in sufficient quantity. With the DC-2s and DC-3s, Pan-American not only made it possible for the United States government to drive out the Axis menace without inconvenience to its southern neighbors, but provided them with better service. It was the Gooney Bird that won the airline war against the Axis in South America before the real war started.

The scene was tense in the Munitions Building in downtown Washington, D.C., where the top brass of the War Department met to discuss the development of the United States aviation industry. There was a faction among the air planners that believed there was a need for development of transport aircraft for the Army to supplement the Army Air Corps' fighters and bombers. Although the DC-2 had been accepted and had proven itself to the civilian airlines, there was skepticism regarding its military use. Ground-bound generals wondered what real value, if any, they would have in a war that seemed inevitable in the late 1930s.

In the midst of the Depression, Congress had taken a dim view of huge appropriations for military aircraft. Each plane that was purchased or was being considered for the military inventory had

A lineup of American Airlines' DC-3s and DSTs. American's president C. R. Smith requested that the DC-2s be stretched to allow sleeping quarters for overnight flights and carry 21 passengers for day operations. (Photo courtesy American Airlines)

to be overly justified. Those who remembered the small part that the airplane had played in World War I were convinced that the next war—if there was one—would still be fought in the trenches.

The Secretary of War appointed a board to determine the types of aircraft needed by the Army and to make recommendations for future requirements of the nation's stepchild air arm. The board believed, and rightly so, that improvements in airplane design always came about through the competition among aircraft manufacturers. Speed, efficiency of operation, utility and safety of flight were among the foremost considerations in determining which should be selected. The board insisted that all new technical developments should be promptly and thoroughly tested by the Army Air Corps. Thus it was that attention was directed toward the revolutionary Douglas transports. Just as there was a growing need for transporting civilians across the country, it was logical to assume that the Army would need planes to transport troops and equipment quickly for national defense if war should come.

By 1938, no other company had produced an airplane, or even a design, to match the Douglas transports. Neither Boeing, Martin, Lockheed nor any other manufacturer had planes that could match it. The Defense Board reasoned that the Douglas company might be able to turn out modified versions of the DC-2 in quantity and still maintain the highest quality. As a result, the Chief of Staff of the Army was directed to study the procurement of Douglas transports without delay.

Air Corps experts poured over the reports of the exhaustive tests made on the DC-1 and DC-2 by TWA. The Air Corps had borrowed the DC-1 briefly from the company to test the Sperry autopilot; Air Corps engineers had installed 1,600-gallon fuel tanks in it which tripled the DC's range.

A report was submitted to the Air Corps Chief of Staff, Major General Benjamin D. Foulois. It recommended that the Douglas design be modified to accommodate Army requirements and that several prototypes be procured for tests under simulated battle conditions.

While the U.S. Army Air Corps was considering the possible adoption of the DC-2 as a standard military transport, four of the early civilian models had found their way to Spain to serve on the side of the Loyalists during the Spanish Civil War. The hard-pressed Loyalists loaded the 14-passenger DC-2s with thirty or more passengers and repeatedly outran the fighters of the Germans and the

American Airlines ran a shuttle service with a DST between Newark and Lakehurst, New Jersey, in 1936 for the convenience of passengers connecting with the German dirigible Hindenburg for the flight to Germany. (American Airlines photo)

To advertise its DC-3 service, American Airlines put the aircraft on display at cities it served across the country. This photo was taken at Boston Common in 1937. (Photo by Leslie R. Jones)

Italians. Francisco Batet, a crew chief on a Loyalist DC-2, told several stories about how they fared during their first taste of war:

"Throughout the thirty months of the war our four Douglas transports were never out of service, and during that time they were never housed in hangars. We always operated from provisional fields either by the seashore or in the mountains. Furthermore, we flew them both night and day, and all during the war we subjected them to punishment no other airplane could have withstood. They gave us courage. They proved that they would not let us down on any occasion.

"Once a crew was pursued by a squadron of Fiat fighters on the Estremadura front. Because of the greater speed of the Douglas, the Fiats soon fell behind.

"When we were transferred to Valencia we accomplished, with the DC-2, 182 liaison flights between Valencia and Santander in a straight line which crossed 311 miles of enemy territory. We did this without fighter protection and without armament, and we were always extremely overloaded. During these operations we were pursued eight times, but the Fiats never caught us or even annoyed us seriously.

"During May 1937, we transferred some troops from Valencia to Tarragona. With enough gasoline for only an hour and a half of flying time, we carried thirty-five men with rifles in each plane on each trip. On one of those flights the pilot of our plane didn't realize that the airfield at Tarragona had recently been bombed. After he was already on the ground he learned too late that the plane was heading for a huge hole made by a bomb. The left wheel dropped with a sickening crunch and the wing on that side was slammed against the ground. The ground crews dragged the plane out of the hole, back to solid ground; then the pilot and crew made an inspection to determine the extent of the damage. Much to their dismay,

When the first Douglas Skysleeper was introduced by American Airlines in 1936, the company put one of them on a nationwide tour and went to great lengths to build the image of safe cross-country air travel. Here a DST is being readied for visitors on a New York City street. (Photo courtesy of Robert Kopitzke)

the wing was bent upward about four meters from its connection with the fuselage.

"While the crew continued to examine the plane, looking at it with both sorrow and disgust, someone shouted that enemy planes were approaching the field. The pilot yelled for his crew to board the crippled DC-2. He flipped the switches, the engines roared, and with complete disregard for the horribly bent wing, the plane took off as if nothing had happened.

"On the ground at Valencia, they continued the aircraft inspection. The flight had seemingly been impossible, yet the airplane limped in safely. It was later ascertained that the upper surface of the left wing formed an angle of seventeen degrees!

"On another occasion a box of ammunition exploded beside one of the DC-2s, killing three men and destroying half the fuselage between the entrance door and the tail. The gaping hole had so distorted the fuselage that a glance indicated the plane might never fly again. Working out in the open at the provisional field where maintenance facilities were practically nonexistent, the crews patched the torn fuselage. When the work was completed, the pilot gave it a test flight. He reported that the old plane flew as it always had.

"We began the war with four Douglas transports. Each one flew more than 2,000 hours during the conflict. They were finally surrendered to Franco, old and with many scars, but they were covered with glory and in good condition."

Major General Benjamin D. Foulois, one of the country's first military pilots, agreed with the findings of the war planning board in that transport planes selected for the Air Corps should be selected "off the shelf" from existing standard commercial types if possible. However, the Army had already pushed the development of a special military cargo plane which was to be delivered in August 1934 by the Fairchild Corporation. He believed it might be good enough to be adopted as the standard military air transport.

The Fairchild plane was finally delivered, but soon developed some aerodynamic "bugs" and was grounded. However, the original concept and specifications were still considered valid. Based on the Fairchild plans, Foulois's staff announced a requirement for a cargo plane whose tactical mission would be to transport military materiel and troops to front line airdromes and to evacuate sick and wounded from the battlefield. Bids were invited from the aircraft industry to supply the Air Corps with a plane that could haul a payload of 3,000 pounds, have a cruising speed of 125 miles per hour, a top speed of 150 miles per hour, and a range of 500 miles. The bid announcement further stated that the plane's landing speed could not exceed 60 miles per hour.

The specifications were sent to the various aircraft companies and several manufacturers put their engineers to work to see what they could develop. Douglas, already tooled up for the DC-2s, was among the first to submit a bid. Based on an order for twenty, Donald Douglas informed the Air Corps procurement office that he could produce them for $61,775 each, plus $20,500 for the two engines.

The American Airlines ground staff at the Newark, New Jersey Airport form the letters "NK" which was the station symbol for Newark when two-letter designations were used. (American Airlines photo)

The unmistakable profile of the ubiquitous Gooney Bird in American Airlines colors. The main wheels protruding beneath the engine nacelles prevented much fuselage damage on gear-up landings. The tail wheel was not retractable. (Photo courtesy Robert Kopitzke)

After all the bids were in, the Air Corps flight-tested all the entries and graded on a point system. The Douglas entry received an aggregate score of 786 points and placed first. The Fairchild plane placed second with 599.7 points. When the test results were sent to Washington, the contracting officer recommended that the contract be awarded to Douglas even though he noted that the aircraft requirement program for 1936 called for thirty-six cargo aircraft of the single-engine type.

When the report reached General Foulois's desk, he sought an opinion from the Judge Advocate General. Could thirty-six twin-engine transports be procured or must only single-engine planes be ordered? He was advised that a purchase of half as many twin-engine cargo planes was authorized but no more. The contract was drawn up for eighteen planes and the new Air Corps plane was eventually designated the C-33.

When the first C-33s rolled off the production line, performance data showed that this version of the DC-2 could carry a useful load of 6,320 pounds, fly at 171 miles per hour, and had a range of 916 miles. Many innovations were incorporated to meet the Army's cargo needs. Two main methods were provided: In one, a hoist was attached to a tripod on top of the fuselage and cargo was lifted from the cabin by a winch permanently attached to the forward bulkhead. In the other, tracks were used and the cargo was drawn into the cabin by a system of pulleys and cables. Other changes were made to allow the C-33 to carry nine Air Corps litters or twelve commercial-type passenger chairs. All the Air Corps specifications were not only met but exceeded.

It wasn't long, however, before someone wanted to change the specifications for a new round of cargo plane procurements. In January 1935, the commanding general of the Air Corps General Headquarters (GHQ) developed a requirement for a personal plane. Besides reclining chairs, the specifications required desks, filing cabinets, and other office facilities. Since the DC-2 (not the C-33) had recently undergone flight tests at Wright Field, Ohio, it was decided that it could serve the purpose with only minor cabin modifications.

But the Secretary of War had other ideas. He had approved specifications for an airplane that could carry a payload of 3,600 pounds or 18 passengers. This automatically precluded the procurement of all standard transports then in production.

Faced with this decision, General Foulois suggested that the minimum specifications be reduced to allow the DC-2 to fall within those limits. A compromise was finally reached and a contract was negotiated with Douglas for one 14-passenger DC-2 which was designated the XC-32. An order for twenty-four C-32As quickly followed. In January 1936, two more were ordered under slightly different specifications and labeled C-34s.

Months passed while the Air Corps tested its new transports extensively. In the meantime, Douglas engineers had designed the DC-3 to meet new airline specifications. The Air Corps promptly asked for changes in its specifications; one C-33 with a DC-3 tail was constructed and designated the C-38. The tests proved successful and an order for thirty-five C-39s was placed which were DC-2s with a DC-3 tail and were modified inside to carry cargo.

As was often the case in the days before the 1941 attack on Pearl Harbor, aircraft research, development and procurement were controlled to a great extent by men who had never flown and who were not even remotely acquainted with aerodynamics or the capabilities of airplanes. Army ground officers who had no knowledge of flight characteristics insisted that the loading door on the C-39 should be made wider to accommodate a 75mm field artillery piece. Others insisted that the floor should be rebuilt so that it would re-

The DC-1 was the prototype for the DC-2s and -3s. Only one was built but it established speed records within a few days after its first flight in 1933. (Drawing by R. G. Smith)

main level while the airplane was on the ground. Another suggestion was that the floorboards should be covered with a certain type of sandpaper so that paratroopers wouldn't slip as they bailed out. To attempt to satisfy all the suggestions, single procurements were made of a C-41, C-41A, and a C-42. However, these were made with plush interiors and were used for transport of VIPs.

While the idea of nonflying officers making suggestions did not appeal to the pilots responsible for procuring and testing the planes, they had to admit that some of the suggestions proved worthy of adoption. The sandpaper idea, for example, was excellent. Strips of tough, gritty material were installed on the floor and used throughout the war.

Donald Douglas and his patient aeronautical engineers listened to all modification requests, studied them and were able to make most of the changes requested; in some cases they were able to improve on the ideas submitted. After the C-39 was modified, for example, it could carry a 75mm artillery piece, drop men and supplies, carry litter patients, and serve as an airborne office. Furthermore, the changeover to carry these varying types of loads could be made in a matter of minutes.

Royal Dutch Air Lines was one of the first foreign air carriers to purchase the DC-2. One of them finished second in the London-Melbourne Race of 1934. (Drawing by R. G. Smith)

During this period of modification requests, so many changes were made inside and out that the Army Air Corps designated the final product the C-47 and hundreds were turned out. However, there were still more modifications made later which earned more designations: C-48, C-49, C-50, C-51, C-52, C-53, C-68, C-84, and C-117. The Navy gave the original model the designation of R4D-1 and dash numbers upward. The Army Air Force called one model the YC-129 which was redesignated a YC-47F and then the Navy gave it a designation of R4D-8. It was later converted to a C-117D. (See Appendix for further explanation of the various model designations.)

Of all the models with minor differences from the basic C-47, only the C-49 and C-53 were produced in quantity. The only major difference between the C-47 and these two was that the C-49 was the Skysleeper version of the DC-3 which was easily adapted into a comfortable air evacuation aircraft. The C-53 was the paratroop version. After World War II plushed-up models of the C-47 became the C-117 and one Super DC-3, designated the YC-129, was purchased by the Air Force. The Super DC-3s are discussed in a later chapter.

With all the numbers used to designate models with relatively minor differences, the C-47 was destined to be produced in the greatest numbers. It was soon found that the C-47 could be produced with all the other modifications built into it at the factory. Besides, it was easier to mass-produce one model of an airplane than four or five which were almost alike.

While the U.S. Army's air arm was struggling mightily to convince a disinterested Congress that the nation needed more planes for defense, the Germans proved what General Billy Mitchell had preached before his death in 1936. The airplane could be the most potent weapon ever devised if properly employed. The Germans blitzed their way with it into Norway and the Low Countries of Europe. Dive bombers preceded troop transports which disgorged parachute troops into carefully chosen areas and thus pioneered the offensive maneuver known as "vertical envelopment."

Stimulated by the German successes, the U.S. Army organized a parachute platoon for experimental purposes in early 1940. By September the War Department ordered the platoon built up to battalion strength. Later, more battalions were organized, and by December 1941, the four battalions then in being had become a regiment which formed the nucleus of the Army's first two airborne divisions.

Until November 1941, however, the Army Air Corps had never been capable of dropping more than one infantry company at a time. The reason: there weren't enough transport planes available to accommodate the newly-formed airborne units.

As early as February 1933, the Army Air Corps had set up air transport units to fly air freight between the several air materiel depots across the nation. These units grew slowly and when war began in Europe in 1939 there was only one transport group of four squadrons with nine or ten airplanes assigned to each. In addition to these, the Air Corps had fifty transports assigned to tactical units, which transported ground maintenance personnel and supplies on maneuvers.

It was ironic that the U.S. Army Air Corps had pioneered in the use of air transports beginning in 1931, and yet had not organized them into permanent units. Driven by the urgent need for fighters and bombers, and influenced by a belief that transports could always be bought off the shelf, no new orders for any type of transport plane were placed in 1939 or the first half of 1940. In June 1940, however, this policy was abruptly changed. It was realized that the Army had not more than a hundred aging transports and that new ones could not be bought so easily merely by ordering them from the manufacturers. War planners now wanted 11,802 transports to support the nation's expanding military organization, but from June to December 1940 only five planes had been delivered. At the end of 1940 the Army had an anemic total of 122 transports, mostly C-33s and C-39s which were modified DC-2s. During all of 1941 only 133 more transports were delivered. Considering these statistics, it is not difficult to explain why the Army Air Corps objected when infantry staff members at Fort Benning, Georgia requested thirty-nine airplanes for paratroop training for the 1941 maneuvers.

By December 1, 1941, the Air Corps was faced with a serious problem. Deliveries were still small and the aircraft in the inventory were already obsolescent. To make up for the shortage, plans had been laid that would permit the Government to call on the airlines to lend their planes to the War and Navy Departments in case of war. Their experienced flight crews, their knowledge of air routes, and their excellently maintained planes and supporting equipment would thus provide a reserve air fleet to make up for the shortage. The airlines, under this plan, would be asked to provide transportation of men and supplies for the armed forces to all parts of the world. They would also train military men in airline operations and convert their airline maintenance shops into modification and repair facilities. The concept was accepted by the entire airline industry. It was to be put into operation sooner than anyone would have believed possible.

On Sunday afternoon, December 7, 1941, an American Airlines DC-3 lumbering along on its popular coast-to-coast run was approaching Phoenix, Arizona. The passenger list included a well-known movie star, several prominent businessmen en route to their respective homes in California, and a few assorted passengers who were happy to be aboard because they had been forced to book passage weeks in advance in order to get a seat. In the cockpit the two pilots relaxed comfortably while the plane was flying on autopilot, one listening to the company radio and the other monitoring the CAA radio range frequency. Without warning, an excited voice on the Phoenix frequency shouted, "American Twenty-One, this is Phoenix Radio. Plan A! Plan A!"

There was silence. No more information was forthcoming. It was a simple message but it had deep significance. It was a code that had been agreed upon several weeks before and meant war had come. Within a few minutes after the word of the Japanese attack on Pearl Harbor, similar coded messages were flashed to every passenger plane plying the nation's airways. The airlines were at war and could be said to be the first commercial enterprise that realized it. This message was part of the detailed plan that would signal the mobilization of the airlines for war.

Meanwhile, in Hawaii on that infamous date, one of the casualties among the civilian aircraft destroyed during the Japanese attack was a DC-3 that belonged to Hawaiian Airlines. A KLM DC-3 was destroyed by the Japanese at Medon Airport in Indonesia later that month.

On December 13, President Roosevelt signed an executive order directing the Secretary of War to take possession of the nation's transportation systems, including the airlines. Fortunately, since the orders for more C-47s were already being carried out, there would be no delay in getting production lines started. However, the large number required an expansion of the Douglas facilities and C-47s began to be produced in a new plant at Long Beach. The Wright engines of the commercial version were replaced by more powerful Pratt & Whitneys; the interior seating was changed to bucket seats along the cabin walls, and the operating weight was increased from 25,000 pounds to 29,300.

It was perhaps prophetic that the flight crew of a DC-3 would be among the first to know of the beginning of World War II for America. What no one did know, however, was the role that the faithful DC-3 was to play in the four-year drama that lay ahead. Certainly no one would have bet that the lumbering, ungainly DC-3 would be called one of the pieces of equipment that won the war by a general who would one day be the President of the United States.

The DC-3 in its airline configuration. It proved to be the first plane that enabled the airlines to make a profit without government mail subsidies. (Drawing by R. G. Smith)

3

The Gooney Bird Goes to War

Four pieces of equipment that most senior officers came to regard as among the most vital to our success in Africa and Europe were the bulldozer, the jeep, the 2 1/2-ton truck, and the C-47 airplane. Curiously, none of these is designed for combat.

Dwight D. Eisenhower
Crusade in Europe

During World War II, more than five million men and women served in the armed forces. There were few who did not depend in some way at some time upon the military versions of the DC airplanes. These planes carried ammunition, gasoline, food, and medical supplies to the fighting men at the front; they carried out the wounded to behind-the-lines hospitals; they carried tired combat crews to rest areas in Australia and New Zealand and brought fresh milk and eggs back to the Pacific islands on return trips; they carried paratroopers and dropped hundreds of them behind enemy lines; they towed gliders to the battlefront; they flew for the partisans in Yugoslavia and for the Chetniks of Mihajlovic; they became bombers, and at least one became a fighter plane with a victory to its credit. The plane became a legend. Wherever it flew its familiar shape and sound could be recognized.

One of the first areas to test the real capability of the C-47 and its Navy version, the R4D, was the Pacific theater, where almost any flight to anywhere was over water and the distances were great. There were few radio facilities to guide the pilots from one point to another, and the Gooney Birds were so slow that unless the navigators stayed alert and could take frequent celestial readings, a strong crosswind could blow them far off course.

One of the first notable flights of the Gooney after Pearl Harbor took place before the famous Battle of Midway. On the eve of the battle, Marine Captain Albert S. Munsch with a three-man crew, 10 Navy passengers, a cargo of machine gun ammunition and airplane spare parts, and a 300-gallon water cart desperately needed because there was no fresh water source on the island, made an unescorted emergency flight from Ewa, Hawaii, to Midway Island. That mission, carried out under the continual threat of interception by the marauding Japanese, proved to be the first operational use of what one writer called, "the most reliable, but mostly unsung, planes in the history of Marine Corps aviation."

The C-33 derivative of the DC-2 was purchased as a cargo plane by the Army Air Corps and many innovations were included, such as a loading hoist and tracks. It was a DC-2 with a larger rudder and tail and a cargo door. Nine litters could be carried or twelve commercial-type seats. (USAF photo)

One XC-32 was purchased by the Army Air Corps. Four additional C-32s were procured, followed by C-34s with new specifications which were DC-2s with DC-3 tails. More powerful Wright engines were installed. (USAF photo)

It was a 1,130-mile round trip flight for Munsch in the unarmed Gooney without radio aids that took 16 hours, 45 minutes elapsed time. When he was about 300 miles east of Midway, he descended to about 100 feet so "I would be harder to find if they [the Japanese] were anywhere nearby." He was not intercepted and delivered the passengers and cargo which were urgently needed by the defenders of Midway. He returned to Hawaii with a special report of the preparations for the coming battle at Midway. He received a special commendation from Admiral Chester W. Nimitz, Commander-in-Chief, Pacific.

The ensuing battle for the beleaguered island ended in disaster for the Japanese; they lost four carriers, hundreds of planes, and several hundred of their most experienced pilots.

The overall American strategy developed in the Pacific was that of by-passing Japanese-held islands in a never-ending island-hopping campaign toward the Nipponese homeland. Some of the islands were relatively flat coral atolls where there was little undergrowth; others contained many kinds of vegetation and mountainous terrain. And some islands were covered with dense jungles that the enemy clung to tenaciously and gave the defenders an advantage. Such an island was Guadalcanal.

Despite their losses in the naval battles of Midway and Coral Sea, the Japanese had succeeded in bringing reinforcements to the Solomon Islands group to which Guadalcanal belonged. It was a key island to which the Japanese had sent enough troops to force the U.S. Marines off. The enemy advantage lay not only in the superior number of troops and air units that could be brought to bear but they were also much closer to their supply bases than the Americans.

American bases were at least 1,000 miles away and the nearest supporting air base to the south was a crude, matted strip cut among the hills and jungle 640 miles away in the New Hebrides: Espiritu Santo Island. However, American troops were able to hold on to Henderson Field on Guadalcanal where a mixed force of about seventy Army Air Force and Marine aircraft operated in spite of day and night enemy air raids. Nightly shellfire from Japanese cruisers zeroed in on Henderson's strip which represented the only offensive base for attacks against enemy naval and air forces, as well as

Interior view of an Army Air Corps C-39 intended for cargo hauling. Note reinforced sides and floor. The radio operator's position in the rear of the cabin was moved forward to the area behind the cockpit in later models. (USAF photo)

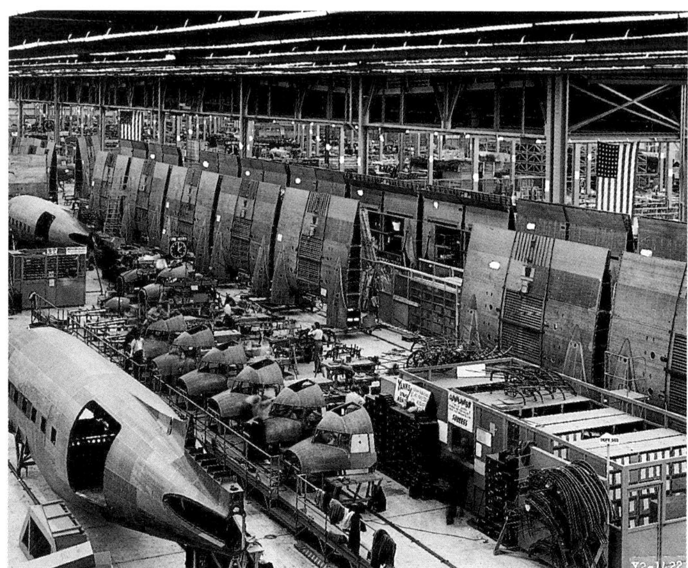

LINE MOVES
108

providing the launching point for air support of American ground forces.

Some four thousand U.S. Army reinforcements and ground forces supplies had been landed on the island by the Navy. However, supplies for air units had low priority and aviation gasoline was in critically short supply. Consequently, the day after its arrival in Plaines des Gaiacs, New Caledonia, the 13th Troop Carrier Squadron teamed with two Marine Air Group squadrons and began to haul gasoline and bombs to Henderson Field in C-47s and R4Ds. It was about 400 miles from New Caledonia to Guadalcanal, and from Espiritu Santo to Guadalcanal and back to Espiritu Santo was a 1,300-mile round trip. None of the gasoline they were flying to Guadalcanal could be used to refuel their own aircraft. By having to make the long trip without refueling, they could not carry very heavy loads.

The route to Guadalcanal was entirely over water, which taxed the ability of navigators to locate their destinations, especially in poor weather. The only prior experience any of them had previously was on the route overseas from the States to Hawaii, Christmas Island, Canton, Fiji, and on to New Caledonia.

On the night of October 11, 1942, a United States naval force comprised of two heavy and two light cruisers with destroyer escorts made a daring midnight interception of some Japanese reinforcement ships, known as the "Tokyo Express." The Americans tore into the enemy vessels with their powerful guns and succeeded in sinking three Japanese cruisers, five destroyers, and an auxiliary ship, with the loss of hundreds of men. The U.S. Navy lost one destroyer and 175 men. But the heavy losses did not stop the Japanese. The American cruiser force had to withdraw from the immediate battle area because of a shortage of fuel oil and ammunition for the big guns; the enemy immediately resumed the Tokyo Express and intensified their attacks on Henderson Field.

Finally, on October 13, all American air operations on Henderson had to be canceled because the aviation gasoline stock was almost exhausted. That night enemy bombers flew across the field and dropped flares to light it brightly. Then Japanese cruisers and battleships standing offshore began blasting the airfield and enemy bombers later dropped their loads until dawn.

The next morning the Americans looked out across the debris-laden, bomb-pocked airfield and their hopes fell. The Japanese now seemed to hold the upper hand in the seesaw battle for permanent possession of the island. Of the nearly seventy aircraft the Americans had the day before, there were now only a dozen that were flyable. In addition, the anti-aircraft batteries and air warning systems were barely operable.

But the Guadalcanal defenders were not defeated. Work crews quickly cleared a grass strip parallel to the original Henderson strip while the Japanese kept up a steady shelling on the workers. Enemy bombers and fighters were now free to bomb and strafe without fear of interception.

OPPOSITE: Views of the C-47 Skytrain production lines in 1942 at the Douglas Santa Monica and Oklahoma City plants. The large clock under the sign "Line Moves" warned production employees how long they have to finish their respective job tasks. (Douglas Aircraft Co. photos)

By using the gasoline found in the few drums around the strip and draining fuel from damaged planes, eleven dive bombers managed to stagger into the air late on the afternoon of October 14 but the damage they were able to do was negligible and two were shot down with antiaircraft fire. Now the gasoline was almost completely gone and the Japanese were more determined than ever to put the defenders totally out of action. However, there was enough gas left for one lone P-40 to get airborne with two 500-pound bombs. He scored two hits on naval vessels, but that was certainly not a deterrent.

That night an enemy convoy anchored offshore only ten miles from Henderson Field, between Kokumbona and Tassafaronga. The ships were loaded with ten thousand enemy troops and while they were being offloaded, Japanese Zeros patrolled the skies overhead.

October 15 seemed like doomsday for the surviving Americans. However, shortly before noon the silhouettes of airplanes were spotted coming from the south and when they came closer they were identified as American C-47s. Strangely, they were not intercepted, and one by one the transports came in for a landing. The defenders wasted no time unloading the precious cargo of drums of gasoline. Each load was enough to put twelve fighters into the air for one hour, and the unarmed transports came and went all day—bringing in gasoline and taking out wounded men. The remaining Guadalcanal fighters could now fight again. Their pilots were jubilant. They looked at the slow, lumbering C-47s and were impressed with these flying boxcars and the pilots who flew them. These planes had no armor, no guns, no great speed, and little maneuverability. It took a special kind of guts to fly planes like that into enemy-dominated airspace.

One Navy pilot, watching one of the Goonies being unloaded, exclaimed, "They couldn't sell me on making that run if they exempted me from paying income tax for the rest of my life. It's the suspense that's so hellish. A fighter pilot always has the feel of a good, fast plane strapped to his rear end with plenty of power at his fingertips. Flying those transports, you're just cold turkey for anybody who sets his sights on you. All you can do is stay in the clouds, and if there aren't any clouds you have no choice but to dive for the ocean and skim the waves all the way home. Do that seven days a week with a few tons of high explosives and inflammables for cargo and you can call yourself a hero in any man's war."

Between the time the transports brought in the first loads of gasoline until they were ready to depart, the flyable fighters had refueled and were ready to take to the air. The Japanese ships were so close to Henderson now that the fighters were over their targets almost as soon as they were airborne. They dove through intense antiaircraft fire to release their bombs. A swarm of enemy Zeros arrived and the few American fighters that were flying more than evened the score that day. In three successive attacks, one naval transport exploded and sank, two damaging hits were made on other

2000

BERL
IVAN
MR. BIG
2000
John
LOMPE
WILMA

BERLIN
IVAN
MR. BIG
2000
John
LOMPE
GLENN ROSS
HUNTER

vessels, and one was probably damaged. One Zero was exchanged for one American fighter.

Although the damage to the Japanese forces wasn't as great as the Americans would have liked, it was a satisfying victory for the American airmen. If the C-47s could keep the gasoline coming into Guadalcanal, the American pilots had a good chance of nibbling away at the enemy fleet until it would either be sunk or forced to withdraw.

B-17s arrived from Espiritu Santo and joined the fighters in their attacks on the enemy vessels. They sank several transports and caused the force to withdraw. But the transports had left empty. During the night they had deposited their human cargo on the Guadalcanal beaches. The bedraggled American troops had to face new, fresh enemy soldiers.

The final outcome is well-known. The enemy was eventually routed but all that saved the weary Americans was the support of their fighters. Had it not been for the C-47s which shuttled back and forth from Espiritu Santo to Henderson with their loads of precious fuel, victory would not have been possible. Official records do not reveal exactly how many Gooney Birds participated in the battle for Guadalcanal but it was a combined effort by Army, Navy and Marine pilots.

The enlarged cargo door enabled the Army ground forces to load field guns, jeeps and other large equipment into the C-47 and its later derivatives. (USAF photo)

During the New Guinea campaign, the 317th Troop Carrier Group, under the command of Colonel John H. Lackey, had the inglorious job of hauling supplies to war-weary troops operating against the Japanese in the dense jungle areas. There was nothing that made the troops happier than to see and hear the Goonies circling to deposit bundles of supplies, ammunition and food by parachute into small clearings. On almost every mission, the C-47s were fired upon by small arms from the ground. Many a transport was peppered by enemy bullets.

When the 317th Group moved to the Philippines it was assigned an assortment of missions quite unlike any it had performed in New Guinea. On February 15, 1945, the Battle of Manila was on. The fighting raged in the streets and fierce artillery duels took place as American and Japanese forces fought for control of the capital city.

On a two-lane dirt highway within sight of the fighting, C-47s of the 317th "Jungle Skippers" landed and took off on a rigid, preplanned schedule. Crews loaded American wounded onto litters in the C-47s, while the walking casualties climbed into the bucket seats. In less than an hour they were being cared for by medics and had clean beds, good food and baths, something they had not had for many weeks.

OPPOSITE: When the 2000th C-47 rolled off the assembly line at Santa Monica, California, employees were invited to sign their names all over the aircraft. Although the chalk was rubbed off before the plane was delivered to the Army Air Force, many "Rosie the Riveters" managed to get their names and addresses into the wheel wells and hidden compartments and started pen romances with the mechanics in the war zones who found them later. (Douglas Aircraft Co. photos)

While the battle for the Filipino capital city was raging, the first American C-47s were landing on nearby Clark Field; it was to be a tactical base as soon as possible. Aviation gasoline, bombs and ammunition had to be flown in quickly so that Fifth Air Force fighters and bombers could continue, uninterrupted, their relentless campaign against enemy targets from the Philippines to China, Indo-China, and Formosa. Service squadrons, combat engineers, communications specialists and antiaircraft units, as well as ground personnel and equipment for the fighter and bomber units had to be flown in from Leyte and Mindoro Islands. With the roads clogged by ground fighting units, it was the job of the C-47s to bring in the necessary men and supplies.

For the next two months the Jungle Skippers streamed in and out of Clark Field to accumulate more than 2,500 plane-days of air

C-47 fuselages move down the production line at the Douglas Santa Monica plant in August 1941 after being painted the drab camouflage color specified by the Army Air Corps contract. (Douglas Aircraft Co. photo)

supply. Filipino crews unloaded the C-47s while other transports circled above waiting for their turns to land. The planes flew with minimum fuel loads so they could carry a few more bombs or drums of gasoline on each trip. During this period the Jungle Skippers hauled more than 3,300 men and over 16 million pounds of cargo to Clark Field. This cargo included 7 million pounds of bombs and almost 3.5 million pounds of ammunition.

During the first days of fighting at Manila the C-47s had to land under artillery fire. Sometimes they made their approaches under the trajectory patterns of American artillery. Some areas of the field still contained land mines, making it extremely hazardous to taxi the planes. When the planes had to remain overnight at Clark Field, the flight crews guarded their own planes to keep the Japanese from sabotaging them during the night. On at least two occasions night-marauding enemy soldiers slipped through sentry lines and damaged several C-47s with hand grenades.

The Jungle Skippers were given a new task in April 1945. Corregidor Island, which had been the last American stronghold in the Philippines, had now been wrested from the tenacious Japanese. The Skippers were assigned to haul the 503rd Parachute Infantry Combat Team and drop them on "Old Topside," as Corregidor was called. First, however, Old Topside had to be softened up.

A-20 light attack planes and B-24 heavy bombers attacked the island. Six minutes after the last bombing plane passed over Corregidor, a lone C-47 followed carrying heavily armed men of the 503rd Combat Team. They were to jump into a very small area with many obstacles. Sticking up everywhere were jagged stumps and the ruins of buildings. Shell holes completely dotted the island. The jump would have to be accurate. After the first "stick" of men parachuted, other Goonies followed in a long line. Because the area was so small, only ten men could be dropped at a time so second passes had to be made, placing the planes in danger from ground fire. This meant a smaller concentration of men on the ground to battle the surviving Japanese.

While the paratroopers dropped toward the shell-scarred earth, the A-20s returned to pin down the enemy and make it easier for the paratroopers to gather their equipment and dig in. The fight lasted all morning and the Americans seized their first objective sooner than anticipated. The C-47s appeared again after noon and dropped more paratroopers to deal the final knockout punch to the groggy Japanese. Old Topside was once more in American hands. Airpower had once again enabled the Americans to have a victory day at the place where American forces had surrendered many months before.

Corregidor was not the last of the islands of the Philippines to be liberated. In other places a few Japanese still held out to the bitter end, sniping whenever they could find a target. Resistance

Airborne infantrymen at a 9th Air Force Troop Carrier base in England await the signal to board their gliders on the morning of June 6, 1944—D-Day. (USAF photo)

was especially bitter on a tiny island in Manila Harbor entrance called Carabou Island.

American fighters and bombers had clobbered the island until the enemy's heavy weapons were useless, leaving the enemy soldiers with only rifles and pistols to defend themselves. Ordinarily, the fact that Japanese still occupied this tiny piece of rock would not have been a serious threat. However, Liberty ships going into Manila had to pass Carabou and snipers picked off crew members easily at close range.

Made of solid rock and corral, the island was honeycombed with caves which kept the Japanese comparatively safe from bombing attacks. A way had to be found to drive them out.

Since the C-47 was capable of flying at relatively slow speeds, could it be used to spread napalm, a jellied gasoline that ignites upon impact, to burn out the enemy?

Fully-equipped troops of the 439th Troop Carrier Group were alerted two days before D-Day to be ready for boarding their gliders. Into Normandy alone, 516 CG-4As carried more than 4,000 glidermen, 95 artillery pieces, and 290 jeeps. (USAF photo)

Two planes and crews of the 317th were selected to try. The planes were loaded with fourteen 55-gallon drums of napalm each and dispatched for this new type of job for the Goonies. The pilot of the lead plane, Major Archie G. Burdette, described this unique bombing mission:

"I don't know who got the bright idea of going in and burning the Japs out," Burdette said, "but they figured we could spread fire all over the island and drive them out of their holes. When that smoke gets down in the holes, they have to come out. They can't breathe.

"I instructed Captain Sheridan, pilot of the other plane, to circle and watch me. I made my first pass, explaining that if I ran into serious trouble dropping my load that he was to return to base and not attempt to drop his. All it takes is one well-placed bullet in a can of napalm and that's all, brother. Napalm is miserable stuff.

"I came in about 50 feet high over the island and slowed the Gooney down to 95 miles an hour. At that speed and altitude you're a dead duck for a man with a gun if he knows how to use it. I dropped my first barrel of fire on one end of the island. On my reverse pass I dropped another one just as I crossed the near end of the island; then I saw something on the ground that made me wish I hadn't made the second run.

"A Japanese soldier was standing directly in the path of my airplane shooting at us with a pistol. At that distance I didn't see how he could miss. I felt something strike the plane but we passed over him and my 'kicker' released another barrel of fire on the other end of the rock.

"On my next trip around I was determined to get the man who was shooting at us, providing he didn't get a lucky shot into the old Goon first. We dropped a barrel on the end of the island, then another on the Japanese soldier who was still plugging away at us. We missed both targets.

"Next time I figured it was going to be that Jap soldier or me. My sole aim on this run was to drop a barrel on top of him. I dropped lower, slowed the airplane a little more, and told the kicker what I intended to do. We didn't get our signals crossed either. The next time around there was a mass of fire where the soldier had been standing, but we didn't see him. I knew several bullets had hit the C-47 but I didn't know how many. Sheridan dropped his load of napalm and when we finished the island was a mass of flames and smoke.

"When I got back to the base, I counted nine bullet holes in my Gooney Bird, but there were none in Sheridan's. Funny thing about that ninth hole—the first eight showed where the bullets had entered the fuselage and where they had gone on through, but the ninth one puzzled me until we figured out what happened. There was only an exit point for the bullet but no place of entry. Since part of the cargo door had been removed, we concluded that the bullet had entered through the open doorway, probably glanced off one of the napalm drums that were piled in the doorway, and smashed through the side of the airplane. It's a good thing that napalm drum

Paratroopers have their equipment inspected before boarding a Gooney Bird for the invasion of France. (USAF photo)

was struck only a glancing blow. Had it been a direct hit, we would have all been blown sky high.

"We gave a repeat performance of the morning mission, except that we were more selective with our targets. We aimed directly at the caves where the Japs were dug in, and we learned what a good bomber the old C-47 can be when given a chance.

"About the only noteworthy part of the incident is that it was widely circulated in newspapers back home. The Army Air Force news release claimed that this was the only officially scheduled bombing mission made by a C-47 during the war."

The press release was incorrect. Another pilot had flown a previous bombing mission with a C-47. His name was Major Richard L. Benjamin who was attached to the First Air Commando Group in India, an outfit that was commanded by Colonels Philip Cochran and John Alison that had been flying men and supplies to points beyond the Japanese lines in Burma. The group had as the mainstay of its operation, thirteen C-47s, each of which could tow two gliders.

One night in 1944 as Benjamin was returning to his base after towing a couple of gliders to their landing point, he saw a string of enemy trucks rolling along a narrow mountain road toward the Imphal Valley. When he landed, he reported the sighting to his commander.

"Too bad we can't do anything about it," his boss said, shrugging. "Our bombers and fighters are on another big deal tonight."

But the major had already mentally turned his Gooney into a bomber and sold his boss on the idea. Ground crews quickly shoved 500-pound bombs and several boxes of fragmentation bombs into the Gooney. Major Bejamin, Lieutenant R. T. Gilmore, Sergeant J. H. Webb, Sergeant R. D. Alexander, and Corporal R. A. Royce piled in and took off. They sighted the convoy about forty-five minutes later.

Since there was no bombsight to give him an idea when to signal for the drops to the men in the cabin, Benjamin explained to the crew that he would have to estimate the bomb release point. And since there was no bomb release either, the men would have to roll the bombs out the side door at his command. However, they had dropped enough bundles of supplies to friendly troops in the jungle to make their judgments fairly accurate.

The Japanese trucks were moving slowly, their drivers unsuspecting as Benjamin made a wide reconnaissance sweep around the convoy.

"We couldn't very well miss," Benjamin said. "It was a narrow canyon and we were only three thousand feet up. Over the target Webb and Royce kicked out the three big bombs, destroying at least one truck. I made another run and the crew peppered the Japanese with the little frag bombs. Even Lieutenant Gilmore went back and joined in. We had a helluva lot of fun for a few minutes.

"When we returned home we could see several burning trucks, and by the light of the fires we saw Japanese dashing around like ants whose hill had been bashed in by a farmer's boot.

"The Japanese were so surprised to have a C-47 bombing them that they didn't fire a single shot." Benjamin concluded. "Safest mission I ever flew."

In spite of seemingly insurmountable obstacles, Major Ray Van Diver was a pilot who could be counted on to deliver his cargo at the proper time and place. Flying a C-47 in the South Pacific to support General MacArthur's island-hopping campaign, his mission was to fly combat cargo to front-line troops and special missions "as may be directed."

Three American fighter pilots had been forced to ditch their planes near a small island and had to swim to shore. Van Diver's special mission this day was to locate them and drop emergency rations and survival gear so they could hold out until a rescue vessel or flying boat could pick them up. When he found the island, he circled and soon three bedraggled figures darted out of the jungle and waved frantically. Van Diver made a low pass over them to be sure they were Americans.

Paratroopers of the 439th Troop Carrier Group await the command to hook up for their drop behind the enemy lines in France. (USAF photo)

The faithful Gooney Bird was an angel of mercy to hundreds of wounded troops in the South Pacific during World War II. From battlefront hospitals in the Marianas, C-47s of the 7th Air Force evacuated serious emergency cases often at great risk to flight crews and medical personnel. (USAF photo)

Ambulances await offloading of wounded Army troops from a South Pacific battlefront. For most, the evacuation by Gooney Birds was the first leg of their homeward journey. (USAF photo)

He made a second pass and signaled the crew chief to kick out the bundle of supplies. After the supplies were dropped, Van Diver banked sharply so he could see where they landed. He was shocked to see that they had dropped into deep water offshore.

Van Diver was mad and knew that the men below would also be extremely angry, too, when they realized that their life-saving supplies could not be recovered. As he circled, wondering what to do, he said to his copilot, "We can't leave them there. I wonder if I could set this bird down on the beach..."

He banked, lined up on the beach, called "gear down" and then "full flaps." The copilot reluctantly did as he was commanded.

The beach was wide enough for a C-47 but Van Diver was more concerned about the debris that littered the beach area. One half-hidden log or rock could cause them to flip over or swerve and crash into the water or the jungle.

The wheels touched down easily, cushioned by soft sand, and he braked to a stop. The three airmen ran to the plane, were hauled aboard, and Van Diver roared off the beach quickly as if he did this kind of thing every day. As far as is known, this was the first—and perhaps only—time such a landing was ever attempted.

After takeoff the flyers went into the cockpit. One said, "Boy, were we glad to see you! If you hadn't landed and picked us up, no telling how long we'd have stayed there."

"Think nothing of it, lads," Van Diver said. "It was routine. But do me one favor when we get back."

"Sure," the fighter pilots echoed. "Anything."

"Please don't tell the Old Man that we dumped that bundle in the ocean."

On the other side of the world the Gooney Bird played a key role in the initial phases of the first full-scale American airborne operation in history. It was to North Africa that the Allies had decided early to take the war to the Axis forces on a grand scale. French forces occupied North Africa but there was disagreement whether or not they would side with the Allies. Negotiations on the highest command level to get French cooperation instead of resistance had preceded the proposed invasion of North Africa. In the absence of assurance as to what the French attitude would be on D-Day, two plans had been prepared for the airborne phase, one to be used in case the other proved unfeasible.

One plan, known as the "War Plan," was based on French resistance, and called for seizing the military airfield at Tafaraoui, seventeen miles from Oran, by an American airborne battalion. The other plan, designated the "Peace Plan," called for a battalion to land at La Senia, a commercial airfield located only five miles from Oran. There, it was hoped, they would be welcomed by the friendly population.

On November 7, 1942, the paratroopers stood by their planes in England on five-minute alert. They had been briefed to put the War Plan into action. While they waited, however, the instructions were changed to the Peace Plan. This change caused the alert to be eased because the Peace Plan called for a later arrival in Algeria than the War Plan.

A short time later the orders were changed back to the War Plan but the word didn't filter down to the paratroop units. Even the mission commander for the airborne forces didn't know that the strategy had been changed back to the War Plan.

Paratroopers of the 503rd Parachute Infantry were committed to the operation, and thirty-nine C-47s from the 60th Troop Carrier Group were to take them to Algiers. The planes were organized into four flights and were to depart from two air bases—one at St.

On Henderson Field, Guadalcanal, a medical evacuee from the jungle fighting in the South Pacific islands is placed aboard one of the C-47s operated by the U.S. Marines. (US Navy photo)

Paratroopers of the Army's 101st Airborne Division seem calm before their jump into Normandy after D-Day. Paratrooper in the foreground is holding a bazooka. (USAF photo)

Eval and the other at Predanneck, England. The bases were about 1,250 miles from the intended drop zone.

The operation was highly classified and even the briefing officers did not know all the details of the nonstop flight. It was intended that the aircraft would fly directly to La Senia only under the Peace Plan. Refueling would have been necessary at Gibraltar only under the War Plan so that the aircraft would have enough fuel to return to a friendly base after dropping the troops.

Not only was the briefing inadequate but apparently there was a mistake in the Signal Annex of the Operations Order which caused confusion regarding the radio frequency of a guide boat stationed near the entrance to the Mediterranean. Nevertheless, the first flight took off at 9:05 P.M. on November 7, 1942. The flight crews and paratroopers, having been on alert for a long time, were already dog-tired. The flight crews had 1,250 miles of flying ahead of them, mostly over water.

The four flights were soon airborne and rendezvoused over Portreath, England. Several collisions were narrowly averted while the planes were attempting to get into formation in the dark without running lights. Finally, in loose formation, they headed south toward Oran.

The flight crews took caffeine pills and drank cold coffee to try to stay awake while the paratroopers dozed. But fatigue began to take its toll. The formation slowly disintegrated as individual planes climbed to 10,000 feet to clear the mountains of northern Spain. Several planes were fired upon by antiaircraft guns along the northern coast. At this point, three planes abandoned the flight. One later landed at Gibraltar and the other two at Casablanca.

By daylight three more planes, low on fuel and with the pilots near exhaustion, landed in Spanish Morocco. For a reason which was never explained, the paratroopers of one plane jumped; all three planes were promptly seized; all the personnel were interned.

Thirty-nine C-47s had started toward Algiers, but when morning came on November 8, only thirty-two, with weary paratroopers and half-awake flight crews, were over the Oran area. Colonel William C. Bentley, the mission commander, still believed that the Peace Plan was in effect, so he ordered the paratroopers in twelve planes to jump after he sighted a column of tanks near Lourmel. They were American tanks so the paratroopers had to march into the city. One of the transports flew low over Tafaraoui and was promptly

The military versions of the DC-3 had small plastic inserts in each of the cabin side windows. The unarmed transports, extremely vulnerable to attacking fighters, could use the combined firepower of the troops on board for protection. Although no enemy aircraft were known to have been shot down in this manner, Army troops felt less like sitting ducks while being transported. (Douglas Aircraft Co. photo)

Students at the U.S. Navy's parachute rigger's school at the Lakehurst Naval Air Station were required to make jumps with 'chutes they had packed. Here, they are making practice jumps from an R4D, the Navy's version of the Gooney Bird. (US Navy photo)

shot at by antiaircraft guns, a greeting which was not anticipated. The pilot warned the other pilots, then selected a suitable place to land at the western end of Sebkra Dioran, a large salt lake south of Oran. He landed, followed by twenty-seven other planes. One of the first planes to land was fired on by two Arab horsemen. A bullet detonated a hand grenade attached to the belt of a paratrooper, killing him and wounding an officer.

Meanwhile, the plane carrying Colonel Bentley had not joined the others. He was aboard one of the planes that had disgorged the paratroopers and had gone on to reconnoiter La Senia and Tafaraoui. He saw evidence of ground fighting near the airdrome, and while his plane circled it was fired on by antiaircraft guns.

Suddenly, one of the engines sputtered, out of fuel. Finding a suitable landing spot, the pilot landed quickly. Bentley got in touch with the American ground headquarters by radio to discuss the situation. While he was talking, another C-47 whose paratroopers had jumped landed nearby. As its engines were shut down, French police arrived from Oran. Bentley and the two flight crews were taken into custody. They were joined by a planeload of paratroopers that had landed in the area earlier. All were held for three days in the St. Philippe Prison Camp before they were released.

Meanwhile, on the afternoon of November 8, Lieutenant Colonel Edson D. Raff organized the airborne troops to support an attack on the Tafaraoui airdrome. He had apparently received a report that the airfield had been taken by the Americans and ordered the C-47s to land there and drop off the rest of the airborne troops. This almost proved disastrous because the C-47s were attacked by both American and French units as they landed. American pilots flying British Spitfires fired on the first transports to land, but did not score any hits. Several French bombers parked near the runway were damaged. One bomber, loaded with bombs, caught fire and exploded. From the surrounding hills, French artillery units lobbed

Troops are lined up before boarding C-47s for a mock invasion of Pope Field, Fort Bragg, North Carolina. Two 37mm field pieces are being positioned for loading in the foreground. (US Army photo)

A .50 caliber machine gun was mounted in the door of a C-47 assigned to the 315th Troop Carrier Squadron. The vulnerability of the C-47 to enemy ground fire and fighters in the CBI was solved by this innovation. It was the forerunner to the side-firing Gatlings used during the war in Vietnam. (Photo courtesy John A. McCann)

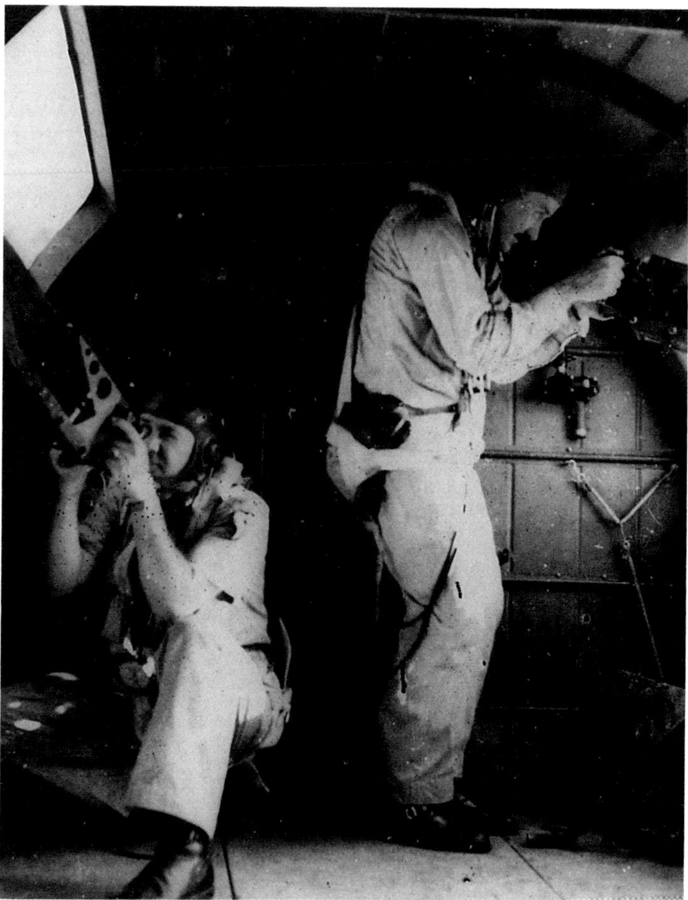

The idea to install a .50 caliber machine gun in a C-47 was the brainchild of Colonel Charles D. Farr (left) commander of the 443rd Troop Carrier Group, and Capt. John A. McCann, group intelligence officer. The gun ship was especially useful in firing on Japanese ground troops who tried to bring down the low-flying Goonies on resupply missions. Two Goonies were modified at Sylhet, India, in May 1944. (Photo courtesy John A. McCann)

shells on the runway, and firing continued for an hour. A few C-47s were damaged by shell fragments. Confused air action went on most of the afternoon, while the Americans slowly mopped up the airfield perimeter and secured the airfield.

Not all the C-47s from the emergency landing area got to Tafaraoui. French fighter planes suddenly attacked the rear echelon planes. One pilot aborted the takeoff when his C-47 was riddled with bullets. Several paratroopers and crewmen were wounded; four were killed. A copilot was killed while crash-landing and another plane was completely wrecked. A third plane was badly shot up, while another became lost and landed at Arzem.

Of the thirty-nine C-47s that had left England on November 7, nine were missing and three were destroyed by the evening of November 8. Of those that reached Tafaraoui, only fourteen were flyable. On November 11, thirteen C-47s delivered 134 paratroopers to Maison Blanche, and on the same day the first elements of the 60th Troop Carrier Group ground echelon arrived at Algiers by boat.

Although it cannot be said that the first American airborne combat operation was a success, much had been learned from the snafus that had developed. The operation demonstrated the capabilities of the C-47 in long-range operations, in addition to pointing out what happens when plans are not coordinated properly from top to bottom. Military analysts would evaluate the mistakes and future planners would try to prevent them from being made again.

When the air war over Germany raged full-scale and the huge daylight raids had begun, many a crippled bomber was escorted by a fighter plane to neutral Sweden, where the crew was interned. It was considered essential that the American and Allied airmen who found safe refuge in Sweden should be evacuated secretly if at all possible and returned to their units so they could fly again. But how could it be done? Flying from Sweden to England meant crossing over or near enemy territory, and German fighter planes patrolled the escape routes, alert to any attempt by the Allies to rescue their flight crews.

Brigadier General Earl S. Hoag, commander of the European Division of the Air Transport Command, came up with the answer.

Waves of American paratroopers drop from Troop Carrier Gooneys near Grave, Holland, in September 1944. Livestock at left graze peacefully near gliders which had landed earlier. (US Army photo)

An unidentified Douglas employee adds her comment to the signatures of hundreds of others as the 2,000th C-47 rolls off the production line at Santa Monica, California, in August 1943. Over 10,000 C-47s and its variants were produced during the war; about 1,000 are still flying today. (Douglas Aircraft Co. photo)

He proposed to evacuate the internees on an unscheduled airline basis using C-47s.

General Hoag's secret airline flew only in bad weather. When the weather was at its worst, the Gooney Birds would sneak across German-held territory, land in Sweden, pick up a load of internees and fly through the foul weather back to England. If the weather improved, the C-47 pilots would wait. Since Sweden was neutral, there was no fear of Luftwaffe attacks even though the Germans knew all about the operation. The only things the Germans didn't know about the operation were the schedule and how to stop it.

Just prior to the invasion of France in June 1944, Hoag's airline carried out the entire Norwegian government-in-exile and flew them to London. It hauled out 2,000 Norwegian soldiers who had escaped German-held Norway and regrouped in Sweden, in addition to diplomats and other high officials.

During their internment in Sweden, American crewmen were constantly followed by German Gestapo agents who hoped that someone would reveal the airline schedule. No one did. Crewmen's quarters were ransacked by agents who looked in vain for evidence of a schedule, but they never seemed to understand that there was no schedule. The airline flew only in the worst weather. Try as they might, the Germans never stopped Hoag's secret airline. In the many months of operations, only one C-47 was lost.

Flying in extremely bad weather is nerve-wracking when it is done frequently, but there are occasions when a pilot would welcome it in preference to being a target for enemy antiaircraft guns. Lieutenant Arthur Douglas, a Troop Carrier pilot, almost didn't make

At a home base in Italy, C-47s of the 51st Troop Carrier Wing line up prior to a mission. They later dropped British paratroopers into Greece and towed gliders loaded with British infantry. Food and medicines were next dropped to starving Athenians. (USAF photo)

it to his English home base one night shortly after D-Day in 1944. He said later that he had, on that particular night, lived a couple of lifetimes. Here is his story:

"From the moment we were briefed and told that this was the real thing, I think all of us wondered how much there was to the old Troop Carrier joke that you train two years for a five-hour job. We were finally going to learn the answer.

"The paratroopers were something to see as they waited for the order to climb into the planes. Some of them seemed very talkative, others relaxed and were at ease, just the way they seemed on practice missions. A few of them spent the last few minutes sharpening a variety of homemade weapons such as spiked brass knuckles and machetes.

"Looking back now, I can say that the takeoff was routine, one airplane and glider lifting off from the runway every thirty seconds. But it sure didn't seem routine at the time.

"This was the mission for which we had spent hours and hours of training, and had gone through scores of missions both in the States and England. This one had to be right. If it wasn't, it wouldn't be a case of the Old Man bawling us out. It would mean a messed-up mission. It might slow up the invasion plan, or the paratroopers might be dropped where they would be easy prey for the Germans.

"I was flying in the third group to go into our target area. That's a pretty good spot. I was impressed how peaceful and quiet it seemed as we flew over Britain and crossed the Channel. It didn't seem possible that anything could happen on such a quiet night. We kept good formation all the way over, and I suppose every pilot was probably thinking this would be a milk run.

"Just before I gave the four-minute warning to jump—we would flick a switch that flashed a green light in the cabin which meant to paratroopers 'Stand up and hook up'—we ran into the awfullest mess you've ever seen. The whole sky lit up. Jerry started throwing heavy lead at us; red tracers arched up lazily and you could see the flashes of the guns on the ground.

"Jerry had our number because we got hit in the center section. I knew we'd been hit, but I didn't know how serious it was. We kept on flying and I reckoned we hadn't been hurt much. We were about seven hundred feet high at the time, our formation was good, and even though we could see other planes get hit, it looked like we were going to do all right.

"I flicked the toggle switch for the drop light, flew over the drop zone and then wheeled for home. Jerry was still throwing up lead and generally making a nuisance of himself. Naturally we all dived for the deck after we'd dropped our troops. I dropped down to one hundred feet and poured on the coal.

"We were clear out over the coast when my crew chief came up to the cockpit. I said to him, 'How'd it go?'

"'You still got a plane full of men, Lieutenant.' Why didn't you give them the green light?'

"As far as I was concerned I had given them the green light, and I told the crew chief so. He said he'd been back there and the

One of the many innovations tried out on the military versions of the Gooney was this factory conveyor powered by a small electric motor. Its purpose was to enable a C-47 to discharge its cargo quickly. Extending from behind the pilot's compartment to the rear of the plane, the belt ran at a rate of six feet per second. A 4,000-pound load could be dropped in about 60 seconds. (USAF photo)

green light didn't show. I had him go back and watch while I tried the light again. It didn't flash, and I knew then that the flak that had hit us had knocked out part of our electrical system.

"There we were over the Channel on our way home. We'd been over the drop zone but hadn't dropped. I wouldn't be able to explain it when I got back, so I had to make up my mind what to do. I figured I had to get those guys back to a place where they could work.

"I don't know why but I turned back. It felt awfully lonesome going back in one C-47. It wasn't hard to find the way back, but it felt funny flying all by myself. All the Jerry flak would be concentrated on us, and that's exactly what happened. If the first sweep over the drop zone had been warm, the second was hotter than the train depot stove.

"As we approached the drop zone, I yelled back, 'Get ready to jump!' The first man was bracing himself in the door frame ready to pop out. At that instant he was hit in the stomach around which he had explosives wrapped—maybe hand grenades. He staggered, looked as if he might clog the door, so the next man gave him a big

Parachutes fill the sky over the coast of southern France after the 12th Troop Carrier Air Division's C-47s carried men and supplies to drop zones over the new beachhead. (USAF photo)

push out. It was a good thing for all of us that he did, for right then the explosives around his middle went off and the plane jumped and rocked like it had been shot in the tail with rock salt.

"For a minute I was certain we'd had it. When the plane finally responded to the controls, I held it on course until the paratroopers had time to drop, then I went down to the deck again and started for home.

"By this time I felt sure I had been kicked in the head by a lucky horseshoe. And when the crew chief came up to say that the explosion had knocked down all the men in their heavy equipment and they hadn't been able to regain their feet until we'd passed the drop zone, I felt like the guy who had hit the jackpot twice and wasn't due again for another century or two.

"On the second pass over the drop zone our instruments had been knocked out. I had only my compass and airspeed indicator and the instruments for the right engine. Should I go back a third time or head for home?

"I'm telling you, that's the time I wished I were back instructing in the States or that I'd gone with the Air Transport Command. There we were, sitting like a crippled duck, with nothing to fire back at Jerry with and not even self-sealing gasoline tanks or armor plate.

"Before I knew it I was making another hundred and eighty-degree turn and heading back for the drop zone. Even though I didn't have any instruments, it was easy to find the drop zone by the gunfire—that's where it was the thickest. This time I yelled to get ready before we got to the drop zone, and when we were over it, I yelled, 'Get going!'

"This time Jerry had everything out and was shooting at us as if the war depended on his knocking down just us. So we all held our breath, and after I had waited long enough for all the men to have jumped I stuck the nose down toward the deck. When I leveled off at about a hundred feet I said to myself 'I wonder if we're going to have to go back again.'

"When we reached the coast, I turned to see what the crew chief would have to say. He said three troopers had been knocked out by the bouncing of the plane, and were still aboard. 'Tell them they're going to have to jump tomorrow because if this crate holds together we're going home right now,' I told him.

"The trip back was in the same kind of weather and somehow it seemed more quiet and peaceful. The three paratroopers were not seriously hurt and were sore as the devil because they didn't get out of the plane over the drop zone. I didn't feel up to explaining to them that we'd stooged all over northern France and had already used up all the luck of a couple of lifetimes.

"Although the plane was flying fairly well, I was losing oil pressure. My tanks had been hit. That wasn't good. We lost most of our oil on the way back, and when we got over the airfield I found that our landing gear on the left side had been all shot up. We finally got both wheels down, though, and landed safely. The airplane looked like a sieve but flew again after only a couple of days in the maintenance shed. Believe me, no other airplane on earth could take what that old bird took that day. There never was and never will be another plane like it."

On March 28, 1944, five C-47s plowed into the darkness to make a pinpoint delivery of supplies on a target in Yugoslavia. This was the first of a series of missions to help the Yugoslav partisans, who were making a last-ditch stand for their country against the Germans.

Having assigned liaison officers with the partisan groups, the Army Air Force's 60th Troop Carrier Group worked up a series of signals so the air crews could make certain they were dropping supplies to the partisans and not the Germans. On the ground the partisans would mark the target area with a lighted triangle, cross or other symbol, and the pilot of the C-47 would flash "the letter of the night." For further identification, the men on the ground would flash back another prearranged letter of the Morse code.

Since the partisans were dug into the hills, practically all supply drops had to be made in extremely treacherous country. It was usually necessary, therefore, for the planes to fly over the small drop area several times in order to get all the load out.

After the first series of drop missions, a number of short landing strips were hacked out in partisan territory on which the C-47s could land. More supplies could be brought in and personnel evacuated. In a record two-night period fourteen C-47s evacuated 585 children and wounded partisans, an average of 42 passengers per airplane.

The Gooney Bird has flown over all the world's continents and oceans. This classic photo was taken during World War II as a C-47 flies past the Pyramids of Egypt on a supply run. Douglas maintained a secret repair base in Ethiopia. (USAF photo)

The first C-47 aircraft to land at Cyclops Airdrome, Hollandia, New Guinea, taxis past a burned out Japanese Zero fighter. (USAF photo)

It wasn't easy to conceal the operation from the Germans, and the partisans were continually harassed by German commando raids. The partisans, realizing that the American C-47s were their lifeline to freedom and liberation, mined the roads and paths with explosives and ambushed the Germans with rifles, grenades and homemade weapons.

On one occasion the Germans attacked a landing strip near Tito's headquarters just two hours after six C-47s had departed. The partisans fought stubbornly for two days against German paratroopers, glider troops, dive bombers, and tanks, finally losing the battle and retreating to the mountains, where they continued to fight for two more weeks before the Germans finally pulled out.

On one of these missions, Captain Joe Bowman got the scare of his life one night when a German fighter plane attacked as he was making a landing at an isolated strip between two steep mountains. Zigzagging the plane on his approach, he managed to evade the German's fire. Bowman landed and, followed by his crew, leaped into a nearby foxhole. The German didn't press the attack and Bowman realized the pilot was probably afraid to make a second pass into the narrow valley. Instead, the German pilot circled high overhead, knowing that it would soon be dawn and the C-47 would be an easy target in the daylight.

Bowman couldn't wait for dawn. As soon as his plane was unloaded he took off into the darkness without lights. He flew low until he reached the coast. Flying high above, the German fighter pilot failed to spot him.

Sometimes, when landing in the darkness on the short strips, pilots damaged their planes by ramming into unseen objects. When this happened, they had to camouflage their planes and remain on the airstrips until the damage was repaired. This often proved risky, especially at night when they had to use lights to work by. That was

A C-47 of the 60th Troop Carrier Group lines up on the approach for a risky landing in the hills of Yugoslavia to supply the partisans serving under Marshal Tito. Pilots had to flash "the letter of the night" for identification before landing. (USAF photo)

exactly what the Germans wanted—they could swoop down and strafe the airplane and crews.

Captain Dan Collifer, who flew one of the first missions for the partisans, related one of his experiences:

"It should have been an ordinary short-field landing, but a heavy ground fog caused me to overshoot. We ran off the end of the runway and nosed up, causing slight damage to the props. They stuck firmly in the mud, and there was nothing we could do about it that night.

"The next day my crew, helped by several stranded bomber crewmen, some partisans, and twenty oxen, pulled the plane out of the mud and we repaired it. All the time we prayed that a German fighter pilot wouldn't spot us, and that day not a single fighter appeared to see what was happening on the airstrip."

Collifer took off that night with his crew and thirty-one stranded bomber crew members. Captain Robert Snyder wasn't so fortunate, however. Approaching a drop zone in a small, deep valley, he signaled the partisans that he would make the drop from low altitude so it would be more accurate. He circled the area once, dropped low, and started into the valley. A jagged cliff loomed in front of him and Snyder turned sharply to miss it. The airplane stalled and, at low altitude, would not respond to Snyder's frantic efforts to recover. The C-47 crashed, and Snyder and his five crewmen were killed instantly. The partisans buried them with full military honors.

Another pilot, Lieutenant Houser, came in over a landing strip early one morning and saw a yellow flare on the ground, a signal that the field was under attack. Suddenly, a German fighter dived on him and sent a 20mm shell crashing through his left wing and engine. The airplane caught fire and Houser gave the signal to bail out, as he fought to keep the airplane under control. His copilot, Lieutenant Largent, ran to the rear hollering to the crew to bail out but the airplane lurched, throwing Largent off balance. By the time he regained his senses, the smoke and fire filled the cabin and Largent couldn't tell whether or not the others had bailed out.

Seeing a large hole in the fuselage, Largent went toward it, fell through, grasped the ripcord of his 'chute and tugged. The 'chute opened and he was safe. Looking up, however, he could see that the others had not bailed out. Helplessly, he watched the airplane swerve out of control and crash into the rocky hillside with the other crew members still aboard.

For his heroic efforts in attempting to save the crew and airplane, Lieutenant Houser was awarded the Silver Star posthumously. The following night Largent was flying another mission into partisan territory.

One of the most interesting missions was flown by Lieutenant Harold E. Donohue, who landed on an airstrip less than 600 yards long. One end of the field ran straight into the side of a mountain, which meant that he would have to take off in the opposite direction from which he had landed. Normally, this would not have been a problem; however, after delivering some cargo, there were sixty-nine pathetic, scared little children to be evacuated; their ages ranged from six weeks to fifteen years.

Donohue looked at the children, scratched his head and wondered how many he could carry out in one load. Placing them exactly right to assure the best weight-and-balance and filling every corner, he crowded all sixty-nine, plus his crew into the plane. Then he wondered if the C-47 could leave the ground with the unusual load—seventy-four people.

In spite of the rough, short runway, Donohue's Gooney Bird clawed its way into the night. Later a crew member said of Donohue,

When the gear was retracted before this C-47 was off the ground at Espiritu Santo, New Hebrides, in 1944, it slid to an ignominious stop. Although the engines and props had to be changed, the main landing gear projecting from the nacelles prevented fuselage damage. (USAF photo)

The C-47 assembly line at the Douglas Santa Monica plant. When aircraft reached this stage, they were readied for a company test flight before being turned over to the Army Air Forces. (Douglas Aircraft Co. photo)

"He's a young fellow, but he's got a kid of his own." That made a difference.

Two of the unsung heroes of World War II were the "food kicker" and the "food pusher"; the men who dragged heavy bundles of supplies to the open door of a C-47, took a firm grip on anything they could reach, and kicked and pushed with all their might to deliver the heavy parcels to troops eagerly awaiting them on the ground. It wasn't an easy job for several reasons, one of them being that sometimes the kicker or pusher would lose his grip and follow the bundle down. More often than not, they would not wear parachutes because their bulkiness hampered their movements inside the airplane. Also, many were wounded by enemy ground fire as they stood in the open doorway preparing to shove cargo out.

Accuracy was also a problem and thousands of pounds of precious supplies were lost forever when they missed a tiny clearing and were swallowed up by the jungle. Too many runs were required, causing flight crews to be exposed to enemy ground fire for extended periods.

Food kickers and pushers needed strong backs and plenty of push power to dispatch their cargo to where it would do the most good. The kicker laid on his back, braced himself and, at a given signal from the pilot, the kicker kicked and the pusher pushed. It usually took many passes to discharge a full cargo. At about 100 miles per hour, the C-47 was a sitting duck for enemy guns. Surprise helped achieve success on the first pass, but each succeeding pass cut down the chances for survival. Occasionally the last box, disgorged as the C-47 pulled up for a getaway, struck and damaged the plane's tail. To solve this problem, Brigadier General Paul H. Prentiss, commanding the troop carriers in the Fifth Air Force, asked Harry Booth, Douglas service engineer in the South Pacific, to devise a cargo hatch to be cut in the floor of several C-47 "biscuit bombers."

This dropping contrivance was given one of its first combat trials supplying fuel for General Patton's Third Army tanks and trucks while they were outrunning their supplies across France in August 1944. During these tests clusters of five to seven 5-gallon cans of gasoline were dropped by parachute through the hatch.

Engineering experts at Wright Field, Ohio, alerted to the problem, commissioned the Douglas factory in Oklahoma City to experiment with an airplane employing a double conveyor and with

The crew chief of this weary C-47 in North Africa kept score of the number of evacuation flights, food drops and flights carrying mules and camels. (USAF photo)

an extra door cut in the fuselage opposite the cargo door. The first trial run was made over Tinker Field, Oklahoma City, in July 1944. The conveyor dropped its simulated cargo packs within a 400-foot circle in six seconds. Authorities at Wright Field, Ohio, accepted the twin conveyor plane for further testing and ordered similar modified equipment to be installed in several C-47s for use in various combat theaters.

A single conveyor with an improved roller launch and a faster belt of greater capacity proved advisable. With the extra door eliminated, the equipment could be installed or removed in an hour at any air base, and the supply-dropping C-47 was not limited to this single purpose.

Occupying the left half of the C-47 cabin aft of the flight deck to the cargo door, a distance of 22 feet, the assembly would support 4,000 pounds on its 22-inch-wide endless fabric belt supported by aluminum alloy rollers. A 3.87 horsepower motor, using power from the plane's 24-volt system, drove the belt at approximately six feet per second, clearing its load of parachute-rigged containers in four seconds. The packs scooted onto a launching platform at the cargo door; static lines automatically opened the chutes as a guardrail deflector nudged the packages out the door.

The conveyor device proved to be worth the cost. In a typical sortie a load consisted of 5,000 K ration packages. One plane dropped 3,000 pounds of gasoline, almost 500 gallons, in seven seconds and within a space of 300 yards. Thirty-three pounds of water, about 400 gallons, formed part of another load. Hundreds of units of blood plasma and whole blood were also dropped.

This new invention might have left a few of the kickers out of a job but it is doubtful that there were many complaints from the men who had stood in the doorways, inviting the sniper's bullets or risking being thrown out by a sudden lurch of the aircraft. No one envied the kickers and pushers nor did anyone ever try to steal their jobs.

Japanese infantrymen, accustomed to shooting at stationery objects on the ground, tried desperately but vainly to bring down low-flying Gooneys that resupplied their American enemies. They aimed at the cockpit, but because of the 100 mph speed of the low-flying planes when on their drop passes, managed mostly to kill or wound the kickers and pushers in the rear. The commanding officer of the 443rd Troop Carrier Group, the main supporting airlift unit for British Brigadier General Orde Wingate's Chindit penetration into Japanese-held Burma, came up with an answer. His name was Colonel Charles D. Farr, a former Navy enlisted pilot who "went Air Force" in 1940. Captain (later Colonel) John A. McCann, Farr's executive officer, told how he proposed to cut down on the losses of his airmen:

"Colonel Farr believed that if a 'gun' ship or ships were fed into these drop patterns, particularly in those areas where high volume of delivery was being affected and where we usually drew a volume of fire, that a good spray job with caliber .50s would suppress ground fire against the aircraft.

"'Mac,' Colonel Farr said to me one rainy night in April 1944 at Syllhet, India, 'You're an aerial gunner—why can't we put 50 calibers on a C-47?'

"I'd known Charley only a short time, but well enough to appreciate that he had a real 'hen on' and wanted to bat the idea around, even though he likely already had it well conceived in his own mind. So I asked, 'Where—in the nose?'

"'Nope—too much stuff to fool with up there,' he said. He thought some more and then said, 'If we made a rig, could you shoot it out of the side window?'

"'Mebbe,' I replied, 'but you wouldn't get much area of fire and it would take up a lot of valuable room right in the middle of the cargo compartment.'

"Then he said, 'You're probably right. How about out the door? That's it,' he continued. 'Sure, we can rig up a tripod and cut a hole in the aft part of the cargo door.'

"'You mean mount a flexible fifty and fire it out of the door without any safety stops? Charley, the pilots would never sit still for that.'

"'Oh yes they would,' he answered. 'Besides, let's not cross that bridge yet.'

"We chalk-talked out the details with pencil and paper until the colonel had a workable sketch drawn up which he turned over to the maintenance gang the next day. The project was launched.

"C-47 No. 315054 was the first ship cut from the herd to undergo the surgery that would transform this placid beast of burden into a deadly bird of prey. As originally conceived, a large aperture was cut out of the aft half of the double-width cargo door from about waist high to slightly above eye level. A tripod of heavy angle iron was attachable by set screw to the floor and lower edge of the new aperture in the aircraft to provide a stable platform for a slotted frame into which neatly fitted the stem of the swivel pin mount of the gun. Thus the gunner standing securely inside the airplane with the gun barrel outside had a radius of action of about 160 degrees of transverse, about 80 degrees of elevation, and a like amount of declination, minus, of course, the contour of the tail assembly and the wing, about which there was still a lot of head shaking."

The experiments by Farr and McCann were entirely successful and another Gooney was modified in the same manner. Both were used in a number of subsequent drop missions. "The ugly duckling of air power," as McCann referred to the Gooney, had proved once again that it could do anything—even defend itself if it had to.

Captain Bob Hartzell and Lieutenant Bob Gray, the latter a pilot who had flown on the 1942 Doolittle Raid on Japan, were scheduled to fly a Gooney Bird from Dinjan, India, in northern India to Kunming, China. It had been left there by a Ferry Command pilot who claimed that the engines would quit whenever he reached 10,000 feet and he refused to deliver it to Kunming in accordance with his orders. Hartzell and Gray flight-tested it up to 17,000 feet and found nothing wrong. They flew it to Kunming with cargo and prepared for the return flight to Dinjan.

Their ship was loaded with wolframite, an extremely heavy ore used in the making of steel. They were asked to carry two wounded Chinese officers on stretchers and one unwounded officer to India where they would get medical care. There were no parachutes for the Chinese but since the wounded men couldn't use them and the third one said he wouldn't use it if he had one, Hartzell reluctantly agreed to take them aboard.

The field at Kunming is 6,300 feet above sea level and even with a heavy load, it was a touch-and-go takeoff situation. As the C-47 passed the halfway mark on the runway and there wasn't much of a sign that it was going to fly, Hartzell knew he had a problem.

A Gooney being readied for a ferry flight to Russia. (USAF photo)

The Oklahoma City Douglas Aircraft plant, producer of the dependable Skytrains, built and modified C-47s for all of the major United Nations, producing more than 3,000 after the plant's completion in March, 1943. Here is a fleet of nations lined up on the Oklahoma City ramp, bearing the insignia (left to right) of the U.S., England, Russia, and China. In addition, a number of C-47s went to the Fighting French.(Douglas Aircraft Co. photo)

Ahead was a P-40 revetment. If he aborted, he'd probably smash into it. He and Gray horsed back on the wheel and barely got it off the ground. The gear hit the edge of a ditch and bounced into the air. While Hartzell fought to gain airspeed, he called for his crew chief, Sergeant Beard.

"Get me that manifest!" he yelled. When he saw it, he blanched. There were sixty bags of wolframite aboard, each weighing one hundred pounds. With the crew, gasoline and three passengers and some other assorted cargo he estimated their load was about 7,500 pounds and at the altitude he was to fly, over 13,000 feet, he was dangerously overloaded. He elected to land at an en route base and get rid of some of the cargo.

When he neared the base, he was on top of an overcast. As he broke through it for an approach, he saw 27 Jap bombers and 17 fighters flying in formation. Three Zeros peeled off toward them just as the control tower operator on the ground radioed, "For Chrisake, look out! The Japs are over us!"

Hartzell and Gray broke away toward the mountains and north up a gorge for about an hour. Paul Gallico, writing in *Esquire*, tells what happened after they found themselves flying between the sheer walls of a river gorge:

"Their pressing idea was to put distance between themselves and the Jap ships since their only armament was the forty-fives on their hips. They flew north up the gorge for an hour, towards Tibet, not daring to show their wings above the rim of the gorge. Hartzell then decided to head back. He did this simply by hauling his overloaded transport into a wingover within the canyon. He says it aged him a little but he got the ship headed south again."

At this point, an engine quit and Hartzell feathered it. He told the crew chief to start throwing out the bags of wolframite. Thinking that there might be a fuel shortage on that side, Hartzell changed gas tanks and unfeathered the engine. Gray worked the wobble pump and the dead engine caught. The crew chief didn't throw out any of the bags.

They began to climb to 10,000 feet over the Naga hills, the last mountains to cross before Dinjan, and went on instruments. Gallico continues:

"Twenty minutes of instrument flying and they would be through. But time was another hazard. The sun was setting. Hartzell gave his ship full throttle.

"They had flown blind for five minutes. Gray reached for the dome light to check the instruments as both engines conked out.

"In the silence, Hartzell told Crew Chief Bob Macklin, 'Get your chute on and get out!'

"Hartzell nosed the ship into a 90-mile-an-hour glide. They were sinking at the rate of 400 feet a minute. 3,000 feet below were the deadly mountain tops.

"It was then Hartzell realized he had three men aboard without 'chutes. He was the captain of that ship and he would not abandon it with those helpless Chinese in it."

Hartzell suddenly had an idea borne of desperation—the wobble hand pump. He began to pump furiously with his right hand and flew with his left. Both engines caught. Gray, realizing that fuel pressure was the problem, grabbed the handle and took over the pumping. Both engines purred smoothly and they continued to the field at Dinjan.

An operations officer met them and looked at the manifest. "Brought quite a load, didn't you?" he said. Hartzell nodded. "Kind of late, aren't you?" Again, Hartzell nodded affirmatively.

"You want to watch that, Captain. You know if you'd been five minutes later you'd never have gotten into this field."

While they were talking, the unwounded Chinese officer climbed down the Gooney's steps and said, "She-She," which means "Thank you" and walked away into the darkness.

Hartzell watched him go, thinking, "It was you who brought us in. If it hadn't been for you, I might be dead now. She-she, fellow."

Hartzell also remembered what he had thought about that ferry pilot who refused to fly the Gooney over the mountains to Kunming. He said he was going to apologize to him.

Although the Russians had been licensed to turn out the Li-2, their own version of the C-47, several hundred American-made Goonies were also ferried from the United States using the great circle course near the top of the world. The route started at Great Falls, Montana where the Air Transport Command maintained a huge base. Here all types of fighter, bomber and transport planes were collected from the factories on both coasts. The red star of the Soviet Union was painted on each plane in place of the American insignia. They were then flown through the Canadian cities of Calgary, Edmonton, Fort Nelson, and Whitehorse to Ladd Field near Fairbanks and Nome where they were turned over to Russian pilots. The American pilots followed the Alcan Highway which had many small emergency strips carved out of the wilderness which paid for themselves many times over.

The route was little known but was first developed in 1942 and by 1944, more than 5,000 combat aircraft had been flown over this northern route. Interpreters were stationed at Ladd Field and Nome. Relations were always friendly and spare time waiting for aircraft to be readied for the long flight to Russia was filled with games of pool and chess which required no language to understand who was a winner.

The entire operation was deemed highly successful and helped to carry out General Billy Mitchell's prophecy that "he who holds Alaska holds the world."

4

The E-X-P-A-N-D-A-B-L-E Airplane

The DC-3 was and is unique, for no other flying machine has been a party of the international scene and action so many years, cruised every sky known to mankind, been so ubiquitous, admired, cherished, glamorized, known the touch of so many different pilot nationals, and sparked so many maudlin tributes. It was without question the most all-up successful aircraft ever built and even in this jet age it seems likely the surviving Douglas DC-3s may fly about their business forever.

Ernest K. Gann

According to Douglas engineers, the C-47 has a weight limit. In wartime, however, pilots paid little attention to limits because of the urgency of their missions. In one theater the gross weight might be pegged at 28,500 pounds, in another 33,000. One unit in the South Pacific limited the payload to 5,000 pounds of cargo because of the need for extra gas tanks, while others said simply, "Cram the stuff in until it won't hold any more."

Although various units had different weight limitations, many of the loads were roughly estimated because of the lack of scales to weigh the cargo. There was also a shortage of slide rules that would show where the cargo should be placed for best weight-and-balance.

One of the first pilots to test the load-carrying capabilities of the Gooney Bird were the pilots of the China National Airways Corporation (CNAC), seven of whom were Americans. CNAC's pilots, flying DC-2s and -3s, had been flying supplies to Chinese troops and evacuating personnel for months before the United States entered the war. One of the pilots who was responsible for much of the exploratory flying over the "Hump" of the Himalayas, and who also set an early passenger-carrying record in a DC-3, was Moon Chin, a native of Baltimore, Maryland, who had been trained by Pan American Airways. On May 5, 1942, Chin took off from the airfield at Chungking with a load of passengers bound for Myitkyina, a military base in Burma. One of his passengers was the famous racing pilot James H. "Jimmy" Doolittle who had just been promoted to brigadier general two weeks before after having led sixteen medium bombers from the Hornet, a US Navy aircraft carrier, to make the first air raid on Japan.

Chin took off not knowing that the destination was under attack from Japanese fighters. Halfway there, he received a radio message about the attack and landed at an isolated emergency field. Doolittle described for the author what happened next:

"We waited there about an hour, then resumed the flight. When we arrived at Myitkyina, the place was in chaos. The airport was jammed with refugees fleeing from the rampaging Japanese. Hundreds surrounded the plane wanting to get aboard. While the DC-3 was being refueled, Chin supervised the loading of additional passengers; soon there were 30 of us in the passenger cabin. He didn't stop. He let 40 get on, then 50. I couldn't watch without saying something. 'I sure hope you know what you're doing,' I said, not believing what I was seeing. Fortunately, they were almost all small people; many were women and children, including babes in arms. They had no baggage, just carry-on bundles.

"Moon Chin was not at all bothered by the number, as if he hauled that many passengers every day. 'We're fighting a war over here,' he said when he saw how perturbed I was. 'You do lots of things here you wouldn't do at home,' he added calmly.

"When the sixtieth person crammed his way into the cabin, Chin shut the door and picked his way among the human cargo to the cockpit. Despite the load, that faithful Douglas Gooney Bird was airborne before we ran out of runway and I breathed a sigh of relief.

"Being jammed in with so many desperate people didn't make for a comfortable ride. We were supposed to go to Dinjan, but Chin decided to go directly to Calcutta, where we arrived after a four-hour flight. As we debarked, however, I got another surprise. Out of the rear compartment, usually reserved for baggage, tumbled eight more disheveled Chinese!"

The 68 passengers and crew of four made a total of 72. Doolittle thanked Chin for the ride but said, "Believe me, Chin, if I had had any idea that you were going to jam that many people into this old crate I would have gone home the way I came."

Captain John Mowat had landed his C-47 at his base in India, thinking he had just flown his last air evacuation mission before returning to the States after a long tour in the China Burma-India theater. He was jubilant as he watched the ambulance take away the load of wounded to the Lido Hospital. He had done his share

The role of the Gooney Bird as a medical evacuation aircraft was repeated during the Korean War. Here Army medics load a wounded soldier aboard a C-47 of the Kyushu Gypsy Squadron. More than half of the 200,000 men evacuated from the combat zone were carried aboard the planes of this unit. (USAF photo)

helping men who were fighting a nasty, dirty war, but he was glad the weary routine was finally finished for him.

As Mowat walked from the Operations shack for what he thought was the last time, the squadron operations officer called to him. "Hey, John, I got another mission for you."

"Not for me, my friend," Mowat said dryly. "I'm going home. So long."

"Not quite, old buddy," the officer said. "The Old Man scheduled this one himself, and you're it."

"That do make a difference," Mowat growled. "So what's it this time?"

Mowat was told that the mission was to haul eighty live sheep to British jungle troops fighting in Burma, so they could have Christmas dinner in style.

"Ugh!" said Mowat. "Mutton? For Christmas dinner?"

That night eighty sheep were jammed into Mowat's C-47. Had there been only eighty sheep, Mowat would have known there would be no weight problem. But, in addition, sixteen Indian sheepherders, each with nearly 200 pounds of baggage, were crammed aboard. All this plus a crew of three began to add up dangerously. Nineteen people—roughly 3,800 pounds. Eighty live sheep at about 50 pounds each—4,000 pounds. About 3,200 pounds of baggage and miscellaneous equipment. Mowat figured he had about 11,000 pounds of payload aboard, yet the cargo handlers insisted he had only 9,400 pounds. But they hadn't weighed the sheep, the sheepherders and their baggage.

John Mowat had flown many heavy loads in the C-47, but not one like this flying barnyard. As if the possible overload wasn't enough, he had to take off at night on an unlighted runway with tall trees towering at the opposite end.

Mowat could tell that this was no ordinary load as he taxied out. The fuselage squeaked and sagged under the weight. The sheep were not tied down and he could feel the plane sway as he turned to line up on the runway for takeoff.

The tower cleared him for takeoff. He revved up the engines to full power, released the brakes and the plane began to move, very reluctantly. About a thousand feet down the runway Mowat forced the tail up; in another thousand feet he had reached an airspeed of only 60 miles an hour, not enough for takeoff. The end of the runway was near. Mowat yelled to his copilot to drop quarter flaps, but this didn't seem to help. There was only one thing to do: haul the wheel back into his stomach and pray.

The plane shook, finally responded to the controls, and hesitatingly left the ground—but only briefly. Not quite ready to fly, the groaning plane bounced and Mowat eased back on the wheel to prevent a stall. Staggering with full power on, the plane slowly picked up airspeed, then Mowat heard what he hoped he wouldn't—the sound of trees scraping the bottom of the fuselage. He waited for the crash into limbs, but none came.

Finally getting its wind, the Gooney Bird inched its way into the night sky, and Mowat completed his mission a few hours later. He had set a record of sorts but he would just as soon have left the honor to someone else. The British fighting men on the ground had their Christmas dinner and Mowat had finally flown his last mission.

The walk-on type of animal cargo was not always to be eaten, however. Sometimes the live cargo in the China-Burma-India theater consisted of mules to be used in their traditional role as beasts of burden by troops on the ground. But how could they be transported to the dense, mountainous areas safely?

The Chinese 14th and 22nd Divisions were being sent to Chanyi, China, in December 1944 because it was believed the Japanese were planning a big push on the city of Kweiyang. The army needed ground transportation—horses and mules. These pack animals were in short supply, however, because Mongolia, which had formerly been one of China's major sources of the animals, was now cut off by the enemy. Tibet was another source, but could supply China with only about 10,000 horses per year, many less than the number needed.

The Chinese were not stock raisers and they knew little about the care and feeding of mules and horses. The number that had been available before the Japanese invasion of China had been seriously decimated. The primary source would have to be India. The commanders of the two divisions had originally planned to use about 2,500 horses and mules to haul the division's supplies across the mountains, but finally decided that 1,500 might do the job. The problem was how to get them over the mountains from India so they would be fresh and capable when they reached the area near Chanyi.

Someone looked at the C-47, measured the girth of an average mule and the inside of the plane and conceived the "Jackass Airlift." The C-47 could carry the animals if stalls were made inside the fuselage to hold the animals in place during the flight. Staff Sergeant C. L. Hathaway of the Army Corps of Engineers was assigned the task of rigging the planes to carry the animals. He and his crew of twenty Chinese soldiers had only one day to get the first airplane ready for the first flight. They began work on December 9, 1944.

First, Hathaway removed the seats from the passenger compartment. He built simple rigid stalls out of large bamboo poles. When the poles were fitted together there was enough room to accommodate one animal in each and its handler who would care for the animal in flight.

When this was finished, Hathaway knew he had to solve another problem. During the flight the animals would have to urinate, unless he could persuade them to do so prior to takeoff. If they urinated inside the airplane it would drain through the floor and slowly corrode the control cables stretching underneath. His solution was to place a tarpaulin on the floor covered with coco matting, and spread 200 pounds of hay throughout the fuselage.

Next was the problem of loading the animals. Hathaway and his men tried using ramps and walking the animals up to the cargo door, but for reasons known only to the animals, they balked at the door and refused to be enticed inside. The loading was finally accomplished by first putting the animals into the rear of a covered truck, then backing the truck up to the cargo door and encouraging them inside using the push-pull method.

Once inside, the animals were lashed into their stalls by halters which kept their heads held tightly so they could not move freely and injure themselves. A rope was tied to the fuselage wall, passed over the backs of the animals and lashed to the other side. Pack saddles were placed on each so the ropes would not cut into the flesh if the plane should encounter rough weather.

The first C-47 arrived without difficulty and the Jackass Airlift soon became routine. The pilots would take off and climb to 14,000 feet for the flight across the Hump. At that altitude the animals were usually well behaved, probably because of the lack of oxygen, but whenever the C-47s hit turbulence the animals pawed and pranced and became extremely agitated. On one occasion, a mule broke loose and the flight engineer, who happened to have had veterinarian experience in civilian life, finally persuaded the animal to lie down in the stall, then sat on its neck until the plane landed at Chanyi.

While several transport units carried mules, the 315th Troop Carrier Squadron was the only unit to drop them by parachute. To the uninitiated this may not seem like a major logistics problem, but it was to the crews of the 315th.

Imagine for a moment that you are the pilot of a C-47 and your squadron commander orders you to fly a drop mission. All you usually need to know is where to drop whatever it is and when you're expected to drop it. Today your C.O. says, "Okay, we've got another drop mission to make in support of Wingate's Raiders. You guys know the pitch. They expect you over the drop zone at 0615 tomorrow."

There's nothing unusual about the order but you wonder what it is you're going to drop and ask. The answer is surprising: "Mules."

This happened to Captain Frank Sweeney, who took part in one of these missions. He tells how he handled a difficult problem with the five animals that were to be airlifted:

"Since we had the mission to perform, we became interested in having questions answered which we never thought would ever concern us as Air Force pilots. What kind of parachute should we use on a jackass? Since we would be at low altitude and probably in rough air, how would we keep these animals quiet? How would we get a balky jackass out the door? After being dropped, would they land safely or would they break their legs and have to be shot?

"With an assist from the medics, we doped the animals to quiet them, loaded them aboard and headed deep into Burma behind the Japanese lines. When we got to the drop zone we got four of the animals out of the airplane in four passes without any problem. But the fifth one gave us trouble.

"Apparently, the dope had worn off this particular jackass who seemed thoroughly aware of what we were about to do with him. As he was led to the door and found his head outside, he panicked. When the handlers tried to push him, he did what all jackasses do—he promptly dug in with all four feet and dared them to dislodge him.

"The handlers pushed and shoved while I made trip after trip over the drop zone flicking the "jump" switch. Time after time it was the same—they couldn't get the critter out.

The C-47 could be converted from a cargo to an air evacuation plane in minutes. Stretchers were stacked four high. Two nurses are shown here tending the wounded while a medical technician assists. The C-47 was used for medical evacuation during World War II, Korea and Vietnam. (USAF photo)

"Exasperated, I turned the plane over to the co-pilot and went back to see what I could do about the situation. There were the four handlers, the crew chief, and radio operator standing there completely baffled by this stubborn jackass. The animal was standing facing the door, all four feet firmly braced.

"We held a conference and finally hit on an idea. It looked like what this animal needed was a little stimulus of some kind from behind which would make him decide that going through the door was the least of his troubles. The only thing we could think of was to build a fire under him but this could be dangerous.

"There was one kind of fire that we thought might work, however. When my co-pilot got us over the drop zone the next time, I took out my Zippo cigarette lighter, fired it up, raised the mule's tail and applied the flame to a tender spot. The mule quivered for a second, suddenly came to life and leaped out the door into the slipstream like a cannonball. I'm sure he was looking forward to the trip."

Lengths of pipe are loaded aboard a Gooney in the South Pacific. Although loads were always to be within weight and balance limits for the aircraft, there were no scales available and crews often didn't know how much the cargo weighed they were loading. Many pilots unknowingly took off dangerously overloaded. (USAF photo)

Although the C-47 was designed primarily for hauling people and cargo, its use for other purposes seemed unlimited. It was a "natural" for flying mercy missions to haul in food and medical supplies to front-line troops and to evacuate sick and wounded to rear-area hospitals. During World War II, a C-47 flew one of the strangest cargoes and it wasn't an overload mission. In fact, the cargo weighed only about 100 pounds. Based on other flights which have been given names such as "Redball Express" and "Fireball Express," this mission became known as the "Lipstick Express."

The mission, to be flown at night, had been assigned by Colonel Frank McNees, commander of the 435th Troop Carrier Group stationed in England. A young lieutenant was chosen and reported to the colonel who told him what the cargo was: several boxes of lipstick. The lieutenant gulped and was shown a circuitous, dogleg route that he should fly to avoid German antiaircraft fire. The ack-ack batteries were circled on the map. Clearly irritated that he was selected to fly a dangerous mission with a cargo of something that only women could use, he asked for but received no explanation.

Colonel McNees didn't blame the lad for being irritated about this flight. He had been chosen because he was a good pilot but McNees knew that if he were told what the lipstick was really going to be used for, he might take unnecessary risks to deliver it and probably would be shot down before he got very far. The Germans would like nothing better than to "zero in" on a lone, unarmed C-47.

The C-47 was airborne and the lieutenant asked his navigator to take a look at the dogleg course the colonel had drawn. "I think the Old Man's wrong," the navigator said. "I was over this course three days ago, and we didn't get a single burst out of any of these places he's marked." He gave the pilot a new course to fly to straighten out the doglegs the colonel had drawn. The plane was turned to a new heading.

Without warning, as they throbbed along, flares suddenly looped up into the sky. The lights covered the plane with such blinding brightness that the pilot didn't need a flashlight to see the map. The plane rocked as heavy black flak followed the flares and the pilot struggled desperately to keep the wings level.

The crew chief came struggling forward and shouted, "Sir, we've been hit! There must be a thousand holes in the fuselage. Does she fly all right?"

The pilot nodded affirmatively but was in no mood to answer questions. He shouted for the navigator to give him a new heading to get out of the area. The flares and flak stopped and the navigator gave him a course to get back to the route the colonel had plotted. The C-47, riddled with shrapnel and bullet holes, had slowed down but eventually reached the drop zone. The pilot made two passes over it for identification and saw the Aldis lamp signal which marked the spot where he was to drop his strange cargo. The crew chief kicked the box out and the plane headed for England. German ack-ack batteries fired on the C-47 several times but it was only token firing and scored no hits.

As they passed over the Channel and the pilot knew they were safe, he began to think about the mission and the strange cargo of lipstick. The more he thought about it, the madder he got. They all could have been killed and for what? A case of lipstick! He wanted to know the reason for such a stupid assignment. After he landed, he wasted no time looking for the colonel and found him in his quarters. "Colonel, I think you owe me an explanation about that stupid lipstick," he said. "We damn near got our fannies shot off over there and we're lucky we made it back. The airplane is full of holes and won't be safe to fly for awhile. I just can't see how dropping lipstick to a bunch of Wacs or nurses will shorten the war!"

The Gooney Bird has served humanitarian causes all over the world. Here an Air Force C-47 is loaded with emergency food supplies at Misawa Air Base for victims of Japan's disastrous tidal waves in the early 1950s. (USAF photo)

"Did you drop the box on the target?" the colonel asked.

"Right on the nose, but...."

"Did you fly the course I gave you?"

"Not at first, I didn't. I changed, though, after the flak hit us."

"I gave you credit for being able to follow orders better than that, Lieutenant. If you had followed the course I gave you, you wouldn't have 'damned near got your fannies shot off.'

"Now if you'll be patient a moment, I'll explain the purpose of that lipstick. First of all, you should know that there are no Wacs or nurses in a combat zone. There were men below you—desperate, weary, wounded, brave men. There were several hundred wounded men where you made that drop who were waiting for that 'stupid' lipstick.

"I still don't understand what it could be used for, Colonel."

"Son, what you don't know is that lipstick is used by the medics on wounded men. When there are casualties the medics rush in and quickly check them over to see the extent of their wounds. They then separate the more serious cases from the less serious and they have to have some way of marking the emergency cases for priority attention. That lipstick that you delivered is being used at this very moment to mark the foreheads of seriously wounded men to distinguish the serious cases from those that can wait a little longer for a doctor's care. That lipstick is actually saving lives tonight because it's the best thing invented for the job. They were out of it and you dropped it right in their laps. Believe me, son, there are a lot of mothers somewhere tonight who will see their sons come home from war because of that case of lipstick."

The colonel looped his arms around the young pilot and said, "I'm proud of the job you did tonight."

The young lieutenant received the Air Medal for this flight but the words from the colonel meant more than the medal.

Of all the overload stories that are told about the Gooney, the one about a mission during the early days of the Berlin Airlift seems to outweigh them all. Someone was responsible for nearly losing a C-47 and its three-man crew because he didn't understand the meanings of "PAP" and "PSP" on the plane's manifest.

Within a few hours after the Russians barricaded the roads and railroads leading into Berlin in the summer of 1948, a lone C-47 winged through the air corridor from Wiesbaden to Germany's old capital city, loaded with vital medical supplies. The Russians had blocked all ground transportation because of "technical difficulties" but they could not put up a barrier to the air corridors linking West Germany with Berlin short of a shooting war. Was this to be the beginning of World War III? No one knew.

The lone C-47 made it through, followed by many others, and the Berlin Airlift, called Operation Vittles, was born. Within four days every available C-47 within flying distance of Wiesbaden was placed on temporary duty under the command of the Commanding General of the United States Force in Europe, General Curtis E. LeMay. Ninety-eight C-47s showed up, most of them from the 60th Troop Carrier Group, which had won battle stars in Algeria, French Morocco, Sicily, and Italy.

The first few flights into Berlin's Tempelhof Airport broke open a new chapter in aviation history. Desk-bound pilots became airline pilots, colonels, and all officer ranks below were marshaled into the cockpit seats of the Gooney Birds. LeMay himself, his famous cigar in hand, flew his share of missions to see for himself what problems his pilots would have. In some cases, colonels flew as co-pilots for lieutenants because the lieutenants had more experience in the Gooneys. Everyone waited for the Russians to capitulate and allow ground traffic to resume. But the Russians were confident that no city could be kept alive solely by air. The three Allied zones of the partitioned city would be starved into submission.

After a week or so with no letup, the cargoes being flown changed from medical supplies to badly needed foodstuffs. Then it became a task of hauling in everything needed to keep the people of the Allied sections of the city alive. The Gooney Birds hauled coal, flour, potatoes, truck parts, fruit, milk, you name it. The crews became dirty, tired, and exhausted as the days wore on. Airplanes were beginning to wear out. Jet fighter pilots with little or no actual experience in weather were transferred from their squadrons at Furstenfeldbruck to fly as co-pilots for the more experienced twin-engine pilots, some of whom had no more than thirty or forty hours in the C-47 before the airlift began.

As it became apparent that the Russians had no intention of giving in, it was also evident that the fleet of C-47s that filled the three air corridors into and out of Berlin could not carry the increasing amounts of cargo needed. More and larger aircraft would be required. Another Douglas product—the four-engine C-54 Skymaster—was the plane for the job. About a hundred were ordered from the Far East, Panama, Hawaii, and the States to replace the C-47s which had borne the load from the beginning.

In his book *Boxcars in the Sky* Richard Malkin said, "At the beginning of the airlift 85 percent of the aircraft were war-weary C-47s, averaging more than 3,000 hours per aircraft prior to Operation Vittles. Lack of parts and qualified ground crewmen created almost insurmountable obstacles, but during this period the group maintained more than 65 percent of its planes in commission. This is far above the average, considering the scope of the operation.

"The 60th Troop Carrier Group accomplished an exceptional feat by averaging 7,000 pounds, loaded weight, per aircraft, when the average load is 6,000 for the C-47. This was made possible by reducing the gas load. At times the planes were carrying up to an 8,000-pound payload."

One day, just before the C-54s took over the airlift, a C-47 pilot checked his load manifest sheet, nodded his satisfaction and boarded his aircraft. It was listed as "PAP" on the manifest which meant "Pierced Aluminum Planking" and was destined to be used for a runway at Tegel Airport in the French sector of the city. He picked his way to the cockpit over the long metal strips, started the engines and taxied out for takeoff. The instruments showed that everything was functioning normally but the plane seemed to need more power than usual just to taxi—"like being bogged down in the mud" was the way he expressed it.

He lined up for takeoff and gave both engines full power. The plane moved slowly down the runway. At last the tail wheel came up and with great effort the C-47 staggered off the ground just before it reached the end of the 6,000-foot runway. The pilot climbed the plane, creaking and groaning, to the assigned altitude and leveled off. Cowl flaps were closed and power adjusted on both engines. The airspeed immediately sank to about 100 miles per hour, far below the normal cruise speed. Something was wrong.

The pilot and co-pilot went over the checklist again, visually checking to make sure that the landing gear and flaps were up. "Guess she's just tired, like I am," the pilot said, and pushed the throttles nearly all the way forward to maintain the airspeed designated for air corridor traffic. The engines resented it and began to overheat.

During the Korean War, Air Force C-47 units were often called upon to evacuate civilians and military personnel hurriedly from war areas. This Kyushu Gypsy Gooney Bird carried 40 passengers with the wounded on stretchers and some sitting in the aisle. (USAF photo)

When Berlin appeared on the horizon after more than the usual time to fly the route, the pilot entered the traffic pattern and made his approach. The airspeed dropped dangerously low when the gear was put down. Almost full power was needed to hold a safe airspeed without stalling. The main wheels banged down on the runway with a jarring crunch and the tail wheel blasted to earth with a thud that rocked the entire airframe. As the puzzled crew taxied to the unloading ramp at Tempelhof Airport, they knew that something was woefully wrong. No Gooney Bird had seemed less anxious to fly than this one.

Before he opened the door the pilot thought he'd better check the load before the Germans swarmed all over to unload it. The manifest was clearly marked "PAP" for "Pierced Aluminum Planking." Bending down, he fingered one of the metal planks, tried to lift it, straightened up with surprise and yelled, "Hey! This isn't aluminum, it's steel!"

It was pierced steel planking and the pilot had good reason to yell. His Gooney had carried a load of pierced steel planking (PSP) that weighed nearly 13,500 pounds-about twice the weight any C-47 ought to carry!

In 1950, the year after the Airlift ended, the Gooney Bird was to fly and fight in a new war that would once more test its load-carrying capabilities and its role as the military services' old workhorse. This time the place was Korea and the task was to engage in a "police action" as it was called when forces from North Korea invaded the southern half of the divided nation. The C-47s went there officially as the 21st Troop Carrier Squadron, but they soon were better known as the Kyushu Gypsies, because after the Communist forces of North Korea crossed the 38th parallel, they had no permanent home.

When United Nations forces were mustered to confront this invasion, Greek and Thai pilots brought in several C-47s to augment the Gypsy squadron and flew as an integral part of the unit. The three C-47s that winged in from Thailand had their original engines but no records came with the planes. Since there were no records, it was impossible to tell how many flying hours each had amassed. Baling wire and coat hangers had long since replaced cotter pins and safety wire. Over the years mud daubers had built nests inside the engine cowlings; most of the instruments were either inoperative or missing entirely from the instrument panels; and the fabric covering the tail surfaces and ailerons was held together with adhesive tape.

The exploits of the Gypsies would fill scores of books, but of all the missions they flew, one operation stands out in their minds as giving them the most pride and satisfaction, not only in their unit but in the planes they flew. It was an operation that the U.S. Marines would not forget either.

The Gooney Bird has handled just about anything that will fit into its fuselage. This tractor is being guided into a C-47 in the South Pacific for transport to an advanced airstrip. (USAF photo)

The weather was frigid as the cold air and clouds pushed in on the peninsula battle ground in Korea and across Japan. Emergency messages flooded in, saying that some C-47s were needed at Hamhung to evacuate wounded Marines out of the village of Hagaru-ri near the Chosen Reservoir. The 1st Marine Regiment had been cut off and other Marine and Army units had concentrated their survivors at Hagaru-ri. On November 30, 1950, the first C-47s departed for Hamhung Airfield. By the end of the day thirteen C-47s sat on the Hamhung airfield ready to work. The next day the planes took off for Hagaru-ri, passing through a saddleback ridge on the way, looking beyond to Koto-ri and the winding narrow road that led across the valley to the reservoir.

Midway between the two towns the pilots saw a convoy stretched along the road. They wondered how this was possible if the Chinese had the Americans encircled. They looked closer. The convoy was not moving. It had been attacked, gutted and every vehicle destroyed. There was no sign of life around the ruined trucks and tanks.

The airstrip at Hagaru-ri was only 2,500 feet long, hardly long enough to operate from safely without a load, let alone taking in heavy loads of supplies and bringing out wounded. On the ground the crews of the C-47s saw more indications of battle. They smelled the stench of men's wounds, of unwashed bodies. They saw the weapons and small fires where the men were huddling to keep warm. They heard the barking of rifles, the chattering of machine guns, and heavy blasts of artillery.

The Marines began loading the stretchers of the seriously wounded into the C-47s immediately. Others not seriously injured walked by themselves to the plane. Several hobbled on canes or crutches made from tree limbs. They moved quietly and with discipline.

One of the first C-47s into Hagaru-ri that day was hit by bullets from small arms fire. Major Paul Fritz, one of the pilots, later said they flew so low over the enemy that the planes could have been brought down by rocks pitched at them.

As they were getting ready for takeoff, a young Marine told Fritz, "It's nice of you to come and get these fellows. Some of them are pretty badly shot up. Tomorrow we're going to convoy out, soon as you Air Force people get the wounded out."

Fritz didn't have the heart to tell him that the convoy they were expecting would never arrive.

As far as load limits were concerned, few Gypsy pilots paid any attention to them at Hagaru-ri. A pilot would take all the wounded that could be loaded into the plane. One crew brought out thirty-eight, but this number was challenged by another crew who boasted they had brought out forty. Fritz's crew did better than that. As they loaded the fortieth man, Fritz looked back at the truck where two more badly wounded Marines waited stoically. Their faces were set in agony. Fritz looked back inside his plane. There was still some floor space, so he motioned to the crew to make way for two more.

When Fritz had first flown to Hagaru-ri, he hit a bump in the runway that had not been smoothed away. On every takeoff it caused the plane to bounce, shudder, then fall back for lack of airspeed. The runway bump was to prove disastrous for one plane. Heavily loaded, it hit the bump, bounced nose high, stalled and plummeted to the ground. It plowed off the end of the runway through a stand of trees and stopped.

Fortunately, no one was injured; however, the plane had crashed in no man's land near the entrenched enemy. Two Air Force fighter pilots flying overhead saw the crash and watched as the passengers and crew streamed from the wrecked plane and hobbled away. When they saw the flashes of small arms fire, they dove on the enemy snipers and held them off until the Marines were all rescued.

The C-47 seemed beyond repair but the fighter pilots wanted to make sure it could not be captured and put into service later by the Communists. Again they streaked in, machine-gunning the Gooney Bird on the ground. Bullets hit the gas tanks and the plane exploded. To the C-47 pilots who had to watch the destruction, it was a sickening sight.

After five days at Hagaru-ri, the C-47 crews could see their efforts paying off. The daily crop of casualties decreased, and those who fought were well-supplied with warm clothing, food and ammunition brought in by the C-47s. But it was time for the Marines to fight their way to the coast. "The way out is the way through," one Marine said.

On the sixth day, as the Goonies went into Hagaru-ri, the advance spearhead of the encircled Marine division was already inching its way from one fire-fight position to the next. Small detachments of men scouted the flanks of the main body, and a handful of vehicles labored behind. The semblance of security they had before in their small defense perimeter vanished. Now they were completely vulnerable and tired. The Siberian winter gave no respite but the Marines were on their way.

By noon of that day it was time to give the airstrip back to the enemy. A C-47 which had been damaged beyond repair on the field was blown up by a hand grenade.

As the Marines slowly made their way toward safer territory, an emergency airstrip was being carved out of the terrain at Koto-ri near where the Marine division would pass. The strip at Hagaru-ri had been short but the new strip was only 2,000 feet long. As soon as it was finished, Gooney Birds landed every few minutes and supplied the Marines for two more days. The Gypsy planes, plus some planes borrowed from other UN units for the Chosen Reservoir operation, had hauled in 547,000 pounds of supplies and ammunition. On the flights out they had evacuated 4,638 men. Two C-47s were lost, but not a single flight crewman was killed or even seriously injured.

Several days after Christmas, the Kyushu Gypsy crews who had participated in the Marine evacuation were standing in formation while a glowing tribute to them was being read over a loudspeaker. Men were decorated with Distinguished Flying Crosses and Air Medals. Behind them in a precise line sat tired, war-weary C-47s that needed new tires, new engines and bullet damage repairs. As the unit commander pinned the DFC on one pilot and congratulated him, the pilot replied, "Thank you, Sir, but I don't deserve it. It's these airplanes here that should get the medals. Without them, no one could have done the job. With them, anyone could."

In the desperate days of the Pusan Perimeter fighting when the United Nations forces were trying to maintain a toehold on the Korean peninsula, United States logisticians of the three services were trying to smooth out the delivery of priority air freight destined for the front lines. Cargo was delivered from the United States by four-engined Douglas C-54s to the Tachikawa Air Base warehouse in Japan where it was classified and stacked to await delivery. When transport planes were available, the badly-needed war materiel was flown to Ashiya, in southwest Japan, the temporary home of the Kyushu Gypsies. From there the Gypsies flew it to the Pusan Perimeter in their C-47s.

In those confused days, an independent communications system was connected directly to the command post in Pusan. Priorities for the supplies were established and the Gypsy Squadron notified. The squadron supply officer would earmark the materiel on hand and ship it according to the priority given. Code words were used to disguise the cargo being shipped.

One day the Gypsy Squadron commander received a call saying that thousands of pounds of graham crackers were required in Pusan with the highest priority. This strange request was relayed to Tokyo, and all other shipments were put aside while hundreds of cases of graham crackers were located and flown to Pusan.

Within a few days cases of graham crackers piled up at several bases in Japan. They piled higher and higher at Ashiya as the C-47s could not deliver them fast enough. The Gypsies even took their planes out of the hangars to make room for storing the piles of boxes.

Supply officers were mystified as to why boxes of the dry brown crackers had suddenly taken priority over ammunition and medical

The 21st Troop Carrier Squadron detachment of the famous Kyushu Gypsies combat cargo unit in Korea lived in these tents at a frontline airstrip. (USAF photo)

supplies, and tried to shut off the stream. When the operation was about 50 percent complete, priorities were suddenly changed and the Gypsies started hauling 3.5-inch bazooka shells as fast as they could move them. The graham crackers were suddenly forgotten in the excitement of war and became, for a time, one of the Far East's unsolved mysteries.

Many of the flight crews thought the South Korean Army had run out of staple food and needed graham crackers to supplement their usual diet. But this explanation was unsatisfactory, because the graham crackers never reached the front lines.

One evening a few weeks later Colonel Troy Crawford, commander of the Gypsy Squadron, overheard a conversation between two Army ground officers at the Tachikawa Officers' Club. They were discussing graham crackers and seemed to be quite amused. Crawford questioned them and discovered that the graham cracker incident was the result of a curious mixture of coded and uncoded messages.

Large quantities of bazookas had been shipped to Korea for use against the enemy tanks at Pusan. The United Nations troops, running low on bazooka shells, had called for resupply with the highest priority. Except during extreme emergencies, code messages were always used in communications between Korea and Japan. This time the urgency was so great that the Army communications men transmitted the message in the clear with the exception of the name of the needed item. The code word for bazooka ammunition the day this message originated had been graham crackers!

The Gooney has played many roles during its years but one event stands out in the minds of Coloradans when the Gooney was the first line aircraft of Frontier Airlines. Beginning in 1946, Captain Everett Aden flew the Frontier Flying Cross every Christmas Eve from Denver for thirteen years. It was a neon-lighted cross attached to the underside of a Frontier Airlines DC-3. Powered by a large battery pack attached to the belly of the Gooney, Aden flew over the Denver metropolitan area for up to two hours. "Viewers used various signals to let us know of their appreciation, from strong spotlights to blinking of outside Christmas decorations," Aden said. "It was one of the real highlights of my flying career, since the cross means so much in my personal life."

Flying the cross over the city of Denver had been an annual event since 1929 with the exception of the World War II years. Ray Wilson, founder of Frontier Airlines, flew the cross in a single-engine Curtiss Robin to celebrate the Yuletide from 1929 through 1941. Various means of illumination were used, including a flare attached to the struts of the plane. When the Gooney was used, it seemed a sort of tribute from the plane that had contributed so much to saving lives during its war years.

5

What No Other Airplane Can Do

Give me fifty DC-3s and the Japanese can have the Burma Road.

Generalissimo Chiang Kai-shek

Of all the attributes of the Douglas DC-3/C-47, the one most comforting to flight crew members is its ability to fly on one engine. While many pilots have had to find out about this the hard way, including the author, the record for distance with only one propeller turning belongs to Major "Skip" Kimball, of the U.S. Marine Corps. Kimball was a member of SCAT—South Pacific Combat Air Transport Group—and was slated to fly a load of cargo in an R4D from Pearl Harbor to San Diego.

At the halfway point between Hawaii and the States—nicknamed "Jones Corner"—Kimball lost power on his left engine and had to feather it. Since the distance was the same either way and the wind was 70 degrees off his course, the choice of whether to turn back to Hawaii or continue on to California was academic. What mattered was how far the plane could fly on one engine.

With the heavy load, it soon became apparent that the Gooney Bird could not maintain its altitude unless some cargo was jettisoned. The crew kicked the boxes overboard, the plane picked up speed, and Major Kimball lumbered into San Diego without further mishap. He had set a single-engine record by flying the R4D more than 1,100 miles.

Aircraft equipped with tail wheels can be difficult to land in stiff cross winds. This Goodyear DC-3 was outfitted with swiveling main gear and experiments were conducted to determine if they would assist in landing. (USAF photo)

The second longest distance ever flown on a single engine by a twin-engine airplane is claimed by Commander Frank E. Kimberling, USN, in a ski-equipped R4D-8, a Super DC-3 (naturally called the Super Gooney), in September 1958. Kimberling was to fly his plane, equipped with long-range tanks, from Quonset Point, Rhode Island, to Antarctica via San Francisco, Hawaii, Canton Islands, the Fijis, and New Zealand.

Kimberling's nonstop flight from Quonset Point to San Francisco was uneventful, but the leg to Hawaii presaged the difficulty he was to have later on the trip. Three times he left San Francisco for Honolulu, Hawaii. Three times he got 500 miles over the Pacific and had to return on one engine. He finally made it after 14 hours, 55 minutes of uneventful and wearying flight.

Loaded with approximately 10,000 pounds of cargo for Antarctic operations, plus an extra 500 gallons of fuel in the fuselage tanks, Kimberling blasted off the runway at Honolulu with the aid of 15 JATO (Jet-Assisted Take-Off) bottles. The time was 6:35 p.m., September 29, 1958. The distance to the Canton atoll in the Phoenix Islands was 1,670 miles.

All was serene as Kimberling, his two co-pilots—Lieutenants Reginald Simmons and Norman Davis—plus seven other crew members, settled down for the long flight. At fifteen minutes after midnight, with 620 miles to go, the hours of boredom were interrupted by the sudden terrifying whine of the propeller on the left side as it ran wild and the engine caught fire. Kimberling immediately tried to feather it but to no avail. The propeller speed governor malfunctioned and if the engine could not be shut down, the whirling steel blades could come off and rip through the fuselage like a power saw.

Nothing Kimberling did could reduce the engine's rpms. The only action he could take was to cut the fuel off to that engine and let the dead propeller windmill until it froze for lack of oil. The unfeathered propeller, however, would windmill and be a tremendous drag on the plane, just as if a huge, round steel plate were affixed to the plane in its place.

Kimberling had been cruising at 8,000 feet when the emergency occurred. Seconds later, by the time the gas had stopped flowing to the disabled engine, the plane was down to 1,000 feet and headed for the ocean below. The good engine was wide open and the plane was in a skid from the excessive weight and drag on the left side caused by the spinning propeller.

"Throw out everything you can move!" Kimberling shouted.

Ten thousand of pounds of cargo is a lot of weight to throw overboard but the seven passengers needed no prompting. To their dismay, the "jump door," a small door which can be drawn inside the plane in flight and replaced after a supply or paratroop drop, had been riveted shut. The only alternative was to rip the pins out of the whole door and push it overboard, which they did. Piece by piece and box by box, the entire 10,000 pounds was unceremoniously dragged to the yawning doorway and shoved out. Each pound dropped gave the crippled Super Gooney and its human cargo a better chance to survive. The plane was now down to 100 feet above the waves and still trying to descend.

"Throw out everything!" Kimberling commanded, and out went suitcases, radios, the radar set, navigation equipment and tools. Lieutenant Davis, fully realizing how dangerous the situation was, personally carried the six 280-pound JATO bottles to the doorway and dropped them out. Davis, who weighed less than 200 pounds, said later he was so anxious to get them out that he didn't think they were heavy at the time.

For the next six hours, Kimberling battled the drag created by the windmilling propeller and the open doorway. He used full right rudder trim and he and his co-pilot took turns holding the right rudder all the way forward with their feet. The plane stayed in a skid at an airspeed of 89 knots—barely above stalling. Mike Ortega, the radio operator, had flashed a Mayday message on the liaison set at the first sign of trouble. Although they were a thousand miles south of Hawaii, the first station to acknowledge was Argentina, Newfoundland. Next, Tokyo answered and sent a message to Canton and around the Pacific.

Reaction was immediate. British RAF air-sea rescue aircraft were dispatched from Christmas Island and two U.S. Air Force planes departed from Pearl Harbor. In the meantime, Captain John Connelly, flying a Qantas Airlines Lockheed Constellation was just departing from Honolulu for the Fiji Islands. Flying at maximum cruise, Connelly caught up with the Super Gooney 120 miles from Canton. As soon as Kimberling spotted the Constellation he radioed: "We expect to run out of gas ten minutes from Canton."

Connelly acknowledged the transmission and relayed the information to Canton. A rescue boat was dispatched from there—an eight-foot rowboat powered by an outboard motor and manned by a lone Fiji Islander. At thirteen miles from Canton, Kimberling fig-

A C-47 of the Troop Carrier Command drops supplies to troops building an airstrip on Bougainville in the Southwest Pacific. The interlocking metal strips were laid down after bulldozers leveled the terrain. (USAF photo)

New Guinea natives crowd around a C-47 that has just landed. Gooney Birds sustained the aerial lifeline between supply bases in Australia and advanced bases to support the "island-hopping" strategy of General Douglas MacArthur. (USAF photo)

ured they had only twenty gallons of gas left. Five miles out, the gas gauges read "Empty."

"I'll never know how we made that last five miles," Kimberling said, "but we did. Just as the wheels touched down, the starboard engine sputtered and died. We had flown for five hours and forty-seven minutes under the most difficult drag conditions any pilot ever had to contend with to stay aloft. Believe me, I've flown lots of hours in lots of planes and had my share of near misses. Of all the airplanes in the world, only the faithful Gooney Bird could have done what we asked it to do that day."

Kimberling's Super Gooney didn't get to Antarctica that year in time to participate in the Navy's Operation High Jump. The next year, however, during an exploratory flight over the Horlick Mountains, the plane's luck ran out and it crash-landed but without loss of life. Today, Kimberling's disabled R4D-8 lies buried beneath tons of Antarctic ice and snow. Someday, if the world's aeronautical engineers give up and decide that no replacement for a DC-3 can ever be produced, someone may resurrect Kimberling's plane and fly it again.

On an earlier occasion during World War II, Major Owen Ross, a Marine pilot, was 500 miles from Espiritu Santo in the New Hebrides Islands when one engine of his R4D stopped without warning and he could not start it again. Unlike Kimball and Kimberling, Ross could not jettison his cargo because he was carrying twenty wounded Marines, all stretcher cases, to a rear-area hospital. Ross chugged ahead dreading what would happen if he lost power on his good engine. He nursed the plane along carefully and finally brought it to a safe landing.

When it comes to weight-lifting on one engine, Air Force Captain J. G. Herring, who found himself 250 miles at sea with a C-47 totaling 29,000 pounds, probably takes the prize. He could have jettisoned his cargo but since he knew it was badly needed in the combat area he refused to let any of it be kicked overboard. He flew tediously to his destination on one engine through cumulus cloud buildups that made his airspeed come dangerously close to stalling.

Whenever a group of aircraft crew chiefs get together for a bull session they usually discuss the experiences they've had with the pilots with whom they fly. For example, take the time when Sergeant Walter E. Jones told a story about a pilot who forgot how long the Gooney Bird's wings were. It is an excellent example of the luck and audacity of some pilots who had blind faith in the Gooney to fly under any circumstances. His story is repeated here in the same colorful words Jones used:

"In the last summer of 1944 I was a member of the 27th Transport Squadron of the 302nd Transport Wing, stationed at Heston Airdrome just a few miles outside London. Our wing had charge of all the ferrying of aircraft and the transport work in England.

"In September, after the breakout at Saint-Lo, we flew gasoline to General Patton before the Red Ball Express was set up. We also flew rockets, blood plasma and other critical items to France and took wounded men and German prisoners to England on the return trips.

"The day I want to tell you about started like any other day. I was the flight engineer assigned to this C-47 and we were to take a load of high-ranking officers of some armored division to Metz, France. The trip over was uneventful until we landed at a strip that was made to accommodate a squadron of P-47 'Jugs.' The strip was a common one for France at that time with steel matting runways, narrow taxi strips, and lots of tents. We landed just behind a flight of fighter planes, and my pilot, being unfamiliar with the layout of the field, started following them around the taxi strip. We didn't get very far. The strip was all right for the Jugs but was too narrow for the C-47. We hit both wing tips on some good-sized trees growing along the strip. The tail came up in the air and bounced back a couple of times as we came to a jolting halt. I ran back to open the door and get the ladder down and was almost trampled in the stampede of passengers trying to get out of the plane.

"After we had all piled out and looked the plane over, I was all for putting it on a red cross [making an X on the maintenance form

A crash-landed C-47 is pulled back onto a New Guinea jungle strip by friendly natives. The natives regarded it as a festive occasion and many are wearing elaborate headresses and necklaces. (USAF photo)

A C-47 has just crashed and burned after being shot down by a strafing Japanese fighter at an American air base in China. The dead Chinese coolie had been working on the runway when the enemy plane made its first pass. (USAF photo)

Chinese coolies break stones for a runway at a base along the India-China air route over the Hump flown by C-47s. The workers became so used to planes zooming overhead that they didn't even look up. (Douglas Aircraft Co. photo)

with a red pencil to indicate the plane was unsafe for flight until repairs were performed], pulling it over to one side and leaving it there until some service squadron could come and fix it or cannibalize it for spare parts. It was beyond my capability to fix it so all I wanted to do was get out of there on the next plane going back to our base.

"The left wing was turned up at about a 60-degree angle for about a foot and a half. The right one was torn and mangled from the nut plates on the wing all the way up to the tip and back to the last spar that holds the aileron on. It was a mess, to say the least, and I would have bet anything I had then against a discharge that that C-47 wouldn't fly again until both wing tips and maybe both wings had been replaced.

"But the captain looked it over and told me to get the crash ax from the ship. Then he got up on the right wing and started chopping the torn metal away from our right wing tip. He chopped off all that he could get at and then we got some mallets and hammers and beat the jagged ends back inside what was left of the tip. It was an awful looking thing, with jagged metal sticking out all over. Then he used his pocket knife to cut off one piece of rubber deicer boot that was hanging down.

"Going over to the left wing tip, we beat and beat on that one trying to straighten it out, but we didn't do much good. The thing was cocked up in the air about 60 degrees. We were tired of pounding on it. It was then that the captain told me we were going to fly it back to Heston. Well, you can imagine what I felt like telling him; but I was young and foolish, so we piled in and taxied to the Operations tent. He told them he was going to take off in spite of the accident we just had, and filed his flight clearance.

"As I was pulling the ladder up, a commander from the Royal Navy came running up puffing like an old ferry boat. He wanted a lift back to England and had just heard we were leaving. What a sailor was doing that far away from the ocean, only the King knew.

"I told him about our damage and pointed to the left wing tip which looked like it was going to flap. He hesitated a minute, uttered a few 'Bless my souls,' then decided that if we were crazy enough to fly the ship that way, he was crazy enough to go with us.

"He was a rather portly man, to say the least, and we certainly had a time getting him strapped in a parachute. We finally made it, but he looked like a sack of potatoes, he was bulging so much from the chute straps.

"By the time we were at the end of the runway to take off it looked as though every man at that base was there to see us kill ourselves trying to get that clobbered bird into the air.

"Well, sir, that old airplane took off and climbed like it was new. We climbed to about 7,000 feet and cruised at 130 miles per hour. I really expected to see that right aileron and the rest of the wing tip go at any second. I could see it fluttering and starting to bend. I told the pilot about it and he slowed down a little bit. The ship flew remarkably well, considering its condition. It required only about three degrees of aileron trim which we attributed to the left wing tip being bent up.

"When we landed at Heston and taxied up to Operations, I think all of the brass in the United Kingdom was out there. They could hardly believe we had flown that C-47 in that condition from Metz, France, to London in one piece.

"In our excitement over the trip, we had completely forgotten about the commander. I found him stretched out under a couple of blankets fast asleep. It's wonderful what ignorance will do some times. Our predicament didn't worry him a bit. He got up, stretched, thanked me and plumped down the steps just like he was getting off a streetcar after a day at the office.

"When we got the C-47 back in the shops and started to change wing tips, we could see how lucky we were. That last spar and one aileron mounting bracket had been cracked. Another inch and we would have had to change the whole wing because it would have ripped all the nut plates out that fasten the wingtip to the wing.

"I often think back on that day and I wouldn't do it again even if I could be Chief of Staff of the Air Force. I've just gotten smarter, I guess. I've long since graduated from C-47s but will always have a soft spot in my heart for the best airplane ever built and will always remember my association with it. No one will ever be able to tell me that another plane can be as forgiving. I know!"

Captain Jack Farris, pilot of the Geronimo, was a man who resented being assigned to fly the Gooney Bird. He had wanted to fly fighters, but after graduating from flying training he had been sent to C-47 transition school and then to England. Almost every day since getting his wings, Farris had been the victim of routine, or so it seemed to him. He called his job "boring" even though many times he had been shot at as he groped his way dangerously low over German anti-aircraft installations to deliver men or supplies in France.

Although the transport pilots had been told many times that their job was just as important as those flying bombers and fighters, Farris wasn't happy about flying an airplane that couldn't defend itself. He found it hard to listen to the fighter pilots on his base telling about how they had been hit by flak or how someone had shot down an enemy plane. He felt he had contributed little to the war effort, although he had dropped paratroopers behind enemy lines, hauled ammunition and supplies, and even dropped enemy agents to work with the French Resistance. But this knowledge didn't lessen the monotony he felt flying his "milk runs."

When a C-47 crashed near the Japanese lines in New Guinea, Major Edward T. Imparato and a crew of the 478th Service Squadron strapped a C-47 wing under his Gooney and flew it 250 miles to a small strip at Bena Bena, New Guinea. Imparato received the Distinguished Flying Cross for this C-47 "first." Later in the war, P-40 and B-25 replacement wings were flown in this manner. (Photo courtesy Edward T. Imparato)

One night Farris was in for the surprise of his life. He checked his load of paratroops, climbed into Geronimo and took off for France with a formation of other C-47s. Nothing happened during the first part of the flight until he neared the drop zone on the southern coast of France. Then all hell broke loose.

An enemy ack-ack shell tore through the fuselage on the starboard side, ripping a six-foot hole. A fragment split the aluminum and damaged every rib from the bulkhead to the vertical stabilizer. Then a second burst hit the plane and carried away a portion of the rudder. The explosion also blew away a large box of equipment inside the fuselage. The impact was so great that Farris thought one of the engines had come crashing into the pilot's compartment.

Captain Joseph Baxter, the co-pilot, went back to survey the damage, and what he saw knotted his stomach. Only the front half of the airplane was intact. The aft section was a sieve of jagged holes. There were so many holes in the fuselage that the wind whistling through them slowed the C-47 to 110 miles an hour. Wounded and dead paratroopers were spilled all over the aisle. Farris and Baxter knew what they had to do. Farris turned sharply, leveled off and headed for Africa. He fire-walled both throttles but the plane lost altitude steadily until it was skimming the wave tops over the Mediterranean. His instruments were useless and the only means of knowing whether he was right side up was to steer by the reflection of the moonlight on the water.

But Farris' number wasn't up that night. He wrestled the airplane all the way across the Mediterranean to a base in North Africa. When he attempted to shut down the engines, one of them was so hot that it continued to run after the switch was turned off. And never again did Farris complain that flying the Gooney Bird was boring.

The Gooney Bird was fired on many times during World War II but not by friendly troops. However, Capt. Louis B. Curdies had the unpleasant duty of shooting one down to save the lives of its crew and twelve passengers.

Curdies, who had shot down seven German planes and one Italian before his transfer to the Pacific, bagged his first Japanese plane over Formosa. It was a Japanese two-engine bomber. Returning from that mission, he and his squadron strafed an enemy-held airstrip on an island halfway between Formosa and Luzon.

As they were leaving, Curdies sighted a C-47 heading for a landing on the airstrip. He said he tried to make radio contact with the Gooney to notify the pilot that the strip was still enemy-occupied, and then tried to head off the transport.

"As a final resort," he said, "I shot out the right, then the left engines and the transport ditched in the bay, about 100 yards offshore. I saw the occupants get into dinghies."

Curdies and his squadron mates strafed the shore to keep the Japanese away from the life rafts. Other planes arrived to fly top cover. Next morning, a Navy Catalina rescued the Americans, including two Army nurses.

This view shows how the replacement wing was strapped onto the belly of "Battling Bishop" for the flight to Bena Bena, New Guinea. A wooden frame was made over the butt end of the wing and covered with aluminum to smooth the air flow. (Photo courtesy Edward T. Imparato)

Combat was not the only trial that the Gooney had to face during World War II. Flying over the frozen wastes of the Far North had prospects that were just as harrowing.

The possibility of going down in the arctic areas where it might be impossible for rescue crews to locate survivors was always present. Many planes disappeared with their crews, never to be heard from again. Theirs was a silent war against the elements instead of the enemy.

Major Ed Crandall and Capt. Bill McGilpin were two pilots who were lucky and they knew it. When forced down on the Greenland ice cap in a C-47 loaded with passengers, they survived to tell the tale. Having flown to an isolated radar site to evacuate a frostbitten mechanic, they had landed safely, picked up the patient and were heading back to Thule Air Base with a Grumman SA-16 Albatross flying cover for them. While on the ground they had a fire in the right engine and had requested the Albatross to escort them—just in case. They anticipated no real trouble but felt better with the SA-16 amphibian nearby. It could land on water, ice or snow.

Thirty minutes from Thule the Gooney's left engine suddenly sputtered and died. Crandall feathered the prop and then increased power on the right engine. A few minutes later the overworked engine began to lose power and the Gooney began to sink toward the forbidding white desert below. Rather than take a chance on landing with two dead engines, Crandall decided to make a landing immediately while he still had enough power to enable him to pick his landing spot.

Choosing a smooth plateau, he landed without difficulty as the SA-16 circled overhead. Two hours later the Albatross landed, took the scared, cold passengers of the C-47 aboard, and left for Thule. Crandall and his crew were left with the C-47. The men packed blankets around the engines of the C-47 and waited. About four hours later the Grumman returned and took them to Thule.

"Now here's where the story gets interesting," McGilpin said later. "The previous January the same type of incident had happened to another C-47. Although the plane was buried in the snow for three months, they managed to uncover it, change the engines under arduous circumstances and fly it out. We had visions of getting our C-47 out by the same means, but it didn't happen that way.

"The maintenance crews wanted nothing to do with changing engines on our plane with the temperatures ranging from 40 to 60 degrees below zero; to wait until the sun came up after the long winter would mean digging the airplane out from under tons of snow.

"What I say now I relate with bowed head. The Army had to pull us out of this one! They took one of their Caterpillar tractors and towed the sick Gooney ninety miles back to Thule. Uphill, downhill, around the treacherous crevasses, between nunataks, and down the side of the icecap; they towed her right into the hangar where she could be repaired. It seemed like that bent, broken old C-47 could always be patched up to go out and do a job that no other airplane could accomplish."

On several occasions the C-47 flew without wing tips, with a fuselage full of holes, with control cables broken, and even with much of its insides shot away. Sometimes it flew with no visible means of support, like one day "down under" when it flew with only one wing. As far as can be determined, this was the only Gooney Bird ever to accomplish such a feat.

The date was March 21, 1945, and the man riding in the co-pilot's seat at the time wasn't a pilot. He was what pilots called a "ground pounder," and his name was Capt. Jack Roberts, a communications specialist attached to the Army Airways Communications Service.

Natives carry a replacement wing to the wounded "Flamingo" of the 374th Troop Carrier Group at Bena Bena outpost on New Guinea in January 1943. Reportedly headhunters, the natives hated the Japanese but were friendly to Americans. (Photo courtesy Edward T. Imparato)

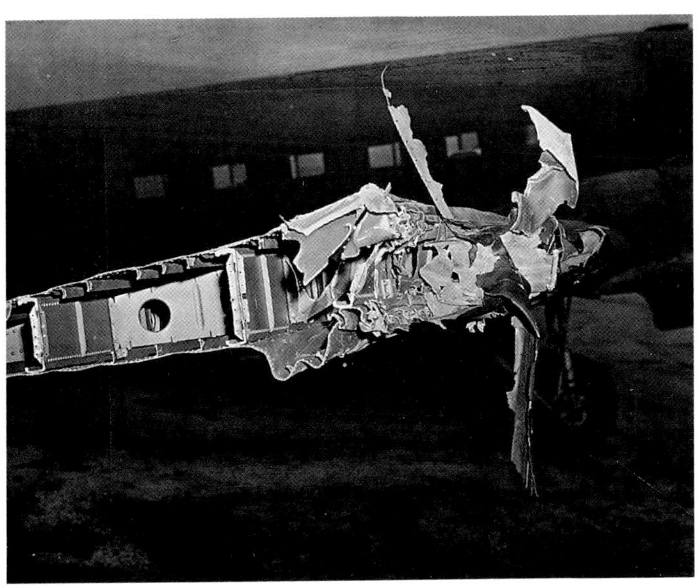

The famous Gooney Bird has been noted for its ability to keep flying despite horrendous damage. A C-53 had thirteen feet of its right wing ripped off in a mid-air collision yet its pilot brought it back home safely. (USAF photo)

Here is more proof that a DC-3 could sustain heavy damage in flight and still manage to return safely to earth. This airliner collided with an Arizona mountaintop in severe turbulence and lost several feet of its left wing tip. A safe landing was made at Phoenix. (Photo by Joey Star)

Although Roberts did not draw flying pay, he had a flying job that kept him in the air almost as much as the flight crews. He was an electronics expert who was required to assist in making periodic checks of low-frequency radio range facilities, the means by which pilots could fly the radio beam and make instrument landings in bad weather. Auckland, New Zealand, had one of these installations and it had to be checked regularly.

Roberts always flew these missions in the co-pilot's seat of the C-47 Dakota with earphones clamped tightly to his head. As the pilot flew back and forth on the four invisible range legs, Roberts had to listen carefully for "bends" and "fades"—conditions which might lead a pilot off course and into the sides of nearby mountains.

Roberts had been doing this for months and he got a thrill from it, because the pilots would let him fly the plane in order to get some "stick time" after the range-checking was completed each day. He had wanted to take pilot training but had been unable to qualify.

One morning, Roberts and First Lieutenant Bade, a New Zealand Air Force pilot, took off from Whenuapai Airdrome near Auckland for a two-hour range check. They crossed the radio range station at 1,300 feet to check the marker beacon receiver but the light on the plane's instrument panel didn't come on, so they made a 180-degree turn and climbed to 2,000 feet to make another pass over the station. Roberts thought perhaps the AACS radio mechanic had forgotten to turn on the transmitter. To make doubly certain that the beacon was not working, Roberts asked Bade to fly the beam outbound for a few miles to the fan marker. Again, the light did not go on in the cockpit.

Roberts shrugged, looked at Bade, and was about to suggest they return to Whenuapei when out of the clouds above them came a twin-engine Lockheed Hudson bomber, headed straight for them. Before Roberts could crank the wheel over and escape a collision, the Hudson smashed into the left wing of the Dakota. The wing exploded into a thousand bits as the Hudson blasted through and disappeared. Bade took over the controls and wrestled desperately to keep the plane level. The rudder and elevator worked, but the ailerons were useless. Bade swung the wheel all the way to the right and added more power on the left engine, but nothing happened. He jammed in right rudder and skidded the plane to compensate for the loss of the left wing. An airplane wasn't supposed to fly with most of the lift gone on one side, but this one did. Slowly, he was able to reverse course and head back for the field.

Bade fought the Dakota all the way to the base trying to maintain reasonably level flight. He made a "controlled crash" on the end of the runway. When he cut the power on the left engine, the airplane veered violently to the left and staggered off the runway into the grass and stopped. Bade cut the switches and, shaking, climbed out to inspect the damage.

The left wing had been sliced off almost up to the left engine fairing as if ripped by a giant knife. Wires and control cables dangled from the stub of what was left of the wing. Jagged metal hung down and gas from the wing tanks was spurting over the ground. Both men knew immediately how close they had come to disaster.

No one knows what kept the Dakota in the air. By all the principles of aerodynamics it should have spiraled steeply to the ground like a maple seed in the fall as had the Hudson which had crashed, killing its pilots. The Gooney Bird, however, had literally come in, as the old song goes, on a wing and a prayer.

No airplane with reciprocating engines will fly without gasoline and oil. This is a fact no pilot will deny. There are many grades of each, and engine manufacturers specify what grades are best for their products to operate efficiently. But, like the aeronautical engineers who designed the venerable Gooney Bird, the Pratt & Whitney engine manufacturers who built the R-1830 engines powering it have been badly shaken by what some pilots put in their gasoline and oil tanks during World War II. Automobile gasoline and extremely high-octane fuel have been used with ratings far below or above that specified by Pratt & Whitney. The grades of oil have varied from the type used in farm tractors to sewing machine oil, when all else was unavailable and a mission had to be flown. But the story that tops them all occurred in the South Pacific in 1944. Pratt & Whitney engineers don't believe it. Any C-47 pilot will.

It seems that a pilot was flying his C-47 to a forward air strip on New Guinea on a resupply mission. He was dozing in the left seat while the co-pilot flew the plane. Suddenly, the crew chief came forward, yelling, "Hey, Captain, we're losing oil out of the left engine!"

The young pilot jerked awake and looked out his window. Flying into a forward airstrip within range of enemy fighters and ground fire was bad enough but engine trouble in enemy territory was worse. Sure enough, oil was streaming out of the cowling, blowing small rivulets over the top of the wing.

"What's our position?" the captain yelled to his co-pilot.

"We've got about fifty miles to go," the co-pilot answered. "We ought to see land in a few minutes."

A bomb planted in the baggage compartment of this airline DC-3 exploded while the plane was in flight. In spite of the damage, the pilot nursed it to a safe landing without injury to passengers and crew. (Douglas Aircraft Co. photo)

The radio operator, a young lad of seventeen, gripped the side of his table. Should he break radio silence and send a distress call? He decided to wait for the pilot to tell him what to do.

The four men waited and watched the ailing engine and its oil pressure gauge as the minutes dragged on. There is no way to tell how much oil is left in an oil tank from inside the plane. If the oil pressure dropped below operating pressure, the engine would have to be shut down. The needle was slowly drifting downward.

Suddenly, the copilot shouted, "I see land! Beautiful land!"

The plane wouldn't let them down. Since they had a normal load, they could still make it to the airstrip on one engine.

After landing, the four men looked at the black streaks that covered the left side of the plane. "Sarge, I'll bet the price of a bottle of scotch that there isn't enough oil in that tank to oil your watch," the pilot said. The crew chief found a stick, climbed up on the wing, and stuck it into the oil tank. "You're right, Captain. The stick isn't even damp."

The sergeant checked the oil connections and fixed the leak but what would they do for oil? The airstrip, simply a rearmament strip with no aircraft using it as a base, was used by the C-47s to supply the infantry which was mopping up the Japanese in the nearby hills. There were no maintenance facilities, no spare parts, no gasoline—and no oil.

The only personnel occupying the strip were a few supply men who controlled the issue of supplies as they were flown in. There were many shortages of supplies and a few huge overages. At mealtime, for example, it was everyone for himself to choose among the cans of fruit cocktail, peanut butter, rice, crackers, and grapefruit juice, plus some odd assortments of dehydrated vegetables, Spam, and canned jelly. For some unknown reason, mountains of these latter food items and little else had piled up at the strip.

The tired flight crew lined up with the supply personnel to eat a noon meal. "Sorry I ain't got any gravy to put on this rice, Captain," the mess sergeant said. "All I got is grape jelly. You might think it's weird but it's all I got for the rice today. After you've been here as long as I have, you'll get used to it," he shrugged.

The captain grimaced. Rice with grape jelly would be something to tell his kids about if he ever got home.

As the crews sat on ammunition boxes to eat, the sergeant stood nearby and continued his apology. "I'm sorry we can't do better on food around here. I got lots of grape jelly and gallons of Wesson Oil. If you like cooking oil, I can get you plenty of that. That's all we had for the rice until the jelly showed up."

At those words the captain stiffened, dropped his fork and said, "You say you've got Wesson Oil by the gallon?"

"Yes, sir. I got maybe a hunnert gallons of it. But you ain't thinking about putting it on your rice, are you? That stuff will give you the runs."

"No, Sergeant. I'm going to use it in my airplane!"

Without continuing to eat, the pilot and crew piled into a jeep and went to the supply area where they found the pile of boxes

In the war zones during World War II, the C-47 quickly became known as "the airplane that always comes home." This view shows the damage sustained by one C-47 when it had a midair collision with another plane. (Douglas Aircraft Co. photo)

labeled "Wesson Oil." They put a few boxes in the jeep and a few minutes later had filled the oil tank with the cooking oil. The crew scrambled aboard as the old mess sergeant stood by shaking his head.

The captain poked his head out the window of the cockpit and yelled, "Thanks a lot, Sarge. We've got to get this crate into the blue before this thin oil burns out. See you next trip!"

The sergeant was open-mouthed as the Gooney taxied out and roared off toward its home base. "Judas!" he exclaimed. "The things you see in this part of the world when you ain't even had one drink!"

The C-47 and its cousins have flown an infinite variety of cargoes in its day. You name it and if it will fit inside the fuselage, chances are it has been flown successfully. During World War II, some cargo was even flown on the outside of the airplane, as witness the times in the South Pacific when P-40, B-25 and C-47 wings were strapped underneath and flown to forward airstrips or rearward for repair of other aircraft.

Passengers, however, have never flown outside the airplane—that is, paying passengers. But there was a time when a hitchhiker rode outside and thus set another "first" for the incomparable Gooney Bird.

October 9, 1950, was a night Captain Jorge L. Guzman, a pilot for LAMSA Airlines of Mexico, will never forget. The run from Torreon to Mexico City was supposed to be routine. The weather was clear and cold, and he carried half a planeload of passengers, some cargo and a little mail.

Guzman taxied into run-up position, checked his engines and lined up for takeoff. He pushed both throttles forward and watched the runway lights slip by as the DC-3 slowly picked up speed. But something didn't feel right. This time the tail seemed heavier than usual and the plane didn't accelerate as quickly as it usually did.

Finally, after what seemed like a long time to Guzman, the tail lifted and the main landing gear came off the ground. The co-pilot pulled up the main gear and as soon as he did, both pilots noticed a slight vibration, the kind that was sometimes caused when the tires are worn and spin unevenly in the wheel wells.

Guzman applied the brakes to the spinning wheels but the vibration continued. He asked the co-pilot to check the cowl flaps, thinking he had forgotten to close them for the takeoff, but they were in the "trail" position where they should have been. Guzman shrugged and watched the instruments in the dimly lighted cockpit, while the co-pilot reduced the power settings for the long night climb out. Then the vibration suddenly ceased and they temporarily forgot about it.

The climb out from Torreon at night was tricky. The safest way was to follow the radio range as if in instrument conditions, but this procedure was "old hat" to Captain Guzman. He had flown the route many times. He leveled off at 12,000 feet and settled down for the long three-and-one-half-hour flight to Mexico's capital.

Guzman went through the usual procedure of reducing power on both engines, closing the cowl flaps, and trimming the airplane for level flight. When he did this, the plane began to vibrate as it had done before. The controls shook back and forth and the rudder pedals fluttered. Guzman checked the instruments but all showed normal readings. He and his co-pilot looked at the engines to see if they were vibrating but they weren't. Puzzled, Guzman continued on course for another ten minutes trying to figure out what could be causing the problem. Were the wing flaps partially down? He checked them visually from the passenger cabin. No, they were full up. Could it be that one propeller wasn't balanced? However, if so, the engine cowling would probably be shaking and it wasn't. Perhaps the cabin door was open? No, it was closed.

He had to make a decision. He had passengers to consider and his decision had to be in favor of their safety. It was night and if he

View from inside the fuselage after the midair collision. This rugged veteran returned safely despite the serious structural damage to its center section. (Douglas Aircraft Co. photo)

had to try a forced landing in the mountains he could expect nothing but disaster. He decided to return to Torreon.

Guzman advised the control tower of his decision and was cleared immediately for a long descent and approach to the field. He had to hold a little more power than usual on the final approach and as soon as he flared out, the plane quit flying and clumped unexpectedly on the ground with a sickening thud.

Guzman wasted no time taxiing to the ramp. As soon as he braked to a stop he unhooked his seat belt and went out the cabin door. He told his passengers to keep their seats while he made a quick check with the ground crew.

When he turned his flashlight on the tail surfaces he saw something he could hardly believe. A human form was draped over the left horizontal stabilizer.

"Que pasa, hombre?" he called. "Get down off there!"

The figure didn't move. Guzman went closer and shined his light into the eyes of the stranger. It was a young boy about sixteen years old. His shirt had been completely ripped off and he was frozen so stiff he could hardly move.

Proof of the ruggedness of the C-47 Skytrain is shown here. This one plowed into a freak hailstorm in Colorado which shattered windows, battered the metal fuselage, and tore strips of fabric from control surfaces. Although hampered by poor visibility because of the shattered windshield, the pilot brought it in for a successful landing. (USAF photo)

Capt. James H. Doolittle, Jr., a test pilot at Wright Field, Dayton, Ohio, and son of famous General Jimmy Doolittle, made this jet-assisted takeoff from a muddy wheat field near Greenup, Illinois, in 1948. (USAF photo)

Captain Guzman reached up and dragged the boy off the horizontal stabilizer, and after a few minutes the lad was able to talk. He had flown for fifty-seven minutes on Guzman's DC-3 by clinging to the leading edge of the tail surface by his armpits!

When he had thawed out enough to give a coherent story, the boy told the pilot that his name was Cliserio Reyes Guerrero and that he had wanted nothing more than a free ride to Mexico City. He didn't get to his destination that night but he had become the first human being ever to ride outside of a passenger-carrying DC-3.

Despite his brush with death, the young Guerrero was impressed with his first flight and had no intention of letting it be his last. He later took flight training and became a pilot in the Mexican Air Force.

As all Gooney pilots know, its windshields always leak when flying through rain. The problem was never solved, at least during the days when it was in military service. Pilots learned to fold their maps so that the water would drain off toward the floor, rather than on their laps.

Another problem that was never really solved was heating the Gooney in subzero conditions. Capt. Robert W. Stevens, former Air Force and airline pilot, recalled that the early airline DC-3s had a boiler with a sight gauge and a few valves placed behind the copilot's seat with the water heated in a muff around the exhaust.

"If on the ground over 30 minutes in frigid weather," he said, "you had to run down below and drain the water from a petcock or the whole rig would freeze up, leaving you with no heat in the air until it thawed out. There were two-gallon spigot cans lashed to the floor. By shutting off a valve you could unscrew the cap of the boiler and add water to it on the ground or in flight. The other can was for adding glycol to a tank for prop deicing. Sure as hell somebody dumped glycol in the boiler and vapor-locked the whole show."

To solve the problem of putting some heat into the passenger cabin, the Russians seemed to have the answer. Their Russian Goonies flying into Ladd Field near Fairbanks, Alaska, to pick up planes under the Lend-lease arrangements with Russia had wood stoves placed near the back of the cabin with a smoke stack up through the fuselage but apparently they were never fired up in flight. They were used by the ground crews who were required to sleep in their planes when on the ground. The Russians also had small household refrigerators installed in some of their C-47s and Li-2s for the use of their ground crews.

And so the ubiquitous Gooney proved over and over how utilitarian and flexible it was wherever it found itself. There never was and never will be another plane like it.

6

Stories for the Hall of Fame

The first daylight jump of the 101st Airborne Division took place on September 17, 1944, a little more than two months after the Normandy landing. We in the Division called it a "parade ground" jump because of its perfection. It was the best that the division had ever made in combat or in training. Much of the credit for the success of the operation has to go to that old workhorse, the C-47. Only three of the 428 planes involved failed to reach the drop zones. Generally, the story was the same for the plane throughout all campaigns. The troopers liked it and the men who flew it.

General Maxwell D. Taylor

More than 10,000 Douglas DC-2s and DC-3s, and half again as many Japanese and Russian copies, have squatted on the world's flight lines during the last six decades. It would be impossible to compile a total of the flying hours attributed to the entire fleet of Gooney Birds; however, we can assume that each airplane that flew for a few years had thousands of hours on its airframe. We can also assume that each airplane took its crew through at least one hair-raising experience. During the preparation for this book, it was found that there were literally thousands of such cases which proved time and time again how indomitable is the plane that Douglas wrought. Some of these stories are repeated here as representative of the reasons why the Gooney Bird will forever deserve a place in the Aeronautical Hall of Fame.

Until the Japanese captured Rangoon in 1942, one merchant had become fabulously rich and was well respected. Now he was just one among the hundreds of refugees that surrounded the DC-2s and DC-3s at the Burmese jungle airstrip, seeking passage out of the path of the rampaging Japanese Army. Every man, woman and child was ready to storm the planes if the guards relaxed their vigil. Terror was in their eyes as they pushed and shoved. Their hands held out pleadingly.

"I'll pay you twenty thousand pounds," the merchant whispered to the China National Aviation Corporation (CNAC) operations manager who was packing twice as many passengers into each plane than it was designed to hold. "Twenty thousand pounds sterling for passage to India," the man repeated softly so as not to be overheard.

The manager didn't even look at the man as he said, "You will have to wait your turn. All the money in the world won't buy you a seat out of turn."

That's the way it was on every transport that flew refugees out of Burma in 1942. Terrified people were willing to pay their last coins and give up all worldly possessions for passage to safety. The CNAC pilots, had they been greedy, could have made fortunes in a few days. To their eternal credit, they were more interested in saving lives than in making money.

For more than a month the steady stream of refugees had been moving northward over the treacherous route to India. Airplanes could evacuate only a small fraction of the total, so thousands took to the mountain trails. The great majority of them were Indian and Burmese, but there were some Americans and British subjects. Many came from as far away as Rangoon, escaping first to Mandalay, then to Lashio, just a few miles ahead of the Japanese. Every motor vehicle that could move was jammed with humanity. Overhead the shark-nosed fighters of General Claire L. Chennault's Flying Tigers cruised, looking for enemy Zeros bent on strafing the endless columns of refugees. The refugees hid during the daytime at concentration points deep in the jungles, and then at dusk, some of the lucky ones who had made their way to an airport were loaded into Gooneys and whisked off to safety.

The evacuation of refugees from the British crown colony of Hong Kong off the southeast coast of China was different. Escape could be made only by air or sea. Escape by air meant sneaking the DCs through Japanese-controlled skies and into the international airport. The Kai Tak airfield at Hong Kong had never been an ideal base due to the hazardous approach near the mountains. There was only one runway and it was pitted with bomb craters; alongside was the wreckage of several planes that had been caught on the ground during the bombings. There were landing lights on the field which were switched on only when a plane was landing or ready for immediate takeoff and extinguished as soon as the plane was airborne.

Because they wished to avoid bringing further excitement to the battle-weary population, the pilots would take off at night at fifteen-minute intervals, swing down the channel toward the Japanese lines, then turn northward toward their destination of Namyung 175 miles away. If they could, they would return for a second trip

One of the strangest hybrids of the Gooney Bird was this DC-2 1/2. The right wing of a China National Airways Corporation DC-3 had been damaged by a Japanese bomb in 1941. The only replacement wing available was for a DC-2. It was flown to the spot and fitted into place. Although the pilot, Capt. Harold Sweet, reported the DC-2 1/2 had a tendency to roll toward the right wing, which was five feet shorter, he had no difficulty in flying it to its destination. (Douglas Aircraft Co. photo)

before dawn. Two of the planes on one night had evacuated a total of 276 refugees, an average of 69 passengers per trip.

Veteran CNAC pilot, Captain Harold Sweet, however, was not so fortunate. When the Japs first attacked Hong Kong his plane had been in the hangar waiting to have the left engine changed because it had developed a bad main bearing. When he took off a few hours after the Japanese controlled the city, he did so with a prayer on his lips, a prayer that the old engine, which had been hastily reassembled without being repaired, would continue to operate long enough for him to get his load of frightened people to safety.

Just as he crossed the border into Free China, the left engine sputtered, backfired and died. Sweet looked down on the blackened countryside hoping to see a place where he could set the Douglas down. The remaining engine wouldn't keep the plane in the air with the load he had. He picked out a tiny field that looked level and landed. As soon as it stopped rolling, the plane sank hub deep into sticky mud. Fifty-four passengers piled out of Sweet's DC-3 to help. They shoved and pushed wherever they could get a handhold as Sweet gunned the good engine in an effort to dislodge the plane from the mud. In spite of their best efforts, the airplane remained stuck all night.

At dawn the next day, Sweet and his passengers gathered leaves, tree branches, and tall grass to camouflage the plane from the searching eyes of the Japanese fighter pilots. Just as the job was finished and they felt certain the plane was well hidden, five Japanese fighters streaked in low and opened up with small-caliber machine guns. Sweet and his helpers scattered for cover and watched helplessly as the enemy planes flew back and forth over the transport, blasting it until their ammunition was exhausted.

Although the Gooney had taken scores of hits, miraculously it did not burn. The propellers, wings, instruments and fuselage were riddled so badly it looked like a giant sieve. Sweet counted more than 3,000 bullet holes in the wings and fuselage alone!

In spite of the holes, Sweet found that none of the main structural members were severely damaged. If parts were available and could be brought in, the old bird might, just might, fly again. Too many people depended upon this plane for their lives; it would have to be repaired, it at all possible.

Sweet hiked to a nearby village where he found a wireless set and was able to contact Chungking. He got in touch with Ted Soldinski, CNAC's maintenance wizard, a man who could breathe life into an airplane if anyone could. Soldinski arrived as soon as he could with supplies and immediately set to work on the engines and replaced the tires, while coolies patched the bullet holes with canvas and homemade glue.

When Soldinski finally pronounced the plane flyable, it was Charles Sharp, operations manager for CNAC, who undertook to fly it to India where it could be reconditioned.

On warm-up the engines ran extremely rough and spat huge streaks of flame out the exhausts. Sharp took off anyway and shortly afterward a rudder control cable snapped, making it difficult to control the plane. It yawed and wallowed, but Sharp managed to keep it fairly level by use of the ailerons. He knew he would have difficulty landing with the broken cable. To save the engines, he flew at reduced throttle on the edge of a stall.

Somehow, and Sharp could never explain how, it took him only 8 hours and 12 minutes to cover the 904 miles to his first objective. He landed without difficulty, despite the broken cable, loaded on seven more refugees whose pleas he could not ignore, and headed the fire-spitting plane back into the night clouds. This time his route took him over the Japanese lines. Controlling the plane was still difficult, but the clouds were his protection and he needed all he could find.

Once inside the clouds, tropical rains battered the plane like sprays of bullets, but above the staccato was the reassuring throb of the engines. Suddenly, a shrill, piercing whistling note broke through the synchronized drone of the engines. The whistling sound became almost deafening. Sharp knew the answer—the rain was washing off the canvas patches that had been stuck on with the coolies' homemade glue!

The weird cacophony of shrill whistles increased in tone and pitch until it reached an agonizing crescendo just as the plane broke out into the clear—headlong into a patrol of six Japanese fighters going in the opposite direction. The Japanese passed so close that Sharp and his passengers could clearly see the orange fireball markings on their planes.

The enemy fighters, recognizing the familiar shape of the unarmed transport, turned and streaked back toward it. As they closed in for the kill, they were startled by the shrieking of the air through the hundreds of holes in the transport's skin. Without firing a shot, the enemy fighters suddenly broke away and disappeared, leaving the DC-3 unmolested.

Two hours later a tired, shaken Charles Sharp approached his destination airfield in India and landed. An Army major met the plane and exclaimed, "Whistling Willie! Why did you bother to radio us? We've heard you coming for the past thirty minutes!"

It was then that Sharp realized that the bullet holes had probably saved their lives. The plane had set up such an unnerving wail that it had actually scared the Japanese away.

Hours later, a cryptic radio report from Radio Tokyo was transmitted in English: "Enemy forces are moving into northern Burma in force. [Actually, there wasn't a handful of Allied soldiers within 400 miles.] Spearhead of their invasion is a new aerial weapon, designed foolishly to unnerve the Emperor's pilots who hold mastery of the Burma skies. This secret weapon spouts streams of flame and screeches in horrible tones as it flies. The white man's folly will forthwith be driven from the Asiatic Heavens!"

The saga of "Whistling Willie," flying while full of bullet holes, is difficult to top, yet this was only one of many incidents concerning the planes and pilots of the China National Aviation Corporation. Another incident, and just as amazing, concerns the DC-3 that flew with a borrowed wing built for its sister ship, the smaller DC-2. After its "operation," it was named the DC-2 1/2.

On a regularly scheduled passenger flight from Hong Kong to Chungking, one of the six DC-3s operated by the "Middle Kingdom Space Machine Family," as the Chinese called the CNAC, was forced down at Suifu because of a Japanese raid on Hong Kong.

The Japanese dive bombers, having completed their destruction, headed home and were looking for more targets of opportunity when one of the pilots spotted the DC-3 on the ground at Suifu. Five bombers pounced upon the transport, sending the grounded passengers and crew scurrying for cover. The Japs dropped more than two hundred bombs on the airfield, and when they left, CNAC Captain H. L. Woods came out to look at the mess.

One bomb had passed through the right wing of the Gooney and exploded underneath. The explosion had torn off the wing just outside the point where it joined the center section. The fuselage, ripped horribly, was marked by about fifty shrapnel holes. The concussion had knocked the airplane sideways more than six feet, but the gasoline tanks had not exploded. Fortunately, other than a ruined right wing and the holes in the fuselage, there was no other serious damage to the engines or other vital parts.

Woods' solution to the problem was plain and simple—the plane needed a new wing. He knew, however, that there were no spare DC-3 wings in Hong Kong. Perhaps someone in Hong Kong could locate one elsewhere, although getting it to him in Suifu would be a problem. Suifu is located about 90 miles in the interior of China, and the only surface means of transportation was over the Burma Road, which might mean a wait of several months, if a wing could be found at all. The enforced idleness of one plane that long would be a bitter blow to the Chinese and there was always the risk that the Japanese fighters would return and finish the destruction.

A China National Airways Corporation DC-2, damaged in a landing accident in 1942, is barged to another location for repairs. (Douglas Aircraft Co. photo)

A lone C-47 drops food and medicine to American prisoners of war on Corregidor in the Philippines. Note the barracks buildings which had been gutted three years before by the Japanese. (Douglas Aircraft Co. photo)

Woods rounded up several hundred coolies. They dragged the crippled plane off the shell-pocked field and three miles down the road to hide it under dense bamboo. Camouflaging it as best they could, they waited. As had been feared, the enemy planes returned, and for three days a total of fifty-seven bombers pounded the field and the town of Suifu. The bamboo camouflage fooled the attackers, however, and not a hit was scored on the hidden DC-3.

Captain Woods radioed Hong Kong and asked the company's representative to try to locate a DC-3 wing. A short time later Hong Kong wired Woods: "Sending DC-2 wing. Try it."

The job of getting the DC-2 wing to Suifu was a major aviation feat in itself. It was impossible to get the wing inside another airplane, so something else had to be tried. Someone suggested that it be bolted to the belly of a DC-3's plane's fuselage, and flown across the mountains to Suifu. It had never been done before but was worth a try.

Two inspection plates were removed from the DC-2 wing's butt end and guy wires attached. The same was done at the wing tip. Then holes were drilled through the floor of the DC-3 and the wires threaded through and made fast inside the fuselage. The wing was guyed fore, aft and sideways. Plywood fairings were fashioned around the butt end for streamlining.

Captain Harold Sweet, of "Whistling Willie" fame, said he would fly the wing to Suifu, if the plane would get off the ground. Sweet was airborne without difficulty and the load didn't seem to bother the DC-3's flying characteristics. He climbed slowly, flying in wide circles to keep out of range of the Jap gunners spotted around the city and harbor of Hong Kong. Except for a slight buffeting and a little longitudinal instability, Sweet found that the DC-3 flew without difficulty. After an uneventful flight, he landed at the Suifu field, now partially repaired, and supervised the unloading of the spare wing.

The DC-2 had a wing span of eighty-five feet, while the DC-3 had a span of ninety-five feet. Fortunately, the butt ends of the wings were identical and the DC-2 wing could be bolted on. However, the DC-2 wing was designed to carry about three-fourths of the gross weight of a DC-3. Supposedly then, it might not be possible to fly a DC-3 with one DC-2 and one DC-3 wing. The shape, area and taper of the two are entirely different.

Nevertheless, the wing was mounted and Sweet flew it back to Hong Kong. The DC-2 1/2, as it was now called, trudged along with little difficulty. It had a tendency to roll toward the shorter wing but Sweet corrected this by setting the aileron trim tab twelve degrees to the opposite side. With this adjustment, and a slight adjustment in the power settings, the plane flew the 900 miles easily, although in a slight crab.

There doesn't seem to be any limit to the capability of the airplane that Douglas built. In the steaming jungles, where corrosion causes considerable damage to metal, rubber, and fabric, the C-47 stood up well. Even when ditched in the ocean, it was surfaced on many occasions, reconditioned, and put back into service.

One of the most unusual stories about the Gooney's stamina and ability to withstand extremes comes from Iceland, where a Gooney Bird tangled with the Vatna Jokull Glacier, known as "the world's deadliest glacier." This plane, Serial Number 1013, belonged to the USAF Air Rescue Service and had been on many rescue missions. This story, however, concerns an incident in which the C-47 itself had to be saved. The man most familiar with the story is Lieutenant Colonel Perry C. Emmons, who was assigned the task of recovering the plane if he could.

"I was on temporary duty in Keflavik in 1950," Emmons recalled, "shortly after an Icelandic Airlines DC-4 was reported missing. I received a message from the commander of Air Rescue Service putting me in charge of rescue operations.

"Our rescue plane searched for three days and finally located the DC-4 on top of Vatna Jokull Glacier in the northeastern part of the island. One rescue plane made contact with the downed crew and learned that everyone was alive and well. They also learned that snow conditions on the glacier were ideal for ski-plane operation.

"I contacted the rescue unit at Bluie West One, Greenland, and asked them to send a ski-equipped C-47 to the crash scene immediately. A short time later Number 1013 arrived at Keflavik.

"The C-47, equipped with four JATO (jet-assisted takeoff) bottles, took off for Vatna Jokull to recover the stranded people. The weather was excellent and I thought it would be a routine mission.

"I was in the control tower at Keflavik, in contact with Number 1013 as it winged toward the crash site, and I talked to the pilot as he made a ski landing on the snow. Everything was perfect for the pickup. The plane took on the stranded survivors. All that remained was to take off and fly to Keflavik. But it didn't work out that way.

"The Gooney Bird pilot goosed the throttles but the plane wouldn't budge from its parking place. He tried again and again, jazzing the throttles, but the old bird was stuck solid. When the metal skis touched the snow on landing the friction had warmed them just enough to slightly melt the snow underneath. Then it had frozen immediately, welding the airplane tightly to the snow. The pilot rocked the plane with throttles, but to no avail; he then told the crew chief to get out and rock the wings to unstick the skis. It still didn't budge.

"Finally the pilot decided to fire two JATO bottles. While the crew chief rocked the wings the pilot flicked the switches which released the blast of air from the cylinders beneath the plane. The Gooney broke loose with full power and moved forward while the crew chief waved for the plane to stop and pick him up. About that time it dawned on the pilot that the crew chief was stranded, so he taxied back for him.

"The sergeant was loaded aboard and the pilot gunned the engines, but the Gooney was stuck again! However, the pilot was sharp this time. He flicked the JATO switches, thus firing the last two bottles. The plane broke loose and inched slowly over the ice and snow; so slowly, in fact, that it wouldn't fly.

"With all four JATO bottles gone, there was nothing left to do but stop the engines and think. He could radio for more JATOs. If two wouldn't get him off, perhaps four would if all were fired at once.

"Well, I sent messages to Greenland requesting JATO bottles but got no immediate response. After the rescue plane got stuck, an Icelandic ground party fought its way to the treacherous top of the glacier and to the stranded C-47. The leader of the party told the pilot that it would be unwise for the crew to remain with the airplane longer than a few hours because he believed bad weather was about to set in. The pilot and crew decided to leave with the ground party and let the Gooney Bird face the weather alone. Even if JATO bottles could be located it might take several days to fly them in. The Gooney was in for a long period of hibernation.

"So old Number 1013 was left stranded on the glacier—one lone C-47 against the elements. I was certain in my own mind that it could be flown off the glacier but I wasn't sure how to go about it. I intended to find out.

"Eight days later I radioed Air Rescue Service Headquarters with a plan for recovering the bird. I told my commander that I wanted approval to get together a qualified group of men and to leave as soon as possible. I would be the mission commander and I would need a C-47 pilot with ski-wheel experience and two top-notch maintenance men. Also, I wanted to take along a pararescue team to be on standby at Keflavik in case we needed them for medical aid.

Before the Philippines were liberated, Skytrains of the 317th Troop Carrier Group dropped infantrymen of the 503rd Parachute Battalion on "Old Topside" headquarters on Corregidor. (Douglas Aircraft Co. photo)

"The boss bought my idea one hundred percent. We assembled the recovery and all the necessary equipment at Keflavik around the middle of October, which was almost a month from the time the bird got stranded. But on the day following the party's arrival in Iceland, I made a flight over the Vatna Jokull to look the site over. I wanted to know if everything was as the crew had left it. There old Number 1013 sat, cold, forlorn and helpless. The weather had changed very little and the snow had not covered it much during the previous month.

"It looked to me as if we could do the job, but at this time a series of uncontrollable delays occurred, which were to spell defeat for the project. I couldn't help squirming at the nature of the delays because at any time bad weather might set in and I felt there would be no getting that Gooney out of Iceland.

"Finally we ironed things out. The recovery party left Keflavik and got to the glacier on November 22nd. As I had feared, however, the weather changed and snow fell heavily. For the next two weeks the glacier was completely closed in by weather. We couldn't even fly over to check on the Gooney.

"On November 14th the weather cleared enough for me to fly there and take a look. When I located the plane it lay buried in the snow with only the tip of its rudder showing through the white blanket. That did it. We canceled all our plans for recovery and abandoned the project.

"The following spring an Icelandic ground party decided to take a look at the Gooney. Kris Oleson and Alfred Eliasson, owners and operators of Icelandic Airlines—now minus its lone DC-4—were close to bankruptcy and wanted that abandoned C-47. They took along a bulldozer, found the plane and set to work uncovering it. They cleaned the snow out and dragged the plane down to the

U.S. 503rd Parachute Battalion infantrymen landing in New Guinea during World War II. Several of the parachutes are seen in various stages of opening, swinging the men at precarious angles close to the ground. (USAF photo)

edge of the glacier. The weight of the snow had collapsed the landing gear, but this didn't bother Oleson and Eliasson too much. They jacked the old bird up and tied some two-by-fours to the gear so it wouldn't collapse again. Oleson got into the cockpit and began playing around with the switches. By all rights, the batteries, after having been buried in the snow for more than eight months, shouldn't have been any good. But Oleson was experienced enough in Far North operations to know that the Arctic often worked strange miracles. Perhaps this was one of them. He flipped one of the starter switches and the engine turned over briefly. (I know what took place because I was flying overhead at the time, watching what was happening.) After a few minutes' wait, Oleson hit the starter switch again. This time the engine started and smoke belched out in huge puffs. I expected the engine to blow up, but it kept on running. Oleson must have been smiling down there in that frozen airplane, and to continue his enjoyment he started the other engine.

"I could hardly believe what I saw—that any airplane after being buried for months in the snow, would start and run smoothly. It seemed to be running as good as the one I was flying overhead!

"Oleson's party kicked a few boulders out of the way and bulldozed a takeoff strip. They climbed aboard like they were at a busy air terminal and Oleson poured on the coal. The snow flew in great clouds. The old bird shifted uneasily on the snow, settled into a straight-forward motion, bounced off the rough, crude strip, and reached for the sky."

The gamble that Kris Oleson and Al Eliasson and their financial backers had taken to acquire the abandoned C-47 paid off. They had offered the U.S. Air Force $700 for the airplane and the offer had been accepted. This sum, plus the cost of renting the bulldozer and pay for the ground party—a total of $5,000—bought them an airplane to replace their lost DC-4. The DC-3 was flown to England for modification but even before work began, a Spanish airline offered Oleson $80,000 for it. The offer was promptly accepted. The $75,000 profit enabled them to make a down payment on a four-engine DC-6. Today Icelandic Airlines plies the northern route between New York and Europe with its jet airliners and is solvent, thanks to the durability and indestructibility of the airplane than can do the seemingly impossible.

Untold thousands of pilots have flown the Gooney Bird in peace and war. But it is in war that the dependable bird and their crews proved their mettle. One who did so was Lieutenant George Walker, just another pilot on the roster of a troop carrier squadron in New Guinea. His airplane was just another Gooney which was christened The Long Island Duck.

Walker was a racing car driver who had made the circuits throughout the United States and South America. He completed Army Air Force pilot training during World War II and was assigned to a C-47 unit for transition at Austin, Texas. Walker was greatly disappointed because he had his heart set on flying fighters. From the beginning he hated the C-47, not realizing that one day he would grow to love the old bird. He grumbled secretly to himself but tried never to let his unhappiness about his assignment show to others.

When the transition phase was completed, Walker was assigned to a Troop Carrier Group and trained to tow gliders and drop paratroopers. He was assigned an aircraft with long-range cabin gas tanks installed and flew to Hawaii, Christmas Island, Samoa, Fiji, New Caledonia, and finally Townsville, Australia. There the long-range tanks were removed and he departed for Port Moresby, New Guinea.

During his first two months in New Guinea he flew all types of cargo in formation with other transports to learn the ropes. Most of these cargo missions were escorted by fighters. On one of the formation flights, Walker's copilot, Lieutenant Howard Zimmerman, was flying the airplane while Walker dozed. Suddenly there was a horrible crash that rocked the plane wildly. It nosed up and threatened to stall, and the two men fought to bring it under control. It took them only seconds to realize that another plane had rammed into them.

When Walker saw the turned up right wingtip and splintered metal whipping in the slipstream, he knew he had been hit hard and had to set the plane down as soon as possible. In the distance he saw a stream bed that he might be able to reach, but quickly discarded that idea when the plane began to buffet violently.

"Bail out!" Walker yelled, knowing the plane was eventually going to crash.

Lieutenant Seymour Rosenfeld, the navigator, ran to the rear of the plane to get parachutes for the crew. He returned quickly, his face ashen.

The attack on Nadzab, New Guinea, by the 503rd Parachute Infantry was at its height when this photo of troops descending from C-47s was taken. White parachutes were used for troops; colored ones for supplies and ammunition. (USAF photo)

"George," he said shakingly, "there are only four 'chutes. There are five of us."

Walker thought a moment, then said, "You fellows bail out. I'll set this bird down in the swamp. Get going!"

No one moved. The other crew members stared at him. Finally Zimmerman said, "We're staying, George."

That was that. Five men—four parachutes. None of them would be used.

Sergeant Braden, the engineer, had been injured in the midair collision. When the two planes had collided, Braden, standing in the cabin, had been thrown against the side of the fuselage, wrenching his back severely.

As the plane continued to vibrate and descend, Walker saw a small clearing and headed for it. The crippled Gooney was steadily losing altitude and he knew he was going to make what pilots call "a controlled crash."

Walker made a good approach and as he leveled off he felt the tall marsh grass scrape the belly of the plane. Zimmerman cut the switches and Walker pulled the control wheel back in his stomach to hold the nose high and tail low. The C-47 squashed into the soft ooze, slid forward for a short distance and stopped, with a prolonged sucking sound as it settled into the swamp. It was over—all but the long trek out.

While they pondered what to do, a C-47 from Walker's squadron flew overhead. Walker and his crew waved to indicate they were down safely. Later that evening other C-47s dropped packages of food, water, and first aid supplies but many of them fell into the swamp and were lost.

That night the crew slept in the plane and battled the ever-present mosquitoes. Several days passed and no more planes appeared. Walker wondered if they had been forgotten but on the sixth day a ground rescue party arrived and they were led laboriously out of the swamp onto more solid ground. They made their way through the jungle to the village of Popo, then down a river on a launch until they reached Terapo where they were able to radio their home base. Just ten days after they had crashed a C-47 landed and picked them up.

Walker described his tour of duty from that point on and told what was asked of the C-47 in that theater of war:

"For the next several months our work was moving and supplying the Australian ground forces as they fought their way up the valley from Nadzab to Kaipit, Gusap, and Dumpu on the southern end of New Guinea. We supplied outposts in the surrounding mountains, and dropped supplies to places with names like Shaggy Ridge. We ate dehydrated eggs, Spam, and bully beef. We flew from dawn to dusk and piled up lots of flying time, most of which was without fighter cover. We hopped from target to target almost at treetop level to evade Japanese pilots, and our landing fields were rough and dirty and much too short for safety.

"One day I was flying a group of Aussie infantrymen back from Dumpu to Nadzab. Near the airstrip I received landing instructions, and as I put my wheels down I glanced out my window just in time to see an explosion of the ground. I wondered what they were blasting. At that moment I saw a B-25 bomber explode, and I knew that I had lumbered in right in the middle of an enemy air raid. Several Japanese Zeros were strafing the field, some buildings were on fire, and when a couple of Jap fighters turned in my direction I knew my bird would be a sitting duck.

"Without waiting to see more, I yanked up the flaps on my C-47 and yelled to the co-pilot to jerk up the gear. With the Zeros in sight, I dove for a small winding stream, part of the Ramu River, which led to Lae. Trees lined both banks. I dropped the C-47 down until I was flying between the trees, trying to keep my wing tips from hitting them. The Zeros either hadn't seen us or had lost us in the confusion as we snaked our way at treetop level down the narrow river. I went on to Lae and landed. Several of my Aussie passengers got out and kissed the ground. These hard-bitten old veterans had seen the roughest kind of war on the ground, but they had been just as scared as I was.

"Several days later, when we were taking off from Gusap, I blew a tire. Since I was already committed for takeoff, I jerked the bird off the ground and staggered into the air. When I reached Nadzab, the tower operator advised me to come in for a belly landing. I thought about it for a while and decided that since we were already short on airplanes, I wasn't about to wreck this one. Luckily we had a good strong headwind to burn up our fuel and the plane was almost empty. I was able to bring it in on one wheel and control the direction with the throttles and brakes with no damage at all. It wasn't a question of my superior flying ability, but rather a tribute to the remarkable flying characteristics built into the C-47.

"Assigned to me as co-pilot was Lieutenant 'Slim' Moore; Sergeant Helm was my crew chief; and Sergeant Gomeringer was my radio operator. One morning just after sunrise we took off, flew up the valley, bypassed the Japanese stronghold at Wewak and landed at Aitape. All troop carrier pilots had been ordered to avoid Wewak because of reports that an estimated 50,000 Japanese had been cut off and trapped there. One of our C-47s had dive-bombed and strafed Wewak one day with hand grenades and a tommy gun, and they vouched for the fact that the Japs were there. Aitape had been taken in April of 1944 and had since served as a bulwark between Wewak and Hollandia. Our job was to work with and supply the units of the 32nd Infantry Division, which was having one devil of a rough time fighting its way in.

"The Aitape airstrip ran parallel to, and was only a short distance from the beach. The surrounding terrain was thick jungle extending back several miles to steep-faced mountains. The intelligence officer briefed us and flew with us on the first mission to point out drop areas—three of which were cinches, but the other looked as if it would be impossible to drop supplies anywhere near the drop zone.

"As luck would have it, the toughest drop site was also the most important. It was at an advanced position approximately fifteen to twenty miles southeast of the Aitape strip. An extremely small clearing, not more than a mile from the foot of the mountain, it was located on the north side of a hill several hundred yards back from a wide, dry river bed which extended from the mountains to the beach.

"The best pattern for this drop was to fly east along the foot of the mountains, approach the river bed, bank sharply to the left around the hill and slow the airplane by dropping partial flaps. The next step was to aim the airplane at a spot which looked greener than the rest of the jungle—the drop zone.

"I pretended that I was landing the airplane and would get the old bird to shiver almost at the stalling point right over the target, because the drop area was so small and so difficult to hit that it was the only way to make an accurate drop. If the supplies dropped into the dense jungle the troops would probably never be able to get to them.

"To regain flying speed after almost stalling over the target, I would dive away down to the river bed at my right, while keeping away from the east side of the river where the Japs were waiting for me with small arms fire. Along the river bed we could see dead bodies scattered over the rocks, and often we could smell the acrid stench of rotting flesh even at flight altitude. Occasionally we saw an L-5 liaison plane directing artillery fire several miles east of the river, but I never envied those liaison pilots because they were sitting ducks even more than we ever were.

"One morning, after I had been using the same pattern each time I flew over the drop zone, I got the surprise of life, and I had no one to blame but myself for my absolute stupidity. I was flying at treetop level between the hills. I had slowed down and was ready to begin a shallow bank to the left when suddenly there was a loud crash which shook the plane violently. Without pausing to see what had happened, I forgot the drop for a moment and executed the maneuver known as 'getting the hell out of there.' There was no question that the noise had been caused by a large Japanese gun.

"Once we were away from the drop zone, the crew chief inspected the plane. There was no damage, but the shell had exploded close. Stupidly I had made all my drop patterns in exactly the same way and the Japanese had figured this out. They had moved a field piece into position to be directly under me when I came lumbering over the next day. If I had made another pass they would probably have zeroed in for a sure kill. This taught me an important lesson and I never made the same approach over a target the same way twice.

"There was another drop area that was almost as tough to find. This one was located in a dense jungle and there was no clearing to mark the exact spot. As we passed over the general area our ground troops would set off a smoke bomb, and I would study the color of the foliage where the smoke rose. Soon I began to distinguish that area from other areas and became so proficient that I could drop accurately even after the smoke gave out. I would approach by an imaginary line that extended from a bare, rocky patch on the mountainside, out over the dropping area, to a cargo ship anchored

Like huge snowflakes, these members of a parachute infantry battalion jump out of a C-47 over the Italian countryside during a test maneuver near Naples in January 1944. (Douglas Aircraft Co. photo)

off the beach. Twice I actually put out the smoke bomb by dropping supplies right on top of it. I've often wondered what would have happened had the Japs decided to light a smoke bomb at the same time that we first started dropping on this target. I might have flown right over their guns and got my tail shot off.

"In addition to our regular drops, we flew a load of supplies to an isolated outpost on the other side of the mountain from Aitape. An intelligence officer of the 32nd Division went along to help locate the spot. The drop area was in a small clearing in which cloth panels were arranged to aid in identifying it. After reaching it, we buzzed it to look it over. For some reason—call it intuition if you like—the intelligence officer told me not to drop the supplies. That seemed odd to me, since the panels had been laid out properly, identifying the areas as belonging to us.

"We returned to Aitape airstrip. The intelligence officer was right in his assessment. The Japanese, just before we got there, had captured it from the Americans and were in full charge. Knowing that the panels were for signaling an airplane, they had left them exactly as the American soldiers had placed them, hoping, of course, to knock us down as we flew over.

"At the end of the third day at Aitape, we were asked to remain for a few more days. Strange as it may seem, my crew was happy about staying because we could actually see what we were accomplishing toward assisting those weary, battleworn foot soldiers. After seeing how those fellows had to fight and live in the jungles, I thanked God many times I was a pilot.

"Almost every day C-47s from our squadron and other outfits landed at Aitape, either on missions or en route to or from Hollandia. I contacted several of the pilots and conned them into helping us with a few drops before they returned to their bases.

I would lead them to the easy drops, point out the drop zone, and take the rough drops myself. It wasn't that I was trying to be brave, but I certainly didn't want to be responsible for those guys getting shot up over a drop zone with which they weren't familiar.

"I explained to their crews that they had nothing to worry about—that I was dropping in the places where there were Japanese on the ground shooting at the planes as they came in.

"On returning to Aitape after one such drop, one of the pilots called me over to his plane. He pointed to a bullet hole in the cockpit. 'I thought you said there was nothing to these drops,' he said. 'A guy could get hurt doing this!'

"Before these missions I begged, borrowed or stole all the cigarettes I could get and dropped them to soldiers on the ground. I enclosed a note with each package which said, 'Compliments of the 66th Troop Carrier Squadron.'

"After twelve days of working at this nerve-wracking pace, I decided to return to Nadzab. My crew had piled up sixty missions during those days, and all of us had about reached the limits of our endurance. We had dropped over a quarter of a million pounds of supplies and equipment. We were all very tired and the old, faithful Gooney was long overdue for maintenance. Since the pilot was responsible for his crew and plane, he had it a bit rougher than the other crew members. Since the rest of the crew were not actively engaged in flying the plane, they had a chance to observe me and must have harbored thoughts about my worn-out condition, and how one simple mistake on my part could wipe us all out. How close they came to having this happen!

"Shortly after we arrived at Nadzab, the commanding general of the 32nd Infantry Division requested that we make a round trip to Aitape. Little did he know then that I was literally 'out of this world.'

"The next night, after I had returned to Nadzab from Aitape, I was extremely restless and spent most of the night walking around the camp area. My mind was cloudy and the whole operation seemed a fantasy. The next morning I was so exhausted that I could not hold my head up, and it took all my strength just to speak. Then things began to fade, and the last thing I remember was when the flight surgeon came to take me to the hospital.

"The next several months were completely blank to me. I gradually had to learn the simple functions of living as I regained my memory. Finally I could recognize my wife, my family, and friends; and eventually I recovered completely."

George Walker did not tell the whole story but he had accomplished one of the most remarkable supply feats of World War II during his days at Aitape. He and his devoted crew and one battered C-47 had performed miracles. Though the Japanese didn't know it at the time, five thousand American ground troops had been completely cut off from their source of supply. Walker and his overworked C-47 crew had kept them fighting.

In addition, Walker was credited with directly saving twenty-six men at River X, so named because its name did not appear on any map. They were members of a patrol that had been trapped and had just enough ammunition left to fire an occasional shot at the Japs, but not enough to fight their way out. Walker and his crew dumped the ammo right into the laps of the patrol and enabled the men to battle their way to safety.

This instance of the part played by Troop Carrier Gooney Birds in the Southwest Pacific was typical of the indispensability of the C-47 during World War II. The troops stranded beyond the front lines on patrol in New Guinea will never forget the sight and sound of a lone airplane with the old familiar shape circling low over their heads every day bringing emergency provisions.

Any collection of stories about the famous Gooney Bird would not be complete without an account of the time this defenseless transport was officially credited with bringing down an enemy plane. It was just one more aviation "first" in the endless list of firsts claimed by this most famous of all transport planes.

When this C-47 landed in Italy after a tour of duty in Burma, it had a record no other C-47 was ever to claim. Some will doubt and dispute this, but what makes the story all the more unusual is that it downed a Japanese Zero while actually assigned to support the Fifth Army in Italy!

In a theater of war where Allied fighters had their sides decorated with swastikas denoting their kills, this old transport brazenly flaunted a small white square with an orange ball in the center—a Japanese flag. The crew chief was the butt of many a joke when the plane taxied to the ramp at a strange airfield. But this C-47, piloted by Captain Hal M. Scrugham of Frankfort, Kentucky, was officially credited with knocking down a Zero. The co-pilot was Lieutenant Elmer J. Jost of Berwyn, Illinois.

The crew and plane had been overseas for about two years and had fought their own kind of war through the North African campaign, hauling supplies to the front and taking wounded men back to rear area hospitals. That phase of their war had ended, however, when they flew paratroopers to Avellino, Italy, for a drop in the hills.

It was an urgent call for help from the China-Burma-India (CBI) theater of operations that changed the routine life of Scrugham's C-47. The plane and crew were sent on temporary duty, along with other C-47s from Africa to Burma to haul supplies over the Hump.

Two weeks after the plane arrived in Burma, Scrugham and Jost suddenly found themselves in a tangle to the death with a pair of aggressive Zeros determined to add a fat transport to their tally.

"We were flying a routine cargo mission—no passengers—when two Zeros jumped us," Scrugham reported later. "I didn't take time to figure out what was happening. I swung the C-47 into a dive and hit the deck as the Jap fighters peeled off after us for what they must have thought was a sure kill.

"The first Zero made his pass at us but we were too close to the ground and he zoomed up without hitting us. The second Zero came right down on us. When he got within what seemed like inches of our plane I jammed the throttles forward another fraction of an inch and got just a little burst of speed.

"That character must have been trying to ram us because he never swerved. The little added speed I had given my airplane caused him to miss hitting us dead center, but he didn't miss entirely and we felt the old C-47 shudder for a minute like it was going to shake to pieces.

"The Jap plane, after it hit us, kept right on going and we watched it explode as it hit the side of a mountain. We didn't know how much our plane had been damaged. I moved the elevators first and then the ailerons and found that we had excellent control there. But when I kicked the rudders, nothing happened. I knew right then he had knocked our rudder off. Jost and I looked at each other and talked about climbing as high as we could and bailing out, but I moved the controls some more and, between elevators and ailerons, we seemed to be able to control the old bird all right. So we decided to keep right on flying rather than have our airplane suffer the same fate as the enemy Zero. We landed without much difficulty at our base.

"Now that I think about it," Scrugham continued, "it never occurred to us to worry about that other Zero pilot. We were so scared that we completely forgot about him. All my life I guess I'll wonder what happened to him. Maybe he thought we had some kind of secret weapon when he saw his buddy go down and simply hightailed it for home to report to his superiors. At any rate we never saw him again."

This rugged C-47 was repaired and back flying again in a few days. It stayed in the CBI theater for two months flying supplies, and then returned to Italy when the group was ordered to help General Mark Clark's Fifth Army in the Italian campaign.

7

The DC-3 Will Do It!

The newer planes are faster, more comfortable and have all the latest gadgets on them, but I doubt if any will ever be any more dependable than the old DC-3.

Capt. Luke Carruthers
Delta Airlines

The DC-3 and its predecessors, the DC-1 and DC-2, were originally conceived to be passenger transports for use on the airlines. However, the demands of military service soon transformed the DC-3 into a cargo transport, bomber, fighter, and a navigators' flying classroom. While its versatility in these operations is well-established, not so well known are some of the odd uses to which the Gooney Bird has been put through the years. It has been used as a flying electronics laboratory, a laundry, an airborne battle command post, a flying loudspeaker, spray plane, wire layer, aerial refueler and even a glider. After its flying days were over, its carcass has been converted into an officers' club, mobile homes, summer cottages, a post exchange, a coffee house and even hoisted to the top of a restaurant to serve as a penthouse for the proprietor's special customers. Following are some of the stories behind these aviation "firsts."

On October 15, 1944, a group of Army Signal Corps experts waited in a small clearing on the western slopes of the Great Smoky Mountains just outside Gatlinburg, Tennessee. They watched the Army Air Force C-47 approaching fast and low through the smoky haze. The C-47 was on a course which would normally call for flying at a higher altitude because of the towering peaks and treacherous air currents ahead. This was a special test mission, however, and the C-47 was hedgehopping across the foothills in defiance of the treacherous downdrafts.

Glider towing was one of the many tasks assigned to Gooney Birds during World War II. A glider snatch is being practiced in this photo taken at Wright Field during World War II. The arresting pickup gear under the belly of the C-47 has just made contact with the nylon rope hooked to the nose of the CG-4A glider. (USAF photo)

A British Dakota maneuvers over a combat glider before engaging the glider's tow rope. Hundreds of gliders were used after the D-Day invasion to take troops into France. The Germans were the first to introduce gliders into warfare. (USAF photo)

As the plane passed overhead and started its climb toward Newfound Gap and the ridgeline, the ground party saw a small white parachute streak from the plane's open door and snap open in the slipstream. As the plane flew on at a carefully calculated 220 feet per second, a tenuous line spiraled out through a tube in the doorway and arced back and down to a connection in the descending parachute.

Men on the ground raced to positions beneath the falling line, opening an Army field telephone set as they ran. Leads were snapped onto the line as it fell into their hands. An engineer placed a receiver to his ear. Looks of apprehension crossed the faces of these men whose months of hard work were being weighed in the crucial test.

Tension dissolved when the man at the telephone began talking to another group on the ground as the C-47 disappeared into the blue haze above Newfound Gap. They were talking through sixteen miles of telephone wire that had just been laid by the airplane.

The wire had been put down between two ground points over difficult terrain, in perfect condition, in six minutes, forty seconds. It would have required days to lay the wire over the same rugged course by ground crews.

Halfway around the world, in the China-Burma-India and Pacific theaters, there were mountain ranges far more formidable than the Smokies. There were jungles, head-deep swamps, and other natural obstacles to plague the men who had to provide the Army's vital telephone links. Laying wire across these barriers meant laying it slowly, sometimes from the back of a truck but more often from the back of a man as he walked, crawled or swam with a reel of wire attached to his shoulders.

The view from the glider cockpit as Gooney Birds tow their charges to a landing zone in March 1945. Eleven percent of the glidermen were killed, wounded or injured during the invasion. (USAF photo)

The Air Force's air-laying procedure was the answer to a long-standing problem. Wire could be laid across terrain that would be impenetrable on the ground. Further, when laid over this kind of country there was less chance of its being located and cut by the enemy.

From the pilot's viewpoint, there was nothing tricky about flying a wire mission. He would be given the required location of the two ends of the line and advised to fly as low as possible to make certain the wire ends would drop accurately. High speeds and sudden changes of direction had to be carefully avoided, and allowances had to be made for the drift of the wire in crosswinds when passing over the line terminal points. Laying wire by air was one more of the jobs assigned to the Gooney Bird that proved its value far above that imagined by its creators.

There is one tale about a Gooney Bird that is a unique part of the plane's colorful history. It once housed the kitchen that served the best hamburgers in all South Africa.

When Cyril Morley, an Englishman, built a roadhouse near Johannesburg before World War II, he did not think about the day when its roof would wear out and would have to be replaced at a time when repair materials would be scarce. The inevitable happened and Morley had to scrounge around for anything that would keep the rain off his customers. Wartime shortages included metals, tar paper, and shingles. As time went on, his problem grew worse.

One day he discovered an old C-47 Dakota, which had formerly belonged to the South African Air Force, lying in a junk pile at an airport not far away. Being a practical man, Morley purchased the Gooney Bird, hoping that he could use the aluminum for roofing material. He soon discovered, however, that the metal, riveted in many places, could not be stripped off intact. Undaunted, Morley secured some help and a derrick and hoisted the plane—engines, landing gear, propellers and all—to the roof of his roadhouse.

Cyril Morley's restaurant became famous and customers flocked from miles around to dine in the most distinctive establishment on the Dark Continent. After twelve years Morley sold the C-47 for a good price. The man who purchased it took the plane down and hauled it away. It was refurbished and is probably still flying somewhere in the world.

Lord Louis Mountbatten, Supreme Allied Commander in Southeast Asia, had troops spread all over that part of the world. To visit each unit or command by ground vehicle was impossible. A C-47 had been assigned to his headquarters and Lord Mountbatten decided to make it his command post. The C-47 was modified to provide complete living facilities, but the most extensive modification was the installation of an entire radio station in the rear cabin. This enabled Lord Mountbatten to keep in constant contact with his land, sea and air forces. Another "first" for the Gooney.

In later years the United States Air Force transformed a number of aircraft into flying command posts for use in battle situations and to provide a continuity of national leadership in the event of enemy attacks. The most recent example of airborne command posts was during the Persian Gulf War in 1991 when giant jet transports provided constant battlefield surveillance and air operations information over the Iraq-Kuwait battlefield.

In order to give the Gooney Bird more flexibility of operation, Douglas engineers were asked to determine the possibility of making some C-47s into amphibians that could operate from land or water. It was thought that amphibious Goonies would enable troops and supplies to be ferried to the Pacific islands as well as effect more rescues of downed fliers if they could be landed on water. Called the "Duck," and on the Douglas drawing boards as the Y-123, a modification contract was made with American Airlines in

The view from a C-47 as two other Goonies tow their gliders on a mission to a landing zone behind enemy lines. (USAF photo)

1943. A subcontract was given to EDO Corporation, named for its founder Earl Dodge Osborn, long experienced in float and pontoon design, to develop and produce amphibious pontoons. American Airlines installed the pontoons on the prototype and supported the aircraft during initial flight tests. The amphibious Gooney was designated C-47C.

According to Fred G. Space, Jr., coordinator for the project between EDO and American, "EDO's design included main and bow wheels for amphibious operations, and a 325-gallon fuel tank in each float. Gross weight of the aircraft was increased by about 5,500 pounds with the float installation, and the cabin door was 14 feet above the ground.

"The water rudders were raised and lowered by a separate retraction control system. When the rudders were lowered, the foot brake control system was diverted from the main landing wheels to the water rudder directional control cylinders. This permitted full steering control when taxiing—whether on land or water."

Lewis O. Hilton, who restored a former C-53D to make it a C-47C amphibian in 1992, gave more information:

"The EDO floats are 42 feet long, five feet wide and five feet high. Each displaces 29,000 pounds of water with 14 compartments and the 325-gallon fuel tank. Each float has two hydraulically-operated wheels, one in the bow enclosed by doors, and the main wheel retracting into a space just aft of the step. The nose wheels are free swiveling, and the mains are fitted with hydraulic brakes.

"Each float has a water rudder that raises and lowers and steers hydraulically. The steering is unique in that it is accomplished by use of the brake pedals, left brake turning the left rudder out to the left. Using both brake pedals causes both rudders to steer out, becoming water brakes.

"Boarding steps are incorporated on the sides of the floats, and steps are integral with one of the rear struts, allowing the crew to climb onto the trailing edge of the wing and enter the aircraft through an emergency door forward of the main cabin doors."

The view from a C-47 navigator's dome as a fleet of CG-4A gliders carry their loads of airborne infantry reinforcements into needed areas in April 1945. (USAF photo)

A C-47 plunges to earth in Holland during landing of the 1st Allied Airborne Army. The aircraft had been hit by German anti-aircraft fire near Zon, Holland, after cutting its gliders loose. The three crew members were able to bail out successfully. (US Army photo)

Initial flight tests on the original "Duck" were flown by Lt. Col. Harney Estes and Major Everett Leach assigned to the project from Wright Field, Dayton, Ohio, in 1943. The first high-speed land taxi run after the installation became the first flight as the aircraft was actually airborne for a few hundred feet over the runway.

The rigidity of the float installation was apparent after the first water landing. Although quite smooth, the landing impact was sufficient to break restraining clips on the instrument panel.

It is believed that only five amphibious C-47Cs were modified from C-47As. After the first modification by American Airlines, the other installations were made at the Douglas plant in Oklahoma City. Although it was thought that the original contract with EDO Corporation of College Point, New York, called for 150 sets of floats, it has been variously reported that somewhere between 17 and 36 sets were actually made. The conversion required several changes in the C-47's structural design to provide reinforcement for the floats. In addition to the first aircraft, American Airlines made up a parts kit to modify a second aircraft. When the initial project was completed, American had no further association with the program.

The actual extent of the amphibious modification program is rather vague. However, Col. Franklin C. Spinney remembers his role in it as one of the project engineers in April 1943. Then a second lieutenant, he had his first look at Bloomer Girl, a C-47 No. 25671, in the American Airlines hangar at LaGuardia Air Terminal two months later. Later that month the plane was delivered to Wright Field to begin flight acceptance tests.

According to Spinney, the tests on land and water were satisfactory except the plane had a tendency to flip on its back without any warning during a power-on stall. "However, she could be pulled out easily," he said.

A C-47 tows a glider over the Chin hills in Burma. Waco CG-4A gliders were used by U.S. forces in the China-Burma-India theater during World War II. Germans used gliders for the invasion of Crete and Allied troops were towed by Goonies into Sicily. British Horsa gliders were towed by American C-47s from England to North Africa, a distance of 1,200 miles. (USAF photo)

A C-47 tows two gliders into war-torn Holland. Glider pilots and passengers wore no parachutes; no copilots were carried on the gliders during combat missions. (USAF photo)

Some of the test pilots who flew the plane during the test period in addition to Estes and Leach were a Lt. Col. Schroeder, Lt. Col. O. J. Ritland, and Capt. Fred Bretcher. Spinney was aboard for every test flight. In July, it was decided that the plane would be used as a medical evacuation plane in the Pacific theater. Equipped with extra fuel tanks for the first leg of the flight from the West Coast to Hawaii, the takeoff would have to be made with 36,000 pounds of weight.

"Therefore, a series of overload flight tests were programmed up to and including this weight," Spinney said. "I recall that the C-47 wings were stressed for 35,600 pounds which did not give us much of a safety factor.

"To shorten water takeoffs we investigated the use of JATO. These were liquid JATO bottles which we attached to external drop racks under the center section of the wing. The JATO bottles were fueled with aniline and red-fuming nitric acid and each produced about 500 pounds thrust. They were normally fired just before the plane got up on the step. After they were fired, the airplane would immediately be on the step and with the lessened drag would shorten the takeoff by about one-third."

In October 1943, Bloomer Girl was flown to Mitchel Field, Long Island, and based there for the overload tests which were conducted in the water adjacent to Floyd Bennett Field. The floatplane version was reportedly sluggish in cruising flight—about 30 miles per hour slower than the conventional Skytrain. Landings and takeoffs were made with as much as 33,500 lbs. One takeoff with 35,000 lbs. was made without JATO and it took one minute, twenty seconds to become airborne.

"When you were in the air," Spinney recalled, "you could look up at the wingtips because of the load. We dumped 600 gallons of water ballast before we landed. The test pilot's comment after that flight was that it handled like a fully loaded B-17."

It was on the thirteenth flight on November 13 that the pilots remember as their unlucky day. Spinney was sitting in as flight engineer to fire the JATOs and tells what happened:

"We were taking off in a quartering wind and, in fact, had actually become airborne. However, because of the overload condition of the plane, there was no acceleration when we broke water. There was a mud bank about a half mile ahead, and the pilots, thinking they might go aground on it, reduced the power.

At this very second the JATOs quit and the airplane stopped flying. We were about ten feet off the water and the airplane hit so hard that the struts went through the bottom of the float.

"As the cockpit was rapidly filling with water, we opened the escape hatch (above the cockpit) and swam away. We had life vests on the navigator's table but we didn't even think about them because we were afraid she would blow up with the hot rockets so close to the fuel tanks.

"The hatch was one inch above the water, and I don't know what would have happened if, when we opened it, the water would have come in. I am not sure we would have thought to run to the tail of the plane in which case we would only have gotten our feet wet."

A navy boat picked up the uninjured crew. The only injury was to Spinney who suffered a cut on one thumb. The plane was recovered and returned to Wright Field for return to its original C-47A configuration.

Of the other four Gooneys that became Ducks, three were reported to have been flown to New Guinea and one was sent to Elmendorf Air Base at Anchorage, Alaska; Jack Shadeck recalls testing the latter one at Ladd Air Base near Fairbanks. However, in March 1944, Lt. Joe Mistrot recalls ferrying one from the Douglas factory at Oklahoma City to Manchester, New Hampshire. He turned it over to a flight crew whose base he believes was to have been Goose Bay, Labrador.

Dogs were used in Alaska for search and rescue missions during and after World War II. Here "Paratrooper Joe" and his handler, Sgt. Francis M. Dawdy, prepare for a jump mission before takeoff in a C-47 from Ladd Air Force Base, Alaska. (USAF photo)

Conversion kits to turn C-47As into C models were sent to a few bases in the South Pacific but it is not known if more conversions were actually made. However, the Form 5 pilot record of Col. Burton S. Barrett, then assigned to the 4th Air Service Command on Biak in the South Pacific, shows that he made eleven water landings as copilot in a C-47A in July 1945, after first making five water landings in a PBY Catalina. It is probable that this was believed converted to a C-47A for the ferry flight to Australia and possibly its designation on the plane's records was not changed back to a C-47C.

Two Gooneys on floats survived World War II and were reportedly "civilianized" back to land-based Gooneys. One was reported flying in the Philippines on short-haul flights among the islands; the other was flown by Sun Belt Airways in the U.S. Both disappeared later from the civil aircraft registries.

One of the early challenges for military aviation planners was how to extend the range or duration of an aircraft. Installing extra internal tanks was not always feasible. Designing aircraft that were flying gas tanks to refuel other planes in flight was one alternative. Dr. Richard Vogt, a German scientist who came to America after World War II, conceived the idea of increasing the range of an aircraft by attaching two "free floating" panels carrying fuel to the wingtips. If these attachments were able to articulate and were self-supported by their own aerodynamic lift, an aircraft could extend its range with little drag penalty. From this concept evolved the idea of having two fighters coupled to the wing tips of a large bomber, thus getting a free ride until needed for combat. If that were possible, perhaps fighters could couple on the wingtips while in flight and thus save fuel.

With a gentle toss to be sure the dog clears the tail, a para-dog starts his aerial descent. The parachute strapped onto the dog's back is released by a static line attached to the plane. (USAF photo)

Sergeant F. M. Dawdy prepares to thrust a reluctant "Paratrooper Joe" to the door of the Gooney for a practice rescue mission. Dawdy will follow immediately. (USAF photo)

In 1949, a C-47 and a Q-14B target drone, similar to the Culver Cadet, were modified to test the feasibility of air-to-air coupling. C. E. "Bud" Anderson tells about the modification:

"In the interest of simplicity, the coupling device was a single-joint attachment which permitted three degrees of freedom for the Q-14. A small ring was placed on a short boom attached to the right wingtip of the C-47. Only local reinforcement was necessary since the Q-14 would be supported by its own aerodynamic lift. A lance was mounted on the left wingtip of the Q-14, and by facing the lance rearward no locking mechanism was required, since drag would keep the aircraft in place. Of course, this added a minor complication requiring the Q-14 to back into the ring which was a little unnatural. To uncouple, the throttle would be advanced and the Q-14 would fly forward out of the ring. There was also an emergency release that could be activated inside the C-47, which would immediately release the ring from the wingtip boom providing instant separation in case of an emergency."

Tests began in August 1949 and as experience was gained, couplings became very easy. The C-47 would stabilize at 95 knots and once coupled, the C-47 could increase its speed to 120 knots where it was found that coupled stability actually improved. Between August 1949 and October 1950, 231 couplings were made. With the concept thus validated, later experiments were carried out with a B-29 and F-84 jet fighters on each wing. Wingtip couplings were

Search and rescue crew, dogs and equipment are shown aboard a C-47 of the Alaskan Command in 1945. They were flown to an off-loading field and made their way overland to a crash site. (USAF photo)

also made with an RB-36F bomber and an RF-84 under Project Tom-Tom in the early 1950s. Later, Beechcraft was awarded a contract to build, install and test a set of small fuel-carrying wingtip "floating panel" extensions on a Beech L-23. This project, code-named "Long-Tom," was successfully completed and, according to Anderson, "a significant improvement in range was demonstrated." Once more, the faithful Gooney Bird had participated in another aviation "first" for the aviation history books.

World War II was more than a war of armies, navies and air forces pitting their power against each other. It was also a war of logistics, of providing for the buildup and support of military forces by transporting supplies, equipment, and personnel where and when needed. The airplane had made surface means of transportation vulnerable. At the same time the airplane had given military logisticians the means to provide materiel over distances at a speed never before possible on land.

The Gooney Bird had contributed immeasurably to these wartime logistical accomplishments. Its dependability and the great numbers available enabled air transport experts to confidently plan large movements by air. The distances of the global war fronts were vast, however, and the demands of Allied commanders for logistical support were always greater than the ability of the supply services to satisfy them. New ways to transport supplies by air had to be sought. Could the C-47 tow gliders loaded with supplies just as it had proven it could tow gliders loaded with troops for air assault operations?

The answer was sought and found by a team from the Royal Air Force and the Royal Canadian Air Force. After weeks of preparation, a giant Waco glider named "Voo-Doo," with an 84-foot wingspread, was lifted into the air from Montreal by a C-47 Dakota. Its destination was England, and the distance was 3,220 miles over the North Atlantic route.

The Dakota used on this "Atlantic Sky-glide" mission was piloted by Flight Lieutenant W. S. Longhurst, a Canadian flying with the RAF. The copilot was Flight Lieutenant C. W. H. Thompson. Squadron Leader R. G. Seys of the RAF piloted the glider, with Squadron Leader F. M. Goebeil, RCAF, as copilot.

The glider carried a ton and a half of vaccines, radios, and aircraft spare parts. The Dakota was loaded with spare parts and survival equipment, and had extra gas tanks installed for the long legs of the flight. Seys explained what it was like after liftoff from Montreal:

"Most sensational of all sensations was my horrible fright as we started out. Towed by a 320-foot nylon rope the glider went on its way. And at times for as long as eight minutes Squadron Leader Goebeil, my co-pilot, and I couldn't see the tow plane ahead of us, as we hit bad weather, many times at very high altitudes.

"Twice during the crossing we ran into bad weather, from thunderstorms to snow, sleet and rains. The turbulence was shocking and the glider was tossed about mercilessly in the sky. But our tow plane, ever seeming conscious of its terrific job, went on and on."

During those minutes when they were unable to see the tow plane, they flew the glider entirely by instruments. "It was a powerful strain on us and we had to watch the tow rope at all times," Seys added.

Despite the hard ride, the glider and its faithful tow plane reached their British destination only 20 minutes off the planned schedule. While the British Air Ministry declared that "the flight opened great new possibilities in air transport," the long-distance haul was not repeated. For this flight, Commander Seys received the U.S. Air Force Distinguished Flying Cross.

A dog team and crew aboard a Gooney en route to the scene of an F-80 crash 60 miles from Elmendorf Air Force Base, Alaska, in April 1951. The team landed at Willow, Alaska, 30 miles from the scene and continued on foot the remaining 30 miles. (USAF photo)

Additional fuel tanks were installed in Gooney Birds for long flights. Upper tier of stretchers was used to carry small packages and spare parts. (USAF photo)

It was in combat operations that the glider tow by C-47s paid off. Thirteen C-47s of the Fifth Air Force proved this in New Guinea in 1944. The unit called themselves "The Skytrain Railroad" and named their planes after famous fast trains in the States.

The group participated in the first mass flight of C-47s to cross the Pacific and later set many similar records, such as being the first to carry paratroopers into Lae and the first to transport a two-and-a-half-ton truck by air. The truck was cut in half and welded together at its destination. The record of the group for the first two years of operation showed 2.8 million flight miles in which 22 million pounds of freight and 47,000 passengers were carried.

An air commando group, under the leadership of the famous Col. Philip Cochran and Col. John R. Alison, moved 12,000 glider-borne troops in six days to points as deep as 200 miles behind Japanese lines in Burma. Eighteen hours after the first gliders landed at the designated clearing, the airborne engineers, together with personnel flown in on the gliders, had cleared a landing field, set up field lights, and an illuminated wind tee. Major Richard L. Benjamin disclosed that in the six weeks of operations, the 13 C-47s had flown 1,200 sorties.

"On three different nights, the C-47 I flew carried three mules and 18 West Africans. On several occasions the cargo included five mules, the muleteers and their equipment. We also flew armored cars, putting the chassis in the gliders, and the wheels, brakes, ammunition, and gasoline in the planes."

Experiments with glider tow methods were conducted throughout World War II by the Army Air Force. One novel idea was an aerial pickup system whereby a damaged Gooney Bird could be saved from having to make a crash landing by being towed back to its base by a companion plane.

A pickup hook was mounted on the left wingtip of the tow plane. This hook was in full view of the pilot. The tow plane could maneuver into position in flight behind the crippled plane so that the pickup hook would make contact with a 250-foot weighted nylon rope which the crippled plane's crew chief would toss outside. The hook on the wing of the tow plane was held in place by an aluminum pin which would break off when the contact was made and swing out behind a conventional glider tow release mechanism. Thus, the tow plane could release the disabled craft just as it would cut a glider loose.

No radio communication was needed between the planes, and all the pilot of the disabled plane was required to do was to maintain a straight and level course. If the speed of the planes was correct—no more than five miles per hour difference between them—the elasticity of the nylon rope would absorb the shock of the join-up.

The system was first tried in April 1945 at the Clinton County Army Air Field at Wilmington, Ohio, with two C-47s, one of which played "wounded" by cutting out one engine. A standard glider tow release was located below the fuselage near the center of the wing, and the nylon rope was stowed inside a metal sleeve that acted as a stabilizer when it was trailing. The other C-47, which had the pickup hook on its wing tip, maneuvered into position, made contact with the dangling rope and continued on its flight, towing the other ship behind it.

After the initial try, many successful pickups were made, including one in which a C-47 had both engines shut down and propellers feathered. The originators of the idea, engineers of the Glider Branch of the Air Technical Service Command's Aircraft Laboratory, believed that the system could be used on any type of aircraft

These metal fuel tanks were an improved version of older long-range tanks. Each carried 200 gallons of fuel which enabled a C-47 to make a 2,000-mile non-stop flight. Baggage and equipment could be carried on top of the tanks with a space saving of 50 percent, enabling eight to ten passengers to be seated instead of the three previously carried. (USAF photo)

As if to prove that a C-47 could do anything asked of it, one was converted into a glider at Wright Field, Dayton, Ohio, during World War II. This closeup in flight shows how the engine nacelles were streamlined. Designated the XCG-17, its stalling speed was only 35 miles per hour. (USAF photo)

including the heaviest of bombers. However, although this was another "first" for the C-47, the idea was never carried any further in combat operations.

But this was not the only unusual experiment with a C-47 at that time. Residents around the same Wilmington, Ohio, air base were startled one spring day in 1945 to see a Gooney without engines or propellers gliding and banking in the morning sun and then gracefully coming to rest on the airfield. The next day they saw two Goonies towing a large transport-type glider. Onlookers did not realize it but they were watching experiments designed to determine if freight could be shipped by glider express after the war was over. What they had seen in these two sightings was a conventional transport made into a glider, and the first "tandem tow," in which two airplanes pulled a huge glider.

The Army Air Force had already developed several models of gliders to carry airborne troopers into battle. All of these gliders, however, were developed for towing behind twin-engine planes, generally the standard workhorse of the Troop Carrier Command—the old reliable C-47 Skytrain. But the work of air transport was moving from twin-engine to four-engine aircraft, and the Air Transport Command began getting the larger Douglas C-54s for their worldwide airline.

At Dayton's Wright Field, headquarters of the Air Technical Command, it was decided to develop a glider suitable as a "Skytrailer" for the much larger and faster C-54 Skymaster and to have that glider ready for the time when the Troop Carrier Command would change from twin-engine to four-engine operations. None of the existing gliders could meet the specifications for this. The problem was given to the Glider Branch for solution.

"We started by figuring the reserve power available in the C-54, and determined a desired cruising speed for plane and glider," said Major William C. Lazarus, acting chief of the Glider Branch. "Then we began to conceive a purely theoretical design and configuration of a glider which would meet the requirements.

"As the specifications for this glider evolved from the drafting boards and slide rules, it became more and more obvious that the size and gross weight of the glider we wanted would coincide with that of the airplane we had been using as a tow ship—the Douglas C-47."

The project engineer assigned to the study was Captain Bernard J. Driscoll, who was not only an aeronautical engineer, but also a qualified glider test pilot. Working with him was Captain Chester Decker, who in prewar days had been one of America's leading sailplane experts.

First to leave the ground in this triple takeoff is the XCG-17 in a demonstration flight at Clinton County Air Field, Wilmington, Ohio. Being towed by two C-47s, the lead plane maintains maximum power while engines of the second plane are throttled back. (USAF photo)

"It has never been done, but let's take the C-47, jerk out its engines and see if it will prove to be the glider we have been trying to design," Decker suggested. As a glider pilot he knew that the C-47 would be a safe and maneuverable glider, and he believed it would meet the test.

The enthusiasm of Driscoll and Decker for converting the C-47 into a glider was quickly communicated to their superiors and they were told to go ahead with the project. Although no one had ever converted a plane of this size into a glider, the plan offered another possible use of an aircraft already in production that had proved itself on every battlefront. Much time and money could be saved by converting an already existing airframe rather than designing and building a completely new glider.

The moment that Brigadier General Franklin O. Carroll, Chief of the Air Technical Service Command engineering division, gave permission to proceed with the project there immediately arose an argument between the power pilots and the glider pilots.

Could a 26,000-pound transport be denuded of engines and handled safely by the average glider pilot?

The power advocates doubted that any pilot could "dead-stick" a transport with sufficient accuracy to make it a successful glider. They believed that the rate of descent of the powerless plane would be so great that there would be no time to judge a proper landing approach. On the other hand, the glider pilots pointed out that with such a relatively clean glider aerodynamically, such as the C-47, the distance covered would be greater than in the powered plane and therefore the pilot would have more time to plan a successful approach.

Aeronautical engineers, agreeing with the glider advocates, pointed out that it would require less power to pull the C-47 in level flight than to pull the conventional glider, which lacked the clean aerodynamic lines of the C-47.

Tests began at the glider experiment station at Wilmington, Ohio. A C-47 with only fuel and crew aboard took off and flew to 5,000 feet where both its engines were cut, the props feathered and the plane dead-sticked to a landing on the airport a number of times. Pilots who flew the airplane on these tests were Captains Decker, Lloyd Santmyer and Norman Rental; the last two were former airline pilots, each with more than 5,000 flying hours.

As the experiments progressed, the altitude where the engines were shut down was gradually lowered until the pilots were gliding the C-47 in from 2,000 feet. Soon everyone was convinced that the C-47 could glide in and hit a landing spot consistently regardless of winds and the amount of load, provided that the pilots were qualified.

The next problem was to determine if the C-47 had sufficient control when being towed as a glider. "In general, being towed in flight is far less stable than free gliding or powered flight," Major Lazarus explained. "All gliders, while in tow, require the constant attention of the glider pilot. For example, when a wing goes down in a gust, the glider pilot must quickly bring it up. Otherwise the wing may get so far down he may not have sufficient control to pull it up again. A glider without adequate control and thus displaced will continue to roll at the end of the tow rope and the only solution is to cut loose from the tow ship. Once in free flight the glider can quickly be righted, of course, but cutting loose means a forced landing.

"All Army Air Force gliders up to this point have been high-winged monoplanes and have been designed specifically as gliders with more aileron, elevator and rudder control than the conventional airplane. Here was a C-47, designed to be flown only as a powered airplane. Would it stand the test at the end of a nylon rope?

"Before we could find the answer to this question the engineers had a problem to solve. Where would we attach the tow rope?

A Consolidated B-24 tows the XCG-17 aloft in experiments in 1944. The engineless Gooney was the world's largest glider at the time and had a glide angle of 14 to 1. (USAF photo)

The pull of a tow rope tugging a 26,000-pound glider through rough air is no small item. A huddle was called one morning with drawings of the C-47 cluttering the big conference table. And there right in front of us was the answer.

"The versatile C-47 had the solution built into it. Douglas engineers, who had never dreamed of towing when they designed the airplane originally, had provided a rectangular inspection door on the belly of the airplane through which mechanics could readily examine the main wing structure where it passed beneath the fuselage.

"The hitch could be made by simply unbolting this inspection panel and replacing it with one specially fitted with a tow release mechanism. Further, it could be done on a C-47 without removing the engines. The rope would not interfere with the props and, since the glider or towed airplane always flies slightly above the tow plane, the rope would not rub against or damage the nose.

"The tow hitch attachment was quickly designed and installed on the belly of a C-47. We were now ready to proceed with the next step in the creation of what was to become the XCG-17, the largest payload glider in the world, carrying in excess of seven tons."

With Santmyer, Rintoul, and Decker doing the flying, flight tests were begun. Two C-47s were hitched together with a standard nylon tow rope 350 feet long. This flight was made to determine the handling characteristics of the C-47 when in towed flight and to test the tow hitch mechanism. The lead C-47 took up slack and applied takeoff power. The towed C-47 applied power but not quite as much as the tow plane, so the tow rope remained taut and the two planes were airborne.

When the two ships gained safe altitudes, the C-47 being towed cut its engines and feathered its props. It handled beautifully and made a smooth landing.

"We were quick to realize that we had something else besides a new glider," Major Lazarus added. "Here was the making of a

One of the five C-47C "Ducks" that were converted to amphibians during World War II. Each float had two hydraulically-operated, free-swiveling nose wheels. Water rudders were steered hydraulically by the brake pedals. (USAF photo)

'tandem tow.' For months, as the gliders became larger and heavier, the need for the assisted takeoff of the tow plane and glider had been felt. The power of one plane was sufficient for level flight once the desired altitude had been gained, but extra power was needed for the climb.

"Could two airplanes be coupled together tandem just as two locomotives are coupled together to pull heavy trains up steep mountain grades? Could a heavy glider be attached behind two C-47s? True, this was a digression from the primary objective of developing the XCG-17, but it would help solve one of our problems, so we went ahead."

The first tandem tow was made using two C-47s pulling a standard fifteen-place CG-4A, one of the smaller military gliders. Pilots were surprised to find that the tandem tow was easy. Later, the two C-47s in tandem took off with a loaded XCG-10A, one of the Army's largest gliders, in tow. At altitude, the lead C-47 cut loose and the other C-47 continued to tow the big glider. One C-47 could not have pulled the loaded glider off the ground. Here was the first real "Skytrain," the official name given to the Gooney Bird. The experiment opened up new possibilities for air cargo development.

These test completed, the next step was to convert a C-47 into a glider. General Carroll imposed only one restriction. He assigned a war-weary C-47 named "Old Miscellaneous" to the experimenters, but he ordered that the plane not be so stripped that it could not be restored as a normal airplane if the experiment were not successful.

Mechanics set to work to reduce the weight of the C-47 as much as possible. The radio operator's and forward baggage compartments were eliminated and a new floor added so that cargo could be loaded farther forward to compensate for the loss of forward weight when the engines were removed. The engines were removed and hemispherical streamlined noses were added to the engine nacelles to reduce drag.

The B-24 tows the XCG-17 over Ohio farmlands. It could be towed at speeds up to 290 miles per hour. (USAF photo)

The first flights of the C-47 that had now become the XCG-17 (experimental cargo glider) were made at the Clinton County airfield in the summer of 1944. Major D. O. Dodd was at the controls.

"The flights were as successful as we had expected," Major Lazarus explained. "The glider engineers had been slightly concerned that some small amount of ballast might be needed to fly the glider in the lightweight condition. On the first flight about 400 pounds of lead shot were added in the nose to ensure that the XCG-17 would not be tail-heavy. After the first few flights it was proved that even this wasn't necessary."

The XCG-17 had a long flat glide angle—a ratio of 14 to 1, which meant that it could go forward fourteen feet while dropping only one foot. By comparison, the smaller CG-4A glider had a glide ratio of ten or twelve to one. The XCG-17 had a remarkably low stalling speed of 35 miles an hour as compared to the 55-mile-an-hour stalling speed of the CG-4. And, most important of all, it could be towed as fast as 270 to 290 miles per hour, whereas the top speed of the conventional glider was only 200 miles per hour. This was proven when it was towed by a B-24 Liberator.

Only one XCG-17 was ever made but once more the lovable Gooney Bird had proved that it had more potential for other jobs than the one the Douglas engineers had in mind.

It may have been inevitable that the Gooney would be turned into a spray plane after World War II was over but this potential role had its beginning in the South Pacific when C-47s of the 13th Air Force were given such a mission. It was on Bougainville in 1944 when the Japanese infantry troops were being driven back into the jungles and were cut off from their supplies. They began to cultivate patches of vegetables. In an effort to drive them back to the beaches and stifle their farming efforts, C-47s were loaded with fuel oil which was dumped on their gardens to kill them before they could be used.

After the war, surplus C-47s were converted to dump fertilizer on farms in Australia and spray weed and bug killers in other countries. So one more accomplishment was added to the long and never-ending list of tasks the indomitable Gooney Bird has been asked to perform. No other aircraft in the history of flight has had such a varied and distinguished career. Whatever the requirement, whatever the job, the DC-3 could do it!

This sequence of photos shows the first C-47C amphibian on takeoff from water. Shortly after the last photo was taken, the JATO bottles used to accelerate the plane stopped operating and the plane nosed into the water. The crew escaped and the plane was salvaged and returned to service as a land plane. (USAF photo)

The floats on the amphibious Gooney were manufactured by EDO Corporation. They were 42 feet long, five feet wide and five feet high. Each contained 14 compartments and a 325-gallon fuel tank. (USAF photo)

A DC-3 modified for crop spraying makes a trial run over a western desert area. (Douglas Aircraft Co. photo)

An unusual in-flight shot of one of the amphibious Gooneys. Only five were converted, although 17 sets of floats weighing 2,000 pounds each were manufactured. (USAF photo)

When deep snow threatened livestock in the western states in 1952, Air Force Goonies participated in Operation Haylift. "Kickers" haul the hay to the doorway and push it overboard to a ranch in Nevada. (USAF photo)

This Air Force C-47, piloted by Capt. Milford Peck, makes a hay-dropping pass to cattle on a ranch northwest of Chadron, Nebraska, in 1952. (USAF photo)

Food and medicine were parachuted to inaccessible areas using canisters attached to the bottom of C-47 fuselages. Reeve Aleutian Airways in Alaska used this method to drop mail and supplies from Gooneys to villages on the Pribilof Islands in the Bering Sea. (USAF photo)

These photos were taken during tests of the first C-47 modified for amphibious operations at the Douglas Aircraft Co. plant, Oklahoma City. Water landing tests were carried out at Lake Worth, Texas, and other locations. (Photo courtesy Mrs. Lee McMurty)

The uses to which a Gooney Bird can be put seems endless. Here a "dung-carrying Dakota" is being loaded in New Zealand. The fertilizer is spread on crops by the propeller blast. Besides the load of "top dressing," the pilot carried a small Fiat in the aft fuselage. (Photo by Fred Tomlinson)

8

Navy and Army Goonies

In Antarctica, many a geographic feature bears the name of brave pilots or hardy crewmen, frequently proposed by a scientist or other recipient of their services. The gratefulness of some of the beneficiaries extended to the airplane itself, and on the map of the Antarctic may be found Dakota Pass, R4D Nunatak, and Skytrain Ice Rise to commemorate, as long as men go to the Antarctic to study its topography, the great contribution that the venerable Gooney Bird made to the first decade of Operation Deep Freeze.

Henry M. Dater
Chief, History & Research Division
U.S. Naval Support Force, Antarctica

The U.S. Navy and Marine Corps flew sixteen variants of the Douglas DC-3, although in much smaller numbers than the original C-47/R4D, during its operation by the military services. First procured for Navy and Marine use in 1941, a total of 568 R4Ds were redirected from Army contracts. Used mainly by the Naval Air Transport Service (NATS) for transport between naval bases in the U.S., they also saw service with the South Pacific Combat Air Transport Service by flying cargo into combat areas and casualties out. The Marines also used them for dropping paratroopers. In a single month, the Marine combat units carried 22,000 passengers, 3.3 million lbs of freight and 941,000 lbs of mail.

As with the Army Air Forces, the Navy and Marine Corps gave the Gooneys a number of specialized roles to fill. They were used for radar countermeasures, electronic equipment and navigator training, and air-sea warfare training. After World War II, the Navy procured 100 Super DC-3s, designated them R4D-8s and used them for trainers and staff transports. During the Korean War, the Marines used the Super Gooneys for close air support at night by dropping flares.

During the period immediately following World War II, the U.S. Navy was given the responsibility to support American research efforts in Antarctica. After examining the aircraft available, it was decided to use six ski-equipped R4Ds to conduct exploratory flights from Little America. Because it was assumed (incorrectly, as later events were to show) that the distance from New Zealand to Antarctica exceeded the planes' range, they would be launched from the deck of the aircraft carrier *USS Philippine Sea* at the edge of the pack ice. This could be done with the aid of JATO bottles, still a relatively new device.

Up to this point, Gooney Birds had been mounted either on skis or wheels for winter operations, but not on both. In order to be launched from the carrier and landed on snow, a combination would be needed. A mechanism was installed so that the skis would have a 1-, 3-, or 6-inch clearance over the deck at time of takeoff. The first R4D, with Rear Admiral Richard E. Byrd aboard, took off from the carrier on January 29, 1947, with USN Commander William M. "Trigger" Hawkes as pilot. Another R4D followed a few minutes later. When it was learned that the two had reached Little America safely, the remaining four were launched.

It was soon found that the ski-wheel combination, which had accomplished its purpose in getting the Goonies off the carrier, had difficulty taxiing in the snow. The wheels were removed on all six aircraft.

Operations over the continent began on February 4, 1947, and terminated on February 21. During this period, 39 flights were made for a total of 250 hours in the air. It was found that a gross weight of 33,000 pounds could be lifted from unprepared snow. At first, JATO

A Navy R4D named the Que Sera' Sera' was the first aircraft to land at the South Pole. Piloted by Lt. Cmdr. Conrad Shinn and Capt. Frank Hawkes, the landing was made on November 21, 1956. Note the shadow of the escorting C-124 circling overhead. (US Navy photo)

Joseph J. Arno poses beside the Que Sera' Sera'. Arno had been selected to accompany the historic aircraft aboard ship for the return to the States for eventual display at the Naval Air Museum at Pensacola. The paint is a preservative to protect the plane's skin from the salt air. (US Navy photo)

was used, but as the temperatures dropped and the snow hardened, unassisted takeoffs were made successfully with the same weight.

The principal use of the Gooney Birds was to explore and photograph the interior of the frozen continent. An exploratory flight on February 15, with Admiral Byrd aboard, crossed the South Pole and flew 60 miles beyond it. The flags of the countries belonging to the newly-established United Nations were dropped as the plane passed over the pole.

When flying was terminated for the season, the Gooneys had to be left at Little America. They could not be landed aboard the carrier and there was no other ship in the task force that was large enough to take them aboard as cargo. They were faced into the wind and their skis were lowered several feet into the snow to anchor them firmly. Oil was drained, classified research instruments were removed, and fabric control surfaces were stored inside the fuselages.

When two icebreakers returned in 1948, the snow was cleared from one of the Goonies and its engines started, but no attempt was made to fly it. When another icebreaker returned in 1955, it was found that about two-thirds of Little America IV on the Ross Ice Shelf, including the airstrip and the aircraft left on it had broken off, sending the Goonies to a watery grave.

During the International Geophysical Year (1955-56), two Goonies were assigned to Operation Deep Freeze I. This time, a new landing gear system was installed on four Goonies that permitted the pilot to use either wheels or skis. Instead of flying from a carrier, four 200-gallon gas tanks were installed in each aircraft which would enable them to fly from nonstop Christchurch, New Zealand, to McMurdo. Three other types of planes were also assigned. However, when the aircraft encountered severe headwinds and it appeared they couldn't make it, they were ordered to return to New Zealand and none were used that year.

Deep Freeze II began in 1956 and the four Goonies that had not made the trip before from New Zealand landed at McMurdo in October. A base was established at the foot of the Liv Glacier and two R4Ds flew men and supplies to the station known as the Beardmore-Scott Auxiliary Base. The base would be used as a supply facility from which aircraft would fly with men and equipment to set up a permanent base at the South Pole.

Rear Admiral George J. Dufek, commanding officer of Deep Freeze, decided that a test landing should be made first in *Que Sera' Sera'* (what is to be, will be), one of the R4Ds. It was to be accompanied by an Air Force Globemaster and a Navy Skymaster to help with the navigation, take photographs and be prepared to drop survival gear if needed. The pilot selected was Lieutenant Commander Conrad S. "Gus" Shinn; Copilot was Captain "Trigger" Hawkes, the Navy's most experienced Antarctic flyer. In addition to the admiral and Captain Douglas Cordiner, squadron commander of VX-6, Lieutenant John R. Swadener was the navigator, and crew members were Petty Officers John P. Strider and William A. Cumbie.

Lt. Cmdr. Conrad Shinn keeps the engines of Que Sera' Sera' running at the South Pole camp which was set up as a scientific observation station. The Gooney Bird has the honor of being the first plane to land and take off from both poles. (US Navy photo)

When Navy teams returned to the Antarctic for summer operations in 1958, one of the first tasks was to dig out the R4Ds that had been left there from previous expeditions. (US Navy photo)

A Navy report of the historic mission explained what happened:

"As the Dakota churned up the Beardmore Glacier, the Skymaster developed engine trouble and turned back. The Globemaster, piloted by Marine Major C. J. Ellen, pushed on to what the navigator calculated to be the position of the Pole. As Shinn approached the area, neither he nor anyone else knew what to expect. One theory held that the plateau would be covered with deep, soft snow into which the skis would sink irretrievably; others had quite the opposite view, that the surface would be hard and ruffled with sastrugi. During the approach to a landing, oil pressure fell off and oil streamed from the engines. Shinn reported that his instrument panel was lighting up like a Christmas tree. From above, Major Ellen soothingly radioed, 'Don't worry, Gus. If you can't get off I'll bellyland this baby and give you a warm house to live in.'"

Shinn made three low-level passes to examine the surface and then landed easily. Admiral Dufek climbed down the Gooney's ladder to become the first man to stand at the South Pole since Amundsen and Scott. He was followed by Captain Cordiner who tried to plant an American flag. In so doing, the argument about the surface was settled; he had to use an ice ax to dig a hole for the flag pole.

While the pilots kept the Gooney's engines running, the rest of the crew set out a radar reflector and tried to take photographs. Only one or two snapshots were taken before the cameras froze, "making this probably the worst recorded event in Antarctic history," according to the Navy's report.

The R4Ds flew a number of trips to establish Little America V and the base at the Pole. The first landing of two Goonies was made on November 20, 1956, with eight men and eleven dogs, plus their gear. When the operation was over for that year, the Goonies had flown over 900 hours and regularly operated with gross weights of over 38,000 pounds.

The Dakotas and other aircraft were left behind in 1956 and then dug out when Deep Freeze III began in 1957. Two R4D-8s were added to the fleet. These were the so-called Super DC-3s that the Navy had procured. "While the Dakotas did not occupy the preeminent place in Deep Freeze III that they had in Deep Freeze II," a report said, "they still continued to be regarded as the workhorse of VX-6, a role they would continue to play during the two following seasons."

In December 1959, after Deep Freeze IV (1958-59) was concluded, the *Que Sera' Sera'*, the first plane to land at the South Pole, was returned to the States. It was later presented to the National Air & Space Museum where it was stored for several years and is now on permanent loan to the US Naval Air Museum at Pensacola, Florida.

The newer versions of the Gooney Bird continued their service in succeeding Deep Freeze operations doing their duty as people and cargo haulers. Although several of the larger C-130 Hercules were added to the fleet in 1961, the Goonies still could not be replaced. There were four assigned at this time and Rear Admiral David M. Tyree stated that the R4D would "be needed for years to come for the support of scientific projects requiring landing on unprepared snow surfaces." At the end of Deep Freeze 62, Commander M. D. Greenwell, then VX-6 commander, gave the Goonies another accolade:

"The R4D again proved herself a valuable friend and the 'Grand Old Lady' of Antarctic operations. She is economical and durable, and her versatility in short range, open field ski operation remains undisputed. It is not difficult to foresee the day, perhaps in the near future, when an equally versatile, longer-range, greater-payload, higher-flying turboprop replaces the old warrior, but until that day comes, treat her kindly, keep her warm, push the right JATO buttons, and navigate clear of all obstacles."

During Operation Deep Freeze 63, the Navy adopted the Air Force's system of aircraft designations. The R4D-5 and -6 became the C-47, and the R4D-8 became the C-117. The latter had more powerful engines and could carry a payload of 2,000 pounds more than the C-47. When equipped for cold weather operations, which usually meant modified with skis, the prefix "L" was added. By this time five Goonies had been lost which were replaced. How-

"Kokora II" with Lt. Cmdr. Conrad "Gus" Shinn at the controls flies over Erebus Bay with Mt. Erebus in the background. The R4Ds were used extensively for Antarctic research activities by the U.S. Navy. (US Navy photo)

ever, they had begun to show their age under the harsh conditions of polar operations and were recommended to be withdrawn. Gradually, they were required to fly less and less, although they continued to fly in subsequent operations until Deep Freeze 1968 when there were three left. The last flight by a Dakota in Antarctica was actually made on December 2, 1967. The remaining three planes were dismantled and prepared for shipment aboard the USNS *Pvt John R. Towle*. However, one of them slipped from the derrick's sling while it was being loaded and was so badly damaged that it was abandoned. A ten-year Deep Freeze veteran, it did not give up easily. Pushed out on the ice of McMurdo Sound, it was expected to drift away and sink. It was still there a year later, plainly visible from the station. One LC-47 that had continued to operate in New Zealand was presented to the Ferrymeade Museum of Science and Industry at Christchurch on April 18, 1969.

The Navy has always been grateful for the dedication of the faithful Gooney to their Antarctic requirements. As the final report of its LC-47 and LC-117 operations noted, "During those early years, despite its limitations, the Dakotas gave to the United States program a flexibility and scope never before achieved in the area. One can only end a review of their accomplishments by awarding them the tested Navy accolade of 'Well Done.'"

While the United States was operating with DC-3s in Antarctica, the Argentine Air Force and Navy were also using them there. During the 1961-62 season, the navy flew two DC-3s to the South Pole by way of a temporary base on the Larsen Ice Shelf and Ellsworth Station. Fuel, JATO bottles and maintenance support was provided by the U.S. Navy. In 1964, the Argentine Gooney had its normal engines replaced with more powerful DC-4 engines and a jet propulsion engine with a 600-kilogram thrust was placed in the tail. This aircraft reached the Pole on November 3, 1965. That same year it also crossed the continent, the first plane to do so.

The Argentines sent three Goonies to the Antarctic in 1967. During their service in the area, they carried fuel, supplies and passengers, and performed photo reconnaissance missions.

The Soviet Union also had its version of the Gooney, the Lisonov Li-2, performing similar duties in Antarctica from their base at Mirnyy Station. Just as the United States had depended heavily on C-47s in the years from 1956 through 1961, so did the Soviets rely upon the Li-2s. They brought two into the area by ship in 1955-56 and increased the number to a maximum of seven by early 1958. After that the number was gradually reduced until there was only one left by the end of the 1966-67 season.

Some of the Russian Goonies were said to have been specially equipped with various types of gear for special undisclosed scientific investigations. One use of their Goonies was to ferry ashore both passengers and cargo from ships unable to penetrate the pack ice. In 1966, approximately 32 tons of goods and 93 passengers were shuttled back and forth between Mirnyy and the expedition ship.

An Air Force C-47 lands on the Greenland Ice Cap in 1947 while participating in the Snowman Project. (USAF photo)

The Gooney Bird had proved that it could operate anywhere on the globe. And it had earned another "first" as the first aircraft to land at the South Pole. But, it also became the first plane to land at *both* poles. On May 3, 1952, a U.S. Air Force C-47 had landed at the North Pole while participating in the establishment of a weather research station there. The pilots were Lt. Cols. William Benedict and Joseph Fletcher. They had to start the engines every fifteen minutes in order to prevent freezing while they carried out geological tests.

The Gooney Bird is well-established in Air Force lore and is not generally associated with the U.S. Army after the Air Force became a separate service in September 1947. As a result, the Army's air arm was limited in the size of the fixed-wing aircraft that it could procure within its own budget. However, before the Air Force and Army came to an agreement, the Army briefly operated borrowed aircraft as large as the four-engine Lockheed C-121 Super Constellation and Douglas C-54 Skymaster.

Although the Air Force was reluctant to allow the Army to have its own fleet of aircraft above a weight limit of 5,000 lbs., it was unable to provide sufficient on-call airlift for Army needs. The Army requested and was granted permission to operate and maintain about 40 C-47s which were acquired from the Air Force and Navy beginning in the early 1950s; they were used widely during the 1960s and through the 1970s.

In 1960, the Army acquired three R4Ds and based them at Fort Monmouth, New Jersey, to be used as flying laboratories in support of research and development activities. A variety of systems for flight control and navigation were installed in each aircraft. A weather radar set was installed that provided pilot, co-pilot and test personnel with a picture of weather directly ahead of the aircraft. An engineer's console was constructed in the aft cabin, in addition to interphone outlets. Wing tanks and various types of experimental antennas were mounted on the plane's exterior during certain types of tests.

Admiral Richard E. Byrd boards a Navy R4D for the flight from the carrier USS Philippine Sea to Little America in 1947. The Navy version of the DC-3 was the workhorse of the early Antarctic expeditions. (US Navy photo)

According to Stephen Harding in *U.S. Army Aircraft Since 1947*, "The C-47 was chosen for Army use for several reasons: there were plenty immediately available; the type was robust and well-suited to the sort of rough field conditions often encountered by Army aircraft; and, almost certainly, because senior Air Force leaders felt that the Army's operation of an elderly and (apparently) obsolescent type would not seriously detract from the Air Force's image."

In addition to transporting personnel and equipment during missile firings at Kwajalein Island in the Pacific, one Army Gooney was "plushed up" for VIP transportation, and others were assigned to the Army Electronics Command. They were designated EC-47s and outfitted with wing racks to test electronic equipment such as sideways looking airborne radar (SLAR). Several were used for mapping missions in Ethiopia and Iran. One aircraft was used for paratroop training and cargo drops.

Heavily-loaded R4Ds were launched from an aircraft carrier for the flight to Little America with the aid of jet-assisted takeoff (JATO) bottles for Operation Deep Freeze. (US Navy photo)

The Army's famous "Golden Knights" parachute demonstration team used at least three C-47s for jump platforms and for support of the Army's precision helicopter team, the "Silver Eagles."

During the years that the Army flew Goonies, there were more than 30 assigned to the Army's Materiel Command, Continental Army Command, the Agency for Aviation Safety and the Strategic Communications Command. Obtained from Air Force and Navy surplus, they were also used in support of topographic activities, paradrops, parachute training, aeromedical research and test support.

Although never used in combat by the Army, the ever-present Gooney Bird played an important role at an important period in the Army's history. The Army was the last of the U.S. military services to operate the venerable C-47; the last one was retired to the Army Aviation Museum at Fort Rucker, Alabama, in 1982 and placed on permanent static display.

A number of Goonies were used by the U.S. Army as a utility transport for several years. One was retained for permanent display at the U.S. Army Aviation Center, Fort Rucker, Alabama. (US Army photo)

A Navy Gooney banks around the famed Sugar Loaf peak while maneuvering for a landing at Rio de Janeiro, one of many stops on the U.S. Navy's World War II airline routes. (US Navy photo)

After landing at the South Pole, dogs and supplies are offloaded from the R4D. The U.S. Navy maintains an airstrip at the South Pole year-round and conducts weather observations and experiments. (US Navy photo)

9

The Vietnam Experience

In an age of supersonic jet aircraft, megaton atomic weapons and sophisticated electronic devices, nothing seemed quite so incongruous as a lumbering C-47 transport evolving into a potent weapon system. Counterinsurgency warfare, as exemplified by the Southeast Asian war, had generated modern weaponry paradoxes such as old T-28 trainers serving as attack aircraft. The gunship fashioned from a transport joined this group as an improvisation that surprised everyone. From a humble modification of the apparently ageless C-47 (DC-3), the gunship grew into a highly complex weapon system. In doing so, it pioneered new research developments and revolutionized aerial counterinsurgency tactics.

Lt. Col. Jack S. Ballard
Author, *Development and Employment of Fixed-Wing Gunships, 1962-1972*

There is no doubt that future historians will label American involvement in the Vietnamese war as the most agonizing ever experienced by its military forces. For over a decade, American air, ground and naval units were required to support the South Vietnamese government by supplying first advisors, then gradually increasing amounts of military materiel and manpower which eventually numbered more than half a million men and women.

When the U.S. Air Force was committed to sending flying units to Southeast Asia beginning in June 1962, it was probably inevitable that the venerable Gooney Bird would have a role to play. To help counter aggression, a number of Goonies had been transferred to the French in the 1950s to transport troops and supplies during military operations against the Viet Minh. The war for national independence from the French lasted for eight years until a conference at Geneva in 1954 created a North and a South Vietnam.

When the tide of communist influence began to spread southward to capture what was called the "rice bowl" of Asia, the United States sent military advisors to assist in the defense of Vietnam, Cambodia and Laos. In July 1955, the Vietnamese Air Force (VNAF) was established as an independent force to protect South Vietnam. The 1st Transport Squadron was formed with 22 C-47s which were transferred from the French units at Tan Son Nhut. Over the years following, more bases and aircraft were added, including helicopters, fighters, and trainers.

The C-47s were used for covert operations by the South Vietnamese beginning in 1961. The missions were conducted at night and always at low altitude. Saboteurs and supplies were dropped behind the lines deep in the heartland of North Vietnam. The turning point in the involvement of the United States came about in July 1962 when Secretary of Defense Robert S. McNamara approved expansion of the VNAF with US equipment and operations against insurgents with American air and ground forces. Joint sorties were flown and the C-47s were used on flare illumination flights. RC-47s were later assigned that had improved infra-red photo systems installed that could locate enemy ground forces through heat-source imagery. EC-47s, equipped with electronic equipment that could locate enemy radio transmissions were also added later. The ancient Gooney, modernized for modern warfare, was once again used to fight aggression. By the end of the war, 40 C-47s, 27 EC-47s and 2 AC-47s had seen action with the VNAF.

There were several hundred C-47s still in the USAF's flying inventory or in storage in the 1960s. Although the Air Force had been preparing for nuclear warfare, once more it had to develop a force capable of supporting ground forces operating in a jungle environment. The concept developed was called "counterinsurgency" and aircraft and tactics were conceived to wage guerrilla-type warfare. The Gooney Bird continued to be called on to do its usual job of flying U.S. and South Vietnamese ground forces to battle zones and keeping them supplied with air-dropped food, medicines and ammunition.

Contrary to popular forecasts at the time, the war did not end quickly. It dragged on month after month as a determined enemy, willing to fight for a hundred years if necessary, stayed in the jungle and infiltrated the entire country. U.S. air and ground forces with weapon systems designed for the nuclear age were relatively ineffective against jungle troops who fought a conventional war in their own country without uniforms and with a seemingly unlimited supply of arms and ammunition.

As always in modern wars, weapons research and technology accelerated during the Vietnam war years. This was particularly evident in the field of tactical intelligence. Using a variety of aircraft and electronic sensors, U.S. tactical reconnaissance forces were gradually able to collect information, process and interpret photographs within ever-decreasing time spans so that air and ground

The ever-faithful C-47 was recalled to active combat duty during the war in Vietnam. One of its most notable modifications was as a gunship, designated AC-47, that was equipped with side-firing 7.62 mini-guns like this one at Nha Trang Air Base in 1967. (USAF photo)

commanders could take appropriate decisive action more quickly than ever before. Gooney Birds, with the designation of EC-47 (for electronically-equipped), were outfitted with a variety of optical, radar and electronic sensors as well as various types of cameras for aerial reconnaissance. The photographic missions included the use of laser beams and flash cartridges to illuminate target areas at night. Infrared cameras were installed in a number of EC-47s to record areas or objects that emitted thermal (heat) radiations. Electronic devices were used to locate and analyze enemy devices emitting electro-magnetic radiation. Radar was used to record either fixed or moving targets by detecting the radar echo of enemy troop concentrations.

In addition to the Gooneys being used for paradrop missions of men, supplies and ammunition, several were flown by Vietnamese crews in conjunction with leaflet droppings. Each aircraft had loud speakers attached to the belly of the fuselage. The aircraft would drop down to less than 1,000 feet, circle the area to be "psyched" at reduced speed, drop leaflets, and broadcast messages in the local dialect. Each voice message would contain the same theme as in the leaflets. Often, the voice missions would follow a USAF defoliation mission, assuring the people in the sprayed area that the defoliant was harmless.

Such tasks were easily accomplished by the ageless Gooney. It had performed most of them in other wars. The basic aircraft was not more sophisticated; the faithful aerial workhorse had the same airframe and engines it always had. There was nothing spectacular about the aircraft or its surveillance missions. It surprised no one that the Gooney Bird, obsolescent by standards applied to every other aircraft in the world, would be doing its part in this latest war.

But the Gooney's greatest role, however, was yet to come. The lumbering C-47 was to develop into a valuable weapon system; despite its age, it was to be called upon to pioneer and revolutionize aerial counterinsurgency tactics in the jet era. And it was to take on an entirely new designation.

The new role in the never-ending saga of the DC-3 grew out of the simple fact that the first-line jet fighters and attack aircraft of the U.S. Air Force of the early 1960s too often could not find or accurately strike enemy targets at night or those hiding under cover

Another view of side-firing guns during experimental flights of the attack version of the C-47 in Vietnam. Three six-barreled mini-guns with 6,000 shots-per-minute capability were eventually used on the AC-47s. (USAF photo)

of a dense jungle canopy. As the success of guerrilla warfare against the sophisticated firepower of the United States was proven daily in Vietnam, it became obvious that not only must the enemy forces be located from the air but a great amount of firepower had to be brought to bear quickly on them before they could slip away using darkness and the jungle to avoid detection. What was needed was an aircraft that had the range to cover any area in South Vietnam, loiter for hours awaiting calls for assistance from friendly ground forces, carry many pounds of the latest electronic detection equipment and then have the capability to remain in the target area and place devastating firepower down on a precise, limited section of the jungle. What was required was a gunship—something akin to the Navy's old battleship—that could rain down overwhelming firepower exactly where it was needed. What was not needed for that job at that time was a supersonic jet fighter plane.

The need, quickly recognized on the battlefield by the ground forces, was not so quickly fulfilled. The answer evolved as the product of several men whose greatest task turned out to be not so much as arriving at a solution to the problem but convincing those in authority that they had truly solved the problem and could prove it.

Credited with being the first to propose a way to counter the threat in South Vietnam was Ralph E. Flexman who, as an engineer for Bell Aerosystems Co., became intensely interested in the problems of limited warfare due to his company's involvement in the development of special hardware for use in combat in Southeast Asia. Coincidentally, he held a Mobilization Day assignment as a major in the Air Force Reserve with the Behavioral Sciences Laboratory at Wright-Patterson Air Force Base, Ohio. In a summary of several ideas he and his Bell Aerosystems colleagues were working on, he reported to his reserve military superior, "with respect to aircraft, we believe that lateral firing, while making a pylon turn, will prove effective in controlling ground fire from many AA (anti-aircraft) units. In theory at least, this should more than triple the efficiency of conventional aircraft on reconnaissance and destructive missions."

Actually, Flexman's basic suggestion was not totally new. Machine guns had been mounted on World War I aircraft so they could be fired laterally by gunners at air and ground targets. Experiments were later conducted at Brooks Field, San Antonio, Texas, in 1926-27 in a de Havilland-4. As noted in an earlier chapter, side-firing .50 caliber guns were mounted in two C-47s of the 443rd Troop Carrier Group supporting Allied forces against the Japanese in Burma during World War II.

The concept of using side-firing guns while in a pylon turn had not surfaced since the Brooks Field experiments when Lt. Fred Nelson flew pylon turns, sighted a ground target through an aiming device mounted on a wing strut and scored hits with a .30 caliber machine gun. What had really inspired Flexman was an article he had read about a South American missionary, Nate Saint, who had perfected delivery of mail and supplies to the remote villages of Arica Indian tribes by lowering a bucket on a long rope. As he made a pylon turn, the bucket would hover over a point on the ground where natives could pick out the contents.

Flexman also recalled his own experiences as a flight instructor when he was required to teach his students how to do pylon eights or pivot an aircraft around a telephone pole or a fence post while they held them in view off the tip of a wing. As Air Force historian Lt. Col. Jack S. Ballard recorded in his excellent study of the use of fixed-wing gunships in Vietnam: "He therefore believed it reasonable that with a very small sight one could fire ammunition along the sight path to a target. All this pointed to possible counterinsurgency applications."

Despite the fact that Flexman's concept seemed to have validity but not wide acceptance, it was a fortuitous contact with Col. Gilmour C. MacDonald that was most influential in the development of the gunship. In April 1942, while Allied shipping losses were extremely high in the Atlantic, MacDonald, then a first lieutenant in the Coast Artillery, suggested a way to increase the effectiveness of civilian aircraft on submarine patrol. He wrote to his superiors: "With a view of providing means for continuous fire upon submarines forced to the surface, it is proposed that a fixed machine gun be mounted transversely in the aircraft so that by flying a continually banked circle the pilot may keep the underseacraft under continuous fire if necessary." Unfortunately, MacDonald's proposal was not considered favorably at that time.

In 1961, as an Air Force lieutenant colonel, MacDonald resurrected his idea and proposed it to the Tactical Air Command. He wrote, "by flying a banked circle, the airplane can keep the gun pointed continuously at a target, and by flying along with one wing low, limited longitudinal strafing can be done without worrying about pullout." Again, his suggestion was ignored.

At a casual meeting of Flexman and MacDonald in late 1961, the former learned of the latter's recommendations and of the Nate

The AC-47's side-firing Gatling, required three crew members to operate them. A1C James H. Schmisser loads the gun while A1C Ronald Snyder, left, and A3C Allen W. Sims observe. (USAF photo)

Smith mail delivery successes in South America. By 1963 Flexman was convinced that the basic idea had considerable merit. As he saw it, there were three main questionable areas that should be investigated. As Air Force historian Ballard states, these areas were "ballistics of the projectiles as they were fired and their dispersion; ability of the pilot to aim his lateral weapon and hold the target; and the reaction time necessary to change from straight-and-level flight to an on-pylon turn."

Flexman, not then on active duty, suggested to Captain John C. Simons that a test program should be formally begun to answer the three questions he posed. Simons, as a research psychologist and pilot on active duty with the Aerospace Medical Laboratory at Wright-Patterson Air Force Base, Ohio, was convinced that Flexman's idea was workable and diligently pursued it through his official channels. He proposed a nine-month study to include test flights to verify the concept but was rebuffed. However, as the Air Force history states, "one of his superiors gave him an under-the-table approval for a few test flights." These flights were conducted day and night in a T-28 trainer with a makeshift sight (a grease-penciled line on the left cockpit window) at altitudes of 500 and 3,000 feet. "He marveled at the pylon turn's simplicity and the ease with which a target could be acquired and held in the sight," according to Ballard's study. These tests by Simons were confirmed by flights in a C-130 cargo aircraft where tracking targets such as trucks, silos, barns, moving horses and even flying geese proved easy from the standpoint of flying and sighting.

To prove how easy it was, Simons conducted tests with three synchronized cameras—one to record the pilot's sight alignment, another fixed on the instrument panel, and the third in the cargo compartment where a side-firing machine gun might be positioned. The success he demonstrated eventually resulted in approval for official flight tests but only after frustrating delays due to lack of priority, funds, and skepticism of the project at higher levels of authority. The main objection was doubt that the C-47 could survive the ground gunfire expected in Vietnam and fulfill its mission. General Walter C. Sweeney, Jr., head of the Tactical Air Command, stated in 1964, "This concept will place a highly vulnerable aircraft in a battlefield environment in which I believe the results will not compensate for the losses of Air Force personnel and aircraft." His opinion slowed down the development of the use of the Gooney as a new weapon system.

Meanwhile, Simons was transferred in 1963 and it fell to Captain (later Lieutenant Colonel) Ronald W. Terry, a Vietnam combat veteran, to try to convince his superiors that the concept was valid. Having flown fighters in Vietnam, he knew firsthand how difficult it was to find and fire on a ground target in bad weather, at night, and when under intense ground fire. Once he became aware of what had gone before and now assigned to the Wright-Patterson laboratory, Terry decided that his role had to be that of salesman because he was convinced that the project was worthwhile. He drafted a scenario showing how a side-firing weapon system could be used mainly for the defense of South Vietnamese hamlets and forts. By the summer of 1964, Terry had won his case and tests were begun to verify the concept at Eglin AFB, Florida, using a C-131 transport.

When the tests proved successful, Terry and a test team traveled to Vietnam in December 1964 and modified two C-47s with gun kits. Flare dispensers were installed in the cargo compartment doors. Converted 16mm cameras with reflex viewfinders and cross-hair reticules were placed in the cockpits as aiming devices for the pilots.

The devastating effect of mini-guns firing from an AC-47 can be seen in this time-lapse night photo. Called "Puff, the Magic Dragon" or "Dragon Ship," the pilot peers through a gunsight while circling a target area and triggers the guns with a button on the control column. (USAF photo)

The venerable C-47 was also used for psychological warfare operations in Vietnam. Leaflets were scattered over Viet Cong concentrations in "the struggle for men's minds." One is shown taking advantage of prevailing winds to blow them toward Vietnam's shoreline villages. (USAF photo)

At this time, members of the 1st Combat Applications Group were conducting tests with equipment and tactics for counterinsurgency operations using C-47s. They asked for and were given permission to install and test .30 caliber machine guns that were fired from the rear cabin; these were later replaced with three rapid-firing Gatling 7.62mm "mini-guns" in the Gooneys that could fire 6,000 rounds per minute. A standard illuminated Mark 20 gunsight was later installed at the pilot's side window near his left shoulder, and the control wheel was fitted with a trigger. These tests were immediately successful but official sanction of the idea was still far off. There was much skepticism at higher command levels about the idea of resurrecting a slow, aging cargo plane for the proposed combat job.

Admittedly, the Gooney was vulnerable to ground fire and interception by enemy aircraft, but the advantages of using the C-47 included its availability in large numbers, along with the qualified crews to fly them. It could carry a large amount of ammunition and flares and could remain on alert and over a target area for long periods of time. The crew could arm, disarm, maintain and repair the Gatlings in flight and assess the battle situation before and immediately after an attack. As to its vulnerability, Terry argued that the C-47 could fly above the range of enemy small arms fire and, since the Air Force held aerial superiority over the battlefield, there were no enemy aircraft to intercept them. "Certainly," he told his doubters, "the C-47 is bound to be less vulnerable than the Army's helicopters" which by that time in 1964 were beginning to be used extensively as gunships.

Captain Terry's arguments eventually prevailed and the order came down from Chief of Staff General Curtis E. LeMay to test the Gatling-equipped C-47 in combat. Upon arrival in Vietnam, a new advantage of using the C-47 as a ground attack weapon system surfaced. It was discovered that its great slant range gave it the capability to strike targets on steep mountain slopes or in similar terrain where the fighters could not attack safely. It was during these initial tests that the new role for the Gooney Bird was validated and caused it to receive a new name. The Air Force history explains:

"The (C-47) gunship fired tracer ammunition on night missions to see where the minigun rounds were hitting. The guns' rapid fire appeared as tongues of flame spewing from the black sky accompanied by a distinctive sound. An impressive sight, it boosted the morale of fort and hamlet defenders but terrorized the enemy."

It didn't take long for the C-47 with an entirely new function to earn a new designation and new nicknames. At first, it was designated FC-47 because of its tactical role but this was changed in November 1965 to AC-47 (for attack version). Its new nicknames became "Puff, the Magic Dragon," and "Dragon Ship." Terry believes that the name "dragon" derived from the fact that 1964 was the Chinese Year of the Dragon and coincidentally from stories from

A Gooney Bird with a loud speaker used in psychological warfare is shown on the flightline at Nha Trang Air Base in 1967. "Surrender or die" messages were broadcast in local dialects to persuade insurgents to come over to the South Vietnamese government's side. (USAF photo)

Two South Vietnamese pilots study the target area for a "voice" mission as Capt. W. P. Kirnan, an Air Force advisor, looks on. The large speakers amplified the psychological warfare messages broadcast to enemy troops below. (Photo courtesy Albert L. Jones)

captured enemy prisoners about the tongues of fire from the gunship. Others trace it to recollections of the child's fairy tale, Puff the Magic Dragon, and the song which was popular in 1964. The name of "Spooky" was given to the Gooneys that flew on armed surveillance missions equipped with powerful magnesium flares and various devices that could detect enemy troop and vehicle movements.

The nicknames and the Gooney's new wartime roles drew renewed interest in it as a potent weapon system for a new kind of war. Reports from Vietnam about its success prompted one Air Force general to say that it had a great psychological impact "way out of proportion to the effectiveness of other aircraft strike efforts and ground force efforts." The result was the assignment of the first 16-plane AC-47 squadron to USAF units in South Vietnam in mid-1965. With typical Yankee ingenuity, a relatively ancient aircraft had been adapted to take part in still another conflict.

As historian Jack Ballard wrote, the idea of using the Gooney Bird in an entirely new role had traveled a "tortuous path." The proposal had almost died on several occasions. "It faced bureaucratic oblivion," he said, "burial in government files, rejection by ballistic experts, plus the usual delaying problems of time, manpower and money. Only the dogged persistence of key individuals enabled the concept to emerge from such a deadly thicket." He gave credit to the four men previously mentioned, and concluded, "Their evolutionary efforts combined to create what was probably the most unique weapon system employed in Southeast Asia—the gunship." He credited MacDonald as the "originator," Flexman the "catalyst," Simons the "tester," and Terry the "seller."

Meanwhile, General Curtis E. LeMay, then Air Force Chief of Staff, ordered the establishment of the 4400th Combat Crew Training Squadron within the Tactical Air Command; later he authorized the formation of the USAF Special Air Warfare Center and the 1st Air Commando Group. In 1965, the 1st Air Commando Squadron became the first USAF unit to win the Presidential Unit Citation since the Korean War. Between August 1, 1964, and April 15, 1965, the six aircraft of its C-47 section flew 3,763 sorties, airlifted 2,187,000 pounds of cargo and 16,862 passengers and airdropped 1,000,000 pounds of cargo and 1,125 troops; 3,341 flares were dropped on illumination missions.

The AC-47 deserved the plaudits it received. In the months following its introduction in 1965 with the 1st, 4th, and the 14th Air Commando Squadrons, the aircraft that was literally pulled out of mothballs flew hundreds of armed reconnaissance missions, not only in South Vietnam but Laos and Thailand as well with outstanding results. These "Spooky" missions were flown around the clock and continually demonstrated the Gooney's versatility for the next four years. They performed a wide variety of tasks from leaflet dropping, "voice" and other psychological warfare missions to flying protective cover for friendly truck convoys and destruction of those not so friendly.

During the four years of their use as gunships, the 53 AC-47s eventually assigned had successfully defended 3,926 hamlets, outposts and forts, according to official statistics. In doing so, the crews were able to boast that "no outpost or village was ever lost while under gunship protection." About a dozen of them had been downed or severely damaged late in the four-year period by Soviet-made antiaircraft rockets.

The year 1969 saw the end of the use of the Gooneys in the hands of U.S. pilots. They were replaced by Fairchild AC-119G "Shadow" and Lockheed AC-130 "Stinger" gunships with refinements such as infrared and laser-beam equipment to enhance night target acquisition. Both aircraft, referred to as Gunboats, could carry more ammunition and loiter longer than the AC-47s and were outfitted with four 7.62 mm and four 20 mm Gatlings.

The AC-47s phased out of American hands but not out of the war. The AC-47s were transferred to South Vietnamese, Laotian and Thai units and continued their special missions. It was inevitable that the Spooky flare and gunship missions would produce their own heroes because of the risk involved.

Although many crew members won the Distinguished Flying Cross and the Air Medal for valor in combat, one of their number was awarded America's highest decoration—the Medal of Honor. His name was Airman First Class John L. Levitow.

On the night of February 24, 1969, Levitow climbed aboard his assigned AC-47, codenamed "Spooky 71," for a combat air patrol over the Saigon area. After 4 1/2 hours of inactivity, Major Ken Carpenter, aircraft commander, was vectored toward Bien Hoa where a U.S. Army base was under attack by a large enemy force. The official Air Force report tells the story:

"As Spooky 71 turned to meet the enemy, the pilot and copilot spotted muzzle flashes on the southern and eastern perimeters of Long Binh Air Base. With hot activity below, they moved into attack orbit and fired about 3,000 rounds. After the second pass, they were directed to give the ground troops more flare illumination and to remain over the area.

"In the cargo compartment, Spooky 71's loadmaster, A1C John L. Levitow. was busily setting ejection and ignition controls on the 2-million candlepower magnesium flares. He would carefully hand the flares to one of the gunners, Sgt. Ellis C. Owen, who hooked them onto the lanyard. The sound of mortar fire rose above the engine noise. A turn of the aircraft indicated the pilot was firing on a new target. Then came the sudden shock of a blast, a white flash, showers of flying metal, and the sinking sensation of the aircraft veering sharply right and down. Crewmembers in the rear of the aircraft were thrown violently about and injured. Unknown to the crew at the time, a North Vietnamese Army 82 mm mortar shell had hit Spooky 71's right wing.

"At the moment of the blast, Sergeant Owen had one finger through the safety pin ring preparatory to dropping a flare. Knocked from his hand, the armed flare rolled on the floor. The crew knew it took but 20 seconds for the flare to ignite—the 4,000-degree Fahrenheit burn and the incapacitating toxic smoke. In that instant of crisis, A1C Levitow, severely injured with shrapnel in his right side, was dragging himself to the open cargo door to pull away one of his injured comrades. Suddenly he saw the armed flare for the first time. It was rolling between number one mini-gun and a jumble of spilled ammunition and storage cans. Filled with terror at the sight of the smoking flare, Levitow knew he had to get it out at once or all would be lost.

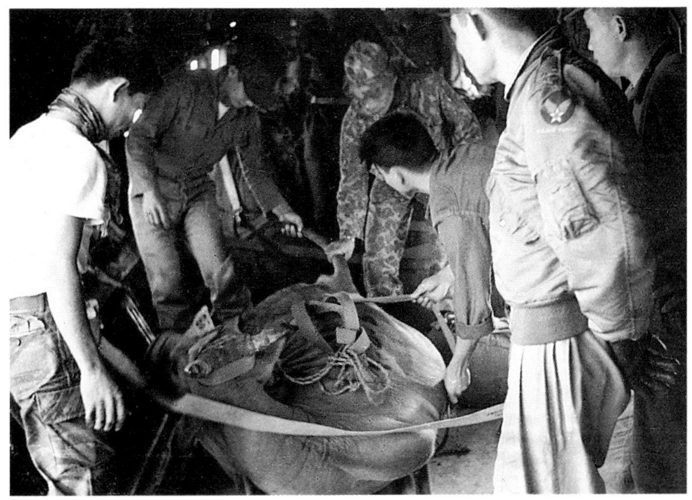

Another of the many functions of the Gooney Bird in Vietnam was to transport livestock for native villages. Here a 700-lb. steer is equipped with two parachutes for a drop to an inaccessible area. (Photo courtesy Albert L. Jones)

"Moving in pain and with great difficulty in the pitching gunship he finally reached the flare. He grasped it and crawled slowly but determinedly to the open door. At last he pushed the flare out; it ignited almost instantly.

"Major Carpenter regained control of the aircraft and managed to get it and the injured crew back to Bien Hoa Air Base. Later, he said, 'It is my belief that this story could not have been told by any other member of my crew had Levitow failed to perform his heroic action.'"

There were not many more U.S. Air Force AC-47 missions after this heroic action by Airman Levitow. The flight of Spooky 71 was a fitting climax to four years of intense flying of aircraft that were then a quarter century old—way past their prime by every known aeronautical standard. To people who know and love the ubiquitous Gooney Bird, it was no surprise—just further proof that this faithful machine does not live by the rules set for other flying machines.

Dropping leaflets was another of the C-47's duties during the Korean War. Two members of the Army's Psychological Warfare Division fight the tendency for the leaflets to return inside the plane. Over 180 million leaflets were dropped from Gooneys during that period. (USAF photo)

Loading ammunition for the 7.62mm cannon for the AC-47 Dragonships was the duty of the armament crew during 1966 operations in Vietnam. (L to R) S/Sgt John R. Boineau, S/Sgt. Carl R. Starwalt and M/Sgt. Norris W. Johnson. (USAF photo)

Inside view of the AC-47 fuselage showing the miniguns in position for firing. The usual crew for Dragonship operations was seven men; three armament specialists operated and reloaded the guns. (USAF photo)

10

The Legend Goes On and On

We badly need an aircraft which will provide the DC-3's reliability, its same ease of maintenance, and a similar low cost. One approach could be to marry a modern turboprop engine to a modern airframe. Surely our design capabilities are great enough to create a plane as advanced...as the DC-3 was in its day.

—Senator A. S. "Mike" Monroney
Former Chairman, U.S. Senate Aviation Subcommittee

There were over 10,600 DC-3s and their military counterparts manufactured in the United States between 1936 and 1946. Today, more than six decades after the last Gooney Bird rolled off the Douglas assembly lines, an estimated 1,000 of them are still flying in almost every nation in the world. Many others are found seemingly abandoned on the edge of foreign airfields stripped of engines and parts. But, just as Senator Monroney hoped in his plea above, turbine engines are being married, not to a new aircraft, but to the old, reliable Gooney Bird by several firms in the U.S. They are being completely overhauled, refurbished and outfitted with the latest turboprops. Or, if desired, new, more powerful Pratt & Whitney piston engines can be furnished.

No one would have dared predict that the Gooney which had done so much for the war effort during World War II would also have an impact on postwar aviation and still be around to participate in wars all over the globe including two more major conflicts in which the United States was involved.

The impetus given to aeronautics during the World War II years brought forth great promise for the future of aviation. "In a short time," the experts said, "the DC-3 will be replaced by newer, faster jet transports and will eventually go to the airplane graveyard like the Stinsons, Boeings and Fords of yesteryear."

The experts were wrong. True, great advancements in aircraft performance have been made. Jets replaced piston engines, and transoceanic flights from the United States to all the other continents are so commonplace that the world might be tempted to forget planes were once as slow and old-fashioned in design as the DC-3. But no one reckoned with the astonishing tenacity of the Gooney Bird to stay in the air, and this includes the Civil Aeronautics Board, which in 1942 decreed that it could not justify certifying the airworthiness of DC-3s to carry passengers past 1947. The deadline was extended year after year until finally, in 1953, the board decided that, in the future, there would be no limitation on any DC-3 that could pass the required routine inspections.

Following the Second World War, surplus C-47s glutted the used airplane market. Twelve hundred dollars and a commercial pilot's license were all that was needed to put an ex-military pilot

This DC-2 was formerly used by the Finnish Air Force and national airline. It was converted into a coffee house in Hameenlinna, Finland, and later preserved in a museum. (Photo courtesy Finnish Air Force)

During the "winter war" with Russia, this Finnish DC-2 was used as a fighter and bomber. Note bomb racks under the fuselage and the single machine gun in the nose. The pilot-aimed bomb sight can be seen outside the cockpit window. (Photo courtesy Finnish Air Force)

Bonanza Airlines flight over the Bouder Dam. Many local service airlines began operations with DC-3s formerly operated by larger airlines. (Photo courtesy Robert Kopitzke)

into the airline business. Although Douglas had discontinued production of all models of the DC-3, thousands of requests for spare parts were being received. Potential operators asked about modifying the austere bucket-seat models into comfortable commercial versions. Requests were made to upgrade the instruments and add new navigation and communications devices.

To satisfy what the company perceived to be a demand for an improved Gooney, Douglas decided to redesign and market its own improvements in a faster, updated model—the DC-3S or Super DC-3.

Three-and-a-half feet longer than the original Gooney from which it was derived, the Super Three had more powerful engines, squared-off wingtips, larger vertical fin, and more streamlined cowlings and wheel fairings. The tail wheel was made partially retractable, the main wheels were made fully retractable, and the outer wing panels were swept back about four degrees at their trailing edges to compensate for the shift of the center of gravity to the rear. These improvements boosted the speed to 200 mph with a load of over thirty passengers. Douglas publicists proudly announced in press releases that the Super DC-3 was "capable of carrying on indefatigably in the noble tradition of its famous ancestor."

Unfortunately, the face lifting didn't prove exciting to commercial buyers. The U.S. Navy procured one hundred and one, which were designated R4D-8s, but orders from other customers totaled only three which were bought by Capital Airlines. Potential Gooney buyers preferred the plain DC-3 without the added frills; some referred to the Super Gooney as "Donald Douglas's Edsel" after the Ford Motor Co.'s disappointing model that was rejected by the public.

In seeking ways to improve the DC-3, many other innovations were tried. In 1949 British engine manufacturer Armstrong Siddeley installed two Mamba turboprops on a Royal Air Force Dakota only

A number of C-47s were modified to train navigators in the Air Force Reserve after World War II. The flying classrooms, designated TC-47s, could accommodate a dozen students. (USAF photo)

to test the engines. It flew successfully and the aircraft was reconverted back to radial engines later.

British European Airways Corporation decided that the old shape of the Gooney was satisfactory but that the new jet technology powerplants might give their DC-3s new life. The company installed Rolls-Royce Dart turboprop engines from a British Viscount in two of their DC-3s to test engine performance of the Darts as well as to see if the planes would deliver more speed and power.

A newcomer to aviation in the immediate postwar era, the turboprop had arrived on the scene without the backlog of military experience which, previously, had proved to be invaluable in launching new engines—whether piston or jet—on commercial carriers. Relatively little was then known about the problems that turboprop operation would impose on the civil operator. The answers to ground handling, maintenance, operating techniques, and traffic control lay in getting as much flying time in flight as possible with this combination of new technology wedded to a proven airframe.

Conversion on two Dakotas was accomplished at Hucknall, England, with only minor difficulties. The result was aircraft with a maximum gross weight of 28,000 pounds, a cruising speed of 202 mph at 25,000 feet, and a jet fuel consumption of 120 imperial gallons per hour.

It was decided that the planes should be used on regular freight runs so that some revenue would be generated during the test program. Regularly scheduled service with these "fast freighters" began on August 15, 1951, between London and Hannover, and later between London, Copenhagen, Paris and Milan.

Interesting developments cropped up as the tests were being conducted. A Pan American crew cruising over Europe in a new pressurized Douglas DC-7C was startled to be overtaken by a DC-3 flying higher than they were. The airline found out quickly that there had to be restrictions on certain types of cargo. For example, an ear-shattering explosion can occur from a case of champagne in an unpressurized cabin at 25,000 feet. It was quickly found that the turboprop version of the Gooney couldn't carry bottled goods, livestock or fresh fruit at the most fuel-efficient altitudes for the engines.

The pilots loved this "new" DC-3. The engine proved very satisfactory from the maintenance point of view and was remarkably free of the minor troubles caused by vibration which plague the piston engine. Mechanics liked it because it was easily accessible and oil consumption was low. Flight crews and passengers liked it in flight because it gave a smooth ride and was exceptionally free of vibration in the air. Once again, the unbelievable had happened. The Gooney Bird had scored another aviation "first." However, lack of interest by the airlines and anticipated problems with certification resulted in abandonment of the idea at the time. It would take 25 years to bring the concept to economic fruition.

It was midnight at Washington's National Airport. An Eastern Air Lines maintenance crew was checking out a Lockheed Constellation for its regular flight to Miami. Inside the maintenance office, a foreman called out to a group of four men, "Ready to go on your midnight ride?"

An Air Force Reserve officer gets a "fix" in the astrodome of a TC-47 used to train navigators in the Air Force after the Korean War. (USAF photo)

A few Gooney Birds were equipped with retractable skis for snow operations. However, they did not provide the required operational flexibility until wheels were included in the assembly. (USAF photo)

"All set," one replied.

"O.K. Two men will ride in the cockpit and two on the tug. The police will meet us at the gate."

The gates at the southern end of the nation's capital airport were opened and several policemen on motorcycles were waiting. Out of the Eastern hangar rolled a wingless DC-3 being towed by an airplane tug onto the airport street. The policemen started up their motorcycles and went ahead to stop traffic.

The plane was being taken to the National Air Museum (now the National Air & Space Museum) because Dr. Paul Garber, chief curator at the museum, knew of the record the DC-3 had written in aviation's history books. In 1948, he had contacted Capt. Eddie Rickenbacker, then Eastern's president, and suggested that the airline should earmark one of its Threes for permanent display in the museum. Rickenbacker agreed and on this date—November 21, 1956—one of their fleet with a distinguished record was selected for permanent display. It had flown eight and one-half million miles, carried 213,000 passengers since its maiden flight in 1937 and had averaged ten and one-half hours of service per day.

Appropriately, the official presentation was made in 1953 during the celebration of the fiftieth anniversary of the Wright brothers' first successful flights at Kitty Hawk.

After its many years of faithful service, there was one mishap that awaited this veteran. It occurred when it was being lifted aloft in the National Air and Space Museum's air transportation gallery in 1976. Walter J. Boyne, then on the NASM staff and later its director, was in charge of displaying all the aircraft. The Eastern DC 3 weighing 17,500 pounds was the heaviest plane to be suspended in the new building. He explains what happened as it was being raised into position by expert riggers:

"Everything went well until there was a sound like a rifle shot and the wing tip dropped, hitting the floor and bending it. The problem was that a clamp on the round trusses of the ceiling had opened, because of a slight side load, and allowed one cable to run out as the clamp slid down the truss.

"I felt miserable, of course, but we got a wingtip from the Air Force and had it installed, buffed out and ready to go again. As it started to go up, a photographer stepped backward on a piece of metal and caused a bang just like the first one. It was a false alarm but it scared the hell out of all of us."

The DC-3 became the 163rd exhibit given to the museum. It enjoys the place of honor it so richly deserves in the world's most

On March 19, 1952, the first ice island landing was made by a ski-equipped C-47. Piloted by Lt. Col. Joseph O. Fletcher, the plane was used to establish a weather reporting and scientific station in the Arctic Ocean called Ice Station Bravo (also known as T-3). (USAF photo)

This Air Force C-47 had made a forced landing on Ice Station Bravo in the Arctic Ocean and could not be flown out. It was "cannibalized" and only the shell remained on this wind-eroded mound of ice. The ice island had to be evacuated in 1961 when a 2,500-foot runway began to break up and drift away. (USAF photo)

The first American plane to land at the North Pole was an Air Force Gooney Bird piloted by Lt. Cols. William P. Benedict (left) and Joseph O. Fletcher. The date: May 3, 1952. Fletcher was the commander of the Alaskan Air Command's scientific expedition on T-3, the floating ice island. (USAF photo)

popular museum. It is permanently suspended in the exhibit area along with a Ford Tri-Motor and a Boeing 247, the latter owned by United Airlines and flown by Roscoe Turner and Clyde Pangborn during the 1934 London-Melbourne race.

More DC-3s were in scheduled airline service at one time than planes of any other type. In the 1950s, one hundred and seventy-four airlines in seventy nations boasted that the DC-3 was still in their fleets. Three nations—Chile, Hungary and the Netherlands—have honored the DC-3 on airmail stamps. In 1953, China issued a paper note, worth about two cents in American money, with the illustration of a DC-3 on it. A church in the Cotswolds in England installed a memorial window commemorating the Dakota's use by the RAF during World War II.

For a number of years, the Federal Aviation Administration (FAA) and its predecessor organization, the Civil Aeronautics Authority (CAA), used as many as 55 DC-3s to check the radio navigation facilities along the nation's airways. When the Gooneys were replaced by small jet transports and were gradually sold by the General Services Administration (GSA), the FAA decided that one should be preserved for its historic value. The one chosen had been born with an Army Air Force serial number but saw service with the Navy as an R4D-7. It was later transformed internally into a VIP transport and designated an R4D-6V. In 1957, it was transferred to the FAA where it was modified with flight inspection equipment. Declared surplus in 1983, it was restored two years later and used at air shows and for educational purposes. In 1994, the last of the FAA's Gooneys was transferred to the GSA for sale to the highest bidder.

The continued demand for DC-3s has kept their price at a high level. The first DC-3s cost American Airlines $110,000 each. Today, elegantly fitted DC-3s cannot be purchased for less than about $500,000. To keep up with their continued usage, there are a few companies still making spare parts. The avionics required to fly safely in today's crowded skies are more expensive by far than the original aircraft itself.

It is not surprising that refurbished DC-3s are still used by a few corporations as executive transports with exquisitely-tailored interiors. One, owned by a Houston lumber company had mink-covered doorknobs, while one owned by a Texas rancher included divans and reclining chairs upholstered in unborn calf skins. Almost all DC-3s owned for use as executive transports have galleys, dressing rooms, beds, hi-fi, and "refreshment consoles" installed.

The fancier they get, the fewer passengers these private planes hold. Those still flying as scheduled carriers around the world invariably have more than the twenty-one passengers originally intended. Instead of a single row of seven seats on one side of the aisle and a double row of fourteen seats on the other, many now seat thirty-two passengers. One foreign airline changed the seat size so that forty passengers could be seated. And another has accommodated fifty passengers sitting precariously in canvas hammocks strung throughout the cabin.

While these passenger loads make FAA inspectors and Douglas engineers blanch, a near record number of passengers is held by a Gooney that was called upon to evacuate refugees from a Bolivian town threatened by floods in 1949. Ninety-three people were crammed inside. True, most of them were children, but this number of humans, plus a crew of three, made this a hard record to beat. But it was. During the Vietnam War, 98 refugee orphans and five attendants were evacuated from the village of Da Lat by a Continental Air Services DC-3 under contract to Air Vietnam. The three crew members aboard made this the all-time record which has yet come to the author's attention.

During World War II, about 700 C-47s were "loaned" to the Soviet Union. With Douglas providing tools and plans, the Soviets produced 6,157 more of various models. Called at first the PS-84, it was later designated the Li-2, for its "inventor" Boris Lisonov who had been sent to the United States in 1935 to arrange for the first licensed production of the Douglas design.

The Li-2 differed from the standard DC-3/C-47 in that it had an extra window aft of the cockpit, modified engine nacelles and cowlings, and a right-hand passenger door. The engines, also copied from American engines, were ASH-62 radials developing 985 horsepower each. Maximum speed is estimated at 170 knots with a maximum range of 1,460 miles.

The Li-2 production line began in Moskva but moved to Tashkent in 1941. The Russian Gooney was the mainstay of Aeroflot for many years and joint ventures were formed with nine post-war satellite nations. A few are still being flown in Poland, Czechoslovakia and Mongolia.

During World War II, some of the Li-2s flew armed. Gun turrets were installed in the top of the fuselage where the navigator's

A ski-equipped C-47 successfully landed and took off from the Greenland Ice Cap in 1950, at the highest known ice cap altitude in the world. The purpose was to determine if air rescue operations were possible in this area. Lt. Gorn Erik Jensen, a Royal Danish Air Force meteorologist, plants the Danish flag for his country. (USAF photo)

Two members of the USAF party that landed at the North Pole place the National Ensign on top of the world, May 3, 1952. At the base of the oil drum monument are glass jars containing dated notes documenting the occasion. (Douglas Aircraft Co. photo)

astrodome was normally located. Two smaller caliber machine guns were mounted in side windows which were cut just aft of the rear door. Some had bomb racks attached to the bottom of the fuselage.

Very few Americans have flown in the wartime Russian version. However, Colonel Howard R. Jarrell, a U.S. Air Force pilot, was accorded a rare bit of Russian hospitality when he was flown from Vladivostok to Tashkent in September 1944. Jarrell had landed a disabled B-29 in Russian territory after a raid on Japan; his crew and the aircraft were interned because Russia was still neutral against Japan.

When the Russians finally decided to release Jarrell and his crew, they were brought to the airport at Vladivostok and driven to the open door of a waiting C-47. To them it was like a bit of home to see that old reliable DC-type airplane sitting there.

Asked about his flight, Jarrell replied, "It wasn't a bad trip after we got used to how the pilots flew. After takeoff from Vladivostok we never got more than 100 or 200 feet above the ground for the entire three-thousand mile trip.

"The pilots, both lieutenants, were between thirty and forty years of age and estimated they had about seventeen thousand flying hours each. This included all of their time in the air. Their training was progressive from ground mechanic to flight engineer, to radio operator, to navigator, to copilot, and finally pilot. They did not keep separate records on how much pilot or copilot time they had.

"The weather was good all the way as it would be almost anywhere in the world at 200 feet and every foot of it was right on top of the Trans-Siberian railroad.

"There were no parachutes on board and it's just as well. But there was one strange piece of equipment that we thought ought to have been copied. In the rear passenger cabin they had a potbellied stove and a cord of wood stacked neatly beside it. The stove had handles on it so that it could be thrown out the door in case of fire.

"The turret, mounted where our navigator's astrodome is, was manually operated and its gun was equivalent to our air-cooled .30 caliber machine gun. The interpreter told us that it was the only weapon necessary because no one could get under them to attack. However, we were told that some models had waist guns installed that could be manned in case of broadside attacks.

"All of the equipment, except the turret gun and stove, was standard American equipment. All the placards were in English as well as all the instruments. When I asked where they had gotten this plane, our interpreter insisted that it had been made in Russia, even when I pointed out that I didn't think so. He insisted that it was their Li-2 and had been definitely made in Russia.

"The way they flew that ship made my hair stand on end. All the landing approaches were the kind our fighter pilots liked to make. They would zoom in under full power at one hundred feet, rack it over in a tight bank, yank back, and wait until the runway showed up again in front of the nose.

"Before each flight, I noticed that a mechanic always boarded and pre flighted the plane before the rest of the crew arrived. He would shut it down and disappear before the pilot came aboard. The pilot would then start the engines, zoom out to takeoff position and barrel down the runway without any kind of cockpit or engine check. There was never any doubt that they liked the airplane and had as much trust in it as did American pilots."

A Japanese Gooney made of plywood sits in a Japanese salvage yard surrounded by all metal sister ships. This photo was taken early in the occupation years. Although the fuselage seems more square, the nose contour was reportedly unchanged from the Douglas design. (Photo courtesy Robert C. Mikesh)

The proud lines of the DC-3 prevail in this Showa-built L2D3 built by the Japanese during World War II. Square windows were added behind the pilots' seats after removal of the forward bulkhead. A round window was added in the forward access door. (Photo courtesy Robert C. Mikesh)

In his book, *Report on the Russians*, William L. White painted a vivid picture of what it was like to fly in the Soviet's commercial version of the DC-3 from a non-pilot's point of view:

"You get aboard. There are no seat belts. There is no sign warning against smoking; if you prefer to burn alive in a takeoff crash, that is a matter of personal conscience and no concern to the crew. Once the door slams shut, the pilot starts the motors, which have been cold since the night before. If they run at all, he releases the brakes, guns the plane on down the runway. You gather speed and clear the runway by maybe ten feet. At this instant the pilot makes his turn by the process of tilting one wing up toward the zenith and the other down until its tip is digging potatoes on the adjoining farm. Once pointed on his course he levels off and, if there are no mountains, he continues at this altitude from 50 to 100 feet, scaring Kolkholz cows, Sovhoz chickens, and the passengers."

The Russians were not the only ones to copy and use the Gooney during World War II. As mentioned in the first chapter, the Nakajima Aircraft Co. of Japan had secured manufacturing rights from Douglas for the DC-2 in 1934. When the DC-3 was introduced, rights were obtained in 1938 to manufacture it, ostensibly to modernize its civil air fleet. Unknown in the U.S., however, the Japanese Imperial Navy instigated the purchase because its leaders saw the aircraft's potential as a military transport to support its aviation units. Despite passage of an embargo against exporting aircraft to Japan later, a loophole in the Embargo Act allowed engines, propellers and parts to be exported as "replacements on commercial airlines in Japan." Douglas engineers went to Japan to supervise production under the licensing agreement that preceded the embargo cutoff date of June 1938. Concurrently, Japanese engineers from Showa came to the Douglas factory to study American aircraft production methods.

Five semi-finished fuselages and related parts were purchased from Douglas and the first Japanese-built DC-3 rolled out to the flying line of the Mitsui-owned Showa Airplane Co. in September 1939. Showa eventually built 430 of their version of the DC-3, including 75 cargo models with reinforced flooring and wide loading door.

Several designations were given to the Japanese-built DC-2s and -3s which eventually became the L2D series. The "L2" signified transport, second Navy type, and "D" stood for Douglas. Thus, the L2D2 was a DC-2 and the DC-3 was labeled as an L2D3. The Allies, early in the war, assigned code names to all known Japanese aircraft to avoid identification confusion. The Japanese DC-2 became "Tess" and the DC-3 became "Tabby."

An outline of the Douglas DC-3 is shown superimposed on the center engine of the McDonnell Douglas DC-10. The normal passenger load on the DC-3 was 21, while the DC-10 can carry up to 380. (Drawing courtesy of McDonnell Douglas Co.)

As the Japanese swung into full production with the Tabby, the shape changed slightly. Kinsei 51 engines of 1300 h.p. were substituted for the 700 hp Wright Cyclones which had been copied by Mitsubishi. Some models carried a glazed blister above the forward cabin section containing a flex-mounted 13 mm machine gun and 7 mm machine guns mounted in the rear window on each side of the fuselage. As Robert C. Mikesh, former curator at the National Air & Space Museum and expert on Japanese aircraft, noted, "These later versions had better performance than the Douglas-built model by virtue of their greater power and lighter weight.

"On the L2D3, the cowling was more streamlined and the propeller was capped with a shapely spinner. More noticeable, however, were the three additional windows behind the pilot's compartment. Internally, the bulkhead behind the pilots' seats was removed which placed the flight crew of four in one compartment. The forward access door on the port side had its own distinctive window."

The shortage of aircraft metals in Japan by 1943 led to substitutions that would have grayed the heads of Douglas engineers. At first, the less critical components of the Tabby were redesigned and made exclusively of wood, such as the ailerons, vertical fin, rudder, horizontal stabilizers, elevators and doors. Thirty aircraft with wooden components were eventually manufactured and flown, apparently with good results.

As the war progressed and materials became even more scarce, a single all-wooden test model, designated L2D5, was produced. According to Colonel George W. Johnson, who saw the fuselage during the Allied cleanup in Japan after hostilities had ceased, "It was recognizable by its shape, but its strangeness didn't hit me for quite a while. This plane and the other parts of it were made of wood...I couldn't believe it!

"After my initial surprise, I was really impressed at how well the plywood skin was shaped with compound curves to fit as smoothly as the normal aluminum skin would have. When I first saw it, it appeared nearly ready to have engines hung on it and to be flown. I heard later that it was a static test fuselage and main wing section. The war ended before the tests could be conducted."

In the 1960s, the Federal Aviation Administration had seriously sought to encourage the aviation industry to come up with a replacement for the DC-3. Former U.S. Senator A.S. "Mike" Monroney (D-Oklahoma), then chairman of the Senate Commerce Aviation Subcommittee, recommended an appropriation of $5 million to assist in the development of five prototypes in the United States. "What this country needs," he said, "is a new DC-3 that still sells for DC-3 prices."

Alan S. Boyd, then chairman of the Civil Aeronautics Board, described the requirements for the DC-3 replacement. It should:

HORSEPOWER & POWERPLANT
985 HP each
2 Ash-62, radial

DIMENSIONS
Span 95 ft
Length 64 ft 6 inches

MAX. SPEED
170 knots 5,000 ft

RANGE
1,460 nautical miles 120 knots

ARMAMENT

The Russians copied the DC-3 design and designated it the PS-84 and later the Li-2. Some Li-2s were outfitted with machine guns located in the navigator's astrodome position. A few had wood-burning stoves installed for passenger comfort and for mechanics to fire up in sub-zero temperatures when they had to stay with their aircraft on the ground. (USAF photo)

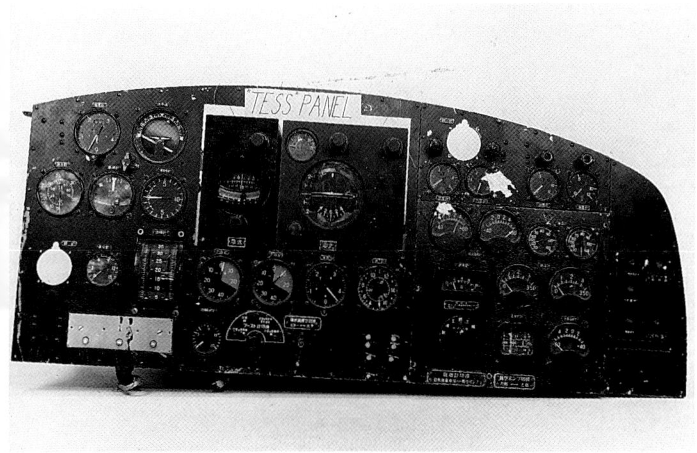

One Japanese version of the DC-3 was labeled "Tess" by the Americans for easier identification. Shown is a Tess instrument panel. (Photo courtesy Robert C. Mikesh)

Another company that is flying DC-3s for nostalgic sightseeing purposes is Vintage Air Tours operating in Florida, mainly between Orlando, Ft. Lauderdale and Key West. Air Cruise America flies an executive-styled Gooney on champagne excursions throughout Southern California from Long Beach. It was formerly owned by John Travolta and several corporations. On April 23, 1995, Laura Burtonboy and Jacob Kuryan were married with a nostalgia theme aboard the Air Cruise America DC-3 with 21 guests in attendance while the aircraft was on a round-robin flight over Los Angeles, Catalina Island, Oceanside and Seal Beach.

Piedmont Airlines, one of the many air carriers that flew DC-3s, decided to acquire a DC-3 and use it for public relations and marketing purposes. Restored to a 19-seat configuration, it began a tour of air shows in the early 1990s. When USAir acquired Piedmont Airlines, it was feared that the DC-3 would be put up for sale. However, proud of its heritage through the acquisition of other airlines such as Mohawk, Lake Central, Pacific Southwest, and smaller carriers, all of which flew DC-3s, the company decided to continue flying it under the Piedmont colors. Former USAir and Piedmont captains ferry it to its scheduled air show destinations where it is put on display.

Continental Airlines also has refurbished a DC-3 for "sentimental flight" usage. Bought by American Airlines in 1940, it flew the system for seven years and was then sold to Trans-Texas Airways where it flew until 1969 when it was sold to a plane broker in San Antonio. Five years later it was back in the air again with Provincetown-Boston Airlines, a Continental Airlines subsidiary. In 1988, it was transferred to Bar Harbor Airlines and then mothballed in Florida where it was located by Capt. Jim Minor, a DC-10 captain with Continental Airlines, who had begun flying DC-3s in 1959 with Trans-Texas. The company decided to purchase it for historical and publicity purposes and provided some support for its operation. The plane was completely refurbished with improved sound insulation and an authentic Forties interior by volunteers who formed the Continental Airlines Historical Society, a separate non-profit organization. Sherri Minor, Jim's wife, flies as stewardess in a period uniform and passes out magazines of the 1940s era while her husband and other former DC-3 captains fly the rejuvenated DC-3 to air shows throughout the country.

Despite its age, the demand for DC-3s continues high. Modifying and updating Gooneys became big business after World War II. One of the most active of the original Gooney Bird renovators was the firm started in October 1945 by Bill Remmert and Bob Werner, of St. Louis. Remmert-Werner made their first conversion of a military C-47 into a civilian DC-3 in December 1946, and subsequently converted scores of Gooneys to private business use from either the military or airline configurations.

As the demand for cleaned-up Gooneys continued through the 1950s and 1960s, Remmert-Werner found that their problem was not finding buyers but locating airplanes. Their search for plane skeletons, parts and pieces widened. Since Gooney Birds have flown in every corner of the world, there was no limit to where they might be found.

C. S. Weaks, advertising manager for Remmert-Werner, told of the origin of some of the planes that may be still flying as plush executive transports even in the 1990s:

"We would put together DC-3s from parts obtained from all over the country. We had our own fleet of large trucks, and occasionally pick up a fuselage here, right wing there, center section over yonder, and so on, until we turned up a whole airplane. I recall one plane in particular where the fuselage came from Minneapolis, the center section from Arizona, one wing from California, the other wing from Florida, the landing gear from New Jersey, the engines from our own shops, and the tail surfaces and controls from various U.S. surplus sales. It took us about three months to overhaul them all, put them together in the shape of a DC-3, dress it up, and get it in the air."

There was a C-47 in Japan that Remmert-Werner wanted. It had been abandoned by the U.S. Air Force and given to the Japa-

A Showa-produced L2D3 Tabby was photographed at an airplane graveyard at Peiping, China, in 1946. Note extra windows behind the pilot's window. (Photo courtesy Robert C. Mikesh)

nese. The Japanese had invited bids, but the company passed this one up. Reason: "The successful bidder must remove aircraft from its present location 200 feet from the top of Mount Fujiyama."

The availability of this C-47 had been occasioned by the bad luck of Major John Fowle, an Air Force pilot, who had become lost in bad weather and crashed into the side of the famous mountain in full flight. The only injury suffered in the accident was Fowle's black eye.

In recent years, Warren Basler of Oshkosh, Wisconsin, has become the world's leading modifier and refurbisher of DC-3s. A fixed base operator and owner of an air freight service, he had his first flight in a DC-3 in 1955. Today, he has more than 10,000 hours in them after purchasing his first one in 1960. He formed a partnership with a Green Bay businessman and began flying freight and passenger charters on fishing trips, and transporting football and hockey teams to their games. By 1995 he had owned and sold about 100 Goonies; his sales agreements include the right to repurchase them if they are put up for resale. He has owned one Gooney five times.

Basler has purchased Gooneys all over the world in an as-is, where-is condition. However, he prefers to purchase military planes because "they tend to be well-maintained."

The Showa Airplane Co. production line of L2Ds in Japan during World War II. Engine and cowl installations were different from that of the C-47. Japanese Goonies were also produced by Nakajima for the Japan Air Transport Co. (Photo courtesy Robert C. Mikesh)

Brig. Gen. Jimmy Stewart, USAFR (right) relaxes on location of "Sentimental Journey," a film dramatizing a senior airline captain's reunion with an old friend, the venerable DC-3. (Left) Ferde Grofe, producer, and Donald Douglas, Jr., represent the Donald Douglas Museum. (Photo courtesy Ferde Grofe Films)

While the turboprop version of the DC-3 mentioned earlier had been an aviation "first," it did not prove successful at the time (1951). But John M. Conroy, a California builder of strange-looking planes like the outsized Super Guppy series used to haul missiles for the U.S. space program, saw a possibility for revival of the basic idea. In 1969, he took two British-made Rolls-Royce Dart turboprops from a British-built Viscount and hung them on a C-53 built in 1942. The result was called the Turbo Three that a test pilot described as "silky smooth and remarkably quiet in flight even though turboprops are noisy outside the airplane." Its first flight was made on May 13, 1969.

From the pilot's standpoint, the only noticeable difference flying the Turbo Three was that besides a rapid acceleration during takeoff, the torque effect was to the right instead of the left. For reasons only the British engine manufacturers know, the props turn in the opposite direction from their American counterparts.

While the Turbo Three handled like any other DC-3 in flight, its true airspeed at 10,000 feet ranged from 182 knots at the start of a trip to 190 knots at the end. At 15,000 feet, speed increased to as much as 235 mph while jet fuel consumption decreased from 100 gallons per hour to 90. Conroy also modified a Super DC-3, called it the Super Turbo Three and first flew it in 1974.

Why would anyone want to buy a jet-age version of an "old" airplane? Jack Conroy answered the question this way:

"Both the airframe and the powerplants are the most reliable in the air today. Engine overhaul and maintenance are drastically reduced and fuel cost per mile is about the same as the piston job because of higher speed and less expensive fuel. The Turbo Three could carry higher gross weights which means greater payloads. It's faster and can fly over most weather and operate from shorter strips at higher altitudes because of power availability."

If two turboprops on a DC-3 can increase the payload, speed and altitude capabilities so much, what could three turboprops do for it?

Conroy decided to find out. On November 2, 1977, he and veteran airline and racing pilot Clay Lacy climbed aboard a DC-3 equipped with three Pratt & Whitney PT6SA-46 turboprops and took to the California skies for another aviation "first" with the Tri-Turbo Three. The flight not only met but exceeded even Conroy's expectations. The Tri-Turbo Three's performance was better than that of the two-engine version with the British-made engines.

The Tri-Turbo Three could cruise at 230 mph and carry up to 12,000 pounds of payload. According to Conroy, "Its increased performance, low operating costs, versatility, and inexpensive acquisition make the Tri-Turbo Three an ideal aircraft for performing either commercial or military missions, particularly maritime surveillance, search and rescue, photographic or mapping missions. It can also be used for Arctic or bush operations by commuter airlines, or as a special purpose aircraft."

The Tri-Turbo Three had outboard wing tanks installed which provided a range of 3,000 miles. It could take off, climb to 10,000 feet cruising altitude, and with the center engine shut off, fly a 3,000-mile mission with one hour of fuel reserve.

One pilot who flew the Tri-Turbo Three commented that "right from opening the throttles it is apparent this is not a modified DC-3. It is a new airplane in terms of performance." However, he added, "on three engines, it becomes noticeably heavier on the controls and response appears to be a little slower."

The Tri-Turbo Three did not become popular. Conroy took the plane on a world tour and it was demonstrated at the Farnborough and Paris air shows. It was sold to Polair in 1979 and was operated on skis in the arctic for research and aerial reconnaissance. It was scrapped at Mojave, California, in 1991. A swing-tail version was proposed for military cargo operations but no buyers came forth.

Another firm that turned to conversions to turbo-props was United States Aircraft Corporation at Van Nuys, California. One turbo-equipped DC-3, called the Turbo-Express and DC-3TP was produced which was eventually sold to an Alaskan operator.

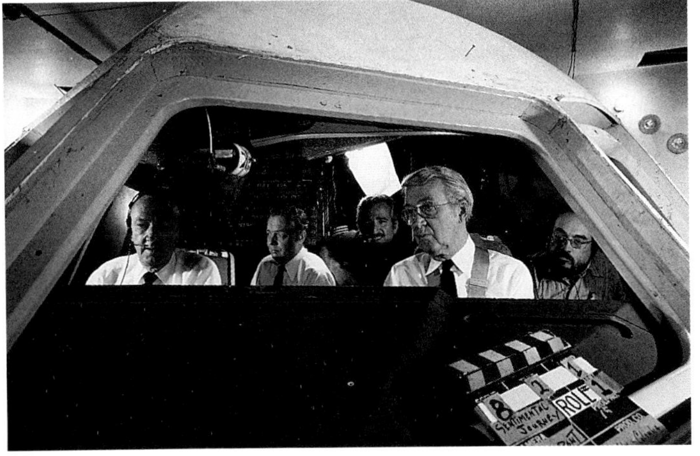

Jimmy Stewart on the set of a DC-3 mockup at the McDonnell Douglas facility, Long Beach, California, is joined by supporting players in a nostalgic tribute to the immortal DC-3. (Photo courtesy Ferde Grofe Films)

Donald W. Douglas, Sr. (left) sits in the pilot's seat of a Super DC-3, with his son Donald Douglas, Jr. Both had high hopes that the Super Gooney would enable the production line to continue after World War II but just over 100 were built. (Douglas Aircraft Co. photo)

It remained for Warren Basler to carry on the twin turbo concept. He stretched the DC-3 by 40 inches, strengthened it and installed two Pratt & Whitney PT6A turbo prop engines that will enable the Gooney to climb to 24,000 feet and cruise at 220 knots. Additional fuel tanks are installed in the wings and engine nacelles. The square windows are replaced with round ones and when used for cargo, it will accommodate five LD-3 freight containers.

Since the original installation of the turboprops, Basler has improved the Gooney even further. He now produces the Basler Turbo 67 (BT-67) which features the Pratt & Whitney Canada PT6A-67R engines and Hartzell five-bladed propellers. The first one flew in July 1989 and was certificated by the FAA the following February.

The BT-67 features a "pilot friendly cockpit" with the most modern avionics, automatic pilot, radar, and navigation systems. The advanced avionics alone may cost up to $250,000. Landing gear, hydraulics, fire control, electrical and flight control systems have been modernized. The maximum useful load is 13,000 pounds, compared to the piston-engine Pratt & Whitney R-1830-powered DC-3s limit of 9,085 pounds. Maximum cruise speed at 12,500

Donald W. Douglas, Sr. poses happily beside the first Super DC-3 to come off the production line before its world-wide sales tour. (Douglas Aircraft Co. photo)

American Airlines Flagship Knoxville greets visitors to the C. R. Smith Museum in Fort Worth, Texas. Retired from the American fleet in 1948, it was purchased by a group of company retirees who restored it for the museum. It had flown 50,549 hours before the restoration. (Photo by Chet Snedden for Viewpoint Publishing Co.)

feet is 205 knots; with long range fuel tanks, the range is 2,140 nautical miles. Single-engine ceiling is 14,000 feet.

Basler points out the advantage of the turbo-equipped BT-67 over the piston engine version:

"Over the years, the DC-3 has proven by experience that it can have a practically unlimited service life with only normal care and maintenance. However, the DC-3 has now found a different kind of limit: an economic limit brought about by its power plant. Piston engines and their components are no longer competitive. Reliability, maintenance cost, fuel cost, and safety are simply not satisfactory in terms of today's technology. Another serious limitation is the increasing scarcity of aviation gasoline."

Basler has reconditioned Gooneys for foreign air forces. Several were made into gunships with side-firing .50 caliber machine guns for the Salvadoran Air Force. Basler fully expects the Gooney to continue to prove its worth well into the 21st century.

In 1943, someone decided to put floats on five Goonies, label them "Ducks" and make them into amphibians as was mentioned in Chapter 7. In the mid-1980s, Louis O. Hilton and members of HBF Inc. located at Folsom's Air Service on Moosehead Lake, Greenville, Maine, decided to revive the idea and put pontoons on a C-53D which, with the seaplane conversion, became a C-47C. One purpose was to start a shuttle service between Greenville and Boston. The sets of floats, made during World War II by the EDO Corporation for the seaplane version, had disappeared; that is, all except two pairs which were owned by B. Savage in Dallas who had obtained them with the intention of making them into a large catamaran. He sold one pair to Hilton.

It took about five years of work but the conversion to an amphibian was finally accomplished at a cost of about $600,000. The toughest part was making the struts and fittings from scratch based on microfilm of the original drawings. This was accomplished by EDO in 1990. The only one of its kind in the world, the new Duck was first flown from Moosehead Lake at Greenville, Maine, in September 1991 and was subsequently exhibited at a number of airshows.

In the event that a Gooney Bird is grounded permanently for any reason, it doesn't necessarily mean that it must end up in the junk yard or have its parts sold off to keep others in the air. H. L. "Smokey" Roland of Cardiff-by-the-Sea, near San Diego, California, knew what to do with one that was destined not to fly any more. A World War II veteran who had flown 42 missions in England, he bought a C-47 from the Air Force "boneyard" at Davis-Monthan Air Force Base, Arizona. He removed the plane's engines, nacelles, wings and tail and trucked the carcass to San Diego.

Next, he located a former Dodge school bus chassis and bolted the Gooney fuselage firmly to the frame. He mounted a 460-cubic inch Lincoln engine between the axles and installed two 65-gallon gas tanks inside. "I had to cut off four feet of the airplane's john to get her down within the 40-foot maximum length allowed," he said. "But I can get about 10 miles to the gallon so I figure I have a cruising range of 1,300 miles without a pit stop."

Built in 1943 as No. 995 on a military contract, Roland's Gooney mobile home was flown previously by Argonaut Airlines for ten years after World War II, then by Allegheny Airlines before it ended up in the airplane graveyard near Tucson. According to

This Gooney formerly flown by Canadian Pacific Airlines was used as a wind direction indicator at the airport at Whitehorse, Canada. (Photo by Gordon Williams)

Roland, it was hijacked to Cuba twice during its lifetime as an airliner.

Asked how much time and money he had spent converting his Gooney Bird, Roland said, "about 3,000 hours of hard work." He estimated it was worth about $15,000 when he finished. Describing the way people reacted when he cruised California's highways, he said, "They did double-takes, triple-takes and quadruple-takes."

The Remmert-Werner Co. of St. Louis, Missouri, specialized in renovating Gooney Birds for many years. This C-47 fuselage had been turned into a chicken coop by an Alabama farmer. It was rescued by Bill Remmert who found wings, engines and parts of other aircraft and had it rebuilt into a plush transport for executives of a large corporation who were unaware of its former status. (Remmert-Werner photo)

Roland was not the only one to convert a Gooney to a mobile home. At least two other families have taken to the road in theirs. In 1986, Robert Pfeiffer, also of Cardiff, California, converted a Gooney carcass into what he called his "Smile Shuttle." While the front portion retained the famous Gooney nose, the aft portion looked like the space shuttle.

Some have used the Gooney as an immobile home such as the DC-2 that was assembled originally by the Fokker plant in the Netherlands in 1936 and eventually ended up in Finland. It was damaged when it hit a snowdrift in 1951 and the fuselage was converted into a family's summer dwelling near Helsinki.

A number of Gooney Birds have been preserved in different ways around the world. A C-47B, in service with Swiss Air Lines from 1946 until 1964, was sealed and placed on a pedestal outside the Swiss Museum at Lucerne. A Soviet Air Force Li-2 is on permanent display in Czechoslovakia, and another is preserved at Chersky, near the delta of the Kolyma River, on the East Siberian Sea of the Arctic Ocean. There is one outside the Lohausen Airport Museum at Dusseldorf, Germany; another is mounted in flying position with gear extended in Stuttgart, Germany. A DC-3 was used as a restaurant in Norrtalje, Sweden, before being moved to a museum.

Old Gooney hulks continue to be found and rebuilt to be flown again. Here a C-47 is being restored to pristine condition after it was fished out of a Canadian lake. (Remmert-Werner photo)

The Australians also venerated the Dakota by suspending it near the parking lot at the Tullamarine International Airport terminal in Melbourne. It is mounted on a 15-degree roll angle with a seven-degree upward pitch to simulate a DC-3 in flight. Another is hanging from a unique arch at an airport in Victoria. A former C-47 has become part of a McDonald's restaurant at West Lakes, South Australia; still another is featured at a McDonald's hamburger establishment in Western Australia. In Japan, a C-47 is on display at a children's playground at Mito Koura Kuen.

Other nations have featured the Gooney in outdoor display areas. One was mounted at a soccer stadium in Antwerp, Belgium, and was often used as a changing room by a local team. Another was used as a night club in Rio de Janeiro, Brazil, until it was struck by lightning and destroyed in 1980. A Varig DC-3 airliner was retired in Rio Grande do Sul, Brazil, and used as a bar at a seaside resort. An Li-2 was put on permanent exhibit at an amusement park in Pecs, Hungary in 1968.

A DC-2, formerly used as a fighter-bomber by the Finnish Air Force, had an unusual history before it was made into a coffee house in Hameenlinna, Finland. Originally assembled by Fokker in 1935, it was bought by KLM and was sold in 1940 to Swedish Count Carl-Gustav von Rosen and presented it as a gift to Finland. It was promptly made into a bomber by modifying the toilet to hold 24 bombs. External racks were installed under the wings and a machine gun was installed in the mid-fuselage. It was used for supply flights during the "Winter War" and the "Continuation War" and for parachuting patrols behind enemy lines. It was retired in 1955, became a coffee house in 1959 but was later moved to the Aviation Museum of Central Finland at Tikkakoski for permanent display.

Guatemala honored the Gooney by putting it on display at a city park in 1981; however, it was reportedly put back into service in Haiti several years later. Another was in use as a restaurant in Plaza Berlin in Guatemala City.

A C-47 that saw service in the China-Burma-India theater was sold as surplus in 1945 to Canadian Pacific Airline. It was abandoned after an accident in 1970 but was restored in 1977 and mounted atop a pedestal as a wind direction indicator at Whitehorse Airport, Yukon, Canada.

In the United States, a fuselage from a former U.S. Naval Air Transport Service R4D, named Air Line Snack Bar, was located near the airport at Santa Cruz, California in the late 1940s. A Gooney, formerly owned for executive transport by Kerr McGee Oil Industry, Inc., was mounted on pylons at the entrance to the State Fair in Oklahoma Cuty, Oklahoma, in 1977.

The USAF has preserved a number of Gooneys for display. In addition to a C-39 at the USAF Museum at Wright-Patterson Air Force Base, Ohio, 29 other models of the Gooney are on permanent loan to other museums. As noted in Chapter 8, the Que Sera' Sera', the first aircraft to land at the South Pole, is on display at the Navy's Air Museum at Pensacola, Florida. It carries the markings of Air Development Squadron 6, the unit it served in Antarctica.

The Douglas Historical Foundation, created by the Douglas Aircraft Co., sponsored the restoration of a flyable DC-2 beginning in 1982. Its first flight took place at Long Beach, California, on April 25, 1987, and traveled to a number of air shows. It is destined for display at the Museum of Flying at Clover Field.

A former Piedmont Airlines DC-3 was restored for the North Carolina Museum of Life and Science at Durham, North Carolina.

An American Airlines DC-3 can be found at the Richmond County Museum in Augusta, Georgia, as well as at the entrance to the American Airlines C. R. Smith Museum at Fort Worth, Texas.

While in level flight under instrument conditions, this C-47 piloted by Major John A. Fowle and Capt. E. P. Kelley inadvertently crashed into the side of Mount Fujiyama, Japan, on March 7, 1956. The plane ground to a quick halt in the snow and the entire crew escaped injury except for a black eye suffered by Kelley. (USAF photo)

The idea of using turboprops to replace the piston engines of the DC-3s was originally tried on two British European Airways DC-3s in 1951. The cabin was not pressurized. At the high altitudes that were possible because of the jet engines, BEA found that they could not carry bottled goods, fruits or livestock safely. (British European Airways photo)

The Gooney Bird has been venerated in another way—by having its famous profile on postal stamps. Donald N. Nelson, an aerophilatelic expert, has found that no less than 77 nations have portrayed the DC-3 on regular postage, air mail stamps, a U.S. Postal card and stamps known as "semi-postals." Five other countries—Japan, Finland, the Netherlands East Indies, Curcao, and Samoa have also honored the DC-1 or DC-2 in that manner.

Panama was the first country to use the DC-3 on a stamp. In 1937, it issued an air mail stamp with a Gooney likeness to commemorate the 50th anniversary of its fire department. The Panama Canal Zone issued a Gooney stamp to observe the 10th anniversary of the first air mail to the Canal Zone and the 25th anniversary of the canal's opening.

The 20th anniversary of the first air mail service in the United States was honored with a DC-3 being loaded with mail. It was marked simply "DC-3, 1938." Some countries have issued a series of stamps in different denominations that show the DC-3; for example, between 1947 and 1953 Egypt printed 54 air mail stamps. According to Nelson, Venezuela is second in that it issued 35 stamps in 1938 and 1939 in a number of denominations with the picture of the DC-3.

Perhaps the most unusual stamp featuring the Gooney is a large one issued by the Republic of Mali which shows the famous 24-cent inverted Jenny beside a DC-3. When the 50th anniversary of D-Day was to be celebrated in 1994, four countries of the British Commonwealth issued stamps featuring the DC-3. As if to prove how much the Gooney is respected, Nelson says that "stamps depicting the DC-3 have been issued in all but twelve of the 60 years since the day of the first rollout on December 17, 1935." The most recent issuance is one stamp issued by Micronesia in a block of eight to honor pioneers of flight labeled "Donald Douglas DC-3."

Even the most devoted of Gooney buffs realize that someday the familiar purr of its reciprocating engines will be silenced and its familiar shape will disappear from the skies forever. How long before that will happen is anyone's guess. However, looking at the plane's record of survival, it is reasonable to say that anyone reading these words will not be around on that day. The Gooney Bird has already outlasted two generations of airline and military pilots and is still to be found in scheduled service at a few locations in the United States and a number of foreign countries. In fact, there is the strong possibility that a United States Air Force Gooney will be ready to fly six centuries from now! Proof of this statement lies buried deep beneath the snow and ice in the Swiss Alps and therein lies the final story of the incredible saga of the beloved Gooney Bird.

On November 10, 1946, Major Ralph H. Tate began a flight that almost ended tragically but instead, by a strange twist of fate, would be newsworthy long afterward. On that day he filed a flight plan for a C-47 from Vienna, Austria, to Pisa, Italy, by way of Istres, France. On board were eight passengers and a crew of four, including Tate. One of the passengers was Tate's mother, along with three wives of military personnel and an eleven-year-old girl—all en route to Italy on official orders from General Mark Clark's headquarters in Vienna.

Tate, an experienced Gooney pilot, had been told that the weather on the first leg of the flight from Vienna west to Munich would be scattered clouds after the first hour. Heavy snowstorms were raging in the Alps on the left of his course and, with radio aids to navigation scarce in postwar Europe, he decided to head west and not tempt fate by deliberately flying directly to Pisa over some of the roughest terrain in the world.

Takeoff was uneventful and Tate went on instruments shortly afterward; he began to climb to eight thousand feet where he hoped to break out on top of the overcast. The Munich radio range was loud and clear as he passed overhead and continued westward. However, the reassuring sound of Munich Radio quickly faded as the plane passed behind the mountain peaks and out of range of the ground station. He did not break out of the clouds, so he would have to continue to fly westward and then turn southward toward Istres still flying on instruments. If the Vienna weatherman's estimate of the winds aloft was accurate and he could soon break out of the murk, there would be no problem. But if the winds were stronger than forecast and from the north instead of the west and he couldn't break out, there were those Alpine peaks waiting to take their deadly toll.

The Gooney droned on as Tate and his copilot, Lieutenant I. S. "Matt" Matthews, took turns flying on instruments. Suddenly, the plane was shaken violently by turbulence and Tate signaled that he would take the controls. He yelled to the crew chief, Sergeant Wayne G. Folsom, "Tell the passengers to fasten their safety belts!"

The last passenger was firmly belted down when a violent updraft sent the Gooney Bird skyrocketing upward. The plane shuddered a moment and then dropped like a stone. The altimeter spun backward and stopped. Out of the corner of his eye, Tate saw ominous black shapes flash by which he knew couldn't be clouds. The plane was only a few feet above the ground!

The familiar lines of the DC-3's engine nacelles are changed drastically with the substitution of turboprops for the piston engines. However, the familiar lines of the trusty Gooney were not otherwise modified. (British European Airways photo)

If two turboprops increase the speed and load potential of a DC-3, what would three turboprops do? With the help of Pratt & Whitney PT6A engines and five-bladed props, John Conroy made a trimotor out of a Gooney and called it the Tri Turbo Three. Cruise speed was 230 miles per hour and, with one prop feathered and extra gas tanks, could fly a 3,000-mile mission. (Photo courtesy John Conroy)

Tate jammed the throttles forward and roared back into the soup. He was again conscious of black shapes flashing by the window and then he felt a shock as though a bomb had gone off inside his head. In that split second he knew they had crashed!

"Everything went white, then black, then white again," Tate recalled. "As I passed back and forth through the gloom of semi-consciousness, I was aware of an awful silence. 'So, this is what's it like to be dead,' I said to myself. My voice scared me at first but then I knew I wasn't dead."

Tate's only injury was a small gash on his head. Miraculously, the only other injury on board was a broken leg suffered by Sergeant Folsom. In one of the flying oddities of all time, Tate's Gooney had smashed into cushioning snow in the Alps in full flight with no loss of life. To add to the miracle, the C-47 was not seriously damaged and could easily be repaired.

While the luck of this dozen people had held out in the inadvertent "landing," they still faced incredible odds in surviving the subzero cold so far from civilization and with no hope of immediate rescue until the weather cleared. There was no cold weather survival equipment on board and no food save a few candy bars that a passenger found in her pocket. Fortunately, a fire could be kindled and kept going by burning everything that would ignite.

It was several days before the weather cleared and search planes could locate the downed Gooney and drop supplies. When the plane was pinpointed among the rocks and crags, it was found to be resting on the only high, level plateau within many miles. Within a hundred yards in every direction were hidden crevices covered by snow bridges.

Even though spotted from the air, Tate and his charges could not yet be rescued. Swiss mountaineers spent several days fighting their way to the treacherous plateau before they finally were able to evacuate the anxious Americans. After the rescue the weather closed in for the next twelve days and heavy snowstorms covered the whole Alpine region. Within a hundred miles of the scene not a single plane was able to get off the ground. When pilots flew over the crash site two weeks later, not a trace of the plane could be found.

The crash, search and rescue of Major Ralph Tate and his crew and passengers made world headlines and added a footnote to history as well. Never before had a transport plane crashed in the Alps without killing everyone on board. The rescue was also a history-making effort that once again proved the courage, determination and stamina of the Swiss mountaineers.

The world soon forgot the incident—but not the Swiss. They collected pictures, magazines and newspapers from all over the

The Tri Turbo Three was used on naval research missions in Greenland in 1979. Shown above at Camp Opal, 180 miles from the North Pole, Jim Wolff and Al Magnuson move supplies by sled from the aircraft to the campsite. (Photo courtesy Tri Turbo Corp.)

world that featured the rescue and placed them in their museum at Bern. The next spring, those who had participated in the operation climbed back up to the plateau and located the plane by probing through the snow with long poles. Digging down, they opened the hatch in the top of the cockpit and placed a sealed capsule inside on the throttle quadrant. In the capsule were copies of many of the magazines and newspapers in various languages telling the whole sequence of events. The hatch was closed and the blowing snow soon covered the site again.

To the Swiss this gesture had a purpose. This rescue had been a classic from beginning to end, with literally hundreds of people of several nationalities pitching in to save lives. But there was another reason for the trek back to the plateau. The plateau was part of a glacier, and Swiss glaciologists believe that Tate's Gooney Bird will sink slowly through the glacial ice until it reaches a point where it will gently slide downhill and will eventually be spit out at the bottom—completely intact! It is estimated that it will take six hundred years for this to happen. So, knowing the historic tendency for the Gooney Bird to continue to make history, it is safe to say that shortly after the turn of the 26th century, this plane will make news around the world. A Gooney Bird will fly again!

Aeronautical engineers tell us that every plane has a definite life cycle and that the Gooney must surely be reaching that point in time when it will disappear from the skies forever. They are wrong. It will still be plodding along the world's airways far below the jetliners long after everyone who reads these words is gone. If anyone doubts this statement, he had better be prepared to be remembered among those who predicted that man would never fly, the world would come to an end, and space flight was impossible.

(Top) United States Aircraft Co., Van Nuys, California, saw the potential of updating the DC-3 with turboprops. (Bottom) The modification included a 40-inch extension of the fuselage and an over-wing exhaust system which ejects gas over the top of the wing. (Photo courtesy U.S. Aircraft Co.)

Basler Turbo Conversions is the largest of the companies installing turboprops on DC-3s. To produce "BT-67s" the fuselage is stretched, wings are reinforced, five-bladed props are installed and metal replaces cloth on the control surfaces in the company's Oshkosh, Wisconsin, shops. (Photo courtesy Basler Turbo Conversions)

The Gooney's clean lines, as well as its performance, are enhanced by the installation of turboprops. Reliability, safety, improved maintenance and fuel costs are also improved. The shortage of aviation gasoline is another factor encouraging conversion. (Photo courtesy Basler Turbo Conversions)

The cockpit of today's turboprop equipped DC 3 is far different from the original Goonies. The instrument panel, overhead switches and control column reflect vastly improved communication and navigation capabilities. (Photo courtesy Basler Turbo Conversions)

Whoever thought there would never be another Gooney on floats didn't know about the dream of Louis O. Hilton of Greenville, Maine. It took a long search for a set of pontoons and five years of work but this former C-53D, the only amphibious Gooney in the world, flies frequently over Moosehead Lake, Maine. (Photo courtesy Louis O. Hilton)

Skis were attached to C-47 landing gear for winter operations on runways and snow. Note airfoils on rear to prevent flutter and vibration of the skis in flight. (USAF photo)

The throttle quadrant of the Tri Turbo Three. Note triple sets of engine instruments for operating the Pratt & Whitney PT6 turbo jets. (Photo by C. V. Glines)

A Tri Turbo Three on a test run off the California coast drops a bathythermograph tube before proceeding to Nord, Greenland for scientific surveys. (Photo courtesy Furman Associates)

A Varig DC-3 on display in a park in Rio de Janeiro brings a large crowd to look it over. DC-3s are still flying paying passengers all over the world. (McDonnell Douglas Co. photo)

Decked out in white topside paint, polished metal and white sidewall tires, this TC-47 was assigned to the Air Force Reserve Navigation Training program at Clinton County, Ohio. With more than 11,000 hours on its airframe in 1963, it was one of the last Gooneys flying regularly scheduled Air Force missions. (USAF photo)

Several DC-3 owners in the United States operate them for nostalgic sightseeing flights. Era Classic Airlines of Anchorage, Alaska, features flight crews in period uniforms, champagne, big band music and original edition magazines. (Photo courtesy Era Classic Airlines)

"Smokey" Roland in Los Angeles traffic in 1978. Describing the way people react to his creation, Roland said, "they do double takes, triple takes and quadruple takes." (AP Laser photo)

When a Gooney Bird is grounded permanently, it can continue to serve in other ways. H. L. "Smokey" Roland, a 42-mission veteran in Europe, bought one from an Air Force plane "graveyard," removed the engines, wings and tail, bolted the fuselage to a school bus chassis and drove it everywhere. (Los Angeles Times photo)

A family of five lived in this Gooney Bird carcass made into a motor home. Others have been made into summer vacation houses, seaside shelters, bars and lunch stands. (McDonnell Douglas photo)

This "Smile Shuttle" was made from a DC-3 fuselage to look like a space shuttle in 1986. It is owned by Robert and Heike Pfeiffer of Cardiff, California. (McDonnell Douglas Photo)

Two views of the C-53D that was restored to a C-47C amphibian in 1992 by Lewis O. Hilton and associates. The gross weight is just over 34,000 pounds with the floats weighing about 2,000 pounds each. (Photos courtesy William K. Jones)

The DC-3 went through more modifications than any other airplane in history. Here "Miss Super Starliner" caresses the nacelle of a C-47 equipped with a "Maximizer" kit made by AiResearch Aviation Service of Los Angeles. The kit guaranteed to give the DC-3s a 20 mph increase in speed at no extra power and 200 extra miles of range. Covered wheel wells and redesigned oil cooler fairings were contributing factors. (Photo by Tom Darling Co.)

The Gooney Bird, known as the Dakota by the Royal Air Force, is honored by this memorial window in Down Amprey church in the Cotswold Hills in England. (Photo courtesy Alan Hartley)

Continental Airlines' DC-3 takes on "sentimental journey" passengers at Houston's Hobby Field terminal. A vintage automobile lends the scene a 1940s ambiance. (Photo courtesy Jim and Sherri Minor)

Sherri Minor, wearing the period uniform of the DC-3 stewardess, passes out 1940s magazines and chewing gum on Continental's nostalgic DC-3 flights. (Photo courtesy Jim and Sherri Minor)

Sherri Minor primps while waiting for husband Capt. Jim Minor to preflight the Continental Gooney Bird before boarding passengers. (Photo courtesy Jim and Sherri Minor)

The clean, squared-off lines of the Super DC-3 are evident in this photo. Engine nacelles were streamlined, wheels covered with fairing doors and the tail wheel was retractable. The US Navy purchased 101 and designated them R4D-8s. A few others were sold to commercial operators. (Douglas Aircraft Co. photo)

A Super DC-3 fuselage receives finishing touches before being moved into position for internal assemblies, followed by wing and tail installations. (Douglas Aircraft Co. photo)

Appendix A
Evolution of the DC-3

Civil Versions

DC-1 Carried 12 passengers. Wright engines. 1 built.
DC-2 Carried 14 passengers. One delivered with Pratt & Whitney Hornet engines; two with Bristol Pegasus VI engines; the rest had Wright engines. 130 built.
DST Skysleeper model with 14 berths. Wright engines.
DST-A Skysleeper model with 14 berths. Pratt & Whitney engines.
DC-3 Delivered to airlines and non-military customers. Wright engines. 455 built pre-World War II.
DC-3A DC-3 with Pratt & Whitney engines.
DC-3B Half Skysleeper, half seats. Pratt & Whitney engines.
DC-3C This designation originally referred to C-47 military versions purchased from the U.S. Government that were completely remanufactured with new serial numbers. Later, surplus C-47s that were updated to the DC-3C configuration also carried this designation.
DC-3D Originally were C-117s built as passenger aircraft rather than as cargo planes. At the conclusion of World War II, Douglas purchased parts from undelivered C-117 stock from the government and remanufactured them as DC-3Ds with new serial numbers.
DC-3S Designation given to DC-3s converted to Super DC- 3s.

Military Versions

XC-32 DC-2; carried 14 passengers. Wright engines. 1 built.
C-32A DC-2 aircraft impressed from the airlines during World War II. Wright engines. 24 had this designation.
C-33 Same as DC-2 with larger tail and cargo door. Wright engines. 18 built.
C-34 Same as DC-2 with VIP interior furnishings. 2 built.
C-38 C-33 with DC-3 tail. 1 converted.
C-39 DC-2 (C-33) with DC-3 landing gear and tail. Wright engines. 35 built.
C-41 and C-41A DC-3s with VIP interiors. 1 of each built.
C-42 Same as C-39 with VIP interior. Wright engines. 1 built.
C-47 DC-3 with cargo door and floor. Pratt & Whitney engines. 953 built.
C-47A C-47 with 24-volt electrical system. Pratt & Whitney engines. 4,931 built.
C-47B C-47 with two-stage blower for high altitude operations. Pratt & Whitney engines. 3,241 built.
C-47C Amphibian model equipped with EDO floats. Pratt & Whitney engines. At least five were originally converted.
C-47D C-47B without blowers. Pratt & Whitney engines. Converted from available C-47Bs.
C-47E Equipped with electronic equipment for checking radio aids to navigation. Pratt & Whitney engines. 6 converted.
YC-47F Redesignated from YC-129 and transferred to U.S. Navy as R4D-8. Wright engines. 1 converted.
C-48 DC-3 originally built for United Airlines. Pratt & Whitney engines. 1 built.
C-48A DC-3A with plush interior. Pratt & Whitney engines. 1 built.
C-48B Same as DST-A Skysleeper. Pratt & Whitney engines. 16 built.
C-48C Same as DC-3A. Pratt & Whitney engines. 16 built.
C-49 DC-3 built for TWA with 24 passenger seats. Wright engines. 6 built.
C-49A DC-3 built for Delta Airlines with 21 seats. Wright engines. 3 built.

C-49B Navy R4D-2 built originally for Eastern Airlines; door on right side. Wright engines. 3 built.
C-49C Troop carrier version with small door, side seats. Originally built for Delta Airlines. Wright engines. 2 built.
C-49D Same as C-49C; built for Eastern Airlines. Wright engines. 11 built.
C-49E through H DC-3s originally ordered by the airlines and converted to troop carriers. Wright engines. 58 built.
C-49J and K DC-3s with side seating for troops. Wright engines. 57 built.
C-50 DC-3s built for American Airlines. 21 passengers. Wright engines. 4 built.
C-50A DC-3s built for American Airlines converted to troop carrier interior. Wright engines. 3 built.
C-50B DC-3s built for Braniff International. Same as C-50A with minor interior changes. Wright engines. 3 built.
C-50C DC-3 built for Penn Central Airlines; passenger interior. Wright engines. 1 built.
C-50D DC-3s built for Penn Central Airlines; converted to troop carrier interior. Wright engines. 4 built.
C-51 DC-3 built for Canadian-Colonial Airlines; troop carrier interior. Pratt & Whitney engines. 1 built.
C-52 DC-3A built for United Air Lines; troop carrier interior with right hand door. Pratt & Whitney engines. 1 built.
C-52A DC-3A built for Western Airlines; troop carrier interior. Pratt & Whitney engines. 2 built.
C-52B DC-3A built for United Air Lines; troop carrier interior. Pratt & Whitney engines. 2 built.
C-52C DC-3A built for Eastern Airlines; troop carrier interior. Pratt & Whitney engines. 1 built.
C-53 Troop transport given named of Skytrooper. Pratt & Whitney engines. 193 built.
XC-53A Experimental model with hot air wing and tail de-icing system; full span flaps. Pratt & Whitney engines. 1 converted.
C-53B Special winterized version for arctic operations. Pratt & Whitney engines. 8 built.
C-53C C-53 with minor interior changes. Pratt & Whitney engines. 17 built.
C-53D C-53 with 24-volt system. Pratt & Whitney engines. 159 built.
C-68 DC-3A with 21-passenger seating. Wright engines. 2 built.
C-84 Originally built as DC-3B (half Skysleeper, half passenger configuration). 4 aircraft impressed from airlines.
C-117A and B Passenger version similar to C-47B. Pratt & Whitney engines. 17 built as C-117As, then 8 reworked to include two-stage blowers and designated as C-117B.
C-117C C-47 type aircraft loaned to airlines and put in passenger interiors. When returned to Army Air Force, they were designated C-117Cs.
C-117D See YC-129.
YC-129 Redesignated YC-47F and then Navy R4D-8. Wright engines. 1 converted, then designated as C-117D.
XCG-17 C-47 with engines removed and used as a glider. 1 converted.

Note: All C-49 through C-52 models, plus the C-68 and C-84, were airline transports impressed from the airlines or at the factory prior to delivery.

Approximately 600 DC-3 type aircraft were procured for the U.S. Navy and Marine Corps by the Army Air Forces during World War II. Given the general designation of R4D, they were used principally for transportation of personnel and cargo. The several models numbered R4D-1 through R4D-7 were equivalent to the Army Air Force variants from the C-47 through the C-53 models.

Prior to World War II the U.S. Navy purchased five DC-2s which were designated R2D-1s. After the war, Douglas converted 105 C-47 or DC-3 aircraft to Super DC-3s. The first was reworked from the YC-129 to YC-47F and finally the R4D-8 (later designated as the C-117D). Three Super DC-3s were sold to Capital Airlines and 100 (in addition to the R4D-8) were converted for the U.S. Navy.

Appendix B
DC-3/C-47 Nose Art

A large number of DC-3s and C-47s have been placed on static display throughout the world. This one rests in a Berlin park to honor the Gooney's role in supplying the city with food and medical supplies during the beginning days of the Berlin Airlift in 1948-49. (Photo courtesy Universa International, S.A.)

Ground crews sweep snow off Goonies after a rare snowfall in south Texas during World War II. All C-47s used as tow ships at the South Plains Army Flying School were named the "We Do'd Its." (USAF photo)

Air Force pilots and crews named the fighters, bomber and transports they flew under combat conditions during World War II, Korea and Vietnam. Gooneys had their share of nose art in Vietnam but they rarely had the drawings of pretty girls that were so common on B-17s and B-24s of World War II. (Photos courtesy of Robert C. Mikesh)

DENNIS
THE
MENACE

THE
ROGUE

GUNFIGHTER
AIRLINES

"WATZAMATA"
YOU

RING DANG
DOO

ANDY'S
ANIMOSITY

Appendix C
C-47 Training Manual

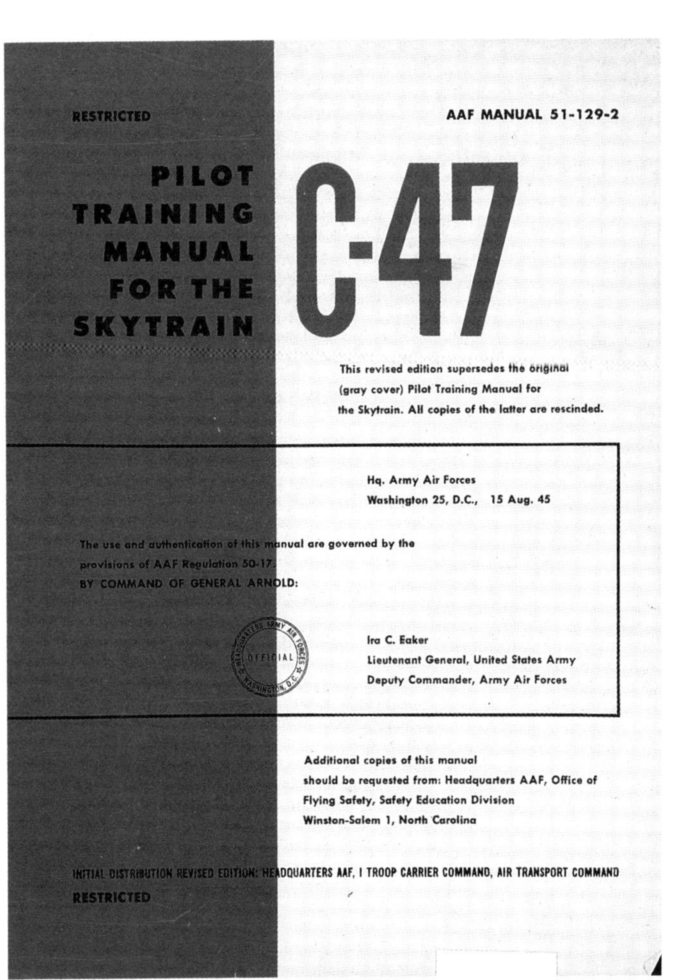

RESTRICTED

AAF MANUAL 51-129-2

PILOT TRAINING MANUAL FOR THE SKYTRAIN

C-47

This revised edition supersedes the original (gray cover) Pilot Training Manual for the Skytrain. All copies of the latter are rescinded.

Hq. Army Air Forces
Washington 25, D.C., 15 Aug. 45

The use and authentication of this manual are governed by the provisions of AAF Regulation 50-17.
BY COMMAND OF GENERAL ARNOLD:

OFFICIAL — HEADQUARTERS ARMY AIR FORCES — WASHINGTON D.C.

Ira C. Eaker
Lieutenant General, United States Army
Deputy Commander, Army Air Forces

Additional copies of this manual should be requested from: Headquarters AAF, Office of Flying Safety, Safety Education Division
Winston-Salem 1, North Carolina

INITIAL DISTRIBUTION REVISED EDITION: HEADQUARTERS AAF, I TROOP CARRIER COMMAND, AIR TRANSPORT COMMAND

RESTRICTED

RESTRICTED

Introduction

This manual is the text for your training as a C-47 pilot and airplane commander.

The Air Forces' most experienced training and supervisory personnel have collaborated to make it a complete exposition of what your pilot duties are, how each duty will be performed, and why it must be performed in the manner prescribed.

The techniques and procedures described in this book are standard and mandatory. In this respect the manual serves the dual purpose of a training checklist and a working handbook. Use it to make sure that you learn everything described herein. Use it to study and review the essential facts concerning everything taught. Such additional self-study and review will not only advance your training, but will alleviate the burden of your already overburdened instructors.

This training manual does not replace the Technical Orders for the airplane, which will always be your primary source of information concerning the C-47 so long as you fly it.

This is essentially the textbook of the C-47. Used properly, it will enable you to utilize the pertinent Technical Orders to even greater advantage.

COMMANDING GENERAL, ARMY AIR FORCES

RESTRICTED

YOUR AIRPLANE—WHAT IT HAS ALREADY DONE

Before the United States entered the war, the Douglas C-47 Skytrain, familiarly known as the commercial airline DC-3, already had flown more than 300,000,000 miles in domestic airline service for a total flying time of more than 2,060,000 hours. In addition, the DC-3 was serving 57 countries on 21 foreign airlines. In

RESTRICTED

this service it was flying daily a distance equal to 17 times around the globe.

The accident rate in this airplane has always been low. As Douglas transports were used more universally, the number of fatal accidents decreased. In 1936, for example, domestic airlines flew 63,000,000 miles and had eight fatal accidents; by 1941, there were only four fatal accidents for 133,000,000 miles flown.

When the United States found itself at war, overnight this country was faced with the problem of transporting troops and supplies and evacuating casualties over long stretches of water and across lands at the far ends of the earth. The DC-3 was the only transport airplane manufactured in large quantities at the time. When it was called into service military men were skeptical that it could do the job. It proved itself without question when in 1942 the Air Transport Command was able to carry 5000% more aerial freight in the C-47 than all domestic airlines had carried during the previous year.

Here are some of the achievements of the C-47 airplane in combat: It evacuated 20,000 wounded from New Guinea in five months, [illegible] 1000 from Alaska, 18,000 from Tunisia, and 14,000 from Sicily.

Shortly after the landing of our Marines on Guadalcanal, C-47's, making their final approach over the Japs who held the edge of Henderson Field, flew in anti-personnel ammunition when not a round was left among our forces. During this operation not a single plane was lost. Later these transports rushed gasoline to our fighter planes when there was not enough fuel at Henderson Field to send the fighters against the enemy.

At Salerno, C-47's dropped 2600 paratroopers in 45 minutes to turn the enemy flank and save the beachhead.

When the Burma Road was lost and the only way to send supplies into China was by air transport, at an altitude of 19,000 feet over the Hump, Chiang Kai-shek was said to have remarked: "Give me 50 DC-3's and the Japs can have the Burma Road."

From the fall of the Burma Road until mid-spring of 1943, C-47's supplied all aviation fuel that the Flying Tigers used. Later they supplied our 10th Air Force, when pre-Pearl Harbor stocks had been exhausted. These airplanes [illegible]

6

RESTRICTED

RESTRICTED

supplies to Guadalcanal when sea communication had been severed. Except for one 24-hour interruption, they maintained a daily service into this area from September 1, 1942, until February 1, 1943.

In New Guinea, when the Japs poured over the Owen Stanley Mountains to advance within 40 miles of Port Moresby, C-47's rushed 3800 troops from Australia to beat back the enemy. Later these transports flew 7000 troops across the Owen Stanley Mountains. This was the force that cleared the Japanese from North Papua and finally from Salamaua and Lae.

In the North African invasion a group of 44 C-47's made a non-stop flight from England to Oran to drop British paratroopers behind the enemy lines. C-47's supported the 8th Army's drive from El Alamein to Tripoli. At Kasserine Pass, C-47's, flying an aggregate of 1,000,000 miles, carried the munitions that beat back the enemy's most dangerous break-through.

We all know the part C-47's played in Sicily, Italy, and in the invasion of the Normandy coast; they not only transported troops and supplies to the battle fronts but saved thousands of lives by flying out wounded.

The C-47 has performed extraordinary feats at times. C-47's flew 19 bulldozers, 32 jeeps, graders, scrapers, field camp equipment, arms, and a crew of engineers into the New Guinea jungles to build an airfield. They carried as many as 74 refugees a trip out of China and Burma. A C-47 carried a 6100-lb. pinion gear 5300 miles in 3 days so that a damaged American cruiser in a foreign port could be put back into service in a week.

And the C-47 airplane can hold up under punishment. During the Sicilian invasion, a large-caliber naval shell passed directly through a C-47, yet the airplane got back to its base. A C-47 got home after one engine had been completely torn out when it struck a group of high-tension wires. Another C-47 was so riddled by shellfire the pilot decided to ditch, but the airplane bounced from the water and the pilot flew it home.

Time and time again the C-47 has proved itself a reliable and safe airplane. It has done its job well in a civilian role and in combat. It is an easy plane to handle, has no bad flying characteristics and gives maximum perform- [illegible] ever, it is an airplane that you can't stunt or dive. You will find it a pleasure to fly.

RESTRICTED

7

FLYING THE C-47

Here is your airplane. As you have seen from the story of its work, it is the workhorse of this war. When the tall tales are spun in the nights to come it will take its place with the *8 chevaux -40 hommes* of the last war.

Your transition training in this airplane covers normal flight procedure, plus the emergency procedures to bring you safely through the tight spots that come to most pilots at one time or another.

The C-47 has no bugs. It has been around a long time doing a magnificent job. The only troubles you will have are those you bring on yourself. Know your airplane. When you check it before a flight know enough about it to spot trouble. Maintenance men are human too—they make mistakes. Your job is to check their work just before you fly.

Know your procedures. Confusion in the cockpit causes far too many accidents. Practice emergency procedures until they are as familiar, and as easily accomplished as normal operation. Some of these procedures you can practice in the airplane. For others, you must use mockups, but know them all.

Make the most of transition training. Spend every hour you can in the cockpit. If you can't take the C-47 up, sit in the cockpit and check yourself on procedures. Get to know your airplane so well that you can close your eyes and visualize every part and just how it works. When you know your airplane that well, you won't make mistakes during tough sledding.

THE AIRPLANE COMMANDER AND HIS CREW

You are the commanding officer of the airplane. It is your responsibility to know your airplane and its accessories and to be familiar with normal and emergency procedures. This manual covers these matters in detail.

As commanding officer of the airplane's crew you must see that each man knows his duties and performs them properly. The airplane and its crew are your responsibility. A C-47 crew normally consists of:

1. Airplane commander or first pilot
2. Copilot
3. Navigator
4. Radio operator
5. Aerial engineer

Your crew must learn to work together as a unit. Under emergency or unpleasant conditions there is no place for lack of understanding of the next man's job, or for clashes of temperament. It is up to you to weld your crew into a working team.

Each member of your crew should learn as much as possible about other crew members' duties so that each can relieve any other under emergency conditions, or in case one is unable to perform his duties.

Besides their particular duties, your crew must know:

1. Position of emergency equipment and its use.
2. Bailout procedures.
3. Ditching stations and procedures.
4. Life raft launching.
5. Lost plane procedure.
6. Health and sanitation precautions in flight.
7. Security precautions and instructions for destroying confidential equipment.

Inspect your crew members before and after each flight. Make sure they have fitted parachutes and proper clothing for long flights and for cold weather operation. Make these inspections a habit, beginning with the first training flight with your crew.

Schedule practice for emergency procedures, including ditching and life raft launching. Drill your crew until it functions as a team.

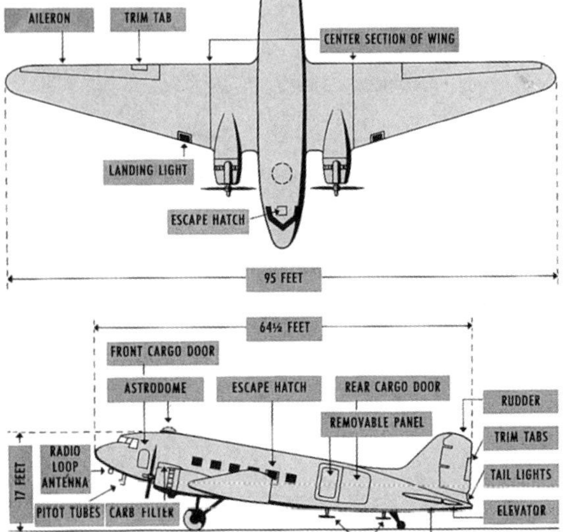

THE AIRPLANE

The C-47, and its modified versions, C-47A and C-47B, is a 2-engine, all-metal, low-wing monoplane, used for transport of supplies, paratroop operation, glider towing, and the evacuation of wounded.

The airplane has two 1200-Hp Pratt & Whitney, 14-cylinder, R-1830-92, Twin Wasp engines, with Hamilton Standard hydromatic full-feathering 3-bladed propellers. The C-47B is designed for high-altitude flying. It has R-1830-90C engines, each with a 2-speed internal blower.

The hydraulic landing gear is of the conventional type. Main wheels retract vertically into the engine nacelles and extend approximately 11 inches out of the nacelles when fully retracted. In this position they are free to rotate and are subject to normal brake action. The tailwheel is non-retractable.

There is a large cargo door at the left of the main cabin and a smaller cargo door on the left side of the airplane behind the pilots' compartment. The plane has four emergency exits: a window on each side of the main cabin, just aft of the wings, an escape hatch over the pilots' compartment, and a removable panel in the main cargo loading door.

The airplane has two main sections.

In the forward section is the pilots' compartment, radio operator's and navigator's compartment, and a space for cargo behind the copilot's seat. Radio equipment is in the forward section.

The rear section consists of main cabin, lavatory, and spare parts compartment. The main cabin is marked off in stations for cargo loading; it has two rows of seats for troop carrying and a static line for operation with paratroops. For long-range operation it carries from two to eight auxiliary fuel tanks in the forward part of the main cabin. There are litter attachments in the main cabin for use when the airplane is employed in the evacuation of wounded.

RADIO OPERATOR
FOLDING SEATS
RADIO
PILOT
MAIN CABIN
FUEL TANKS
LAV.
MISC. CARGO
RADIO
NAVIGATOR
FOLDING SEATS

Dimensions:

Span . . . . 95 feet
Length . . . . 64 feet 5½ inches
Height (at rest) . . . . 17 feet

Weight:

Empty:
C-47 . . . . 17,087 lbs.
C-47A . . . . 17,257 lbs.
Basic:
C-47 . . . . 17,400 lbs.
C-47A . . . . 17,700 lbs.
Recommended takeoff, maximum gross . . . . 29,300 lbs.
Restricted takeoff, maximum gross . . . . 31,000 lbs.
Recommended landing, maximum gross . . . . 26,000 lbs.

Other Figures of Interest :

Cruising speed at 10,000 feet . . . . approximately 185 mph TAS
Stalling speed . . . . 67 mph TAS
Service ceiling . . . . 24,100 feet
Wingloading . . . . . 25.3 lbs. per square foot
Power loading . . . . 12.0 lbs. per Hp
Seating capacity . . . . 28 passengers

RESTRICTED

C-47 SERIES CHANGES

Your airplane, like all airplanes used by the Air Forces, has been changed to meet the ever shifting needs of tactical operations. To fly the Hump run in CBI the C-47 needed more power at higher altitudes, so two-speed superchargers replaced the single speed superchargers then installed. To make long overwater hops additional fuel was needed. Fuselage tanks were added to all airplanes doing this work. Changes were made on all series of the airplane to carry paratroops, to drop supplies, to evacuate wounded.

At the present time three series of the airplane are in use, the C-47, the C-47A, and the C-47B. There is an occasional reference in the text of this manual to early and late series airplanes. The following chart gives you the major changes that have been made in the different airplanes.

If at any point the references are puzzling, refer to this chart or to the technical orders for the specific series.

	C-47	C-47A	C-47B
R-1830-92 Engines	★	★	
R-1830-90C Engines			★
Needle Blade Prop	★		
Paddle Blade Prop		★	★
Non-Ram Airscoop			★
Electric Solenoid Primer	★	★	★
Wobble Pump	★	★	
Electric Booster Pumps			★
Cross Feed	★	★	
2-switch Ignition	★		
1-switch Ignition		★B	★
Demand Oxygen System		★B	★
Sperry A-3 Auto Pilot	★	★B	
Jack & Heintz A-3A Auto Pilot		★B	★
Steam Heat System	★		
Hot-Air Heat System		★	★
Elastic Bungee (landing gear)	★	★B	
Hydraulic Cushion (landing gear)		★B	★
Electrical Altimeter		★B	★
Glide Path Indicator		★	★
Remote Indicating Compass		★B	★
Venturi Voltage Regulator Cooling			★
Hydraulic Blower Control			★
Circuit Breakers (Main Elec. Junction Box)			★
Fuses (Main Elec. Junction Box)	★	★	
VHF	★A	★B	★
Wooden Personnel Seats	★B	★	★
Canvas Personnel Seats		★B	★A
Aluminum Litter Racks (3-high)	★A	★A	
Canvas (web-straps) Litter Racks (4-high)		★B	★

A. INCLUDED IN MODIFICATION　　B. PART OF SERIES

12　　RESTRICTED

RESTRICTED

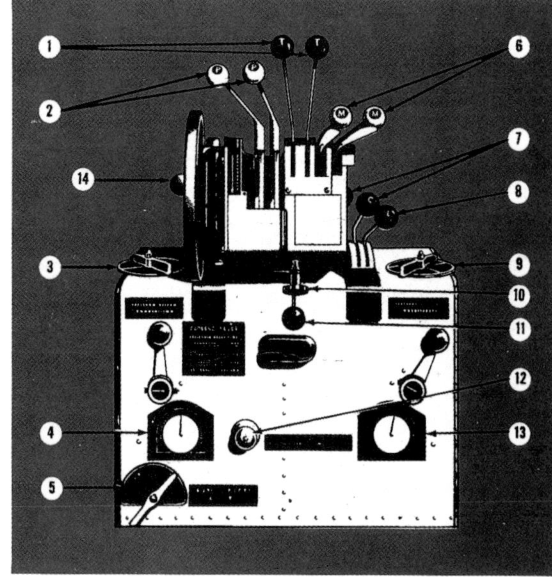

CONTROL PEDESTAL

1 Throttles
2 Propeller controls
3 Left engine fuel tank selector valve control
4 Rudder trim tab control
5 Automatic pilot servo units ON-OFF control
6 Carburetor mixture controls
7 Carburetor air temperature controls
8 Carburetor air temperature control lock
9 Right engine fuel tank selector valve control
10 Throttle friction brake
11 Tailwheel lock
12 Parking brake
13 Aileron trim tab control
14 Oil cooler control levers

RESTRICTED　　13

RESTRICTED

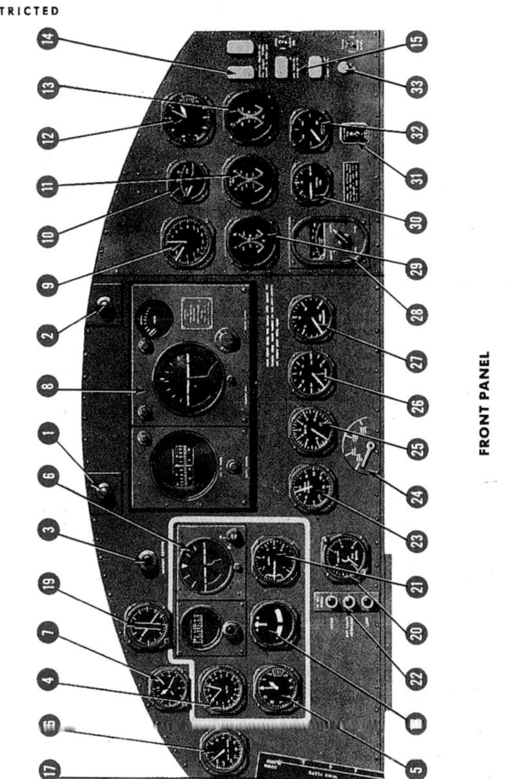

FRONT PANEL

14　　RESTRICTED

RESTRICTED

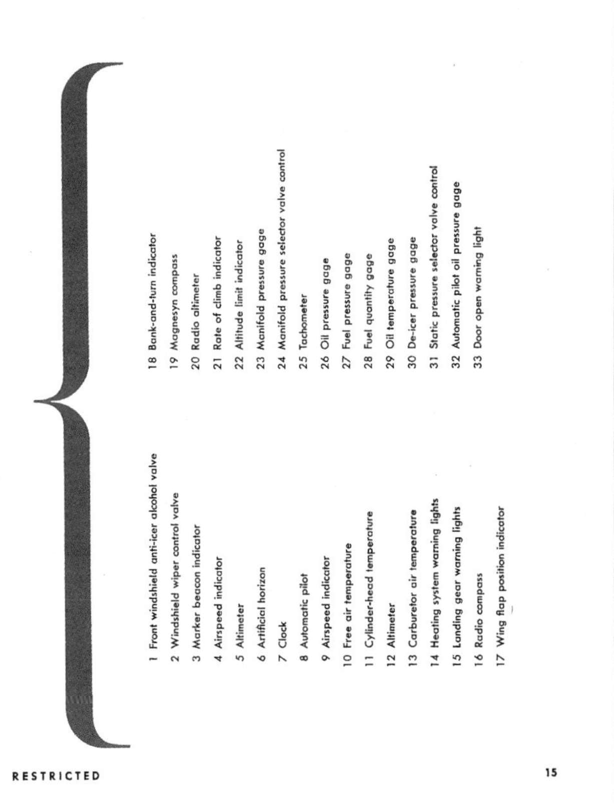

RESTRICTED　　15

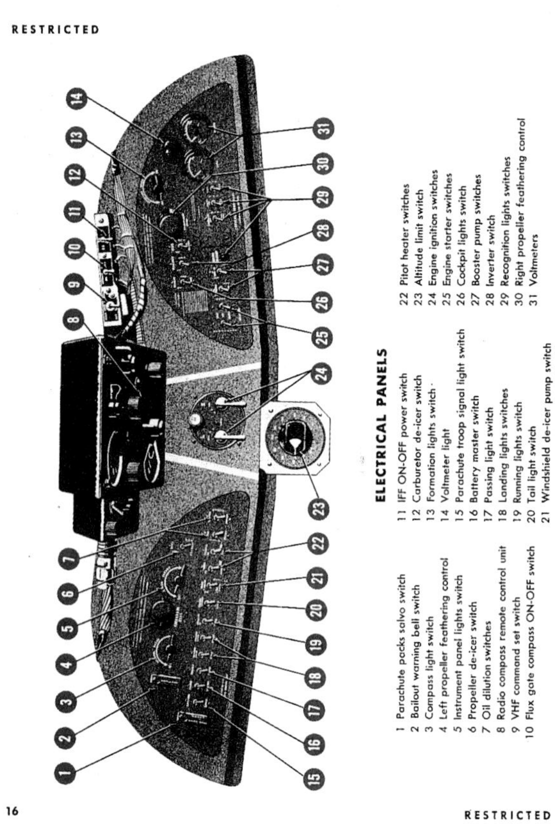

ELECTRICAL PANELS

1 Parachute packs salvo switch
2 Bailout warning bell switch
3 Compass light switch
4 Left propeller feathering control
5 Instrument panel lights switch
6 Propeller de-icer switch
7 Oil dilution switches
8 Radio compass remote control unit
9 VHF command set switch
10 Flux gate compass ON-OFF switch
11 IFF ON-OFF power switch
12 Carburetor de-icer switch
13 Formation lights switch
14 Voltmeter light
15 Parachute troop signal light switch
16 Battery master switch
17 Passing light switch
18 Landing lights switches
19 Running lights switch
20 Tail light switch
21 Windshield de-icer pump switch
22 Pilot heater switches
23 Altitude limit switch
24 Engine ignition switches
25 Engine starter switches
26 Cockpit lights switch
27 Booster pump switches
28 Inverter switch
29 Recognition lights switches
30 Right propeller feathering control
31 Voltmeters

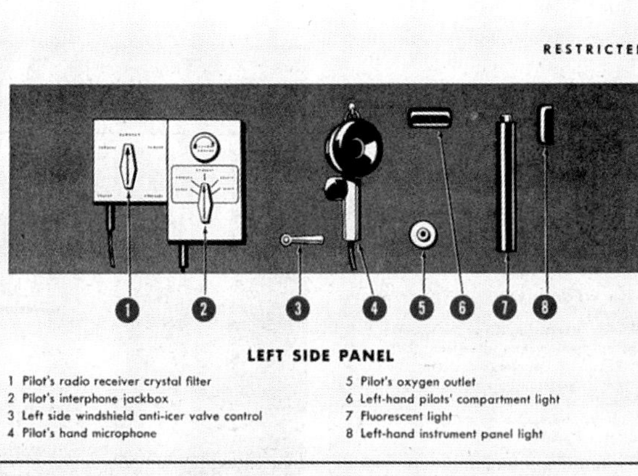

LEFT SIDE PANEL

1 Pilot's radio receiver crystal filter
2 Pilot's interphone jackbox
3 Left side windshield anti-icer valve control
4 Pilot's hand microphone
5 Pilot's oxygen outlet
6 Left-hand pilots' compartment light
7 Fluorescent light
8 Left-hand instrument panel light

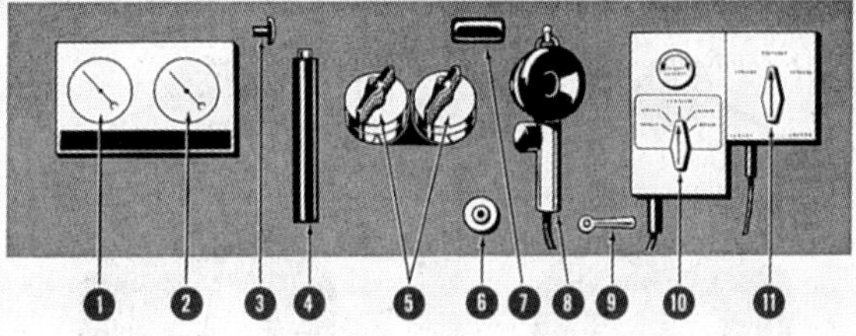

RIGHT SIDE PANEL

1 Landing gear hydraulic pressure gage
2 Hydraulic system pressure gage
3 Side windshield anti-icer hand pump
4 Fluorescent light
5 Engine cowl flap valve control
6 Copilot's oxygen outlet
7 Right hand pilots' compartment light
8 Copilot's hand microphone
9 Windshield anti-icer valve control
10 Copilot's interphone jackbox
11 Copilot's radio receiver crystal filter

SURFACE CONTROL SYSTEM

This system consists of elevators, ailerons, and rudder, which are made of metal frames covered with fabric. There are all-metal trim tabs on the elevators, the right aileron, and on the rudder. Operate trim tabs for the elevators by means of a wheel on the left side of the pedestal. Operate trim tabs for ailerons and rudder by means of hand cranks on the lower part of the pedestal.

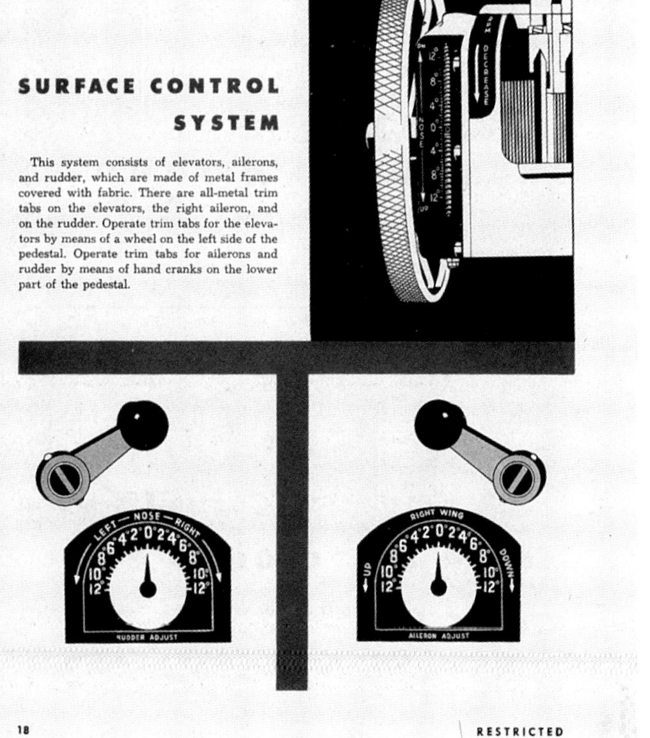

HYDRAULIC SYSTEM

The C-47 has a pressure accumulator type hydraulic system. It operates normally between 675 and 925 psi.

The hydraulic system operates the landing gear, wing flaps, cowl flaps, windshield wipers, automatic pilot, and brakes on all series of the airplane. It operates the non-ram carburetor air filter mechanism when it is installed, and the blower controls on C-47 airplanes using R-1830-90C engines.

The control panel is in the center aisle, behind the copilots' seat. The hydraulic gauges are at the right of the copilots' seat.

Two engine-driven hydraulic pumps supply pressure for the hydraulic system. One pump supplies pressure for the main hydraulic system; the other, for the automatic pilot. You can select either engine pump by means of a selector valve on the hydraulic control panel.

There is a hydraulic hand pump between the pilot's and copilot's seats. A valve on the hydraulic panel controls flow of pressure from the pump. When you open the valve, pressure is built up in the accumulator. When you close it, the accumulator is separated from the hydraulic system and pressure is applied to the hydraulic lines.

Never operate system at less than 500 psi.

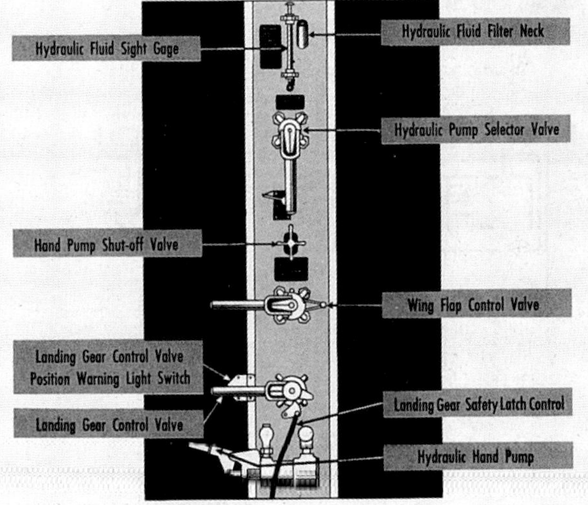

DIAGRAM OF HYDRAULIC SYSTEM

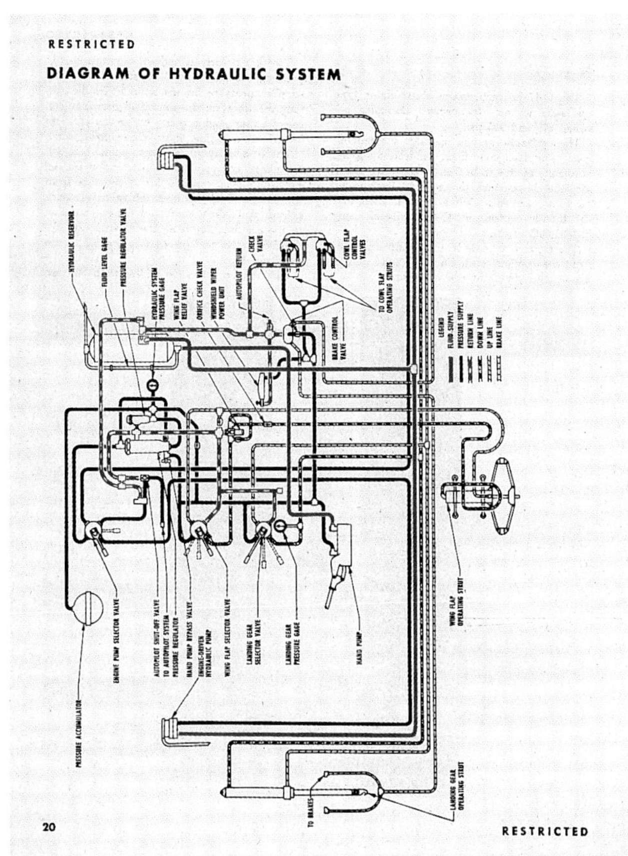

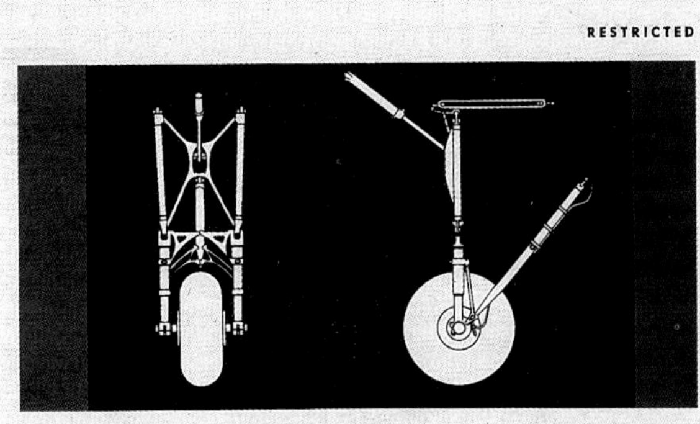

LANDING GEAR

Three controls govern the operation of the C-47 landing gear. A lever on the main hydraulic control panel raises and lowers the two main wheels. A tailwheel lock on the pedestal centers and locks the tailwheel. The tailwheel does not retract, but swivels through 360 degrees when not locked. The third control, a safety latch, on the floor by the pilots seat, controls movement of the safety latch and the landing gear lever.

This latch has three positions: full down, half up, and full up.

Full down (positive lock)—In this position the latch is locked and can be moved only by the latch control. The landing gear lever cannot be moved UP with the latch full down.

Half up (spring lock)—In this position the latch is spring locked. The landing gear lever cannot be moved UP with the latch spring locked.

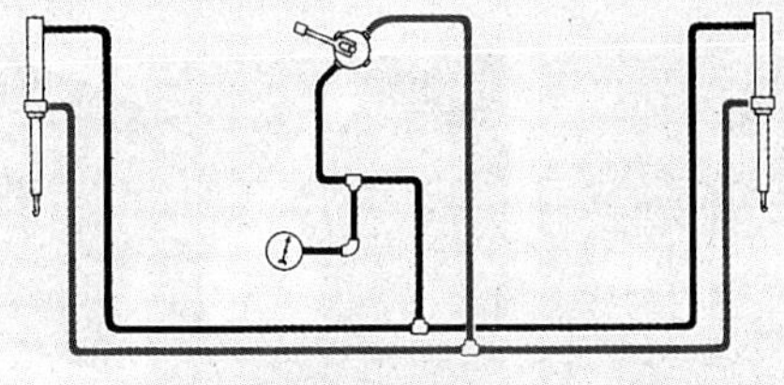

Landing Gear Hydraulic System

Landing Gear Down — Landing Gear Up

PRESSURE OIL
RETURN OIL
LANDING GEAR CONTROL VALVE
PRESSURE LINE
PRESSURE MANIFOLD
FROM HAND PUMP
PRESSURE GAGE
GEAR DOWN LINE
GEAR UP LINE
RETRACTOR STRUT CYLINDER
STRUT ROD EXTENDED
RETRACTOR STRUT CYLINDER
STRUT ROD EXTENDED
NEUTRAL POSITION
UP POSITION

How Fluid Is Trapped in Lines

Full up (unlocked)—In this position the latch is unlocked and the gear lever is free to move UP.

Move the gear lever UP, when the gear raises, move the gear lever to NEUTRAL and the latch will automatically move to spring lock position. The latch lever remains in this position until you have lowered the gear and are ready to lock it down.

CAUTION: Keep the safety latch full down and secured by the catch on the floor until the pilot signals "gear up."

Never move the latch to full down or positive lock until the gear lever is in NEUTRAL.

Keep the gear and flap levers in NEUTRAL for normal operation. This traps fluid in the line and provides a fluid lock to hold gear and flaps in the desired position.

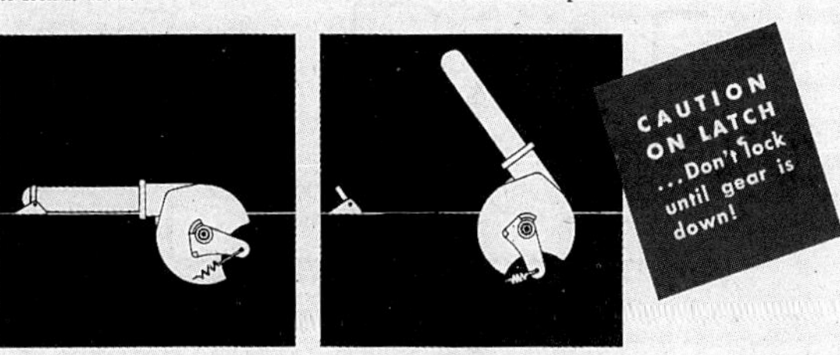

Pressure Drop When Gear Is Down

If landing gear pressure falls below 500 psi, place gear handle in the DOWN position until pressure is equal to the hydraulic system pressure.

Pressure Rises

When gear is retracted and the handle is in neutral, landing gear pressure should be zero. If pressure creeps up, place latch in vertical position and move handle to full UP position, then return to neutral.

Warning horn: Horn sounds when either throttle is closed if:

(a) One or both wheels are retracted.
(b) One or both wheels are unlatched.
(c) Valve handle is not in neutral.

Warning lights: There are green and red warning lights at the right-hand corner of the instrument panel. The green light burns only when the gear is down and latched and the valve handle is in neutral. Under any other condition the red light burns.

2. **Wing flaps:** Your airplane has all-metal wing flaps. A valve lever just above the landing gear lever operates these flaps. To raise or lower the flaps, first clear the slot that holds it in neutral by swinging the lever toward the aisle. Move the lever down to lower the flaps, up to raise them, and return to neutral when flaps are in position. There is a flap position indicator below the instrument panel directly in front of you.

3. **Cowl flaps:** The C-47 has cowl flaps around each engine directly behind the engine cowling. They control engine temperature by regulating airflow through the cowling.

Cowl flap controls are on the right side of the copilot's seat. They are marked: CLOSED, OFF, TRAIL, OFF, OPEN. Operate by moving them clockwise and counterclockwise.

4. **Brakes:** Conventional toe-operated brake pedals on the rudder controls give independent braking action on each wheel, with immediate reaction to toe pressure.

Since the wheels do not retract fully into the nacelles you have braking action on the wheels even though they are retracted. Thus, when the C-47 makes a belly landing, it can be steered by the brakes just as though the wheels were extended.

You must have a minimum of 500 psi pressure in the brake system to get satisfactory brake action.

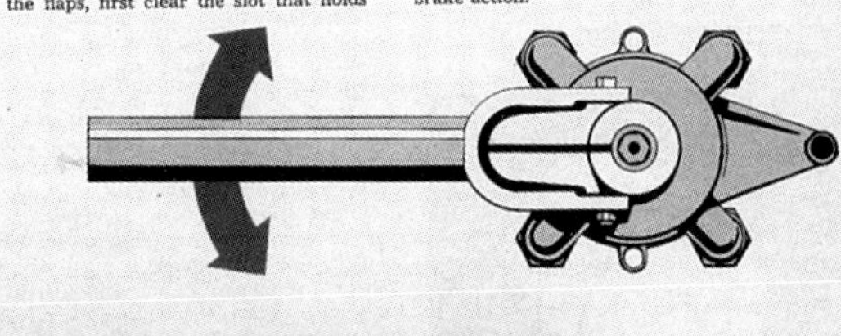

RESTRICTED

Apply brakes smoothly and evenly in order to avoid swerving

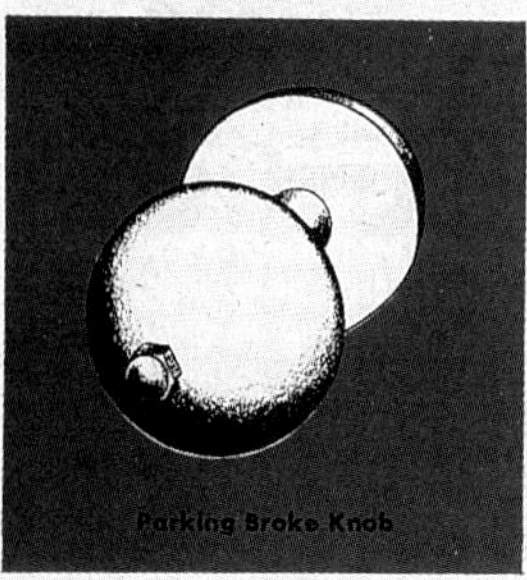

Parking Brake Knob

Parking brake: Set parking brake by pushing the brake pedals all the way down and pulling out the parking brake knob on the lower part of the pedestal. While holding knob out, release the brake pedals. To release parking brake, push the brake pedals down again. If the parking brake doesn't release when you push brake pedals down, push the knob manually.

5. **Carburetor air filter:** The C-47 has three types of carburetor air filters. You will find electrical, manual, and hydraulically operated filters on different series of the airplane.

These filters are installed to protect the interior of the engine from thick dust and blowing sand. They should not be used under any other conditions.

The electrical and manually operated filters are ram filters screening air from the front of the nacelle into the carburetors. The hydraulically operated filters allow the engine to use ram and non-ram air. The non-ram intake is on top rather than in the front of the nacelle.

A control lever behind the pilots seat operates the hydraulically controlled filter. It has 3 positions: Filter, Unfilter, and Lock.

Turn the control to FILTER, then back to LOCK in order to open the filter gate.

Turn the control to UNFILTER, then back to LOCK in order to close the filter gate and use ram air.

6. **Automatic pilot:** The automatic pilot control box consists of a directional gyro, ball bank indicator, bank-and-climb gyro, horizon bar, and suction gauge. It is on a panel in the center

24 RESTRICTED

RESTRICTED

Carburetor Air Filter Control

of the instrument board. The automatic pilot keeps your airplane in straight and level flight by mechanical control of the rudder, ailerons, and elevators. Its operation is described in the section entitled "Cruise."

7. **Superchargers:** Early series of the C-47 have integral single-speed blowers with an impeller ratio of 7.15 to 1. For operation at higher altitudes late series were equipped with 2-speed single stage blowers. These superchargers have an impeller ratio of 7.15 to 1 in low blower and 8.47 to 1 in high blower. Controls for the blower are at the pilot's left.

To check for proper operation:

1. Prop controls .... INC. RMP
2. Throttles .... 1700 RPM

A **minimum** of 45 psi oil pressure is required to operate the blower clutch. If oil pressure is low at 1700 RPM advance the throttles until oil pressure reaches 45 psi.

3. Blower control .... HI BLOWER

Shift blower controls quickly.

4. Throttles .... 30" Hg.
5. Blower controls .... LOW BLOWER

Watch the manifold pressure. A drop in manifold pressure indicates proper clutch operation.

CAUTION

Superchargers must be de-sludged before every flight and at least once every two hours in flight.

To de-sludge:

1. Throttle .... 1400-1600 RPM
2. Blower controls .... HI BLOWER
3. Adjust RPM and manifold pressure as required if in flight.
4. After 10 minutes return blower controls to LOW BLOWER. Don't use high blower at low altitudes. The impeller is geared to the engine and is driven by the engine. At low altitudes it takes more power to drive the impeller in HI BLOWER than you gain by the shift.

Panel of Automatic Pilot

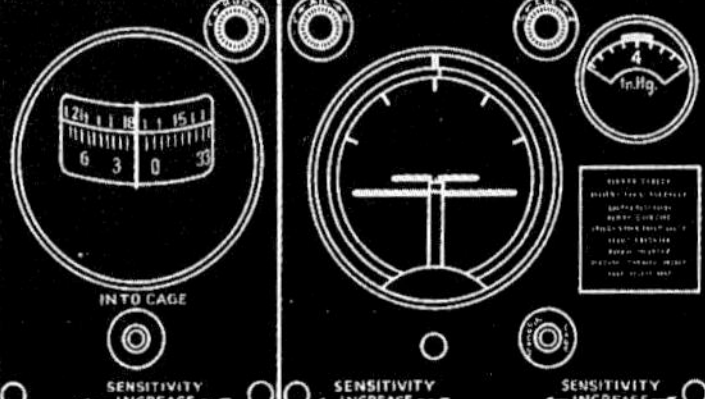

RESTRICTED 25

RESTRICTED

DIAGRAM OF FUEL SYSTEM

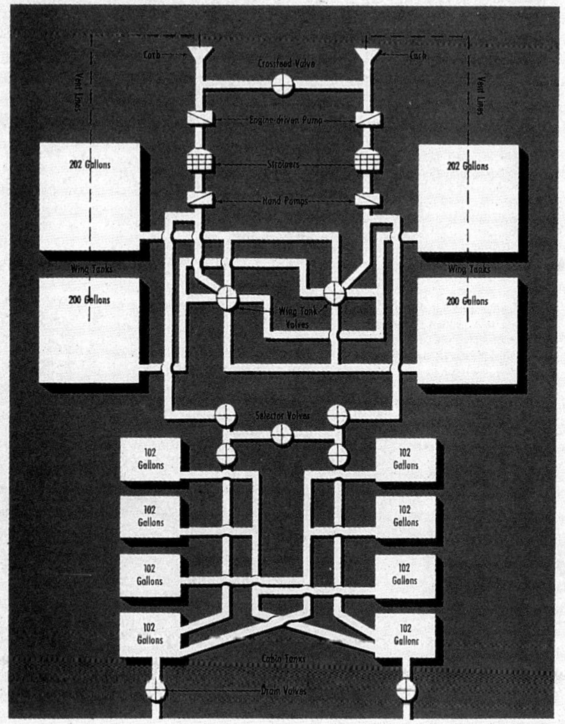

26 RESTRICTED

RESTRICTED

FUEL SYSTEM

Use Grade 91 fuel under normal conditions, Grade 100/130 fuel under critical and combat conditions.

1. **Fuel tanks:** The C-47 airplane has four center section tanks, two on each side of the fuselage. Main tanks are forward; each has a capacity of 202 U. S. gallons. Auxiliary tanks are aft of the main tanks; each has a capacity of 200 U. S. gallons. Each tank is independent of the others.

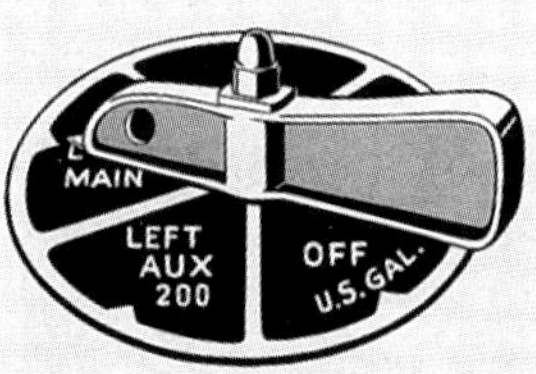

Fuel Selector Valve
(One for Each Engine)

2. **Fuel selector valves:** On each side of the pedestal is a fuel selector valve. The right valve controls flow of fuel to the right engine, the left valve to the left engine. Valves read: LEFT MAIN, RIGHT MAIN, LEFT AUX., RIGHT AUX., and OFF. Select fuel tank for either engine by turning selector valves to the desired position.

3. **Crossfeed system:** Some C-47 series have a fuel crossfeed system that permits either fuel pump to supply both engines. In those series, if one pump fails, you can maintain fuel pressure on both engines by turning the crossfeed system control ON.

Crossfeed control is at the lower right-hand corner of the pedestal. Turn the control ON only when needed; otherwise, keep it in the OFF position.

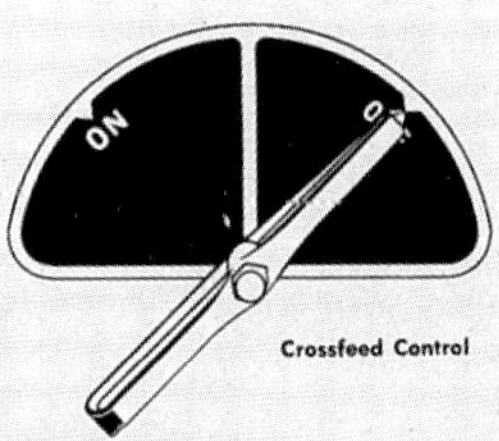

Crossfeed Control

4. **Booster pumps:** On late series of the C-47 booster pumps replace the crossfeed system. The booster pumps maintain pressure in the fuel lines if an engine-driven fuel pump fails. Booster pump switches are on the right-hand electrical panel.

For normal operation, turn the booster pumps ON for all operation below 1000 feet and above 10,000 feet. If fuel pressure drops on either engine, while fuel remains in the tank, turn on that booster pump. If this fails to return fuel pressure to normal, turn the fuel selector valve to the tank from which the other engine is operating. If this fails, feather the engine.

Land as soon as possible if you cannot keep both engines operating normally.

5. **Wobble pump:** C-47 models have a hand or wobble pump to supply fuel pressure manually. It is behind the pilot's seat. Some C-47A airplanes have a wobble pump, others have replaced the wobble pump by electric fuel booster pumps.

Wobble Pump

RESTRICTED 27

6. **Carburetor mixtures:** Carburetor mixtures are controlled automatically for most efficient engine operation at different altitudes. There are four mixture control positions: EMERGENCY, AUTO RICH, AUTO LEAN, and IDLE CUT-OFF. Mixture controls are at the right top of the pedestal.

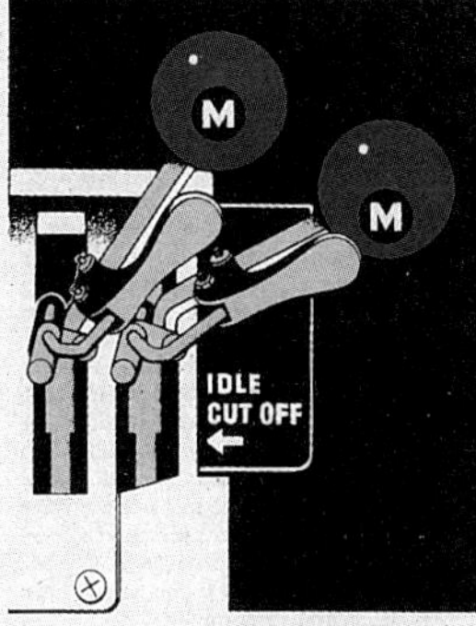

Carburetor Mixture Controls

To lean the mixture move the controls from EMERGENCY to AUTO RICH, and AUTO RICH to AUTO LEAN. Move them back to enrich the mixture.

Here are the effects which the controls produce at different positions:

EMERENCY—full rich mixture. This position eliminates the automatic feature of the carburetor.

AUTO RICH—rich mixture.

AUTO LEAN—lean mixture.

An automatic feature of the carburetor functions in either of these positions. This feature is an altitude compensator unit. As the airplane climbs or descends a diaphragm in this unit measures the pressure of the outside air. It is very sensitive, reacting to the minute changes in pressure and temperature. As the diaphragm expands and contracts, it meters fuel into the induction system to keep the fuel/air ratio at its most efficient level.

IDLE CUT-OFF—stops flow of fuel.

Note: AUTO RICH and AUTO LEAN are sometimes called, respectively, "Takeoff and Climb" and "Cruise."

7. **Carburetor heat controls:** Controls are located below the instrument panel on the right side of the pedestal. Positions: HOT and COLD. When you need carburetor heat to offset icing conditions, move the controls to HOT. This brings heated air from around the cylinder heads into the induction system.

Leave this control in COLD for all normal operations.

Carburetor Heat Controls

OIL SYSTEM

There are two oil tanks, one in each nacelle, with a capacity of 29 gallons each. Servicing these tanks with 25 gallons of oil allows adequate space for foaming and expansion.

Check the quantity in the tank by removing the filler cap and observing the fluid level. When the fluid level is at the top baffle the tank contains 25 gallons of oil.

There is a two-gallon reserve supply in a standpipe at the bottom of each tank. By this means you can feather the prop even though all normal engine oil supply is lost.

Oil pressure and temperature gages and oil pressure warning lights are on the instrument panel in front of the copilot.

Keep oil pressures between 75 and 90 psi in normal flight operation. Don't let them go below 60 or above 100 psi, if you are flying under emergency conditions. If pressure falls below 50 psi, the red warning light above the pressure gage lights.

Oil cooler shutter controls are at the left side of the pedestal. Adjust shutters to keep temperatures within operating limits of between 60°C and 75°C, or, under emergency conditions, between a minimum of 40°C and maximum of 100°C.

ELECTRICAL SYSTEM

Two engine-driven generators supply electric current to your airplane and charge two 88 ampere-hour batteries. Early series of the C-47 have a 12 volt ground-return electrical system. Late series of the airplane have a 24 volt ground-return system.

There is a generator on each engine. One alone, or both of them, supply current to the batteries. Select generators with one of two switches in the main electrical junction box. On some early series the switches are on the right hand electrical panel.

Open or close battery circuits with switches on the left-hand electrical panel. On late series airplanes there is only one switch.

Fuses or circuit breakers are installed to protect instruments and equipment from overloads.

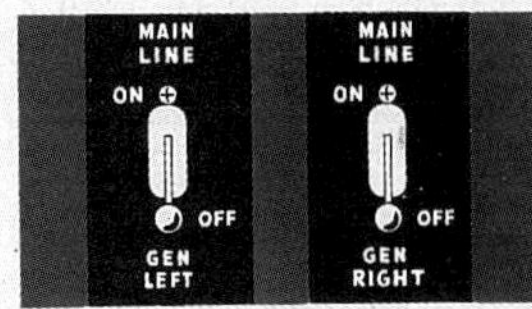

Generator Switches

Spare fuses for the system are in the main electrical junction box on early airplanes. These have been replaced by circuit breakers on late airplanes.

Battery Cart Plug

Always start engines by use of a battery cart, if a cart is available. Battery cart plug-in is under the fuselage, forward of the leading edge of the wing. When a battery cart is connected, keep the master switch or switches in the OFF position. Turn switches ON only when engines are started and battery cart is disconnected, or when battery cart is not used.

PROPELLERS

The C-47 has three bladed Hamilton Standard Hydromatic propellers. These propellers will feather and unfeather quickly in an emergency. A governor, operated by engine oil pressure keeps the props at a constant speed.

A standpipe in the oil tank retains a two gallon supply for emergency feathering if the engine oil supply is lost. Loss of oil pressure, or oil supply, allows the prop blades to move to full low blade angle.

Don't feather this propeller completely more than once every 15 minutes. The feathering pump motor will heat up and probably burn out if it is not allowed to cool.

Don't keep a prop feathered more than 20 minutes for single engine practice. Oil collects in the bottom cylinder heads making starting dangerous. This fluid can cause a fluid lock and blow off the cylinder heads when you attempt to start.

AUXILIARY EQUIPMENT

1. **Heaters:** Your airplane has either a hot air or a steam type heating system.

Hot air heating system: In this type of heater, scooped air is warmed by heat exchangers attached to the engine exhaust tail pipes and mixed with cold air to obtain desirable temperatures. Heat from the right engine exhaust goes to the pilots' compartment. Heat from the left engine exhaust goes to the forward cargo, radio operator's, navigator's, and the main cargo compartments, and to the defrosting system. Valves regulate the amount and flow of air, either to the defrosting system or to the main cargo compartment or both. The valves are in the navigator's compartment.

A valve to regulate mixture of heated and cold air, heat controls for the pilots', navigator's and radio operator's compartments; valves to spill excessively heated air, and a red warning light that indicates excessive air temperatures in the system, are all in the radio operator's compartment. A red warning light that indicates excessive temperatures also is on the pilots' right-hand instrument panel.

In some series there is a bypass control valve in the radio operator's compartment to direct the flow of hot air from either exhaust to the entire heating system.

Dampers that control the amount of hot air flow are in each outlet.

Restrict system to cold air (ventilation) by valve mixture control in the radio compartment.

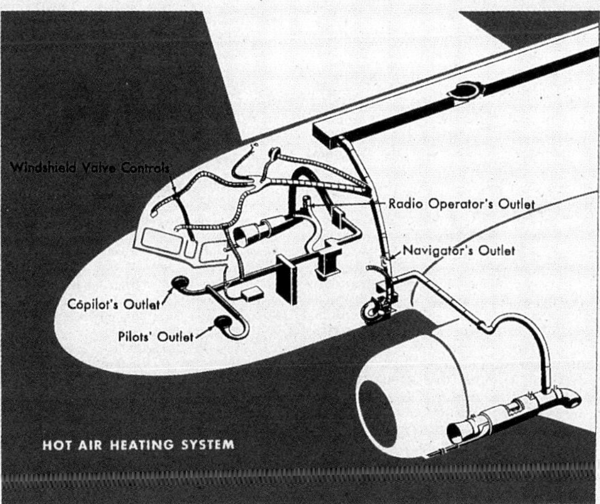

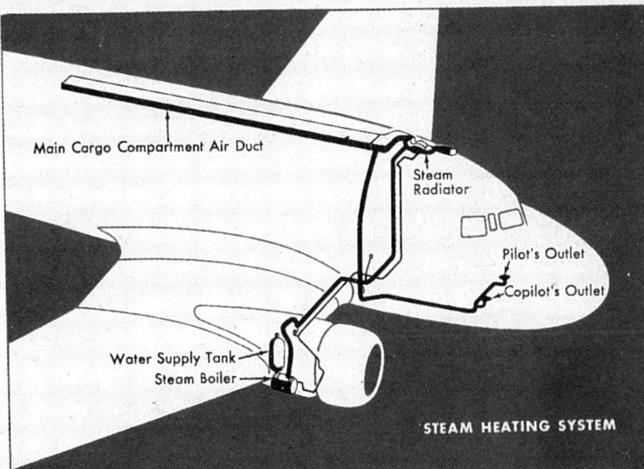

Steam heating system: In this type of heater, steam, supplied by a boiler in the right nacelle, heats air introduced by airscoop to a radiator in the top left side of the forward section. A valve in the radio operator's compartment controls the flow of steam from boiler to radiator. Flow of air from the radiator to the pilots' and radio operator's compartments is controlled by a valve near the ceiling, between the radio operator's and navigator's compartments. Another valve, to the left of the air duct in the main cargo compartment, controls the flow of air to this compartment. A slide valve, near the floor of the radio operator's compartment, controls the flow of air into that compartment.

Use system for ventilation by bypassing air around radiator. A mixture control, directly forward of the radiator, allows air to flow through the radiator, the bypass duct, or both.

Drain system by opening drain cock in bottom of steam boiler.

2. **De-icers:** De-icers are installed to remove ice from the leading edges of the wings and the vertical and horizontal stabilizers. The de-icer control, behind the copilot's seat, has ON and OFF positions.

To remove ice, turn the control ON after a film of ice builds up on the surfaces. Turn the control OFF after the film is cracked and removed. Repeat this operation until you are out of the icing conditions.

Don't turn the de-icers ON and leave them ON. Ice may form a shield around them leaving the de-icers in operation inside the shield of ice.

When you turn de-icers ON, a vacuum pump on each engine pumps air through a de-icer rotary distributing system, which in turn pulsates the air to bladders within removable de-icing boots that form the leading edges of the wings and tail surfaces. Alternating inflation and deflation of the bladders causes ice to break off these edges.

3. **Anti-icers:** Anti-icers remove as well as prevent ice from forming on a surface of the airplane. A fluid, usually alcohol or alcohol-glycerine, pumped to the surface, spreads and causes ice to loosen and break off. Note: Anti-icer fluid works well with rime ice, is not very effective against freezing rain or snow.

Propeller anti-icer system: A pump behind the pilot's seat supplies anti-icer fluid from a 4-gallon (U. S.) tank, next to the pump, to a slinger ring aft of the propeller hub. Start flow of anti-icer fluid by turning on petcock at tank and turning on pump switch on left-hand electrical panel. Regulate volume of flow by means of the rheostat next to supply tank.

Carburetor anti-icer system: A pump in the forward cargo compartment supplies anti-icer fluid to the carburetor from a 10-gallon (U. S.) tank, also in this compartment. Pump switch is on the right-hand electrical panel. Turn ON for continuous operation, to MOM for momentary operation; OFF to stop pump.

Windshield anti-icer system: There are two windshield anti-icer systems. Each is supplied by a 6-gallon (U. S.) tank of anti-icer fluid in the forward baggage compartment.

To open and close panels frozen tight by ice: Pump fluid to perforated tubing around panels by means of hand pump below the lower right-hand corner of the instrument panel. While using pump, two ON-OFF control valves, below window level on either side of pilots' compartment, allow you to free either one panel or the other or both panels at once. Note: Some models have a plunger under each panel. Use plungers as you would a hand primer.

To remove ice from surface of windshield: Open line valve on small panel on the left side of the instrument panel. When the line is open, turn on electric alcohol pump switch found in some C-47 models on the same panel; in others, on the left-hand electrical panel.

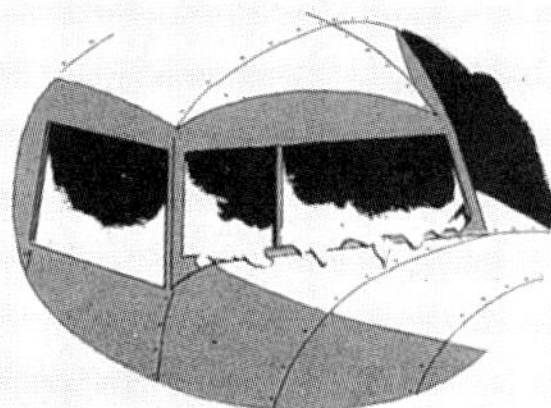

Pitot heater: Two switches on the left-hand electrical panel operate integral heaters, installed in pitot static tube heads. These heaters prevent ice from forming in these heads.

4. **Vacuum system:** Two engine-driven pumps operate the vacuum system. They provide air suction for the operation of the artificial horizon, directional gyros and the turn indicator.

Check suction gage on automatic pilot instrument panel for vacuum indication of 3.75" to 4.25" Hg. The normal reading is 4" Hg. If reading is not within these limits, have system checked.

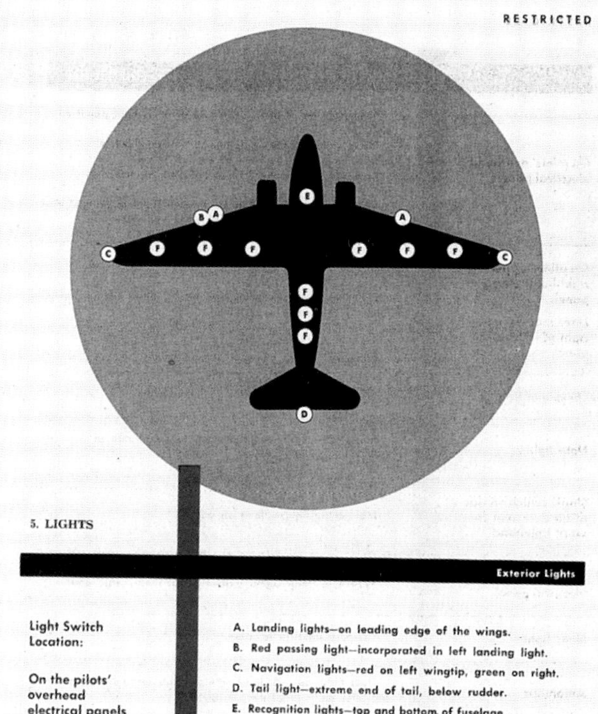

5. LIGHTS

Exterior Lights

Light Switch Location:	
On the pilots' overhead electrical panels	A. Landing lights—on leading edge of the wings.
	B. Red passing light—incorporated in left landing light.
	C. Navigation lights—red on left wingtip, green on right.
	D. Tail light—extreme end of tail, below rudder.
	E. Recognition lights—top and bottom of fuselage.
	F. Formation lights—(later model airplanes) top of wings and tail assembly.

Interior Lights

Location	Light
On pilots' overhead electrical panels	Instrument panel light—at bottom of instrument panel on pedestal. Pilots' compartment lights—on both sides of pilots' compartment at lower front of window panel. Compass and automatic pilot lights—incorporated in instruments. Command receiver remote tuning unit light—to right of dial. Voltmeter light—above and between voltmeters.
On pilots' upper right-hand electrical panel. *Later models*—on right of instrument panel	Fluorescent lights—one on each side of pilots' compartment, and one at front of pedestal.
On side of light	Companionway light—over companionway.
Near lights	Radio operator's, navigator's compartment lights—in respective compartments.
Single switch on side of air duct near forward bulkhead	Main cabin lights—along air duct.
Pilots' left-hand electrical panel	Parachute troop signal light—right of main cargo door.
Near light	Lavatory light—in lavatory.
Automatic	Door light—on right-hand side of instrument panel. When on, indicates main cargo door is open.
On pedestal, below propeller pitch controls	Red signal light—astrodome.

6. **Oxygen system:** All late series of the C-47 have a low-pressure demand oxygen system. It is supplied either by ten small or five large oxygen bottles located under the main cabin floor. New series have five oxygen outlets: two for the pilots' compartment; one to the right of the companionway, behind the copilot; one in the radio operator's compartment, and one in the navigator's compartment.

Each outlet is an individual unit, complete with pressure gage and flow indicator.

Most new series have three or more A-4 walk-around bottles. Two are in the forward cargo compartment and one in the navigator's compartment.

Some older series have no oxygen outlet in the companionway. As a rule, the oxygen system in these series is of the high-pressure type and is supplied by one large bottle in the forward cargo compartment. On this bottle are a high-pressure oxygen gage, an oxygen regulator, and a shut-off valve. An altitude pressure gage for this system is on the instrument panel.

7. **Communications system:** The following communication equipment is in your airplane: In the radio operator's compartment:

Command Set SCR-274N—For plane-to-plane and plane-to-station short-range voice or MCW communication. Operate from either the pilots' or radio operator's compartment.

Liaison Set SCR-187A or SCR-287A—For plane-to-plane or plane-to-station long-range communication. Operate from radio operator's compartment, and from pilots' compartment once necessary adjustments are made from radio operator's compartment.

Interphone Set RC-36—For communications among crew. Installations at pilot's, copilot's, navigator's, radio operator's and jumpmaster's positions. Intercommunication furnished at all positions with selector at INTER position.

VHF Set SCR 522—For two-way voice communication from plane-to-plane or plane-to-ground station. The receiver-transmitter unit and dynamotor are forward of the radio operator's position.

The VHF control box is aft of the copilot's seat and the VHF-MED FREQ switch is at the right of the radio compass control box. Move this switch to VHF position before operating the VHF control box.

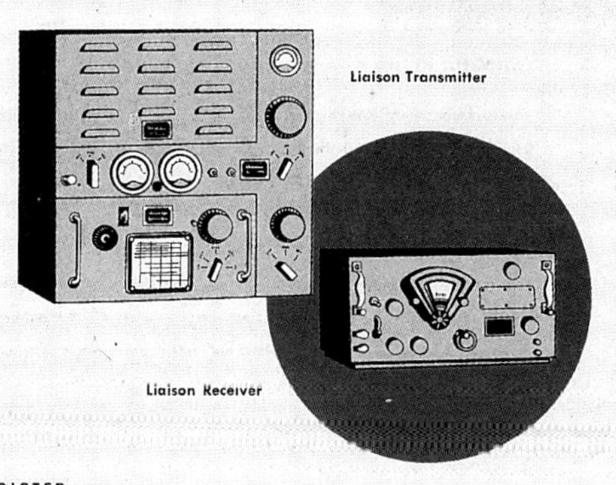

In companionway:
Radio Compass SCR-269G–For homing, loop work and for other navigational purposes. Operate at radio compass control panel, on ceiling of pilots' compartment.
Marker Beacon Receptor RC-39 or RC-43-2. Operate by turning on radio compass which supplies the necessary power for the receiver. Indicator lamp, on pilots' left-hand instrument panel, lights when passing marker beacon transmitters.
Frequency Meter SCR-211–For checking frequencies on radio receivers and transmitters. To use, attach an antenna to antenna terminal on top of frequency meter cabinet. Plug in headset and turn on set's switch to CHECK position. Once warmed up, rotate tuning control until desired reading is observed.
At rear of main cargo compartment:
Identification Set SCR-595-A or 695A–IFF (Identification, Friend or Foe). Operate by turning ON-OFF power switch in the pilots' compartment and radio operator's compartment. When set is ON, turn selector switch to desired numbered position. For emergency operation, use emergency switch either in pilots' compartment or radio operator's compartment. If necessary, destroy set by simultaneous pressure on two push-switches in pilots' compartment.
Emergency Radio Set SCR-578 A or B (emergency dinghy transmitter)–For emergency use after ditching. Instructions for operation on radio.
AN-APN1–Radio Altimeter. When properly set, it indicates changes in ground altitudes. Set at required altitude by means of altitude limit switch above center of windshield. Red, green, and white lights and an altitude indicator are on the instrument panel in front of the pilot. High and low deviations, above and below set altitude, are indicated by green and red lights.
AN-APN2–Rebecca. Homing device.

CHECKLISTS

INSPECTIONS AND CHECKS

As you know, there is a checklist in the cockpit of every army airplane. AAF Regulations require that it be used on every flight. If you have 200 hours, or 12,000 hours, use it. That checklist is designed for qualified first pilots on a particular series and type airplane. When you are checked out as first pilot on the C-47 use that checklist.

The checklist in this manual is designed for *you*. It is a set of operating instructions you need for transition training. Use it on every flight. It not only gets you into the air safely, and down safely, but teaches you to know your airplane.

Visual Outside Inspection–

NOTE: Before you make this inspection, turn on the battery switch and booster pump to raise pressure in the fuel system. With pressure up you can visually check fuel system leaks. Also check the hydraulic gages to be sure that hydraulic pressure is up.

Wheel Chocks	In place
Control Locks	Removed
Pitot Head Cover	Removed
Landing Gear Pins	Removed (only when hydraulic pressure is up)
Control Surfaces	Freedom of movement, fabric for general condition, hinges for condition, trim tabs for condition
De-icer Boots	For condition and security
Nacelles (outside)	Excessive oil, wheel wells for leaks in fuel and hydraulic lines
Tires	Proper inflation, slippage, general condition
Brake Hydraulic Lines	Leaks, condition
Fuel Sumps	Safetied
Landing and Running Lights	Lenses for condition
Fuel and Oil Caps	Secure
Propellers	Blades for nicks and general condition
Glider Pick-up Equipment (if installed)	Security
Glider Tow Hitch	Metering pin, freedom of action

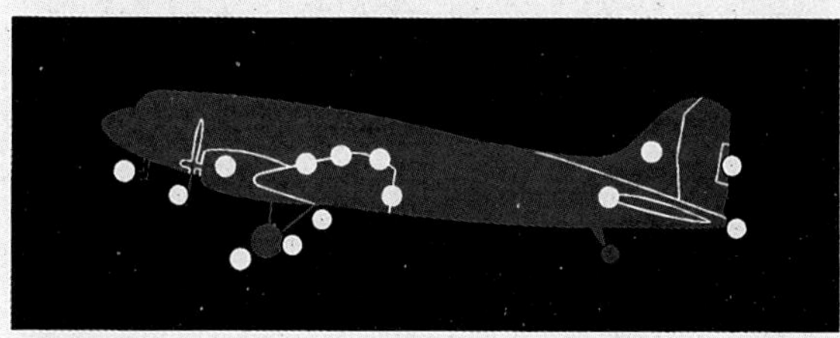

VISUAL INSIDE INSPECTION

Cargo and Ballast	Position check against Form F or F-1, security
Cabin Tanks	Tanks and lines for leaks, valves closed
Safety Belts	In place for each passenger
Parachutes	Available for each passenger
Emergency Equipment	As necessary, proper position and security

BEFORE STARTING ENGINES

Forms 1 and IA	Status of aircraft (consult aerial engineer)
Hydraulic Fluid Level	Normal
Hydraulic Pump Selector	Left engine operating hydraulic system
Gear Latch	Down and locked
Flap Handle	Flaps up, then to neutral
Gear Handle	Neutral
Battery Switch	Off (if battery cart not available, On)
Generators	On
Fuel Gages	Amount of fuel
Cowl Flaps	Open
De-icers	Off
Anti-icer Pumps and Valves	Off
Automatic Pilot	Off
Lights	On (night only)
Flight Controls	Free
Carburetor Air Filter	Unfilter, then locked
Crossfeed	Off
Trim Tabs	Neutral
Parking Brake	On
Tailwheel	Locked
Throttle Friction Brake	Snug
Oil Shutters	Adjust as required
Carburetor Air	Cold
Fuel Selector Valves	Left to left main; right to right main
Propellers	Full forward, high rpm
Throttles	Cracked
Mixtures	Idle cut-off
Pitot Heater	Off
Inverter	On

STARTING

NOTE: Have member of ground crew pull propellers through at least three revolutions, and post fire guard before starting.

Battery Switch	Off (if battery cart is not available, On)
Fuel Booster Pumps	On

Call "Clear" to ground crew, energize 10 to 15 seconds, and engage starter

Master and Ignition Switches	On (after prop is turning)

AFTER ENGINES ARE RUNNING

Fuel Booster Pumps	Off
Battery Switch	On
Fuel Pumps	Checked

BEFORE TAXIING

Crew and Passengers Aboard and Door Secured

Hydraulic Pressure	675-925 psi
Radio	On and checked
Altimeters	Set
Clock	Set
Gyros	Set and uncaged
Flight Controls	Free

WHEN GIVEN TAXI CLEARANCE FROM CONTROL TOWER

Parking Brake	Off
Tailwheel	Unlocked

ENGINE RUN-UP

Parking Brake	On
Tailwheel	Locked
Fuel Booster Pumps	Off
Oil Cooler Shutters	As desired
Mixtures	Auto Rich
Cowl Flaps	Open
Fuel Selectors	Main tanks

Propellers Through Full Range
Carburetor Heat
Generators
Ignition
Hydraulic Pumps
All Instruments and Gages

BEFORE TAKEOFF

Mixtures	Auto Rich
Cowl Flaps	Trail
Oil Shutters	As required
Propellers	Inc. rpm
Gyros	Set and uncaged
Fuel Booster Pumps	On
Friction Brake	Tightened
Tailwheel	Locked (when lined up with runway)

AFTER TAKEOFF

Landing Gear	Up
Wheels	Stop rotation with brakes

Power Reductions

Fuel Booster Pumps	Off

CRUISE

Cowl Flaps .... As required
Mixtures .... Auto Lean
Fuel Selectors .... To desired cruise tanks
Oil Shutters .... As required
Adjust Power as Desired

BEFORE LANDING

Automatic Pilot ...... Off
Altimeters .... Set
Fuel Selectors .... Left to left main, right to right main, or both to full tank
Mixtures .... Auto Rich
Carburetor Air .... Cold
Fuel Booster Pumps.... On
Ignition .... Check
Propellers .... Set
Landing Gear .... Down and latched, gear handle neutral, pressure up, green light: check wheels visually

Tailwheel .... Locked
De-icers .... Off
Parking Brake .... Off (brake pressure on pedals)
Flaps .... As desired

AFTER LANDING

Flaps .... Up
Cowl Flaps .... Open
Fuel Booster Pumps.... Off
Elevator Trim .... Neutral
Propellers .... Full forward, high rpm
Tailwheel .... Unlocked

PARKING

Parking Brake .... On (after chocks are placed, Off)
Cowl Flaps .... As desired
Tailwheel .... Locked
Mixtures .... Idle cut-off
Fuel Selectors .... Off
Ignition .... Off
Radios .... Off
Battery Switches ...... Off
Generators .... Off
Landing Gear .... Pins in
Landing Gear Handle.. Down
Flap Handle .... Up
Flight Control Locks.... On
Pitot Cover........... On

INSTRUMENT *Markings*

C-47B
GRADE 100/130 FUEL

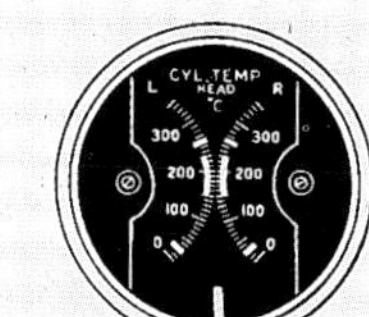

CYLINDER HEAD TEMPERATURE
Short Red .... 25°C
Green Arc .... 150-232°C
Short Red .... 260°C

MANIFOLD PRESSURE
Short red line...................... 48" Hg.
Green Arc .... 43-32" Hg.
Blue Arc .... 32-28" Hg.

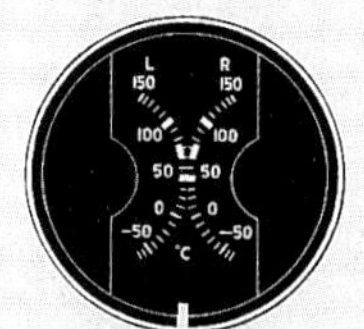

OIL TEMPERATURE
Short Red .... 40°C
Green Arc .... 60-75°C
Short Red .... 100°C

TACHOMETER
Short Red .... 2700 rpm
Green Arc .... 2550-2250 rpm
Blue Arc .... 2250-1700 rpm

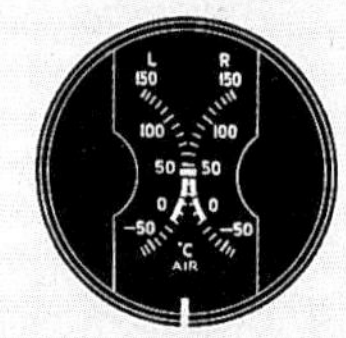

CARBURETOR AIR TEMPERATURE
Yellow .... —10°C + 15°C
Green .... 15-38°C
Red .... 40°C

FUEL PRESSURE
Red .... 14 Psi
Green .... 16-18 Psi
Red .... 19 Psi

SUCTION
Red .... 3.75" Hg.
Green .... 3.75" Hg.-4.25" Hg.
Red .... 4.25" Hg.

OIL PRESSURE
Red .... 60 Psi
Green .... 75-90 Psi
Red .... 100 Psi

AIR SPEED INDICATOR
Yellow .... 112 IAS
Red .... 255 IAS

DE-ICER PRESSURE
Green .... 7.5"-8.5" Hg.
Red .... 9" Hg.

HYDRAULIC PRESSURE
Green .... 675-925 Psi
Red .... 1200 Psi

STARTING

Note: Location and operation of the controls of this airplane are explained in the second section of the manual, "The Airplane." A thorough acquaintance with that section helps you understand this and the following sections that describe the airplane's operation.

Battery Switch....... Off (if battery cart is not available, On)

Fuel Booster Pumps.... On

Copilot builds up fuel pressure by turning on booster pump to right engine or by using wobble pump. Keep pressure built up to between 3 and 5 psi.

Master and Ignition Switches.... On

When your C-47 is equipped with an induction vibrator starting coil, leave the ignition switch OFF until the engine is turning over. This prevents a possible kickback and resulting damage to the engine.

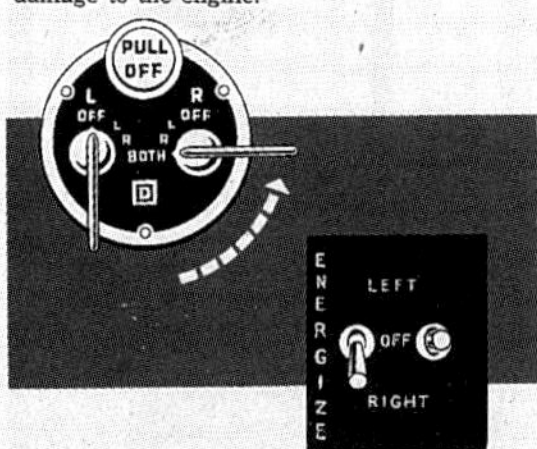

Turn ON the master switch and the ignition switch to the right engine. While the copilot builds up fuel pressure, energize and mesh starters. At the same time you energize, prime engine as much as you feel is necessary. If the engines already are warm, or it is a hot day, you may find it unnecessary to prime.

Be sure not to overprime your engines.

You have left the mixture controls in IDLE CUT-OFF before starting, to keep the engines from flooding. When the engine fires, move mixture control for that engine from IDLE CUT-OFF to AUTO RICH.

Start the left engine in the same manner. If you are using a wobble pump, continue pumping, if necessary, to maintain pressure.

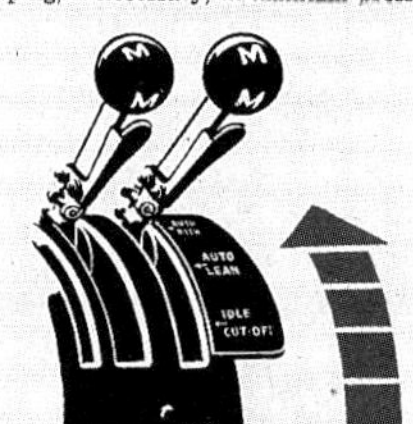

AFTER ENGINES ARE RUNNING

Fuel Booster Pumps.... Off

Battery Switch.... On

Turn battery switch ON as soon as battery cart plug has been removed.

Fuel Pumps.... Checked

Turn fuel selector to one engine OFF. As soon as fuel pressure drops on that engine, turn crossfeed ON. If the engine continues to function, you know at once that the one remaining pump can supply both engines with fuel. By repeating this operation with the other engine, you know whether or not the other pump can supply both engines.

While starting engine watch out for:

1. Engine fire. See that a fire guard is posted beside engine you're starting.
2. Starters burning out. Do not energize and mesh the same starter excessively. If your first or second attempt at energizing and meshing engine does not succeed, start other engine.
3. Overloading. Excessive priming sends too much fuel into the cylinders and causes backfiring. Backfiring, in turn, may result in serious damage to the engine.

RESTRICTED

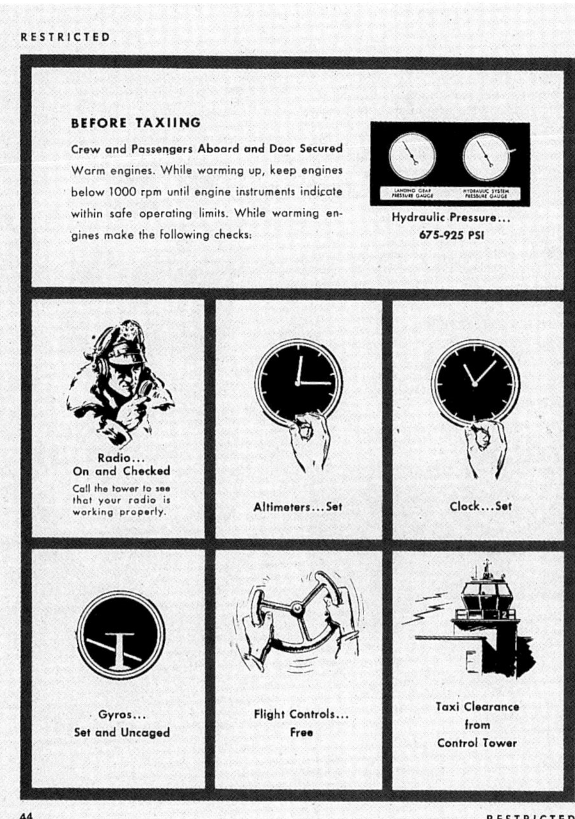

44 RESTRICTED

RESTRICTED

As soon as all instruments and gages indicate within safe operating limits, obtain taxi clearance from tower and clearance from lineman. Taxi to run-up area.

TAXIING

Remember, the C-47 is a large, heavy airplane. Although you taxi it like any other 2-engine airplane with conventional landing gear, its size and weight tend to exaggerate its movement in the air and on the ground. You will soon learn its characteristics, but until you know the airplane, handle it with extreme care.

In straight taxiing, keep the tailwheel locked and use throttles as evenly as possible.

In crosswind taxiing, a locked tailwheel and correct use of throttles help you maintain direction with minimum use of brakes. When you are taxiing crosswind, use additional power in the upwind engine.

Anticipate your turns. Momentum gathered in straight taxiing is much greater than in a lighter airplane and carries into your turns. Before you turn, slow your airplane down and unlock your tailwheel. In starting or completing turns, use throttles in coordination with your brakes. If you use throttles properly, you take a great load off your brakes and thereby increase their life.

Keep rudders neutral when braking so that you can apply full action to the brake you are using. You can keep rudders neutral by applying pressure on the opposing rudder pedal; at the same time, you must take care not to apply pressure to the opposing brake.

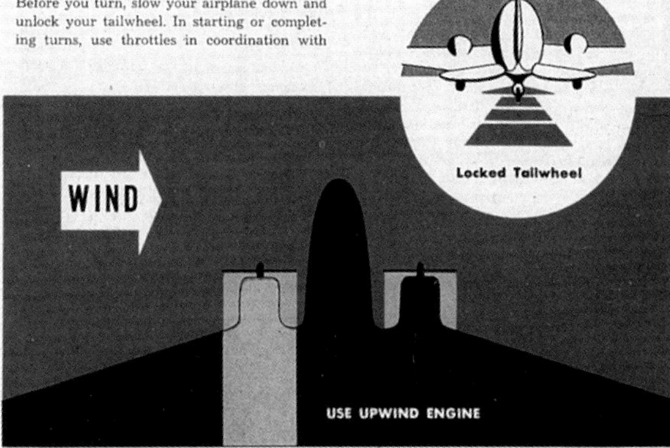

RESTRICTED 45

RESTRICTED

TAXIING DON'TS

Don't make pivot turns.

If you keep the wheels rotating through the turn you save rubber, thus reducing the chance of tire failure. Pivot turns can pull a tire off the wheel and may even strain the landing gear.

Don't underestimate the wing span.

It is 95 feet from wing tip to wing tip. Give yourself plenty of room.

Don't taxi too fast.

Taxi accidents still comprise the greatest number of all accidents. Remember, taxi accidents can be prevented. They are caused by carelessness.

Don't overload one or both engines by excessive idling.

While you are taxiing out to takeoff, check your turn-and-bank indicator and your gyro instruments to see that they are functioning.

ENGINE RUN-UP

Normally you make your engine run-up in an area just clear of the runway. If traffic permits and you are cleared to takeoff position, you can make your run-up on the runway.

The less you idle your engines between run-up and takeoff the better. If there is a slight delay between run-up and takeoff, keep your engines running at a minimum of 1000 rpm to prevent fouling. At the same time watch head temperatures to prevent overheating.

When you park for engine run-up, face directly into the wind. In strong, gusty winds the C-47 will nose up when sufficient power is applied to the engines. Keep the incoming traffic in view if possible. If you cannot do this and still face into the wind, be sure to check incoming traffic before moving out onto the runway for takeoff. Keep as much of your airplane as possible on a hard, clean surface during run-up so that pebbles and rocks won't be thrown into propellers and against airplane surfaces.

Once in position, make your checks:

Parking Brake....On

Tailwheel [illegible]

Fuel Booster Pumps....Off

Oil Cooler Shutters....As desired

Set oil cooler shutters, as necessary, to keep oil temperatures within safe operating limits.

Mixtures....Auto rich

Cowl Flaps....Open

Open cowl flaps to permit maximum cooling while running up engines on the ground. If the outside air temperature is cold and the engine itself is running cold, adjust cowl flaps as desired.

Fuel Selectors....Main tanks

Propellers....INC. RPM

Advance throttles until RPM reaches 1500. Lock throttles and move control to DEC. RPM. This operation checks governor operation and flushes the prop dome with warm clean oil.

Carburetor Heat

Apply heat and note gages for temperature rise. Return to COLD.

Generators

See that generators are charging by checking ammeter.

Ignition

Increase one throttle at a time until manifold pressure gages indicate 30" Hg. Check magnetos by turning switch from BOTH to LEFT, back to BOTH, then to RIGHT and back to BOTH. Check magnetos on both engines in this manner.

Hydraulic Pumps

Lower flaps, change selector, raise flaps. Note pressure rise on the hydraulic gages. Return selector to normal position.

All Instruments and Gages

Check engine instruments on the same engine you are checking magnetos before you retard throttle.

Now you are ready [illegible] clearance to taxi out to the takeoff position.

46 RESTRICTED

RESTRICTED

RESTRICTED 47

Either before takeoff or before you taxi for takeoff position, tighten friction brake to prevent throttles from slipping during takeoff.

Tailwheel. . . . Locked

Lock your tailwheel when you are lined up with the runway.

TAKEOFF

Now you are ready to advance your throttles for takeoff. Advance them evenly and steadily until you reach takeoff power. This forward movement of the throttles should take a full 5 seconds.

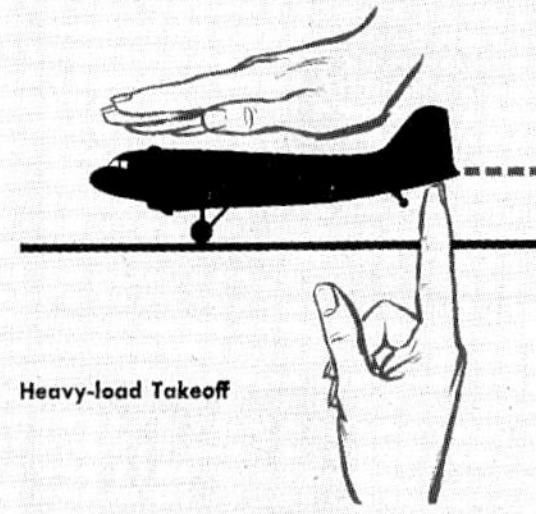

Heavy-load Takeoff

Maintain takeoff direction by using your rudder and, if necessary, your throttles. Rudder control is available directly after you reach takeoff power. Use throttles in crosswinds or to offset swerves of the airplane. As in taxiing, maintain direction in a crosswind by applying additional power to the upwind engine. You can advance one throttle ahead of the other. by a slight twist of the hand.

In a normally loaded airplane the tail usually comes up by itself. You can assist this tail lift by a slight forward pressure on the control column. When the airplane has attained flying speed (85 to 90 mph under normal load conditions), you can break ground.

Heavy-load Takeoff: When you are taking off with a heavily loaded airplane, definitely bring the tail up to straight and level flight position as soon as possible and hold your airplane on the ground until you attain a safe airspeed as determined by your load.

Short-field Takeoff: In taking off from a short field, hold airplane with the brakes until you have advanced throttles to from 25" to 30" Hg. manifold pressure. Release brakes, raise the tail to straight and level flight position as soon as possible, and ease your airplane off the ground as soon as you attain minimum flying speed. Do not allow the airplane to fly itself off the ground. You can use flaps to shorten the length of your takeoff run.

TAKEOFF POWER SETTINGS

RPM	M.P.	MIX.	MAX. CYL. HEAD TEMP.
Grade 100/130 Fuel 2700	48"	AR	260°C.
Grade 91 Fuel—R-1830-92 Engine 2700	46"	AR	260°C.
Grade 91 Fuel—R-1830-90°C. Engine 2700	43"	AR	260°C.

HOLDING

TAIL UP

LEAVING GROUND

Crosswind takeoff: When you make a crosswind takeoff, gain sufficient speed to insure positive rudder control before lifting the tail. As long as you have rudder control, you can coordinate rudder and throttles to maintain a straight takeoff path. Attain enough speed to remain airborne once you have broken ground.

Since your airplane begins to drift when it becomes airborne, you must crab into the wind to maintain straight flight. Once you have begun to crab, do not allow the landing gear to touch the ground. Damage to the gear or to the airplane may result.

AFTER TAKEOFF (CLIMB)

Landing Gear. . . . Up

To retract landing gear

1. Pilot signals ...."Gear UP"

Use the hand signal and a voice command.

2. Release the safety latch from the floor catch.
3. Safety Latch ....Full up
4. Gear lever ....UP
5. When the landing gear pressure gage reads 0 move the gear lever to NEUTRAL. The red light should go out.

Note

When the gear lever is turned to NEUTRAL the safety latch control automatically returns to spring lock position. On a few early series airplanes the red light stays on even though the gear is fully retracted.

Occasionally the gear will sag or start to extend in flight. This is caused by a slight pressure leak in the landing gear lines, because there is no positive up lock on the gear.

You can usually tell if your gear is not fully up by these three checks:

1. Red Light ....ON
2. Loss of airspeed
3. Landing gear pressure gage not indicating 0.

To correct simply follow Gear UP procedure.

To extend landing gear

1. Airspeed............160 mph IAS or less
2. Pilot signals..............."Gear Down"
3. Safety Latch..................Spring lock
4. Landing gear lever.............DOWN
5. Hydraulic Pressure.....500 psi minimum
6. Landing gear lever...........NEUTRAL
7. Green light.........................ON
8. Safety Latch.....DOWN AND LOCKED

Caution

Proper sequence in operation of the latch and gear handle is important. **Any operation of the latch out of sequence results in inability to latch gear in down position.**

Remedy

If inadvertently you operate the latch out of sequence, return to normal by the following steps:

1. Pull latch to vertical position.

2. Raise gear handle to UP position.
3. Return gear handle to NEUTRAL.

Alternate

If you desire to bring latch and gear handle into sequence without retracting wheels, or if you experience difficulty with the foregoing procedure:

Trip the dog, on the hub of the gear handle, by pulling UP.

Wheels. . . . Stop rotation with brakes

As soon as the airplane is clear of the ground retract the gear. Hold a minimum climb until you get safe single engine speed. This speed varies with the gross weight of the airplane, but is between 110 mph and 120 mph IAS.

Power reductions

Once you have attained a speed of 120 mph it is safe to make your first power reductions.

REDUCE POWER TO THESE CLIMB SETTINGS

RPM	M.P.	MIX.	MAX. CYL. HEAD TEMP.
Grade 100/130 Fuel 2550	43"	AR	260°C.
Grade 91 Fuel R-1830-92 Engine 2550	42"	AR	260°C.
Grade 91 Fuel R-1830-90C Engine 2550	42"	AR	260°C.

Note **Maximum cylinder head temperature may exceed 232°C., but *only* for takeoff and climb. At no time allow cylinder head temperature to exceed 260°C. For all level flight conditions, regardless of altitude or power, keep cylinder head temperatures at or below 232°C.**

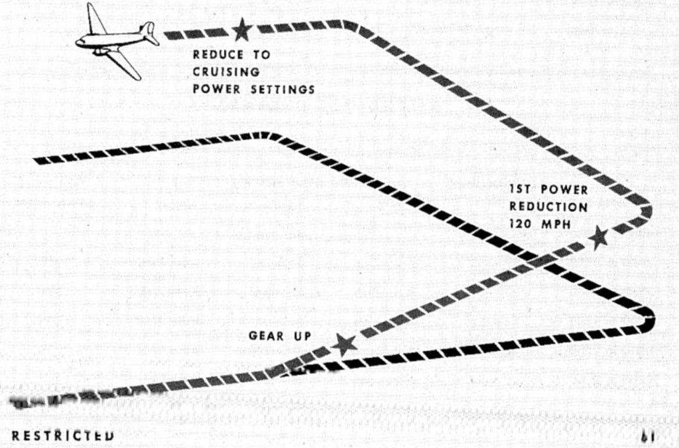

CRUISE POWER SETTINGS

At cruising altitude reduce power to cruise conditions. For Grade 100/130 settings, consult technical orders for the series airplane you are flying.

The recommended power settings for cruise on Grade 91 fuel are:

R-1830-92C ENGINES

RPM min. max.	M.P. min. max.	MIX.	MAX. CYL. HEAD TEMP.
2450 to 2550	39" to 42"	Auto Rich	232°C.
2350 to 2450	36" to 39"	Auto Rich	232°C.
2250 to 2350	32" to 36"	Auto Rich	232°C.
2000 to 2250	28" to 32"	Auto Lean	232°C.
1700 to 2000	24" to 28"	Auto Lean	232°C.

R-1830-90C ENGINES

RPM min. max.	LOW BLOWER M.P. min. max.	MIX.	HIGH BLOWER M.P. min. max.	MIX.	MAX. CYL. HEAD TEMP.
2450 to 2550	39"—42"	Auto Rich	34"—36"	Auto Rich	232°C.
2350 to 2450	36"—39"	Auto Rich	32"—34"	Auto Rich	232°C.
2250 to 2350	32"—36"	Auto Rich	30"—32"	Auto Rich	232°C.
2000 to 2250	28"—32"	Auto Lean	27"—30"	Auto Rich	232°C.
1700 to 2000	24"—28"	Auto Lean	24"—27"	Auto Rich	232°C.

Cowl Flaps....As required

Normally close cowl flaps. Open cowl flaps have a buffeting effect on the tail.

Mixtures....Auto lean

Fuel Selectors....To desired cruise tanks

Since your fuel system has a return line to both main and auxiliary tanks, use at least 60 gallons of fuel from these tanks before using fuel from fuselage tanks. By using fuel from the main and auxiliary tanks first you provide space for return flow fuel as it comes back to these tanks. If this space is not available excess fuel is lost through overflow.

Oil Shutters....As required

Adjust power as desired

You are now ready to trim your airplane for cruising flight.

AUTOMATIC PILOT

When you are flying long distances you can keep your airplane in straight and level flight by means of the automatic pilot. It detects flight deviations the instant they occur and corrects them immediately and with precision. Use this pilot only in ordinary weather conditions, never in extremely turbulent air. To set the automatic pilot in operation, trim your airplane, then:

1. Align index cards in directional gyro.
2. Align bank-and-climb follow-up indicators in bank-and-climb gyro.
3. Check suction gage; it should read between 3.75" and 4.25" Hg.
4. Turn shut-off valve control on hydraulic panel to ON position.
5. Turn automatic pilot servo unit's ON-OFF valve control, on the pedestal, to the ON position.

Note: When pilot is in operation, trim ship with automatic control until airplane is in straight and level flight on desired heading.

Servo controls for rudder, aileron, and elevator are on the automatic pilot. They control the speed of reaction of the control surfaces. Adjust these knobs as needed.

To release automatic pilot, turn pilot servo unit ON-OFF valve control to the OFF position. Turn shut-off valve to the OFF position.

Warning

Whenever the autopilot is in operation a rated pilot must be on duty in the cockpit.

FLIGHT CHARACTERISTICS AND LIMITATIONS OF YOUR AIRPLANE

Your airplane has the normal flight characteristics of a 2-engine, low-wing monoplane. It has no unusual tendencies.

Maneuvers: The following maneuvers are prohibited: loops, Immelmanns, spins, dives, rolls, vertical banks, inverted flight, and all other acrobatic maneuvers.

Limit speed and load factors: The C-47 is designed to operate within designated limits under various load conditions. If you exceed these limits you place undue strain upon the airplane, and structural damage or failure results. These limits are:

Item	26,000 lbs. Gross Weight	29,000 lbs. Gross Weight	31,000 lbs. Gross Weight
Max. Level Flight (IAS)	204 mph	187 mph	170 mph
Max. Glide (IAS)	255 mph	207 mph	191 mph
Max. for Extending Landing Gear (IAS)	160 mph	160 mph	160 mph
Max. for Extending Wing [illegible]	[illegible]	112 mph	112 mph

Turns: Normal flight characteristics. Remember the size and weight of your airplane.

Stalls and recovery: All stalls give warning of their approach by light buffeting of the tail.

Power-off stalls: Power-off stalls give warning sooner than power-on stalls. If gear and flaps are down, this warning is more apparent and the airplane tends to stay in level flight during the stall. If gear and flaps are up, stalls

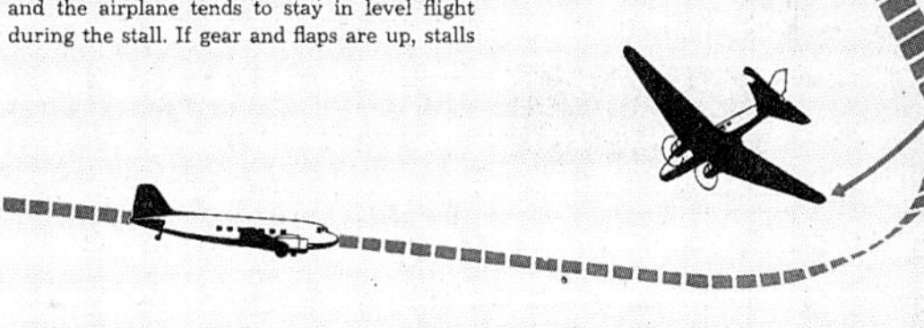

occur with less warning and the airplane has a tendency to fall off on one wing.

Power-on stalls: Power-on stalls occur more suddenly and with less warning than power-off stalls. If your airplane is not in straight and level flight, stalling speed is increased. In steep banks, for example, your down wing stalls and your airplane rolls. Under these conditions the stalling speed of your airplane can reach values of over 100 mph.

Stalls in turns: Stalls in turns are more sudden than stalls in straight and level flight. The down wing stalls first and drops quickly.

Recovery from stalls: You need between 500 and 1500 feet to recover from a power-off or power-on stall. Method of recovery is normal.

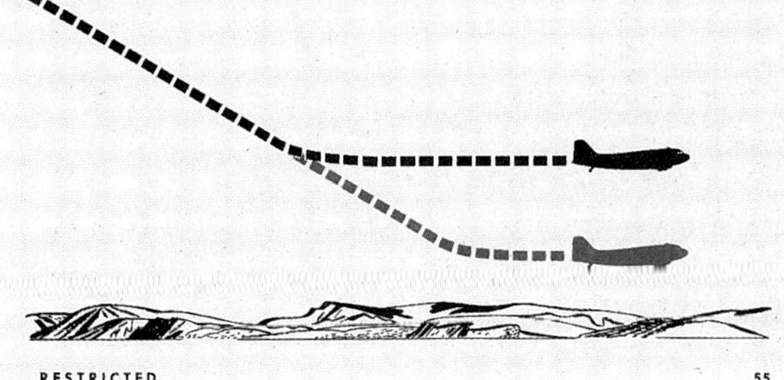

However, avoid excessive airspeed when you are recovering from a stall, to keep loss of altitude to a minimum.

Effect of de-icer equipment on stalls: De-icer equipment in operation disrupts the flow of air over the leading edges of the wings and horizontal and vertical stabilizers. Consequently, it increases the stalling speed of the airplane. Turn off de-icer equipment, therefore, when you are taking off or landing.

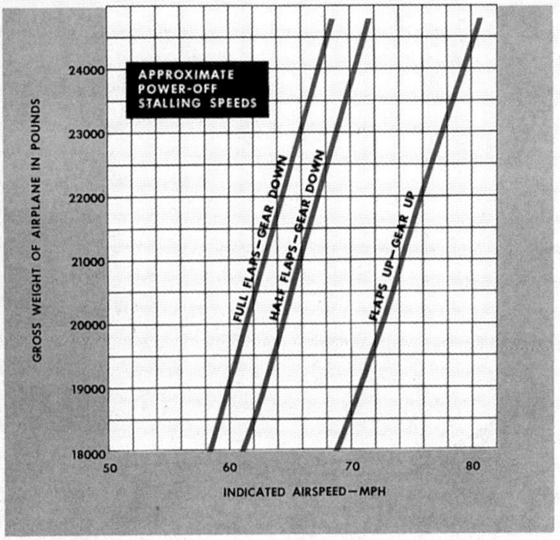

STALLING SPEEDS

Stalling speeds of the C-47 vary greatly under different conditions. Changes in load, power, flap and gear position, and even slight changes in pressure and temperature affect the stalling speed. Your own technique also affects the stalling speed. If you fly smoothly, with coordinated control pressures, you can fly at slower speeds than another pilot who is rougher on the controls.

The chart of stalling speeds tells you **approximately** when the airplane will stall power-off. Use this chart as a guide until you are thoroughly familiar with your own airplane.

Effect of cowl flaps on stalls: When cowl flaps are open during flight they cause tail buffeting. This in turn increases the stalling speed of the airplane.

BEFORE LANDING

Automatic Pilot . . . . Off

Altimeters . . . . Set

Fuel Selectors . . . . Left to left main, right to right main, or both to full tank

Mixtures . . . . Auto rich

Before you enter the traffic pattern, set mixtures at AUTO RICH and change fuel selectors to the main tanks. If one main tank contains less fuel than landing minimum (approximately 90 gallons), set both engines on the fullest main tank. It is permissible to land on auxiliary tanks if they are full or are fuller than the main tanks.

Carburetor Air . . . . Cold

Fuel Booster Pumps . . . . On

Ignition . . . . Check

Propellers . . . . Set

Landing Gear . . . . Down and latched, gear handle neutral, pressure up, green light: check wheels visually

When you have turned on the downwind leg and have arrived opposite the runway, extend and lock your landing gear. Check the landing gear green light indicator, and be sure to **check your gear visually.** Increase propellers to 2250 rpm.

Tailwheel . . . . Locked

De-icers . . . . Off

Parking Brake . . . . Off

When you have extended your landing gear and have increased your propeller rpm, make a power reduction sufficient to lose altitude at between 300 and 400 feet a minute.

Once you have turned on your base leg, make another power reduction. Maintain 120 mph until you are on your approach leg. When you are straightened out on the approach leg, make a third power reduction. Do not make this reduction at too low an altitude, as it might necessitate a quick increase in power just prior to landing.

Note: As every pattern differs in altitude and distance from the field, and as wind conditions vary, use your own judgment in making power reductions.

Flaps . . . . As desired

Approach runway at airspeeds of between 85 and 95 mph.

LANDING

There are three types of landing: (1) A 3-point landing. (2) Tail-low landing (tail approximately 1½ feet above the ground when wheels touch). This is actually a wheel landing. (3) Wheel landing (airplane is in a level attitude when wheels touch).

1. You can make a 3-point landing in a C-47 airplane, but this type of landing is not advisable. Reason: Weight of the airplane causes undue strain if you happen to drop in.

2. Normally, make a tail-low landing. You can reduce manifold pressure to a minimum during roundout in this type of landing, and cut engines after making contact with the ground—or you can cut power before roundout and land without power. As speed is dissipated, tail lowers and contacts the ground by itself. You can aid this lowering of the tail by slight back pressure on the control column.

3. Although a tail-low landing is desirable under normal conditions, you can make a wheel landing with the C-47. In this type of landing, hold roundout to a minimum and allow airplane to settle on the wheels from a level-flight position. Contact ground approximately 10 to 15 mph faster than in a tail-low landing and hold the wheels on the ground by a slight forward pressure on the control column. As speed

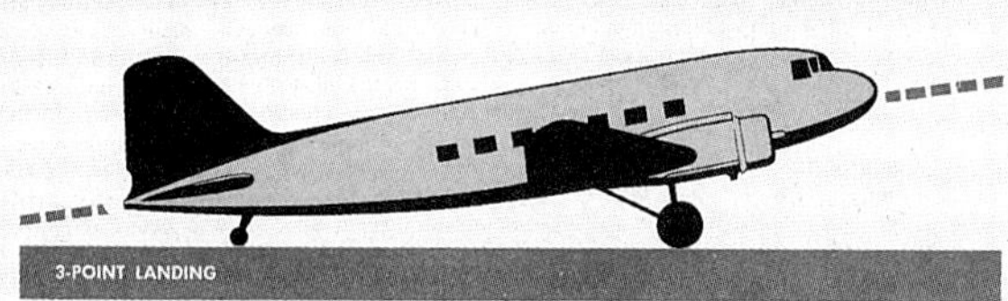

dissipates the tail lowers and contacts ground by itself. Aid this lowering of the tail as you would in a tail-low landing.

CROSSWIND LANDINGS

There are three possible ways to land crosswind: (1) Hold the airplane straight and level toward the landing strip and drop one wing into the wind just enough to counteract drift. (2) Head the airplane into the wind enough to keep a straight path (crabbing). (3) Combine the first two methods.

The best method is the third: head into the wind and lower the upwind wing. This method keeps the bank and the crab to a minimum and makes it easier to straighten the airplane when close to the ground. Crab just enough to avoid slipping. Any uncoordinated movement may raise the stalling speed of the airplane.

In crosswind landings correct for drift as soon as possible on the approach. If the airplane is making a straight path to the landing strip, the only correction needed on actual landing should be the angle of crab.

Use flaps at your own discretion. Less flaps should be used in stronger and more direct crosswinds. In a strong 90° wind, or in gusty crosswinds, it is best to use no flaps at all.

As the airplane begins the roundout for landing, bring low wing up and straighten airplane so there is no side load on the gear as it touches the ground.

In a crosswind, wheel landings are desirable as direction is easier to maintain. You can hold your airplane on the wheels by slight forward pressure on the controls.

Once on the ground, maintain directional control by use of rudder, power on the upwind engine, and by use of brakes.

Remember, you have not finished flying your airplane until you have come to a full stop—especially in a crosswind.

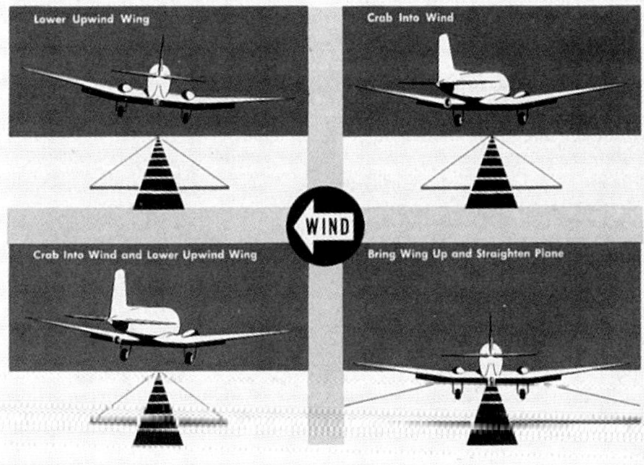

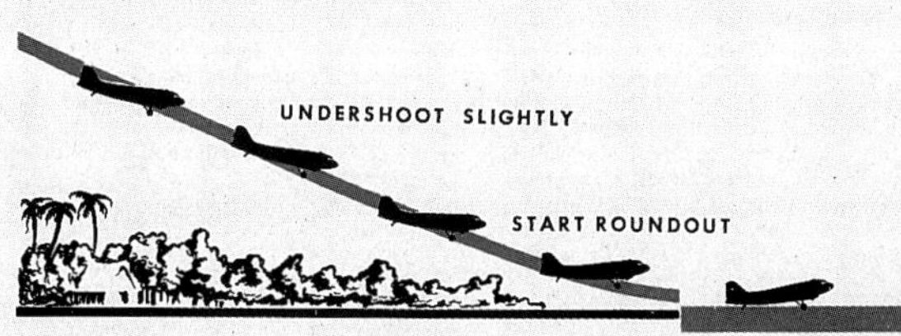

SHORT-FIELD LANDINGS

Tactical operation of the C-47, especially in combat theaters, often requires you to make short-field landings. Field conditions and approach clearances vary in different parts of the world. Landing fields may be small, or bombed so heavily that little landing space remains. Runways and fields may be rough, making fast wheel-landings dangerous, or they may be ice-coated, making the brakes useless. The following landing technique, however, gets you down safely under all these conditions.

Technique

Set the base leg to establish a normal power approach. Set the glide to **undershoot slightly.** This is the key to a good short-field landing.

Hold a normal approach speed from the top of the approach to the start of the roundout. Make the roundout in the shortest possible forward distance.

Make corrections early on the approach, if you are undershooting too much. Use power to clear obstructions—don't depend on judgment alone from high on the approach. Correct by varying power and angle of glide to maintain a constant airspeed.

Increase the power slowly, and go into an approach to slow flying as the airplane approaches a tail-low attitude. Keep the airplane in this attitude for as short a time as possible. You should be slow flying, at an airspeed at or slightly above power-off stalling speed, just before you touch the ground. Reduce the power completely when you contact the ground.

If you are making an actual short-field landing, use the brakes as much as necessary. For practice, however, let the plane roll to a stop as you would if the brakes were not functioning.

Tips

Don't undershoot and slow fly long distances to reach the field. This leaves you helpless if an engine fails.

Don't use excessive speed early on the approach. This prevents a low roundout before you reach the field.

Don't drop below a safe airspeed early on the approach.

Don't use excessive power in the last of the roundout. This causes the airplane to balloon and destroys the value of the procedure.

NO-FLAP LANDING

Make your approach to a no-flap landing lower and with speed slightly higher than in the ordinary approach. As you normally approach in a tail-low attitude it is better to make a tail-low than a wheel landing.

FLAT TIRE LANDING

Make normal approach and a normal tail-low landing. Keep the weight of your airplane off bad tire as long as you can, by use of the ailerons. Be sure the tail is on the ground before you allow weight to settle on bad tire. The airplane turns into the bad tire. Control its direction by using the opposite brake.

OVERSHOOTING A FIELD....BOTH ENGINES

When you mess up an approach and find yourself overshooting, don't be too proud to go around.

Increase rpm and apply power as necessary.

Get the gear up immediately.

Hold the nose down as you raise the gear and apply power. With trim tabs set to hold the airplane in an approach glide, there is a strong tendency for the C-47 to lift her nose. Correct as you apply power. Retrim as soon as possible.

Raise the wing flaps slowly as you gain airspeed (100 to 110 mph IAS). As the flaps come up they decrease the angle of attack of the wings. Use back pressure on the elevators to hold this angle constant, thus preventing uncontrolled sinking and loss of altitude.

Reduce drag further by setting the cowl flaps at trail. Use normal climb procedure and go around for another crack at landing.

AFTER LANDING

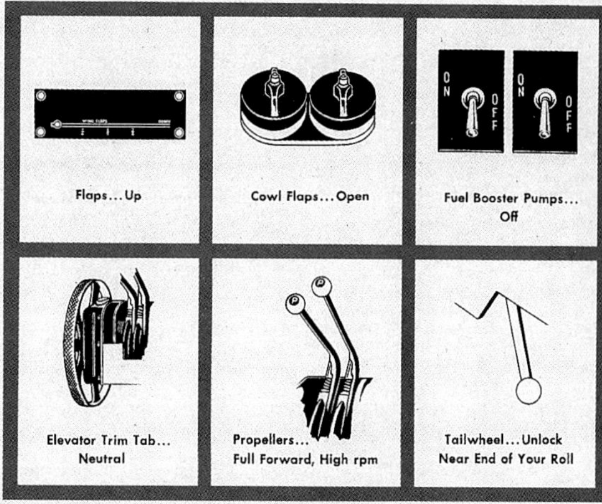

During the roll, pull your flaps up, open cowl flaps, turn off booster pumps, place elevator trim tab in neutral, and put your propellers in high rpm.

Rudder control is available for the major part of the roll. Use your rudder rather than your brakes to maintain direction. At the end of the roll, apply your brakes evenly.

PARKING

Parking Brake....On (after chocks are placed ....Off)

Cowl Flaps....As desired

Mixtures....Idle cut-off

When you park your airplane, lock tailwheel, lock parking brake and pull mixtures to IDLE CUT-OFF to stop your engines. Once your engines have stopped firing, push the throttles forward to the stops.

Fuel Selectors....Off

Ignition....Off

Turn off the ignition switches when the propellers have stopped rotating.

Radios....Off

Battery Switches....Off

Generators....Off

Landing Gear....Pins in

Landing Gear Handle....Down

Place gear handle in full DOWN position.

Flap Handle....Up

Flight Control Locks....On

Release your parking brake only when the wheels have been chocked and you have inspected them.

Pitot Cover....On

MOORING

If it is necessary to moor your airplane, see that it is tied down by ropes attached to each landing gear chassis and to the tailskid. Keep airplane level by attaching ropes to the tie-down rings in the slots in each wing. Be sure all ropes are tied at an angle from the ground, never straight up, and that sufficient slack is left in them in case they tighten. Main stress of wind should be taken by the landing gear lashings, rather than by the wings.

Tie-down cable for the tailskid is kept in a canvas bag next to the rear wall of the forward cargo compartment.

NIGHT FLYING

CHECKS ON LIGHTING EQUIPMENT

If you intend to fly at night, make visual checks of all external lights before you start to taxi. Check formation lights, if they are to be used. Check all cockpit lights necessary to safe night operation.

TAXIING HINTS AND PRECAUTIONS

Remember these points when you taxi at night:

(1) Have on running lights and passing light.

(2) Allow more clearance from other airplanes and obstructions.

(3) Never shine landing lights into traffic approaching the field for landing.

(4) Run up airplane with landing lights off.

NIGHT TAKEOFFS

When you sit in the cockpit of a C-47 airplane you are approximately 12 feet off the ground.

Consequently, it is considerably different from a smaller airplane in reference to ground lights. Bear this in mind, especially during takeoff.

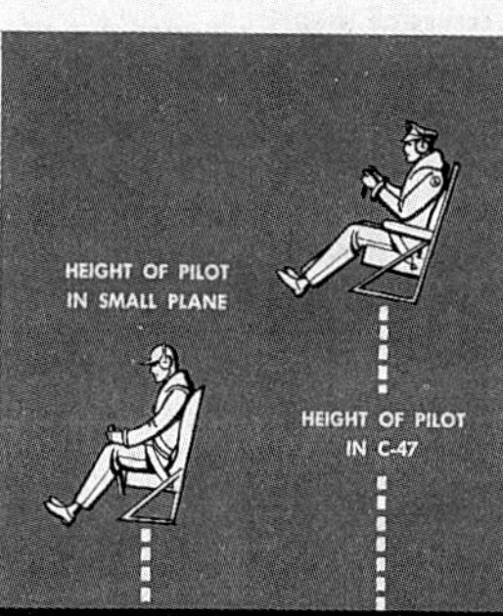

Make takeoff and climb at night with smooth increases and reductions in power and smooth changes of the airplane's attitude.

Use of landing lights during takeoff depends upon your knowledge of the field and of obstructions in the takeoff path. If you are forced to make an emergency landing after takeoff, landing lights are of value.

Make continued reference to instruments. Depth perception at night is poor and ground lights can create illusions. Do not rely upon them for reference, particularly when you are unfamiliar with the airplane.

NIGHT VISION IN THE C-47

There is considerable reflection on the windshield of this airplane from cockpit lights. Adjust these lights to a minimum glare before takeoff. Turn off all cockpit lights and all lights aft of the pilots' compartment that are unnecessary to the safe operation of your airplane. Unless you need other cockpit lights, use fluorescent lights only.

Caution your crew against turning on any unnecessary light. Your copilot, for instance, might inadvertently turn on a flashlight and cut off your vision just as you are making an approach. Warn him to be careful.

NIGHT PATTERNS AND LANDINGS

Land on First Third of Runway

In flying night patterns, be especially careful to maintain correct altitudes and airspeeds and be alert for other aircraft. Use compass to line up with the runway. Remember, you are flying a large airplane and recovery from a mistake takes much longer than if you were flying a smaller plane. Until you are thoroughly familiar with the airplane, make a normal approach and land within the first third of the runway. Do not attempt to land on the end of the runway. It is easy to undershoot at night. Keep alert at all times.

During night operation make continued reference to your instruments in this and other large airplanes.

WEATHER FLYING

The C-47 is an excellent instrument airplane. It is stable and easily controlled. Bear in mind, especially during instrument approaches, however, that the airplane needs more room to maneuver than a smaller airplane.

HANDLING AIRPLANE IN TURBULENT AIR

Slow your airplane down in turbulent air in proportion to its gross weight and the amount of turbulence. You can slow your airplane down by power reductions alone, or by lowering landing gear at the same time you reduce power slightly. The second procedure is more desirable, as you are able to maintain engine power and pressures while you are reducing your airspeed to the desired rate.

CARBURETOR ICING

Whenever there is a probability of flying through carburetor icing conditions, turn on your carburetor heat. If you are flying through a carburetor icing condition and you cannot eliminate carburetor ice by carburetor heat, turn on the anti-icer system. Remember, it is easier to prevent than to remove ice.

FLYING WITH ICE

The C-47 is stable even with an appreciable load of ice. However, because the stalling speed of your airplane is higher under ice load, decrease the amount of bank in turning by increasing the radius of your turn. Remember, a proportionate amount of airspeed is required to compensate for the increase of stalling speed, resulting from the ice load.

Note: Be sure that de-icer equipment is turned off and that de-icer boots are deflated before making a landing.

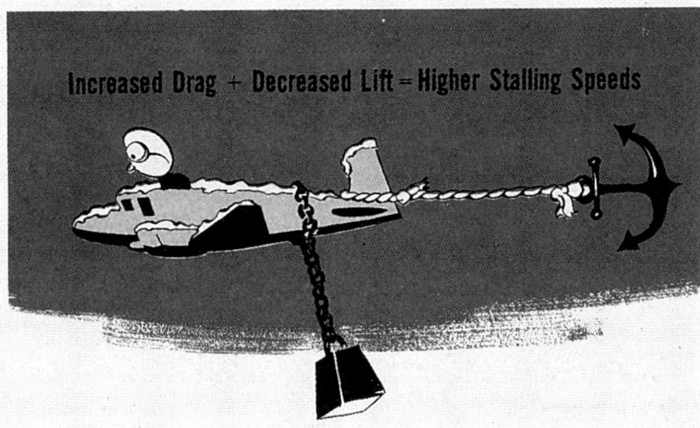

INSTRUMENT APPROACHES

On instrument approaches, maintain airspeed to provide ease of control. On low approaches, establish airspeeds according to the gross weight of the airplane. When you have made visual contact with the ground on a low approach, avoid slow airspeeds, quick turns and steep banks.

APPROACHES WITH PRECIPITATION

When you are making a contact approach, forward visibility is often restricted even though windshield wipers are operating. Under this condition, make continuous reference to instruments when you approach for landing so that you can maintain correct pattern and altitude.

On approaches with low visibility, follow this technique:

1. Fly along the desired runway in the direction opposite that in which you intend to land, setting the directional gyro on 0°.
2. As you pass the edge of the airport, turn 45° to the right (or left). Fly for 45 seconds on this heading, then start a standard-rate turn in the opposite direction.
3. Turn until you reach a heading of 180°. This heading should put the airplane on the landing approach lined up with the runway. Lower landing gear and ½ flaps.
4. Small corrections with this heading line up the airplane exactly with the runway, once it has come into view.
5. Take wind direction and velocity into consideration in executing this maneuver.

EMERGENCY PROCEDURES

Single Engine Procedure

To feather or not to feather? When an engine goes out, do not be in a hurry to cut off the engine and feather the propeller. If you are at a safe altitude, 500 feet or more above the ground, usually you can take time to find what is wrong and correct it before single engine procedure is necessary. Some simple thing may be wrong with the engine or fuel line that you can correct easily if the cause is known. For instance, if an engine goes out because a fuel pump stops functioning, you can continue to supply fuel to the dead engine by an electric booster pump, or, if the model you are flying has no booster pumps, by turning on the crossfeed and using the wobble pump.

The reasons you cut throttle and feather the propeller when an engine goes out are: (1) to prevent destruction of the engine; (2) to eliminate the drag of a windmilling propeller.

Sometimes you can get enough power from a failing engine to override propeller drag. In this case, if there is no destruction of the engine, there is little reason to feather it. Where there is a partial loss of power in an engine, it still may be of definite assistance to you in flight.

Again, circumstances may make it necessary to keep an engine in operation and allow it to damage itself in order to save your airplane and crew. A decision of this kind depends upon your own judgment.

You might feather an engine that obviously is damaging itself, in order to save this engine for landing or for a time when you will need it most during the flight. Again the decision rests with yourself.

Remember, the important thing is to bring back equipment and people safely.

Steps for Single Engine Procedure

A simple 7-step procedure is the basis of single engine operation:

1. Airspeed
2. Directional control
3. Adjust power
4. Reduce drag
5. Reduce fire hazard
6. Trim
7. Trouble Search

1. Airspeed

Get safe single engine speed ([illegible] mph) even though you have to lower the nose and lose altitude to do so. It is better to fly into the ground under control than to spin in.

2. Directional control

Once you have safe single engine speed, directional control is simply a matter of coordinating rudder and aileron properly. Use the trim tabs to aid control if it is difficult to hold the airplane manually.

3. Adjust power

If the power settings are high and the airspeed low (as in takeoff) you may have to reduce power to prevent loss of control. If the power settings are low and the airspeed high (as in normal cruise) increase the power on the good engine. Use as much power as you need. 120 mph IAS is a safe single engine speed, but any additional speed you can get and maintain without overworking your good engine is highly desirable.

4. Reduce drag

Check the gear and flaps. Get them up if they are down.

Cut the throttle, mixture control, and prop control.

Feather the prop.

Readjust trim tabs if necessary.

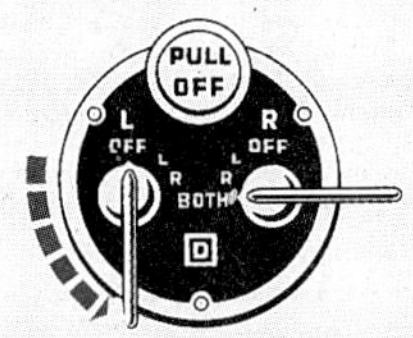

5. Reduce fire hazard

Fuel shut-off valve to bad engine OFF.

Fire extinguisher selector switch to bad engine

Ignition switch OFF after prop stops turning.

Cowl flaps and oil cooler CLOSED on bad engine.

Hydraulic and vacuum systems to good engine.

6. Trim

Make final adjustments on trim tabs.

7. Trouble search.

In case of abrupt engine failure, check ignition switches and fuel valve positions while starting single engine procedure. Try to find out what caused the trouble and make temporary repairs. Check all fuses, switches, circuit breakers, valves, lines and wiring as well as you can.

Don't try to start the bad engine if you don't **know** what is wrong. It is much simpler to make a single engine landing than to fight a fire in the air.

Reduce weight if the plane is excessively heavy. Drop tools, cargo, and anything that will come loose, if it is necessary, to maintain safe flight.

Now let's apply this procedure to the varying test of flight conditions.

Engine Failure on Takeoff

Observe these three rules when an engine fails on takeoff:

1. Cut the throttles and stop straight ahead if an engine fails before you leave the ground.
2. Cut the throttles and land straight ahead if an engine fails after you leave the ground, but before you reach safe single engine speed.

If you have not retracted the gear and enough runway remains, land and stop the plane with the brakes. If you have not retracted the gear and there is **not** enough runway remaining, **retract the gear immediately.**

3. If you have reached safe single engine speed before the engine fails, follow normal single engine procedure.

Engine failure during normal flight.

Use normal single engine procedure.

Engine failure in, or approaching a stall.

Cut the power and lower the nose if an engine fails at low speed. Make your recovery exactly as you would for a power-off stall recovery. As soon as you reach safe single engine speed use the normal single engine procedure.

Single Engine Approach and Landing

In making an approach on single engine, it is better to turn into the good engine and to keep the degree of bank to a minimum. Therefore, you have to make a wide approach.

Maintain sufficient altitude to reach the field in case your good engine fails. Lower your gear only when you are sure of reaching the field; do not delay lowering gear too long, however, or there is danger of overshooting.

Make your final approach slightly higher than usual so that you can keep your good engine at minimum power and can straighten your rudder tabs before getting too close to the field. Keep airspeed at 110 mph until you are sure of getting into the field. Use flaps only when you are certain of reaching the field without power.

Once you have lowered your landing gear and your flaps, with airspeed approximately 100 mph, it is imperative that you land. When you have reached this point, get your airplane on the ground. Do not attempt to go around.

If you have landed on single engine, do not taxi your airplane with your good engine.

Failure of Hydraulic System

Remember to close the hand pump shut-off valve in emergency operations where it is necessary to use the hydraulic hand pump. If this valve is left open, you build up pressure in the accumulator only.

Landing Without Hydraulic Fluid Pressure

If you wish to land but have no hydraulic pressure:

1. Put hand pump shut-off valve in closed position.
2. Put gear handle down.
3. Pump landing gear down by hand pump. Note: If you cannot lower gear by pumping,

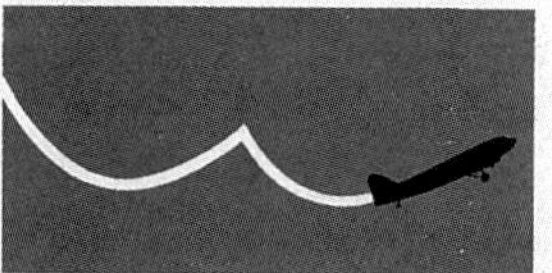

allow gear to lower of its own weight, then zoom airplane to snap gear into latch position.
4. Fasten the safety latch down.
5. Return the landing gear handle to neutral.
6. When the green light burns, you know that landing gear is latched and that you can land. If green light does not show, repeat operation.
7. Remember, when you have no hydraulic pressure, **you have no brakes on landing.**

Landing Without Safety Latch Engaged

You can land without the safety latch being engaged if:

1. Your wheels are down.
2. Fluid in the struts is under pressure (at least 500 psi).
3. You return the landing gear handle to neutral to lock pressure in down lines.

If you land without the safety latch engaged, the red warning light burns and the warning horn sounds, because they are connected to the latch.

Do not use brakes if you land with the safety latch disengaged. Limit pressure on the landing gear hydraulic pressure gage to 1500 psi.

As soon as you have brought your airplane to a stop, and before taxiing, insert landing gear pins. Do not use parking brake if your hydraulic system gage shows pressure of less than 500 psi.

Landing With Simultaneous Failure of Hydraulic Fluid Pressure and Safety Latch

If both hydraulic fluid pressure and safety latch fail:

1. Close hand pump shut-off valve.
2. Put landing gear handle down.
3. Pump hydraulic hand pump several minutes, until just before you touch the ground.
4. Do not use brakes.
5. Make belly landing if necessary. You cannot trust gear to remain extended without pressure and safety latch.

Loss of Normal Hydraulic Fluid

Do **NOT** use the hydraulic hand pump unless absolutely necessary. Save the fluid for brakes and wing flaps.

1. Airspeed ....160 mph IAS or less
2. Safety latch...............Spring locked
3. Landing gear lever..............DOWN
4. Shake the gear down
5. Landing gear lever...........NEUTRAL
6. Green light ....ON
7. Safety latch......DOWN AND LOCKED

Braking When Hydraulic System Pressure Drops

If your hydraulic system drops below 500 psi, use the hydraulic hand pump to build up pressure for emergency braking. Procedure:

1. Place all hydraulic valves in neutral or off.
2. Operate the hand pump while depressing brakes.

Emergency Operation of Wing Flaps

If you cannot lower wing flaps:

1. Close the hand pump shut-off valve if it is open.
2. Lower the flap handle and pump flaps down to the desired setting by using the hydraulic hand pump.
3. Lock pressure in the down-line by returning the flap handle to neutral.

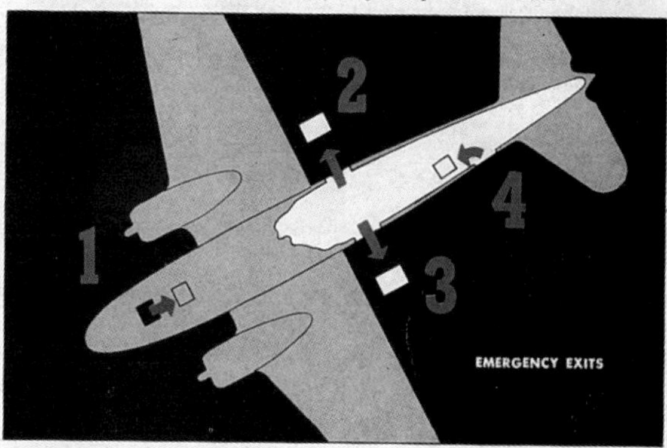

EMERGENCY EXITS

Emergency Exits

There are four emergency exits:

1. **Escape hatch**—above pilots' compartment. To open, twist emergency handles and push from airplane.
2. **Main cargo door**—removable panel. To open, turn emergency release on door and pull panel into airplane.
3. **Two windows in main cabin.** To open, turn handle at bottom of windows and push out and up to clear airplane.

Fire on Board Airplane

You and your crew must know where hand fire extinguishers and engine fire extinguisher control are located.

Hand fire extinguishers are located:

1. One behind the pilot's seat.
2. One to the right of the main cargo door.

Engine fire extinguisher control is located:

Between the pilot's and copilot's seats, on the floor of the compartment.

Procedure When a Fire Is Discovered on Board Your Airplane

1. Order crew members and passengers to attach parachutes.
2. Crew acts on your orders to combat fire.
3. Use fire-fighting equipment.
4. If possible, make a normal safe landing immediately, or
5. Gain as much altitude as possible.
6. If the fire continues to burn, it is up to you to decide whether to land or abandon the airplane. Your decision is final.

Note: Fire-fighting equipment installed in the C-47 is practical for small fires only. Use as soon as the fire starts.

Cabin Fires

To combat cabin fires:

1. Close all windows, exits and vents.
2. Turn fire extinguishers on fire.

Note: Extinguishers of carbon tetrachloride type upon release cause gases which, if inhaled, result in drowsiness, headache, and inability to keep the eyes open. For this reason,

FIRE EXTINGUISHER CONTROL

LEFT MOTOR
EXTINGUISHER
RIGHT MOTOR
TO OPERATE SET VALVE THEN PULL RED HANDLE

LOCATION OF HAND FIRE EXTINGUISHERS

open windows immediately after the fire has been extinguished.

3. If the fire is electrical, turn off main switches.
4. If there is a leaking fuel line, turn off valves to stop fuel flow.
5. Use carbon dioxide extinguishers, if available, on fuel or oil fires.

Engine Fires

1. Open cowl flaps
2. Shut off fuel and oil
3. Feather propeller
4. Turn off ignition
5. Set extinguisher selector valve to the proper engine
6. Pull release handle
7. Lower landing gear
8. Do not start engine again
9. Open emergency exits
10. Land as soon as possible to determine the cause of the fire and correct the conditions before continuing the flight.
11. If engine fire extinguishers are not installed, follow the above procedures omitting the instructions 5 and 6.

If you have used the built-in extinguisher to put out the fire never try to restart the engine. Your CO_2 is exhausted and you have no defense against a recurrence of the fire.

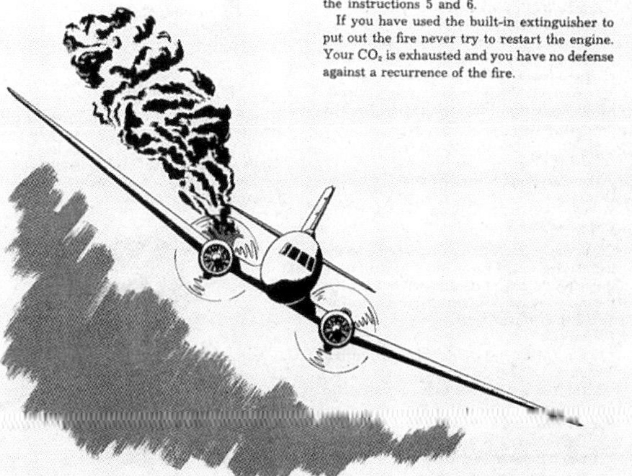

Engine Fuel Pump or Valve Failure

If an engine fuel pump or fuel valve fails:

1. Turn on crossfeed and operate wobble pump; or, in models where there is no crossfeed but where there are booster pumps,
2. Turn on booster pump to the dead fuel pump side.

Relief Valve Failure

First try the foregoing procedure for fuel pump or valve failure. If pressure does not come up, fuel is probably being pumped back to the tank through a defective relief valve. In this case, turn off engine selector valve on the defective relief valve side so that you can feed both engine carburetors through the crossfeed or by means of the booster pump.

Broken Fuel Line

A broken fuel line is indicated by loss of fuel pressure. Remedy by:

1. Turning on the crossfeed (C-47 series only) and trying the wobble pump or by running the booster pump. If pressure does not come up,
2. Turn off crossfeed and engine selector valve and continue on single engine. Land as soon as possible.

Fuel Dumping

There are no provisions for dumping fuel on C-47 models.

Emergency Signals

The emergency warning bell switch is on the left-hand electrical panel. The bell itself is on the left-hand side of the forward bulkhead of the main cargo compartment. Approved bailout and ditching signals are:

For bailout:

(a) 3 short rings, crew takes bailout stations.

(b) 1 long ring, crew bails out ("Abandon airplane").

For ditching:

(a) 6 short rings, crew takes ditching position ("Prepare for ditching").

(b) 1 long ring just before impact, upon which crew braces for ditching.

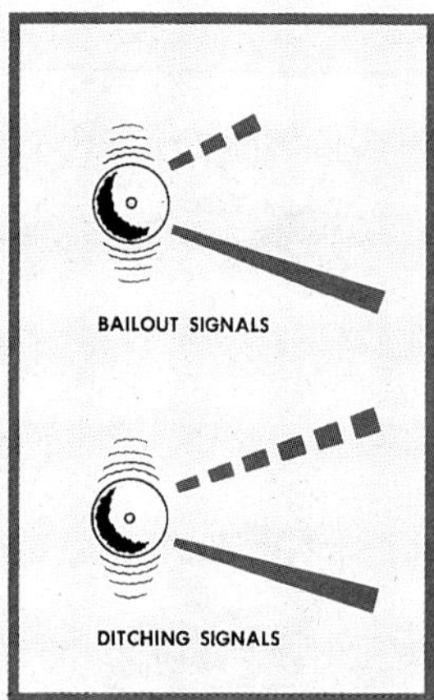

While you are giving the alarm on the emergency warning bell, use interphone to contact all crew members possible.

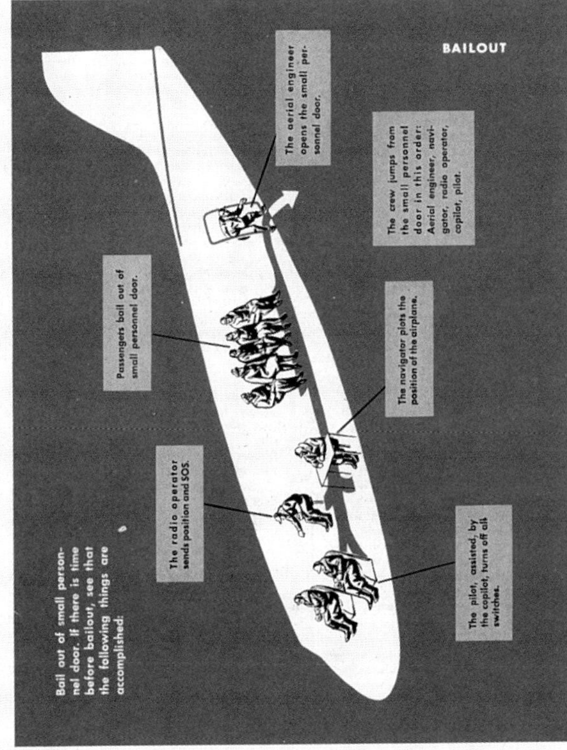

Ditching

> **Practice ditching until your crew knows its positions and functions as a team.**

Before making an over-water flight see that:

1. Water containers are full.
2. Emergency equipment is in order and is lashed down near exits.
3. Retaining lines, at least 12 feet long, are attached to lift rafts.
4. A static line is attached to the retaining line so that it will automatically open the CO_2 cylinder valve when the raft is thrown overboard.
5. A retaining line is attached to the emergency radio set.
6. An emergency radio message is prepared. Leave blank the location, date, and hour of ditching.
7. Mae Wests are in usable condition and are being worn by passengers and crew.
8. Crew members know ditching positions and duties.

Ditching Stations and Duties

> **On taking ditching positions, crew members should pad their heads and backs as much as possible and clasp hands behind their heads. Do not leave ditching stations after airplane's first contact with the water. The second shock is more severe and is the important one.**

When you give the attention signal ("Prepare for ditching"):

1. **Pilot and copilot:**

(a) Pilot gives any necessary instructions to copilot or aerial engineer about disposition of passengers and cargo or equipment to jettison.

(b) Copilot—transmit "Mayday" 3 times. Follow this with the call sign of the aircraft repeated 3 times. Depress the microphone button but do not transmit by voice. At the end of 20 seconds repeat the call sign of the aircraft.

Immediately prior to ditching, bailout, or crash landing, if the aircraft is equipped with VHF: Copilot break the safety wire on the VHF control switch and throw the switch to transmit position. If this is impossible, use any other means to obtain continuous transmission.

After sending distress signals, if the emergency is brought under control, a message cancelling the state of distress must be transmitted.

(c) Attach safety belts and shoulder harness. Copilot assists pilot.

Note: On several occasions pilots have instructed their copilots to leave their seats prior to contact with the water and assume a braced position either on the companionway floor or in the cabin. By using this procedure it has been possible for the pilot to swing his feet up and over into the copilot's seat at the last moment, thus avoiding any possibility of becoming trapped by breakage in the nose or floor section. Inasmuch as no instances of such breakage have been reported, this notation is given only as a suggestion.

2. **Navigator:**

(a) Pass speed, course, altitude, position, and estimated position of ditching to the radio operator.

(b) Places instruments, charts and informational data in brief case or bag and lashes near main cargo door.

(c) Destroys secret and confidential papers and equipment.

(d) Helps in preparing plane for ditching.

(e) Sit in a rear seat if available. If no seat is available sit on the floor facing to the rear with back against the right rear main cargo fuel tank, cargo, or against the right forward bulkhead in the main compartment.

3. **Radio operator:**

(a) If emergency is not imminent, transmit information furnished by the navigator on air-ground frequency and request a fix.

(b) Turn IFF to EMERGENCY, if ditching is imminent. Transmit SOS 3 times, followed by the call sign of the aircraft repeated 3 times. Transmit a 20 second dash and the call sign of the aircraft on CW. Make the first transmission on the liaison set on the assigned air-ground frequency. If contact is not established on the assigned air-ground frequency, use one or more of the following:

(1) The international distress frequency—500 kc.

(2) U.S. emergency and safety frequency —8280 kc.

(3) Any other available frequency in an effort to establish contact with a ground station.

Immediately prior to ditching, bailout, or crash landing, tie down the CW key.

After transmitting distress signals, if the emergency is brought under control, a message cancelling the state of distress must be transmitted on each of the frequencies used.

(c) Remain on interphone until time to assume ditching position.

(d) Assume ditching position in radio operators seat facing to the rear.

4. **Aerial engineer:**

(a) Checks passengers to see that each is wearing his Mae West, and has his safety belt properly buckled, or is properly braced on the floor.

(b) Ties down all emergency equipment near main cargo door so that it is easily accessible.

(c) Jettisons as much cargo and equipment as time permits; lashes down what equipment he cannot dispose of.

(d) Place an article, glove, anything, in crew compartment doorway to prevent jamming.

(e) Sit facing the rear, with back against the end of the left rear fuel tank, cargo, or left forward bulkhead in the main compartment.

5. **Passengers:**

(a) Remain in seats, if possible, with safety belts fastened. Pad the man nearest the forward bulkhead with sprung parachutes or other material. See that remaining passengers lean forward with arms hooked under knees and heads against knees.

6. **Nurse and medical technicians:**

(a) Assist patients with safety belts, litter straps, and life vests.

(b) Prepare first-aid equipment for removal to rafts.

(c) Assume ditching positions authorized for passengers, or positions recommended in paragraph 7 below.

7. **Approved ditching positions:**

(a) Secured by safety belt and harness.

(b) Sit facing the rear, back braced against a forward bulkhead, hands clasped behind head.

(c) Lie on the floor feet forward, braced against a forward bulkhead, knees slightly bent.

Place injured crew members in one of the approved ditching positions to prevent further injury.

SEE DIAGRAM ON NEXT PAGE FOR APPROVED DITCHING POSITIONS

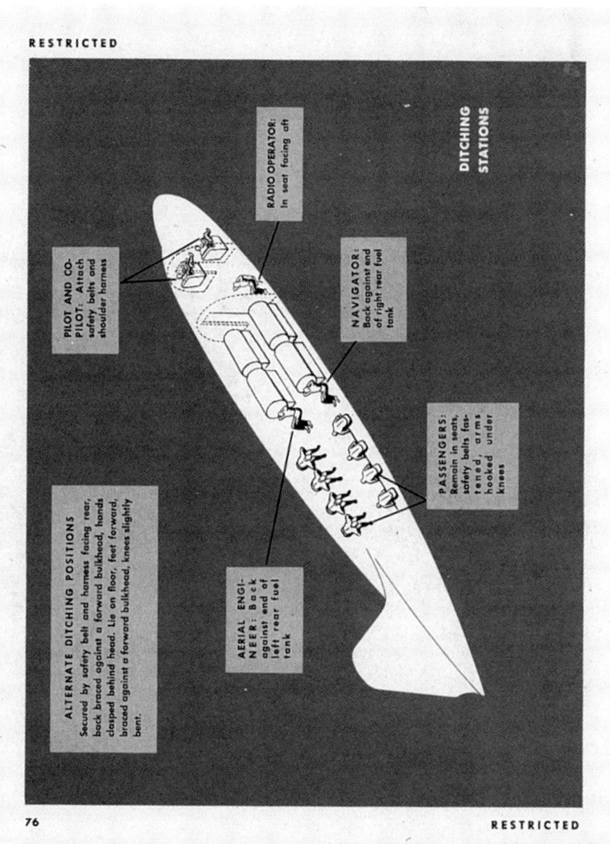

RESTRICTED

Ditching the Airplane

Although conditions of the water determine how and where you should ditch your airplane, there are certain points to bear in mind in **any** ditching:

1. Give your crew as much time as possible to prepare for ditching. Before you land be sure that every person on board your airplane is wearing a Mae West and is in his ditching position.

2. See that as much weighty equipment as possible is jettisoned. The lighter your airplane is, the easier it lands and the longer it is likely to stay afloat.

3. Keep landing gear up and ditch with fuselage parallel to the water. Because of its construction your airplane has admirable water landing characteristics.

4. Approach in a normal landing glide with minimum speed consistent with control. (C-47's have been ditched at speeds as low as 75 mph.)

5. If possible, choose your landing spot, but do not be indecisive about landing. Progress at a low altitude for any extended period of time may allow spray to hit the windshield and lower or eliminate visibility.

6. Keep your wings level or parallel to the water. If a wing hits, the airplane is likely to disintegrate and sink in a few seconds.

7. Use power, if possible, to flatten the approach. For this reason, do not delay in making a decision to ditch.

8. Use flaps at your discretion.

9. Touch down in tail-low attitude so that a stall or near-stall results. The large under surface of the airplane acts as a surf board.

10. Lower landing gear **after** landing to add stability in rough water.

RESTRICTED 77

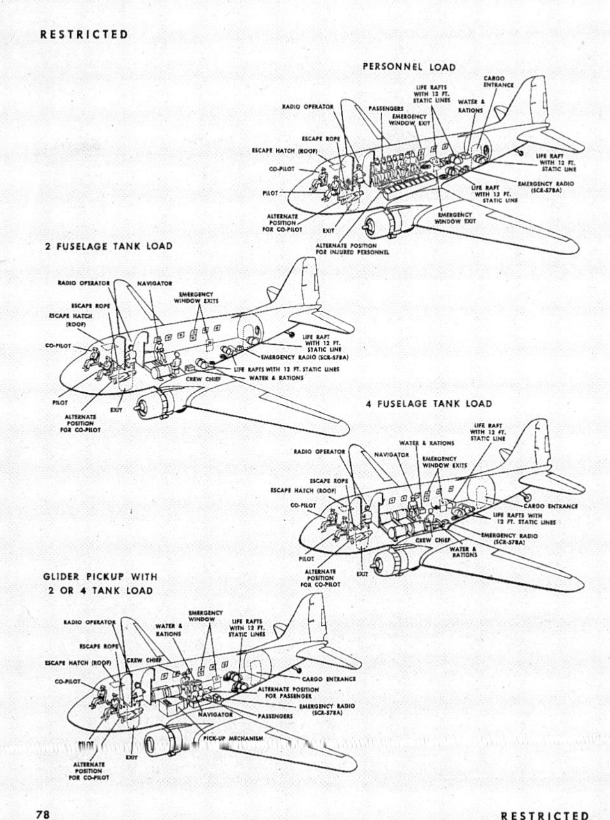

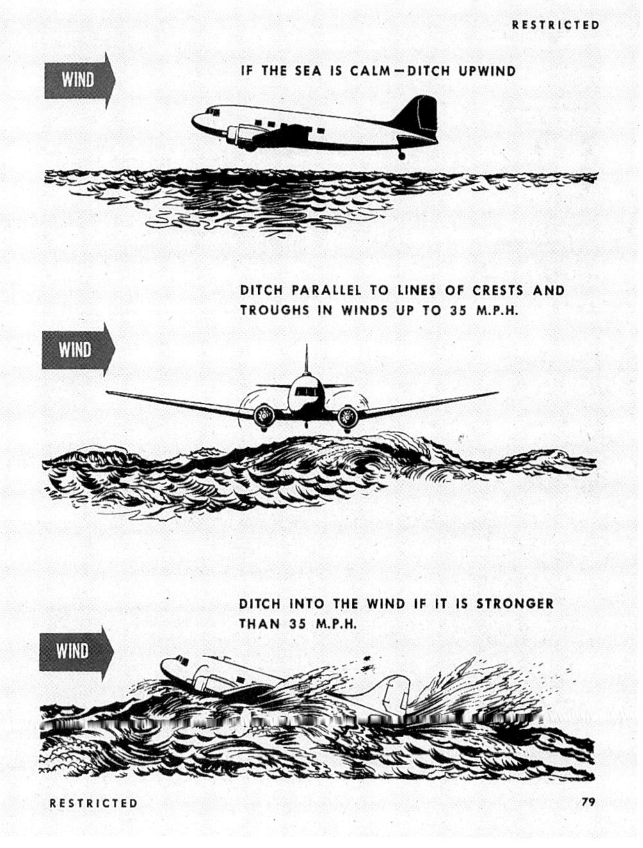

AFTER DITCHING POSITION OF CREW AND LIFE RAFTS

When the Airplane Has Been Landed

Proceed on the principle that the airplane will sink in 30 seconds, but don't hurry so fast that you leave emergency equipment behind or lose it. Drill makes for speed without careless haste.

In all previously reported ditching cases, the main cargo door has never been more than 2 feet above the water. It has been found to be the speediest and best exit. Emergency windows also can be used, and copilot usually leaves through escape hatch over the pilots' compartment. In leaving the emergency windows, step onto the wings.

When You Abandon the Airplane

1. Pilot destroys IFF.
2. The aerial engineer, navigator, and radio operator uncase and throw life rafts overboard, through main cargo door or through emergency window exits. Be sure lines are attached to the airplane. Do not inflate rafts before you throw them overboard.
3. Aerial engineer gets into raft. He keeps raft straight and prepares to receive emergency equipment.
4. Navigator climbs into raft with case containing his equipment. He stands by to receive emergency equipment.

5. Radio operator makes sure that the emergency radio set (SCR-578A or B) is stowed in life raft. He helps to pass out emergency equipment before he abandons the airplane.
6. Copilot climbs out through emergency hatch above pilots' compartment and stands on wing where he helps stow emergency equipment on board life raft.
7. Pilot goes into main cabin to supervise and aid in passing out emergency equipment. He makes final visual check of cabin and is the last to get into a life raft.
8. Passengers climb into life rafts in an orderly manner, after emergency equipment has been stowed. They climb from the main cargo door directly into the rafts, or climb through the emergency windows onto the wings and then onto the rafts, whichever is expedient.

After Airplane Is Abandoned

1. Lash all emergency equipment onto the rafts as soon as it is stowed.
2. Tie all rafts together.
3. Cut rafts loose from the airplane. Put out sea anchor and stay near the airplane until it sinks or until you are rescued.

Note: C-47 airplanes have been known to stay afloat for long periods. On the Pacific Coast, for instance, a DC-3 was still afloat when rescue parties arrived, while passengers and members of the crew who had jumped into the surf were drowned.

Emergency Landings on Land

When it is necessary to make an emergency landing on land, crew and passengers take the same positions as in ditching. Safety measures, such as attachment of safety belts and shoulder harness, and the securing of loose equipment, are the same as in ditching. Crew members have the same individual responsibilities.

If you are making an emergency landing in a place other than an airfield, crew members must where possible:

1. Plot position of airplane and send by radio.
2. Destroy secret and confidential papers and equipment.
3. Prepare airplane for landing by jettisoning as much equipment as possible, and tying down emergency and other loose equipment.
4. See that passengers have attached safety belts or are tied down properly.
5. Moreover, in cases of emergency landing on land, **the aerial engineer must open all doors and emergency exits except the escape hatch above the pilots' compartment. This hatch should be opened by the copilot just prior to landing.**

Landing the Airplane

When you make an emergency landing on land:

1. Make a normal approach, with gear up (unless you are absolutely sure you can accomplish a safe landing with gear extended).
2. Lower flaps.
3. Cut all switches just before touching.
4. If you are landing in densely wooded terrain, stall airplane out directly over the tops of the trees and mush into the trees.

If you are in open country, land airplane normally with fuselage parallel to the ground. (See section on short-field landing.)

When you make a belly landing, either on an airfield or on rough terrain, remember this point: Your landing gear extends approximately a foot when retracted. Not only does it take the greater part of the shock of a belly landing, but you can use the wheels and brakes as you would if the gear were extended. Because of this fact, you **never** actually make a belly landing!

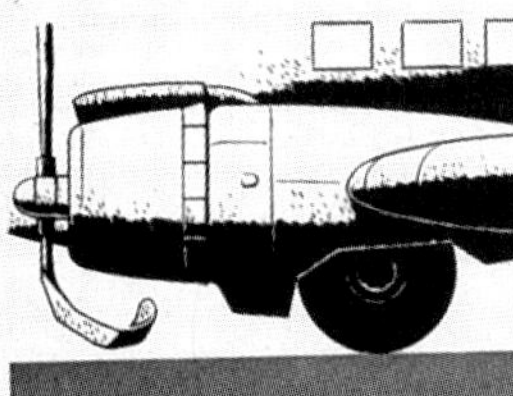

Additional Notes on Ditching and Emergency Landing

Emergency stations for crew members vary with the load carried. If the plane does not carry cabin fuel tanks, the navigator and aerial engineer brace themselves in the main cabin by sitting with their backs against the forward bulkhead. **However, they must not place themselves between this bulkhead and cargo that cannot be jettisoned.** If cargo is in the main cabin, they take positions with backs against the most solid cargo in the rear of the airplane, or tie each other down with feet pointing towards front of airplane, **between cargo and back of airplane.**

COLD WEATHER OPERATION

You will be flying in cold weather from time to time and therefore you must know what to do under normal cold weather conditions. Some of you will be assigned to fly in extremely cold weather. The section following this one touches the highlights of extreme cold weather operation. If you are to fly the C-47 in extremely cold weather, read this section first. It contains basic cold weather information.

OUTSIDE CHECK POINTS

CHECKS FOR NORMAL COLD WEATHER OPERATION

If you are flying under normal cold weather conditions make these additional checks:

Outside Check

1. Engine sections for freedom from ice.
2. Landing gear and landing gear latch mechanism for freedom from snow and ice.
3. Airplane for freedom from excessive amounts of ice, snow and frost. Even a small amount of ice or snow or frost on or within a wing or tail control surface causes a change in balance and a loss of flight performance.
4. Normal position of shock absorber struts.
5. Check around oleo strut for leaks. Note: Cold weather hardens the oleo packing and may cause hydraulic oil leaks.
6. Propeller dome for freedom from ice and snow.
7. All flexible hydraulic lines to see that they are not frozen. Freezing makes them brittle and they can break easily. Do not check hydraulic lines by kicking.
8. Brakes for freedom from ice and snow.
9. See that engines have been preheated.

Inside Check

1. Preheating engine covers installed in the airplane.
2. Tanks full of anti-icing fluid and a sufficient reserve supply in the airplane.
3. Pilots' compartment sliding windows for freedom.
4. Move all controls, including trim tabs, through their entire range to check for ice that may have lodged in the controls.

Starting

Procedure is the same as normal weather operation, except that the starters need more energizing and engines may need more prime.

Taxiing

Taxi slowly when there is snow or ice on the runways. Remember, you are taxiing a heavy airplane. If you start sliding, you may not be able to stop short of an accident. When you get ready to stop anticipate the need for space. Slow down and taxi very slowly.

Run-up

In making the run-up, be doubly sure the engine instruments are within operating limits. Run propellers through pitch range two or three times to make sure the oil in the propeller domes [illegible] same as in normal operation.

Climb and Cruise

Climb and cruise is the same as in normal operation. Turn on the pitot heater before entering visible moisture.

If in extremely cold weather you encounter high oil temperatures, open the shutters to cool the oil. This may result in continued high oil temperatures, caused by oil congealing in the coolers. If this occurs, close the oil shutters until the oil temperature drops. Keep a constant check on engine instruments to be sure that congealed oil, and not loss of oil or other trouble, is causing high temperatures.

Landing

Watch landing roll. Apply brakes slowly and evenly. Release and reapply if the wheels skid. Remember the weight of your airplane.

Parking

Dilute oil by pushing the oil dilution switch while engines are running

Operate engines at 1000 to 1200 rpm.

Maintain oil temperature below 50°C (122°F) and oil pressure above 15 psi.

DILUTION TIME IN MINUTES

4°C to —12°C (40°F to 10°F)	—12°C to —29°C (10°F to —20°F)	—29°C to —46°C (—20°F to —50°F)
2 minutes	4 minutes	7 minutes

Add 1 minute dilution for each 5°C (9°F) below —46°C.

Caution

Be sure to dilute the prop feathering system, when diluting your engine oil in cold weather. Check the technical orders for your series airplane for the proper procedure.

If the plane has a steam heater, drain water from boiler and from the heater system. Drain water by opening drain in wheel well of right nacelle and by opening control valves in companionway.

See that engine, wing, and empennage covers are placed on the airplane, if the covers are available, to protect these parts.

Extreme Cold Weather Operation

Consider extreme cold weather operation to be operation in temperatures of —29°C (—20°F) and lower. You find such temperatures mostly

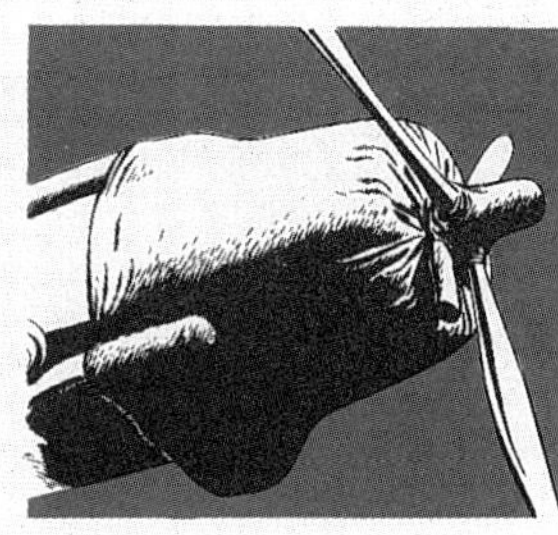

on the Alaska, Alaska-Siberia and Greenland runs. If you are assigned to fly these areas you will be briefed in cold weather operation at your departure base.

Here are a few essential points you must know about extreme cold weather operation of the C-47 airplane:

1. **Brakes:** Do not use your brakes except in extreme emergency. When brakes are used, cold air, striking heated surfaces in the brakes, causes condensation. The collected moisture immediately freezes and locks the wheels. Land slower and shorter than normally. In taxiing and in landing use motors rather than brakes. If it is imperative that you use your brakes, continue to taxi around until brakes have cooled off.

2. **Instruments and gages:** Until your engine is heated your instruments do not function or function sluggishly. The colder it is, the slower the instruments react. Gages that are actuated by liquid pressure can freeze in flight. In particular, extremely cold weather affects your:

(a) **Gyro instruments.** They will probably be slowed by contraction. Check during taxiing and run-up.

(b) **Bank-and-turn indicator.** It slows down, but usually does not freeze.

(c) **Manifold pressure gages.** They may not give a correct reading as a result of congealing and freezing of oil and fuel in the lines. To check reading, bleed the line.

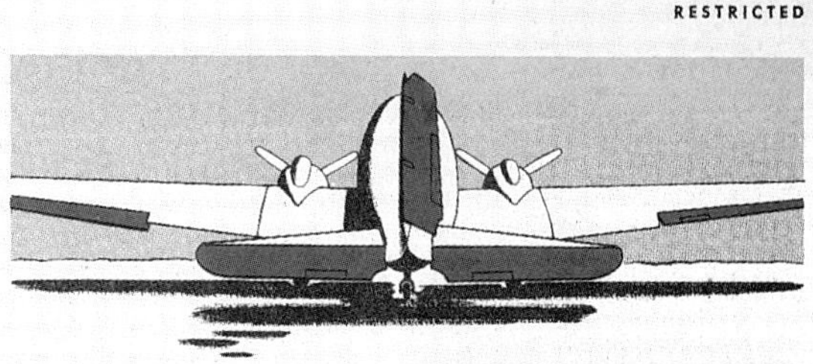

(d) **Magnetic compass.** Lag in this instrument increases because of a tendency of instrument fluid to solidify. However, it is very seldom that the fluid becomes fully solid. In cases where this has happened, solidification resulted from too much mineral oil in the fluid mixture. Check instrument in turns while taxiing.

(e) **Airspeed indicator.** Cold weather has very little effect on this instrument. Any trouble comes from the pitot tubes and can be remedied by the pitot heaters.

(f) **Oil pressure gages.** They can freeze while in flight because of congealing of oil in lines.

(g) **Temperature gages.** They are electrical and consequently there is no trouble.

(h) **Hydraulic pressure gages.** There is no trouble with these gages because fluids now in use are non-freezing down to —70°F.

(i) **Magnesyn compass (installed in C-47A).** Transmitter in wing has tendency to freeze.

(j) **Other pressure gages.** As gages are actuated by liquid pressure, congealing of fluid in the lines can make them sluggish or cause them to cease functioning in flight.

3. **Controls:** When you move an airplane from a heated hangar and allow it to stand for a few minutes in extremely low temperatures, there is condensation and subsequent freezing of moisture on heated surfaces. As a consequence, unless controls are kept free they freeze so tight it is impossible to move them.

Keep moving controls from the moment the airplane is taken from the hangar. If controls are frozen or are difficult to move, do not get rough with them.

Procedure in extremely cold weather is to allow an airplane that is taken from a heated hangar to freeze on the ground while **keeping controls free.** Reason: It is better to discover failures resulting from freezing on the ground, where they can be remedied, than later when the airplane is in the air.

4. **Oil radiators:** Oil radiators can burst as a result of solidification of oil. To prevent bursting of radiators, see that they are drained when you park your airplane in the open.

(a) **Freezing in flight:** An excessive rise in oil temperature indicates an oil radiator freezing in flight. Under normal conditions you would open oil shutters to lower oil temperature. With such an indication in extremely cold weather, however, you reverse the procedure. Close oil shutters in order to build up heat around oil radiator and prevent complete freezing. When oil temperature has been reduced, open the oil shutters as needed.

5. **Communication equipment:** Cold weather does not affect this equipment. However, Northern Lights cause extreme blackout conditions for short periods.

6. **Hydraulic system:** Although fluid now used in the C-47 hydraulic system does not freeze down to —70°F, trouble has been experienced in hydraulic gear creeping down. Reason: Extremely cold weather contracts fluid, causing gear to sag. When you raise the gear, fluid accumulates on the oleo strut packings, freezes when it comes in contact with outside air temperatures, and hardens. This condition again causes gear to sag.

To counteract sagging of gear, move landing gear handle to full UP position and keep it there until warm fluid from the hydraulic system circulates to oleo strut packings. Leave gear handle in the UP position for 10 minutes or more, if necessary. You will probably have to repeat this procedure from time to time while you are flying in extremely cold weather.

In extremely cold weather you experience inversions of temperature. That is, at times you have low temperatures near the ground, relatively high temperatures at altitude. Temperatures may vary as much as 30 to 50°F. When you are climbing or descending into low temperatures, hydraulic fluid sometimes contracts and causes your gear to sag. When climbing or ascending into higher temperatures, landing gear hydraulic pressure can build up.

Watch gages closely. Re-circulate fluid frequently by moving the landing gear handle to the UP position.

7. **Heaters:** In temperatures of —20°F and lower, steam type heaters freeze and are of no use. Airplanes used in extremely cold climates are now equipped with hot air type heaters, rather than steam heaters.

8. **Landing and taxiing:** You will do much of your landing and taxiing on packed snow. Packed snow is entirely safe and provides a firm, hard surface.

9. **Parking in extremely cold weather:** When you park your airplane in the open:

(a) Do not set parking brake. Use chocks.

(b) Put on engine covers.

(c) Use portable heaters to keep engines warm while your airplane is parked, or it will be impossible to start them. See that they are connected as soon as possible.

(d) Dilute oil to help keep it from solidifying. Remember, however, oil dilution alone is not sufficient to facilitate starting of engines.

(e) See that all cargo that might freeze is properly taken care of.

Danger: New parts installed on an airplane in extremely cold weather may fit at the time of installation, but upon reaching higher temperatures they can expand to such a point that they lock with surrounding surfaces. Such a condition is especially true of control surfaces constructed of metals that have different coefficients of expansion.

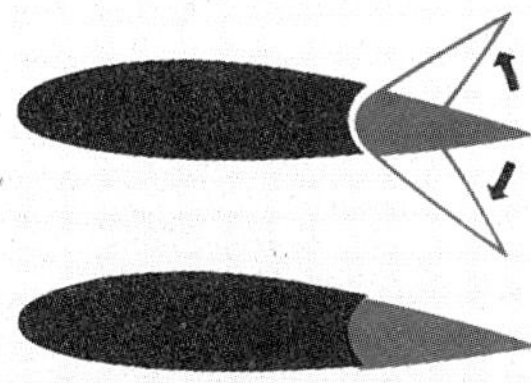

10. **Operations that are the same as under normal conditions:** Single engine operation, operation of propellers, use of tires, anti-icing and de-icing operation, removal of frost and snow, and mooring are the same in extremely cold weather as in normal operation.

11. **Cold weather emergency equipment:** Airplanes flying in extremely cold climates carry special emergency equipment you can use if forced down. Equipment consists of such articles as special signal rockets, a toboggan, and cooking units. If you are flying [illegible] weather countries it is up to you to see that this equipment is on board your airplane and is in working order.

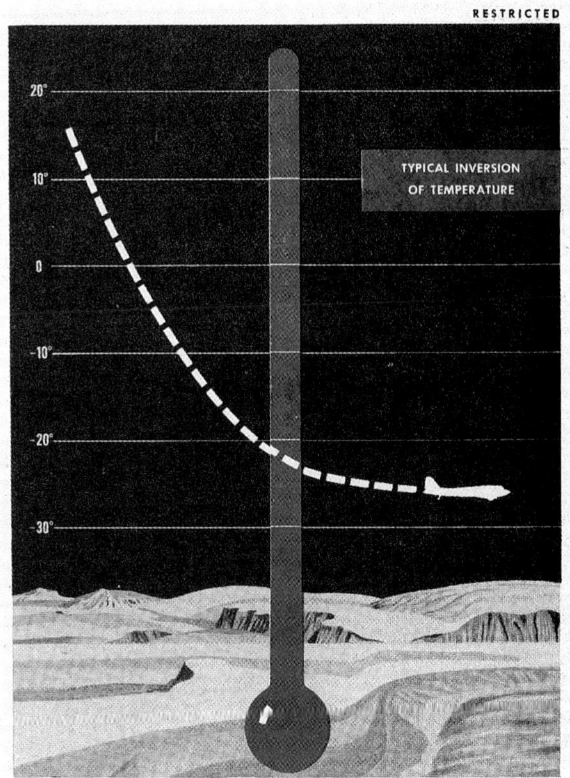

WEIGHT AND BALANCE

The primary job of the C-47 airplane is the transportation of cargo and personnel. Therefore, as a C-47 pilot, you must learn all you can about weight and balance. Although your airplane is loaded under the direction of a weight and balance officer at the point of departure, you will often need to redistribute cargo in flight. You must know when to make the shift and what cargo must be shifted.

Again, it is possible that you may have to take cargo or passengers on board your airplane at a remote place where no one but yourself knows the principles of loading.

Undoubtedly you have already taken a course in weight and balance and are familiar with the load adjuster, charts, form F, and the method of calculating load distribution. If you are not clear on a particular point consult your weight and balance officer.

Here are a few things that you should check before every flight:

Total Load

Before takeoff you must know that your airplane does not exceed the maximum gross weight for safe flight. Before landing you must know that your airplane is at, or below, the allowable maximum gross weight, and within CG limits.

Securing Cargo

Make sure that cargo is properly secured to prevent shifting. Sometimes even a slight shift can unbalance your airplane. A combination of poorly secured cargo and strong turbulence can seriously damage or even wreck your airplane.

Passengers

Make sure that passengers are secured in their seats or riding stations. Accident reports show that severe injuries occur when passengers are not protected during turbulent weather.

Fuel Consumption

During most normal flights you remain within safe weight and balance limits as fuel is consumed. Therefore, your safety factor does not decrease. When you start with a critical loading, however, or when you make extremely long flights, CG position shifts through greater ranges. Under these conditions the stability of your airplane decreases, and cargo must be shifted to restore balance.

As an example, when you burn large amounts of fuel from main and auxiliary tanks weight is taken from the front of the airplane and it becomes tail heavy. To offset the loss of weight, shift cargo forward.

If there are main cabin tanks in your airplane, you normally burn fuel from these tanks before you use an appreciable amount from main and auxiliary tanks. In this case the airplane becomes nose-heavy. Shift cargo to rear to restore balance.

Note

When your loading is supervised by a weight and balance officer, he will instruct you as to redistribution of cargo in flight.

As fuel is consumed shift cargo forward

LONG-RANGE OPERATION

Planning

When making a long-range flight, particularly with a cargo load, have a definite plan in mind as to range, ceiling, climb, speeds and maneuverability of your airplane. Know your safety limitations in regard to maximum landing weights, permissible airspeeds, proper CG and minimum takeoff and landing distances. A long-range flight presents enough problems to occupy the pilot without adding problems by ignorance and lack of planning.

Cruising Charts

Your best insurance of a safe flight, properly planned, is to make use of long-range cruising charts. These charts are designed from the viewpoint of safe operation in takeoff and climb, cruise and landing. They give proper power settings for takeoff and climb and for maximum range.

When you are flying long distances it is important for you to get maximum performance from your fuel as you use it. By using proper power settings, with a given amount of fuel you can reach your objective easily. On the other hand, with the same given amount of fuel, you can fall short of your objective if you disregard power settings, even though you maintain the same airspeed.

Note: On certain long runs, pilots who have not planned their flights, and have disregarded power settings established after long experience, have failed to obtain efficiency in fuel consumption, and as a consequence have been unable to reach their destinations.

LONG-RANGE LEVEL CRUISING CHART (ZERO WIND)

Use settings indicated in the chart for the gross weight of your airplane and the altitude at which you intend to fly. Fly at these settings for the time and distance shown with the settings. At the end of this time and distance, change to settings in the next column, at the proper altitude, and continue with these new settings for the time indicated.

Allow approximately 60 gallons of fuel for warm-up, run-up, takeoff, and climb to 10,000 feet.

Extreme range is computed on the following basis (1200 gallons maximum, at 6 lbs. per gallon; four fuselage tanks; no reserve):

31,000-27,000 lbs. gross weight with 7200 lbs. of fuel.

*25,000 lbs. gross weight with 5200 lbs. of fuel.

*23,000 lbs. gross weight with 4000 lbs. of fuel.

Extreme Alternate Gross Weight		31,000 to 29,000	29,000 to 27,000	27,000 to 25,000	25,000 to 23,000	23,000 to 19,000	Extreme Range Figures T-O Wght	Range/Mi	Hrs-Mins
14,000 to 16,000 feet	IAS	137	136	135	133	128	31,000	2411	13:37
	rpm	2350	2200	2100	2000	1900	29,000	2668	15:13
	Hg.	26.5	25.0	25.0	24.0	23.0	27,000	2823	16:23
	Fuel lbs. per hr.	657	529	488	447	410	*25,000	2420	14:14
	Fuel gals. per hr.	109	88	81	75	68	*23,000	1640	9:45
	Range, hours	3:03	3:47	4:06	4:29	4:53			
	Range, miles	550	676	733	780	820			
12,000 to 14,000	IAS	139	138	137	135	129	31,000	2515	14:26
	rpm	2200	2100	2000	1900	1800	29,000	2705	15:45
	Hg.	26.5	26.0	25.5	25.0	24.0	27,500	2848	16:50
	Fuel lbs. per hr.	566	511	473	435	401	*25,000	2448	14:36
	Fuel gals. per hr.	94	85	79	73	67	*23,000	1660	10:00
	Range, hours	3:32	3:55	4:14	4:36	5:00			
	Range, miles	622	689	736	782	830			
10,000 to 12,000	IAS	141	140	138	136	130	31,000	2551	14:58
	rpm	2000	2000	1900	1800	1700	29,000	2701	16:07
	Hg.	28.5	27.0	27.0	26.0	25.5	27,000	2835	17:13
	Fuel lbs. per hr.	530	[illegible]	[illegible]	427	392	*25,000	2418	14:53
	Fuel gals. per hr.	88	[illegible]	[illegible]	71	66	*23,000	1640	[illegible]
	Range, hours	[illegible]	4:01	4:22	4:41	5:07			
	Range, miles	[illegible]	[illegible]	742	778	823			
8,000 to 10,000	IAS	143	141	139	136	131	[illegible]	[illegible]	15:27
	rpm	1950	1850	1800	1700	1700	[illegible]	2700	16:42
	Hg.	29.5	29.0	28.0	27.5	25.0	27,000	2825	17:49
	Fuel lbs. per hr.	519	482	[illegible]	[illegible]	381	*25,000	2408	15:22
	Fuel gals. per hr.	87	81	[illegible]	[illegible]	64	*23,000	1630	10:30
	Range, hours	[illegible]	[illegible]	[illegible]	4:52	5:15			
	Range, miles	[illegible]	[illegible]	742	778	813			
6,000 to 8,000	IAS	145	143	140	137	132	31,000	2557	15:49
	rpm	1900	1800	1750	1700	1700	29,000	2707	17:05
	Hg.	30.0	29.5	28.5	27.5	25.5	27,000	2822	18:09
	Fuel lbs. per hr.	508	467	436	402	374	*25,000	2406	15:41
	Fuel gals. per hr.	85	78	73	67	63	*23,000	1625	10:42
	Range, hours	3:56	4:18	4:36	4:59	5:21			
	Range, miles	648	700	740	781	813			
4,000 to 6,000	IAS	146	144	141	138	133	31,000	2556	16:06
	rpm	1900	1800	1750	1700	1700	29,000	2697	17:20
	Hg.	30.0	29.5	29.0	27.5	25.5	27,000	2812	18:25
	Fuel lbs. per hr.	495	460	430	396	369	*25,000	2395	15:55
	Fuel gals. per hr.	83	77	72	66	62	*23,000	1615	10:51
	Range, hours	4:03	4:21	4:40	5:04	5:26			
	Range, miles	656	696	737	780	810			
2,000 to 4,000	IAS	147	145	142	139	134	31,000	2528	16:17
	rpm	1900	1800	1700	1700	1700	29,000	2659	17:31
	Hg.	30.5	30.0	29.5	28.5	27.0	27,000	2761	18:35
	Fuel lbs. per hr.	489	456	423	392	366	*25,000	2347	15:02
	Fuel gals. per hr.	82	76	71	65	61	*23,000	1582	10:56
	Range, hours	4:06	4:24	4:44	5:06	5:28			
	Range, miles	652	690	728	765	792			
S-L to 2,000	IAS	149	147	144	140	135	31,000	2501	16:31
	rpm	1900	1800	1700	1700	1700	29,000	2828	17:44
	Hg.	[illegible]	30.5	30.0	28.0	26.0	27,000	2747	18:55
	Fuel lbs. per hr.	476	456	416	[illegible]	[illegible]	*25,000	2313	16:19
	Fuel gals. per hr.	79	76	69	64	60	*23,000	1550	11:07
	Range, hours	4:12	4:23	4:49	5:12	5:34			
	Range, miles	[illegible]	[illegible]	[illegible]	763	790			
Maximum Endurance IAS		137	136	132	126	120 (Min.)			

SAMPLE CHART
ATC LONG RANGE CRUISE

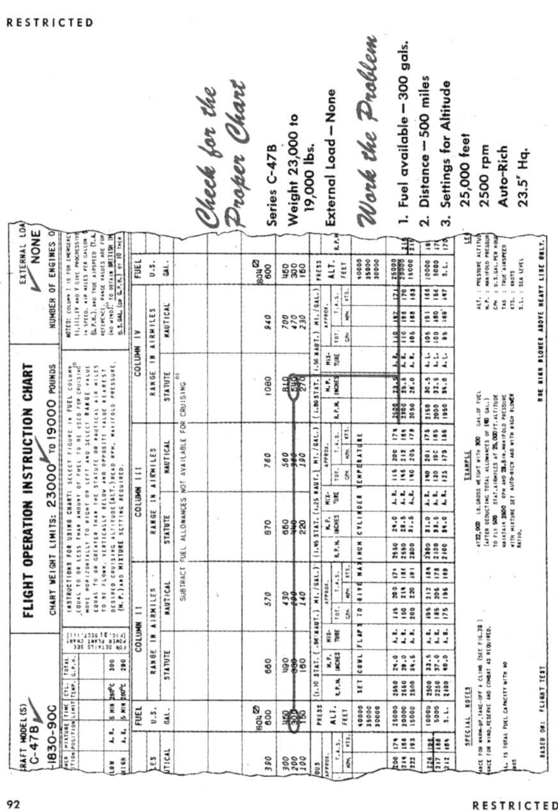

The accompanying cruise chart was worked out by Headquarters, Air Transport Command, Washington, D. C., for the C-47 and C-53 airplanes. It is presented here as an example of a chart used in long-range operation. If you are flying long range you will be given this or a similar chart by your organization.

Preflight Inspection

Before leaving on a long-range flight, check:

1. **All emergency and auxiliary equipment.** See that it is properly installed and is operating satisfactorily. This equipment consists of:
   (a) Main cabin tanks and main cabin fuel system.
   (b) Life rafts (two) secured in rear of cargo compartment, near main cargo door.
   (c) Emergency radio lashed down near life rafts.
   (d) Emergency rations in or near life rafts.
   (e) Extra supply of hydraulic fluid.
   (f) Pyrotechnic pistol stowed in companionway.
   (g) Emergency exits.
   (h) Water containers. Fill personal canteen for use in case of water landing.
   (i) Life lines of strong rope, knotted every 24 inches, placed near exits.
2. **Radio.** Check with crew members and, if flying formation, check radio frequency with other pilots. See that your radio operator has a distress signal prepared in advance for quick transmission.
3. **Navigation.** See that navigator has all necessary charts and maps and that his equipment is in working order. If astrocompass is not aboard, swing compass.
4. **Weight and balance.** Check weight and balance of cargo in airplane against Form F for proper distribution of cargo weights. (See previous section on weight and balance.)

Points to Remember in Flight

1. Proper attitude of your airplane is important. Keep the wings level and trim your airplane to fly hands-off. Any irregularities in attitude may shorten the range seriously.
2. Use proper power setting as set forth in cruise charts.
3. Check flaps and wheels frequently to see that they are fully retracted.
4. See that tailwheel is locked on takeoff and remains locked throughout your flight.
5. Consult with your navigator frequently and follow his instructions to the letter. An error of even 1° will place you several miles off your course in a long flight.
6. Use navigator's ETA over destination to begin your descent far enough from your destination to take full advantage of your altitude. If you descend at 200 feet per minute you can

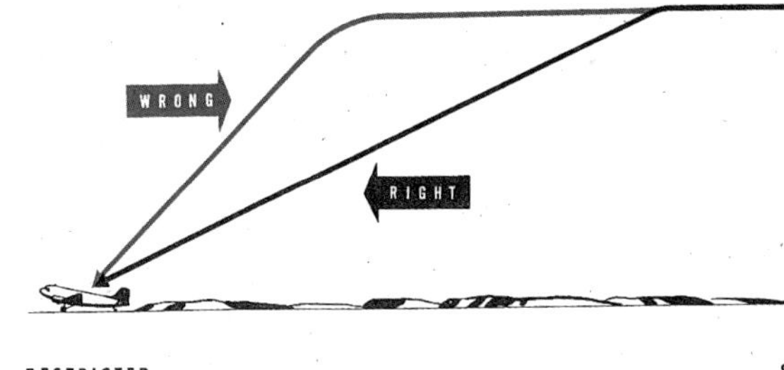

conserve fuel that may be necessary for continued flight.

There are from two to eight extra 102-gallon (U.S.) fuel tanks in the main cabin for long-range flying.

Switch to these tanks only after using 60 gallons from each main tank, followed by 20 gallons from each auxiliary tank. Reason for using fuel from forward tanks first: To provide enough room in these tanks for the return flow of fuel which otherwise would be lost through the overflow.

Five valves control the flow of fuel from the cabin tanks to the main fuel system. Use these valves to route fuel from all tanks to one or both engines, or from a combination of tanks to one or both engines.

To place the cabin tank fuel system in operation, follow this procedure:

1. See that the crossfeed valve is closed.
2. Open the main line selector valves (there are two for each bank of tanks).
3. Immediately after you open selector valves, turn off the engine selector valves in the cockpit. Never use wing tanks in conjunction with cabin tanks.
4. Use wobble pump or booster pumps to aid in starting flow of fuel.

For Single Engine Operation

1. Close selector valve on line to dead engine.
2. Open crossfeed valve if you desire to feed live engine from all cabin tanks.

Drain cabin tanks by opening two drain valves at rear of cabin tanks. When tanks contain fuel, be sure that these valves are closed and safetied.

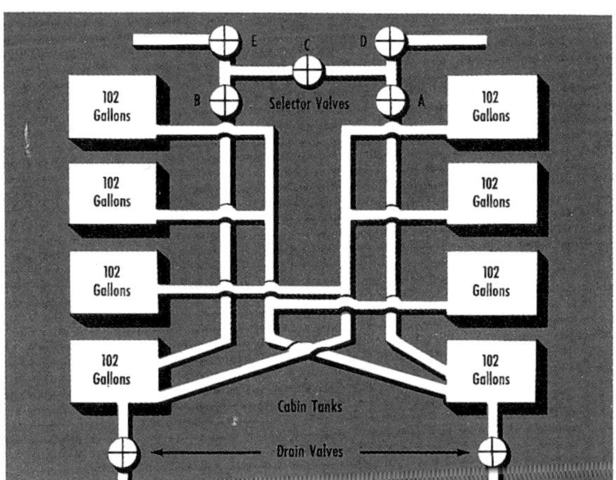

AIRBORNE OPERATIONS

Operation With Paratroops

The C-47 is equipped to carry 28 paratroops, including the jumpmaster. However, the number of paratroops can vary, depending upon type and length of mission, equipment carried, gliders in tow (one or two) and the number of paratroops carried in gliders.

Normally paratroopers jump at an altitude of 800 feet. Again, this altitude can vary, depending upon terrain, weather and combat conditions.

Except for [illegible] detailed in this section, operation with paratroops is the same as normal operational technique.

Airplane Check in Paratroop Operation

Besides the normal checks, outlined in this book, the pilot makes additional checks when operating with paratroops. These additional checks are made together by pilot and jumpmaster. But bear in mind that, as commander of your airplane, **you** as well as the jumpmaster are responsible for seeing that paratroop equipment is in order.

Outside Check

1. Aircraft fittings and external projections in the vicinity of the exit (cargo) door are completely masked.
2. If parapack racks are used, racks must be checked for positive operation before takeoff.

Inside Check

1. The **red** (caution) and **green** (jump) lights are in working order.
2. Emergency bell is in working order.
3. The static line is not frayed or defective in any way.
4. Matting around the exit (cargo) door is unwrinkled and fastened securely to the floor.
5. All loose equipment is stowed so that it does not interfere during the jump.
6. Each seat and safety belt is in correct working order. (Pilot's responsibility alone.)
7. Sufficient buckets are in the aircraft.

Procedure Before Paratroop Drop

Before paratroop drop, you must:

1. Alert the jumpmaster 10 minutes before arrival at drop zone by ringing a predetermined signal on the alert (emergency) bell.
2. Flash **red** caution light ("Stand to the door" signal) approximately 2 minutes before reaching drop zone.
3. Flash **green** jump light ("Go" signal) when the airplane is at the proper speed and proper altitude, on the prescribed course, and over the assigned drop zone.

Procedure During Drop

During paratroop drop, you must:

1. Maintain an indicated airspeed of 110 mph, with wheels and flaps up.

2. Maintain airplane in jumping attitude (level to slightly tail-low position) and take particular care to maintain a constant altitude and gyro heading.
3. Advance throttles to maintain jump attitude.

Note: During combined operations with paratroops and glider tow, drop tow line before paratroops jump.

Operation With Pararacks

From two to six pararacks may be installed at designated positions under the fuselage of the C-47. These racks are used to transport equipment and supplies that may be dropped from the airplane.

Installed pararacks increase drag and materially affect the performance of your airplane. It has been found that six installed pararacks are equivalent to the approximate drag of one glider in tow.

In loading pararacks, compute weight and balance by including load of:

First two racks..........in loading station D
Second two racks........in loading station E
Third two racks..........in loading station F

Note: When you install two pararacks only, it has been found that because of airflow conditions you obtain better flight performance by placing racks in Positions 3 and 4.

Operation With Gliders in Tow

Either one or two gliders are used in glider tow operations. The C-47 is commonly used to tow the CG-4A glider, although it can tow the large CG-13 and the British Horsa glider.

For your information, here are some facts about the CG-4A glider:

Crew.......................pilot and copilot
Number of troops carried................15
Weight empty (with fixed landing gear)....................3655 lbs.
Useful load (approximate)...........3750 lbs.
Wingspread..........................83' 8"
Normal towed speed...........120 to 140 mph
Maximum towed speed...............150 mph

Note: When towing the CG-15 glider, maximum towing speed increases to 180 mph IAS.

Additional Equipment for Glider Tow

Your airplane has the following equipment for glider tow and glider pick-up:

1. Glider tow release unit. This unit is on the lower aft end of the fuselage. Operate by pulling a handle on the pilots' compartment aft bulkhead above copilot's seat.

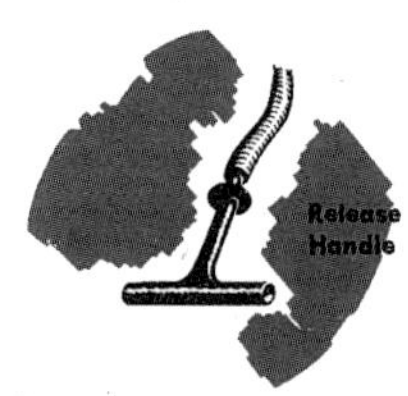

2. Astrodome, installed over the companionway.
3. Red signal light in astrodome, now being installed on all glider towplanes. Switch for this light is on the pedestal just below the propeller pitch controls. It has ON and OFF positions.
4. Glider pick-up unit, which consists of an energy absorbing unit, a contact unit, and cable guide system.

(a) **Energy absorbing unit:** Located on the forward left-hand side of the main cargo compartment. This unit is made up of (1) **a drum** around which is wound the pick-up cable. This drum incorporates a brake, a time adjustment mechanism, and a brake adjustment mechanism to determine the interval of brake delay and the final brake pressure; (2) a built-in reversible, 2-speed, 24-volt DC, compound-wound electric motor. This motor is rated at 2.6 Hp at 460 pinion rpm at high speed. Although provision is made for winding the cable on and off the drum by hand, normally perform operation by this motor. Facilitate even distribution of cable as it is wound on drum by level-wind mechanism on drum.

(b) **Contact unit:** Consists of a hooked cable held by a welded steel torque tube that protrudes through a hole in the aft part of the wing fairing. This tube supports a steel and wood arm that carries a track along its length to guide the hook into the hook retainer. The arm retainer is capable of rotating to extend the arm downward in the pick-up position or to retract it against the side of the airplane. A bolt action latch in the arm retainer holds the arm in the retracted position. The arm latches after it is retracted by closing door on selector valve. A cable fastened to the retainer bolt releases the latch so the arm falls free.

The extending and retracting assembly is operated by a hydraulic cylinder.

The arm retainer release and the hydraulic arm valve are both controlled by interlocking handles on the same bracket. Interlocking handles make it impossible to apply force to extend the arm while it is still being held by the retainer.

(c) **Cable guide system:** A guide system leads the cable from the energy absorbing unit to a point outside the airplane in such a way that it is clear of the airplane structure. This system consists of twin pulleys aft of the unit which lead the cable from the level-wind mechanism through the floor into the hawse pipe. Hawse pipe in turn feeds the cable through the skin to an aft pulley assembly, just outside and below the forward end of the main cargo door. The aft pulley is placed in such a way that it prevents the cable from fouling the tail group or the tailwheel when the airplane and the glider are in normal flight attitude. The pulley also provides easy accessibility to the hook, so that it can be gaffed from the pulley and placed on the track while the airplane is in flight.

Note: An explosive cable cutter is installed

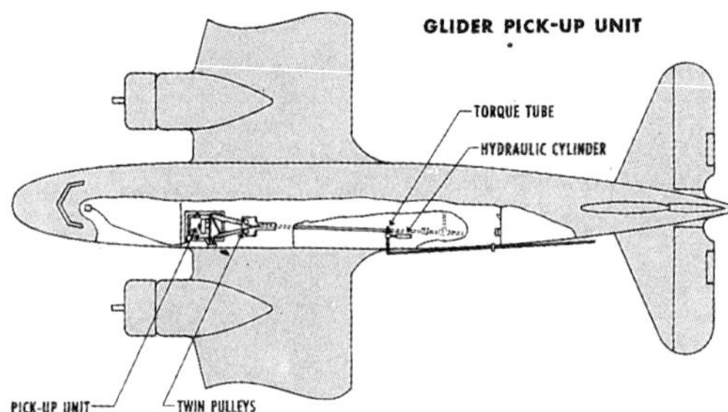

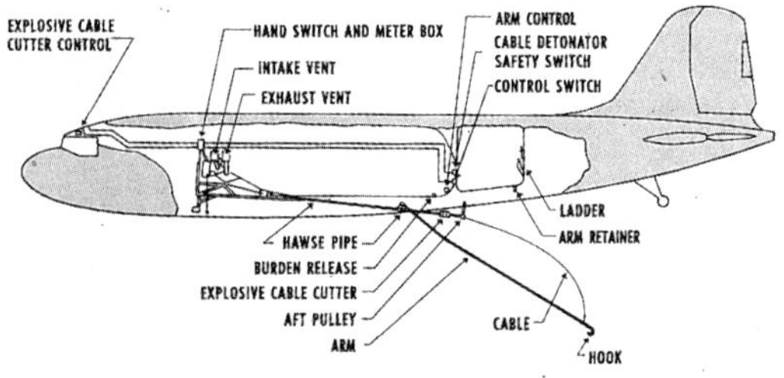

near the end of the torque tube to enable the pilot to disconnect the glider quickly in an emergency. Operate [illegible] switch located on ceiling of pilots' compartment above pilot's head. A toggle switch, above the arm retracting hydraulic selector valve, must be in the ON (armed) position before the button detonator operates.

(d) Ground station unit. This unit is made up of two steel and wood pole assemblies, to the

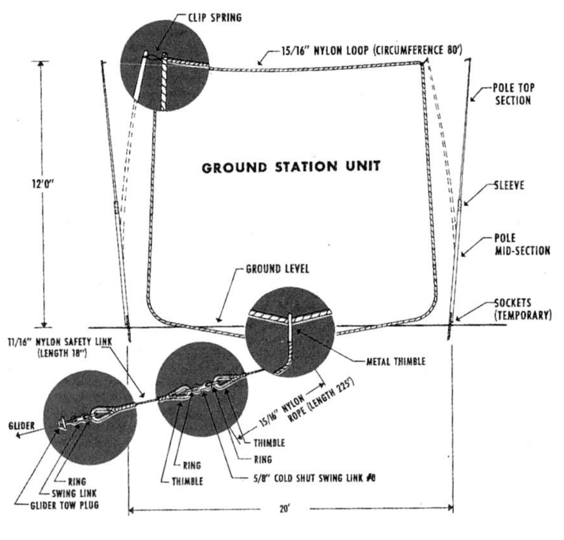

top of which are fastened spring clips. The spring clips support the loop of the towline assembly. The other end of the towline assembly is fastened to the glider through a release assembly, which the glider pilot operates.

Normally pole assemblies are erected in [illegible], built for this purpose.

Check for Glider Tow Operation

Besides your normal check, make these additional checks for glider tow operation:

1. Release mechanism – **for operation and clearances.**
2. For night operation: Red light in astrodome for operation.

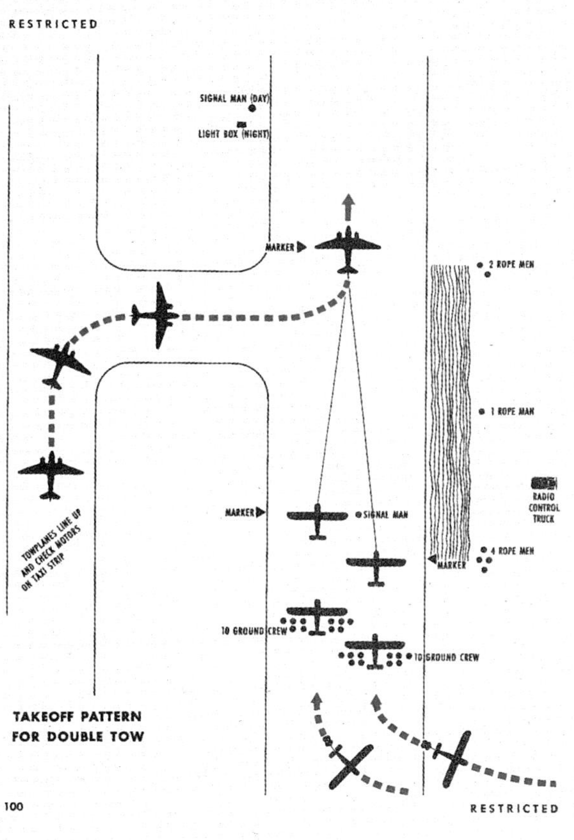

TAKEOFF PATTERN FOR DOUBLE TOW

Readying for Glider Tow

Be sure exit (cargo) door is not removed during glider tow. Absence of door reduces airspeed 3 to 5 mph.

Here are the steps prior to takeoff in glider tow:

1. See that a crew member, usually the aerial engineer, is stationed in the astrodome to observe and inform you of any trouble glider might encounter during takeoff.
2. When airplane ahead has taken off with glider or gliders in tow, taxi from feed-in area to position on runway or feed-in strip. Position is designated by a flag in the daytime and flare-pots at night.
3. Signal man stands by runway approximately 100 feet ahead of the towplane.
4. Glider towlines are laid on field to one side of the runway, between the towplane and the gliders.
5. Gliders are parked between 350 and 425 feet behind towplane and are moved into position by jeeps or other vehicles. In single-tow operation, gliders are stationed in one or more lines behind tow plane. They are attached to the towplanes by 350-foot lines. If there is double-tow operation, gliders are parked in a double row behind the towplane. Glider on the left is attached by 350-foot line; glider on the right is attached by a 425-foot line.
6. Towline ends are attached to the tow release mechanism in the towplane and a tow release mechanism in the nose of the glider. Slack is left in the towline.

Takeoff for Single and Double Tow

Take off on main fuel tanks, land on main fuel tanks or fullest fuel tanks. Minimum fuel in main tanks for takeoff and landing should be approximately 90 gallons.

1. Upon first motion from signalman, release brakes and apply 12" to 15" manifold pressure until slack is taken from towline. Move forward slowly.
2. Upon receiving clear for takeoff, or high-ball, signal from the signalman, immediately apply throttles smoothly and rapidly until you reach 47" Hg. and 2700 rpm. **Have full power on at the end of 5 seconds.** Your engines are so constructed they can take power rapidly if you apply it smoothly. Reasons for rapid acceleration of power:
   (a) Glider pilots get more and quicker control of their gliders, thereby becoming airborne sooner.
   (b) You shorten takeoff run and consequently quickly gain airspeed sufficient for engine cooling.
   (c) You vacate takeoff position quicker, so that succeeding airplane can move into position sooner. Five to ten seconds of time gained is valuable, particularly in formation takeoffs.
3. Position of controls before and during takeoff:

	Grade 100	Grade 91
Mixture	AUTO RICH	AUTO RICH
Cowl Flaps	TRAIL	Full Open
Carburetor Heat	COLD	COLD
Prop Control	INC. RPM	INC. RPM
Crossfeed	OFF	OFF
Trim Tab	0	0
Landing Gear	Positive Lock	Positive Lock
Tailwheel	Locked	Locked
Takeoff	48" Hg., 2700 rpm	46" Hg., 2700 rpm* 43" Hg., 2700 rpm†

*R-1830-92 Engine †R-1830-90C Engine

Note: **Use Grade 100/130 fuel in all 2-glider towing, except in an emergency.**

4. One-fourth flaps may be used at the discretion of the towpilot However, use of flaps is advised for double tow on short runways in order to break ground quickly.
5. Hold tailwheel on ground until you reach 40 to 50 mph. Holding tailwheel on ground keeps prop wash from hitting gliders and also

helps you maintain directional control of the towplane.

6. Take off at 85 mph airspeed, minimum 80 mph. Do not take off at less than 80 mph except under extreme emergency conditions.
7. Retract landing gear immediately upon becoming airborne, **never before you leave the ground.**

Warning: When you begin takeoff on an uphill, graded runway, the sensation is similar to that of leaving the ground. Do not retract landing gear before definitely becoming airborne.

Climb

1. Hold the airplane to a minimum climb until you have reached an airspeed of at least 100 mph IAS. When you have reached 100 mph IAS, reduce power to climb settings for the grade fuel you are using. Maintain at least 100-110 mph IAS throughout the climb.
2. Climb at the rate of approximately 300 feet per minute until you reach tactical altitude of approximately 400 feet above the terrain.

Cruise

1. Maintain between 115 and 120 mph IAS during tow. Don't exceed 150 mph IAS except with the CG-15 glider. The maximum safe airspeed for the CG-15 glider is 180 mph IAS.
2. Do not exceed a 30° bank in any turn, except in an emergency. Make each turn with a smooth entry and smooth carry-through. Smooth, shallow banks with smooth carry-through enable the glider pilot to control his glider with ease and in turn make it easier for you.
3. Keep cylinder-head temperatures within the following limits:

Minimum	25°C
Maximum	232°C
Desired	180°C-200°C

To cool cylinder heads, use cowl flaps as necessary.

4. Keep oil temperatures within the following limits:

Minimum	40°C
Maximum	100°C
Desired	60°C-70°C

5. Formation flying:
   (a) Use ¼ wing flaps at your discretion. Use of flaps gives your airplane stability while flying in-trail formation in rough air and reduces the stalling speed of the towplane approximately 8 mph.
   (b) Unless you are in the leading airplane, set your propellers at 2300 rpm. This setting maintains power necessary to keep formation during single or double tow without having to change propeller setting constantly to conform with changes in manifold pressure.

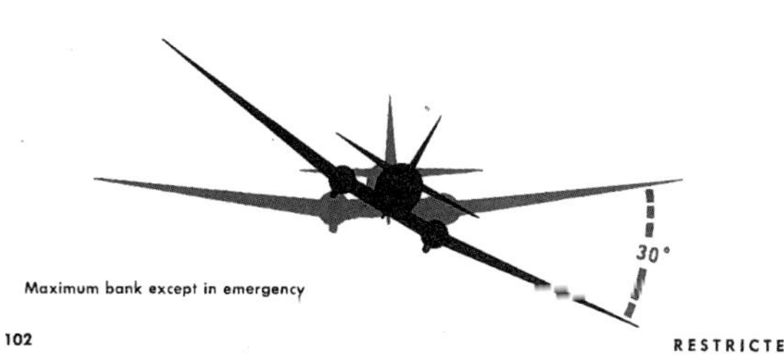

Maximum bank except in emergency

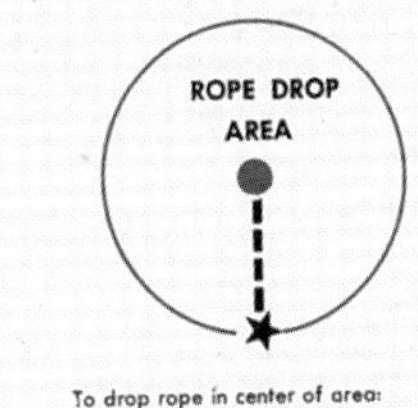

To drop rope in center of area:
If no wind...release rope approximately 150 feet from center of area
If there is a wind ... adjust point of release so that direction and velocity of wind carries rope to center of area.

Emergency Precautions

1. Copilot must have one hand on or near the glider release handle during takeoff and the initial part of the climb in case it is necessary to release glider or gliders in tow. If you have a partial or total engine failure on takeoff, you must give an emergency signal **immediately** and release gliders **within 3 seconds.**

If you have an engine failure on takeoff and do not release gliders immediately, there is extreme danger of both towplane and gliders crashing.

2. If you have an engine failure below safe minimum altitude of 800 feet with two gliders in tow, or 400 feet with one glider in tow, signal individually and release gliders.
3. If it is possible to establish single engine procedure and maintain a minimum airspeed of 100 mph, you may attempt to tow glider or gliders to a safe landing field, so long as you maintain safe minimum altitudes.
4. In case of partial engine failure (substantial loss of power) do not assume that the engine will not go out entirely or will have sufficient power to tow gliders to a landing field.
5. If a glider releases from your towplane at an altitude below 400 feet above the ground, climb immediately and sharply to between 400 and 500 feet to prevent fouling of towline on trees, buildings, wires, or other obstructions. Fouling of a towline can result in injury or

death to people in the air and on the ground and damage to your airplane and equipment.

6. Emergency signals for glider release are:
Day—rocking of wings.
Night—red light in astrodome.
Do not allow more than a 3-second interval between the emergency signal and the glider release. Glider pilots are cautioned to keep alert for emergency signals. Immediately upon observing an emergency signal they cut loose.

Note: Glider towlines stretch approximately 15% of their length during tow. If released from the towplane before the glider makes release, a towline may snap back and severely damage the nose of the glider or foul glider controls.

Procedures for Glider Pick-up

1. Pilot signals the pick-up unit operator to prepare for a pick-up. Maintain an airspeed not in excess of 110 mph in order to facilitate pick-up unit operators' work.

The unit operator then notifies pilot that unit is prepared for a pick-up.

2. Upon visual signal or radio message from the ground station that all is ready and the pilot of the glider is in his seat, approach the ground station on the right of the glider at the following indicated airspeeds:

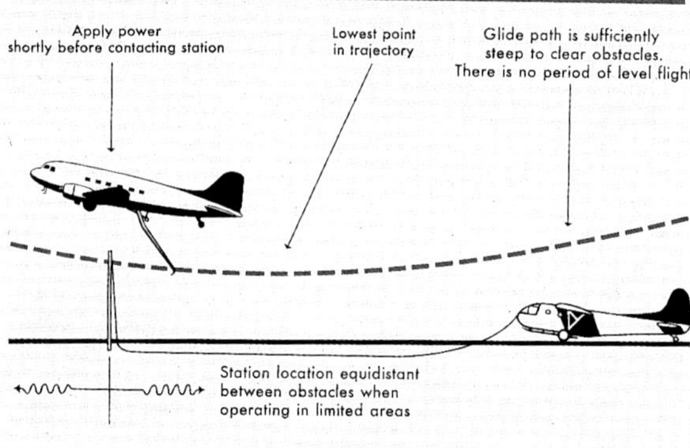

Excessively sharp pull-ups may result in damage to the tail surfaces or may stall the airplane.

Glider weight in lbs.	Conditions	Contact Speed in mph
4900	On wheels in firm ground	130
4900	Skids or wheels in soft ground	135
6000	Skids or wheels in firm ground	130
6000	Wheels in soft ground	135
6000	Skids in soft ground	140
7500	Wheels in firm ground	135
7500	Wheels in soft ground	140
CG-4A of unknown weight	Unknown	140

3. Use a power glide to keep the engines clean and warm.

4. Start increasing power approximately 100 feet before contacting the station.

5. Use takeoff power for the pull-up and continue until you clear all obstacles. Reduce power to 40" and 2550 rpm and continue the climb until there is no danger of dragging the towline because of a safety link failure or because of emergency cut-off by the glider pilot.

Do not exceed 15° in pull-up. Maintain a minimum airspeed of 105 mph except in cases of emergency.

6. If you intend to fly cross country, hold reduced airspeed in order to allow the unit operators to reel in the glider to a distance of approximately 350 feet. Normal towing procedure follows.

Hints for Pick-up

1. Warn all aircraft in the vicinity by radio of your activities and the presence of a 1000-foot trailing cable during part of maneuvers.

2. Circle left and use a close 90° approach to keep the ground station well in sight.

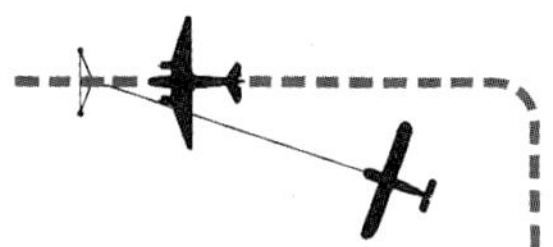

3. If in doubt about the glider and ground station being ready, stay in the vicinity until receiving a definite radio or visual signal.

4. Do not turn during the pull-up after contacting the ground station.

5. If you think you missed the station or made a knockdown, climb to 500 feet to eliminate the danger of dragging the loop and leader. The glider pilot may have released his end of the rope and you are trailing from 250 feet to 350 feet of rope and cable.

6. Communicate with the unit operators by conversation method rather than by bells or lights, with the exception of dropping the line loop and leader. (Flash the jump light to signal this operation.)

7. After some experience you will be able to maintain a constant glide or rate of descent during let down towards the ground station. There should be no period of straight flight. Go from a glide to a climb and apply the right amount of power in one smooth continuous motion.

8. Before landing, signal unit operator to prepare for landing and allow him time to retract the pick-up arm.

Index

Also from the Publisher

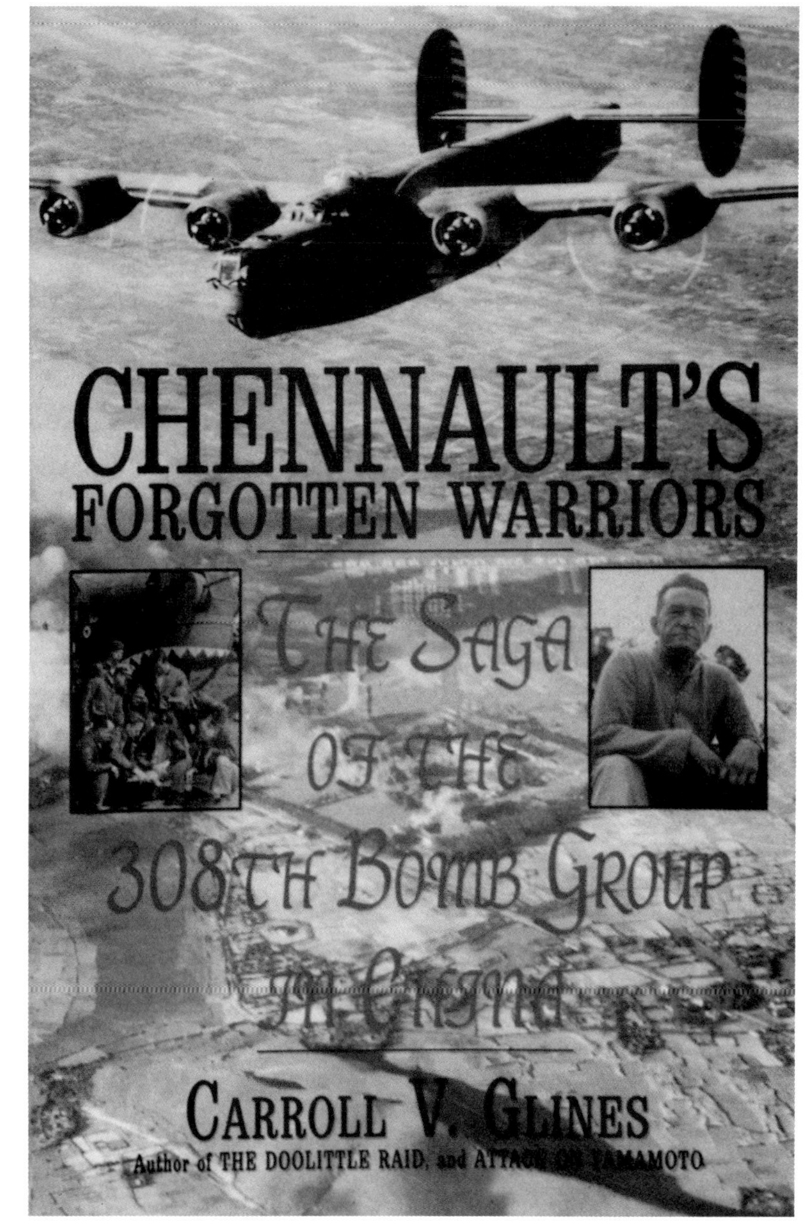

CHENNAULT'S FORGOTTEN WARRIORS

THE SAGA OF THE 308TH BOMB GROUP IN CHINA

CARROLL V. GLINES

The 308th's wide-ranging activities through nearly three years of bitter air warfare are described here by reknowned author C.V. Glines.
Size: 6" x 9" over 130 b/w photos
416 pages, hard cover
ISBN: 0-88740-809-5 $29.95